Research Reports Esprit

Project Group HCI · Volume 2

Edited in cooperation with the European Commission, DGIII/F

Esprit, the Information Technology R&D Programme, was set up in 1984 as a co-operative research programme involving European IT companies, IT "user" organisations, large and small, and academic institutions. Managed by DGIII/F of the European Commission, its aim is to contribute to the development of a competitive industrial base in an area of crucial importance for the entire European economy. The current phase of the IT programme comprises eight domains. Four are concerned with basic or underpinning technologies, and the other four are focused clusters aimed at integrating technologies into systems. The domains are software technologies, technologies for components and subsystems, multimedia systems, and long-term research; the focused clusters cover the open microprocessor systems initiative, high-performance computing and networking, technologies for business processes, and integration in manufacturing.
The series *Research Reports Esprit* is helping to disseminate the many results – products and services, tools and methods, and international standards – arising from the hundreds of projects, involving thousands of researchers, that have already been launched.

Springer
Berlin
Heidelberg
New York
Barcelona
Budapest
Hong Kong
London
Milan
Paris
Santa Clara
Singapore
Tokyo

K. Varghese S. Pfleger (Eds.)

Human Comfort and Security of Information Systems

Advanced Interfaces for the Information Society

Volume Editors

Kadamula Varghese
European Commission
Rue de la Loi 200, B-1049 Brussels, Belgium

Silvia Pfleger
Technical University of Munich, Dept. of Computer Science
Orleansstr. 34, D-81667 Munich, Germany
and
Expertise Information Systems GmbH
Budapester Str. 21, D-81669 Munich, Germany

Cataloging-in-Publication Data applied for

Die Deutsche Bibliothek - CIP-Einheitsaufnahme

Human comfort and security of information systems : advanced interfaces for the information society / K. Varghese ; S. Pfleger (ed.). - Berlin ; Heidelberg ; New York ; Barcelona ; Budapest ; Hong Kong ; London ; Milan ; Paris ; Santa Clara ; Singapore ; Tokyo : Springer, 1997
(Research reports Esprit : Project group HCI ; Vol. 2)
ISBN 3-540-62067-2
NE: Varghese, Kadamula [Hrsg.]; Research reports Esprit / project group HCI

CR Subject Classification (1991): H.1.2, H.2.0, H.4-5, K.6

ISBN 3-540-62067-2 Springer-Verlag Berlin Heidelberg New York

Publication No. EUR 17530 EN of the European Commission, Dissemination of Scientific and Technical Knowledge Unit, Directorate-General Information Technologies and Industries, and Telecommunications, Luxembourg.

Typesetting: Camera-ready by the editors
SPIN: 10554491 45/3142-543210 – Printed on acid-free paper

Foreword

The Commission of the European Union, through its Fourth Framework R&D programme is committed to the development of the Information Society. There is no doubt that there will be many radical changes in all aspects of society caused by the far-reaching impact of continuing advances in information and communication technologies. Many of these changes cannot be predicted, but that uncertainty must not stop us from moving forward. The challenge is to ensure that these technologies are put to use in the most beneficial manner, taking fully into account the rich cultural and linguistic backgrounds within the peoples of Europe. We have a duty to ensure that the ultimate end-users of the technology are involved in the development and application of that technology to help shape its use. Without this active involvement, designers will not understand the individual and organisational requirements of the users, and the users will not understand the impact and applicability of the new technology. Failure on either account will lead to a sense of resentment on the part of the users and a lost opportunity to improve the quality of human life.

The work, sponsored by the Human Comfort & Security sub-domain of the ESPRIT programme, has a central part to play in the creation of the Information Society, lying as it does at the interface between the technology and the user. Improvements in the design process will lead to better methods for user involvement in product and system design. These in turn will result in feelings of increased user satisfaction and reduced threat from the introduction of new technology. New user interface technologies will enrich the process of human-computer communication, thereby making products easier to learn and more satisfying to use. These technologies will also facilitate the development of new applications, such as virtual reality, which are critically dependent upon a high degree of interaction with the user. All users can be expected to benefit from these advances, including the young, the disabled and the elderly, thereby ensuring that the Information Society is for everyone, not just the computer literate.

October 1996

Reinhard Büscher
European Commission

Preface

This book is the lasting record of the second workshop on Human Comfort & Security, organised by Esprit, and held in Brussels in October 1995. The workshop had three objectives: *(i)* share results from Esprit and other projects in the area of Human Computer Interaction, *(ii)* solicit views from the Esprit community regarding useful changes in emphasis for future calls in this area, and *(iii)* define a series of leverage actions, to ensure that experience accumulated in technology projects is widely applied to the benefit of users and suppliers.

This volume addresses the first objective. The aim is to give the reader a view of what is happening in the field of Human-Computer Interaction, and to provide a perspective on trends and future issues. Progress towards the Information Society will be considerably affected by progress in this field in two ways. Firstly, the technologies of the user interface are important for increasing the flow of information between people and the information systems that will increasingly underpin their lives. Secondly, improvements in the design process ensure that human needs and characteristics are taken into account in a more disciplined engineering manner than hitherto. This remains a considerable challenge, because continuing technological developments are constantly raising new questions about our understanding of human behaviour. The field of Human-Computer Interaction is very broad and diverse in nature. To help the reader, the book has been divided into a number of sections, each focused around a particular set of related topics.

The first section focuses on *general topics*. The keynote address at the workshop was given by Greg Garrison, Director of the Usability Group at Reuters in London. Reuters has been dealing with information since its inception, long before the advent of electronic information technology as we know it today. Garrison's paper describes their achievements in implementing a user-centred design process in a global business. Benefit to the business is what matters, hence Garrison's process is customer-centred. Moreover, the whole scale introduction of a customer-centred process ultimately points to a dramatic re-organisation of company structures and operations. Looking to the future, Purcell identifies the challenges arising from the widespread introduction of digital technology for the handling of all forms of static and dynamic information. He postulates that user interface designers are going to be severely challenged to handle the new forms of interactive media that digital technology will facilitate. Wejchert gives an outline of the new Esprit Long Term Research action concerned with intelligent information interfaces. This was launched in September 1995 with a call to create a master plan for the programme, and sets out to deliver new models, techniques and technologies for interface design, addressing, amongst others, the challenges raised by Purcell in the previous paper.

Four papers in the section *User-Centered Design* are all concerned with improvements to the design process so that systems and products satisfy all aspects of human needs and characteristics. There is a strong need to move away from craft-based approaches towards consistent engineering methods of system design.

The paper by Mumford outlines the well established ETHICS methodology, which is particularly appropriate for the development of bespoke systems, where it is important to understand and obtain a good organisational fit. This paper also provides an introduction for anyone wanting to understand the benefits to be gained from using a user-centred approach to design. In the author's words, today's systems are so complex they need user participation. Marti and Normand propose improvements to user-centred design through the use of task modelling and analysis. They advocate a more structured approach to the normal iterative user-centred approaches through using task analysis and modelling as a shared resource throughout the development process. They report on their experiences of using the techniques in a number of applications. The MAPI project described by Kirakowski and Bevan is an Esprit trial application of the MUSiC approach to user-centred design, developed in an earlier EU-funded project. It is concerned with the integration of that approach into overall system and product life-cycle processes. The intention is to offer professional services based upon the MUSiC methodology at all stages of the product life-cycle. The EU Directive on health and safety requirements for screen-based work and the adoption of ISO 9241 standards are both helping to force the pace to ensure that products and systems meet human requirements. Oppermann describes a software-based tool which is a guideline-based evaluation tool for assessing the conformance of products under development to ISO 9241 requirements.

Research has been conducted over many years into *Speech-based Communication* with IT systems, on the premise that such systems will be easy to learn and to use. Steady advances in speech recognition technology mean practical real world applications are becoming feasible, that do not require the speaker to make major changes in speaking habits or train the system on his/her voice prior to use. Systems employing speech recognition over the telephone are likely to offer advantages to both service provider and user alike, overcoming the need to restrict access to those with special terminals. The paper by Piper reviews the range of data collection techniques used in market research and then goes on to describe the results of trials using speech recognition to conduct telephone-based market research. One of the major requirements for application domains where speed is essential, such as market research, is reducing the length of time it takes to create a new application or service using speech technology. Fraser describes a recently funded project designing service creation tools to accommodate multiple languages, an important factor in the European market. There are two papers on the MASK project, providing multimedia access to information systems by the general public. An important design issue here is the extent to which the technology can accommodate how people behave, and the extent to which people have to adapt to the limitations of the machine. Chhor gives an overview of the project, and includes some preliminary results from trials using a simulated system in a Paris railway station. The design of the spoken language components of the system is dealt with by Gauvain et al. To ensure readily customisable applications, it is necessary to separate the task dependent and independent activities; successful speech recognition requires the application of domain specific knowledge to remove ambiguity. Dybkjaer et al are concerned with the design of the spoken dialogue that takes place between humans and systems. Much of the work to date has been empirical, based upon common sense, experience, intuition, and not least trial and error. This paper proposes and validates some design principles to help dialogue designers create co-operative human-computer dialogues. Usability evaluations of spoken dialogues for automated telephone banking services are addressed in the paper by Jack and Lefevre.

Systems to support *co-operative working* are becomingly increasingly important and are only possible because of the conjunction of developments in computing and telecommunications. Haake and his co-authors describe a hypermedia-based system for supporting the market introduction of software products. In today's global marketplace, this takes place across a number of organisations, each playing different roles in a geographically separated environment. The paper includes an analysis of user requirements in this testing domain, and describes in outline the system being designed to address them. Computer-based training in a distance-learning environment is described by Davarakis and Harissis. Their aim was to produce a training environment that could be either stand-alone or operate remotely using digitally transmitted information in broadcast TV signals. Pfleger and Krauß address the information navigation aspects of computer-based teaching in the university environment. The decision support services of the GeoSol system for monitoring water quality and crisis management are presented by Pfleger at al. together with the user requirements generated within two European projects (Esprit project GeoWorks and ENS project ENVIRONET). User support for estimating the passenger flow in airport terminals is discussed by Heyde et al.

The *design of user interfaces* is the most challenging and time-consuming aspect of information system design. The role of the designer is to ensure that overall human-system performance is optimised through balancing the activities on both sides of the interface and obtaining the most effective flow of information across it. The interface designer needs a range of methods and tools to handle both the formal aspects of system design and the cognitive capabilities of the users. There are four papers concerned with these issues. Boutrouche and Kärcher describe a trial application of the DIADEM user interface design methodology, developed under previous Esprit funding. As a trial application, the objective is to validate the method in the design of real systems, and to quantify the risks and benefits from using the new methods. Three different application areas are here presented, including computer-telephony. Darzentas et al. report on the transfer of results from a previous basic research project (AMODEUS2), concerned with deriving a set of models and tools for user interface design. Their paper describes the design of a Designer's Decision Aiding system, an intelligent decision support system which helps designers with specific interface design problems identify which design techniques to use. This approach is appropriate to handle the qualitative knowledge represented in the system. A particular concern in the design of multimodal user interfaces is the coordination and fusion of the user's intent from their use of different input modalities. A formal approach for doing this is addressed by Faconti, that is equally applicable to the analysis of existing systems as for the design of new ones. The paper by Cavallaro et al. describes a structured approach to the design of interfaces to hypermedia databases. The objective is to provide users with more navigational type interfaces to enable them to explore the information in a more intuitive interactive manner. They describe approaches to link the different representations and structures of hypertext and relational databases.

Intelligent Interfaces are capable of providing the user with an explanation of the underlying system's reasoning and thus generating increased user confidence. This topic becomes more important as system complexity continues to rise and will doubtless be addressed in the Long Term Research action Intelligent Information Interfaces referred to earlier. Three papers are each associated with a different application demonstrator of the I-SEE project, concerned with tools and techniques for co-operative explanatory behaviour. The paper of Lambert and Ringland contains a high level description of the overall system architecture, and its application to the monitoring and diagnosis of problems in the operation of sewage plants. They produce preliminary evidence of the value to be gained by users from the use of such a system. The theme is further developed by Quemeneur and Brossier, who describe the explanation toolkit that permits the construction of explanation modules as well as intelligent interfaces. Their architecture is readily adaptable to different application domains; they illustrate its use in the generation of intelligent help for a high level scheduling tool. Thomas et al. provides a good overview of the limitations of conventional user interface management systems and toolsets, and describes how these can be overcome to generate dynamically produced explanations. The results are illustrated for a numerical modelling program predicting the effects of oil spillage at sea.

Improvements in human-computer interaction would not be complete without a discussion of the developments in *User Interface Technology* that increase the bandwidth of communication between user and IT system. Much of this work is currently driven by the need to provide users with more realistic sensations in virtual reality environments. Bergamasco describes novel work on haptic interfaces; those concerned with providing the hand with sensations of touch and concentrates on the detailed requirements for integrated force and tactile feedback. Whilst the primary objective is for use in virtual environments, there are important applications in Rehabilitation Technology, which are also being explored. Another interface technology partly motivated by the needs of people with disabilities is described by Kalra et al. They review the techniques available to extract information from video images of the human face, and describe how their techniques overcome some of the limitations of the existing methods. A range of potential applications are discussed, including animation, computer control and low bandwidth video conferencing systems. Animation is also the prime motivation for the work described by Boulic et al. on the animation of human motion, an important aspect of games, simulators, and virtual environments. They review the limitations of current techniques for modelling human 3D motion which are still computing intensive, despite advances in computer technology. They propose improvements in techniques for handling dynamic problems such as collision avoidance and goal-oriented motion.

We acknowledge the assistance provided by Dr. Michael Underwood and Anda Pfleger in editing this book.

October 1996

K. Varghese
S. Pfleger

Contents

Beyond the Final Frontier: Usability at Reuters

Greg Garrison
Director of Usability Group
Reuters
85 Fleet Street, London EC4P 4AJ, U.K.

Abstract

This paper presents the Reuters Usability Group and its Customer Centred Design process both of which pivot around their life-force - the customer. We describe how to build this process into an evolutionary, self perpetuating and continuously evolving life cycle of ever more relevant and responsive products. Everything that we do revolves around the centre of gravity set by our customers, creating energy and synergy that launches our product into the future.

1. Introduction

Reuter customers in dealing rooms across the world are like top fighter pilots. In the action-packed financial service market-place, dealers are in daily dog-fights. To compete and perform, they rely upon Reuters to equip and arm them for battle. A second's delay is fatal. A miscalculation catastrophic. As we all know from recent financial disasters, a missed opportunity carries an all too real opportunity cost. At Reuters, we are striving to improve the performance of our customers, giving them the systems they need, the data they want, the way they want it. Reuter customers need cutting edge technology. They expect fast and accurate information. They demand immediate response, effective training and instant help. Without this support, they're unarmed, exposed and vulnerable.

But who are Reuter customers? Are we really giving them what they want? Simple questions. But our industry, like many others, has a tough time finding the answers.

This paper describes how usability is giving Reuters a competitive advantage by putting and keeping our customers at the centre of the design process: Empowering our customers through usable technology. We will show awareness. Meeting the usability challenge means making no assumptions about what customers want, but gathering hard data from them. It means moving from

you how we have gone beyond the final frontier that separates us from our customers, pulling them into our design teams and putting them at the heart of everything we do. The following describe some of the key challenges that we have addressed:

Fig 1. A typical dealing environment

1.1 Diversity

Like many industries, we face a key demand from customers for usability, a demand that few are meeting. Serving the world's financial community presents the most extreme of challenges. Our customers work in diverse markets, using varied instruments. They live in cultures scattered over 150 countries, using a variety of languages. They want to use systems in wildly individualistic ways. They need to run all range of products on all types of platforms, combine all kinds of applications in many varied ways, using all levels of skills. The technology to make this happen is fantastically advanced and complex, but people are even more so.

1.2 Change

The challenge facing us all is to create systems that customers can use in the way they want to use them, not how we think they should be used. Usability is about changing from technology-driven product development, to customer-driven evolution. Each step of product design and development must be rigorously centred around the customer, blending the latest technology with real-world just getting the system to work, to getting the system to work the way our customers want it to. By giving our customers a competitive edge, we are enhancing our own.

2 Why is Usability so important in Today's Marketplace

Reuters produces highly sophisticated and comprehensive financial information systems. At considerable cost we gather data from right across the globe. It takes cutting edge technology to send this information at the speed of light to customers' workstations world-wide. All this investment of time, talent and technology to transmit data direct to customers, wherever they are: Just to have it crash, burn and die on the last millimetre of its journey at the user interface of the screen.

If systems are too complex, if customers can't find the data they want when they want, the bottom line is that they simply don't have it. All efforts and competitive advantage die as dead as the customer deal.

For most of us ten years ago, usability was a non-issue. Five years ago it was a nice to have. Last year it was a value-added benefit of products. Forget the past. Now usability is a core requirement and expectation of computer systems.

Usability and user interface design have been considered soft sciences when compared to "real", "hard" programming skills. In fact, they're really a highly-refined combination of science and art. But it's certainly not art-for-art's sake. As the leading authority on user interface design, Ben Schneiderman says:

> "User interfaces are no longer the glossy paint splashed on at the end of product development, rather they're the steel superstructure upon which we hang all of the details"

The sad fact is, until recently, if you really dug around in the superstructure of many systems you could find an awful lot of rust, dust and barnacles. Those days have gone.

3 Changing to Meet the Needs of the World's Financial Community

Meeting the global usability challenge for diverse customers means not changing the rules, not bending them, but creating a whole new rule book. We need to take an imaginative leap, and that's what I'm going to ask you to do now. Let's go beyond the final frontier and look at how we rose to meet this new challenge.

4 Vision

Back in 1993, we set out with a vision for usability. We wanted to develop products that are easy to learn, intuitive to use, and efficient to support. Products should have inherent brand strengths, be highly customisable, and very importantly, have a high degree of interoperability. It means creating products that are engaging, that customers can use without fear or effort. When users switch on for the first time, they want to pop up a screen that's reassuring not frightening, intriguing not mystifying, fun not frustrating.

5 Customer Centred Design

To turn this vision into reality, we must follow a consistent methodology across the world, whether products are developed in New York or Singapore, Paris or London. The process must involve customers at all critical points in a product's life cycle. At each stage, the product must be evaluated with customers, and the results instantly fed back to development teams. The net result of adopting such a methodology will be that our systems are designed to be consistent interoperable, and usable.

Reuters have developed a Customer Centred Design process which ensures that developers world-wide take advantage of to the same design styles techniques and standards.

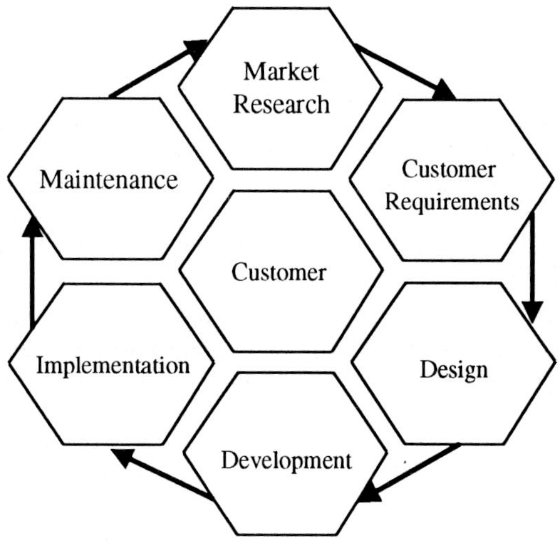

Fig. 2: The Customer Centred Design Process

As can be seen, the process is at once iterative and evolutionary, comprising the following basic steps:

- MARKET RESEARCH - Monitoring existing products and the marketplace in real-time.
- CCUSTOMER REQUIREMENTS - Clearly tracking customer task flows not only through products, but across products.
- DESIGN - Designing products that map user interface navigation systems directly onto task flows.

- DEVELOPMENT - Developing products in constant consultation with the ultimate users.
- IMPLEMENTATION - Launching products into the marketplace that have effective user interfaces and responsive support systems built in from the outset.
- SUPPORT - Supporting products proactively in full awareness of how the product is likely to perform based on continuous customer feedback through usability evaluation.

A frequently asked question is, doesn't involving customers to this extent add time? We all recognise that time to market is more critical than ever. In real terms, the process actually saves time by:

- Preventing over-engineering
- Cutting rework
- Speeding up market acceptance
- Removing unnecessary training and support.

These are some of the benefits, but how does it all work? We will now describe critical aspects of the process in more detail.

5.1 Market Research

The first step is collecting, managing and analysing the information we get from every interaction with our customers across the world. We need a free-flowing pipeline of data on what customers do and how they do it. We need to understand the subtleties and complexities of the diverse markets we serve.

We conduct a baseline usability evaluation of existing products, checking how they perform in the market place, and comparing their performance with that of competitor products.

Help desks are our goldmine of information, right in the front-line to customers. Thousands of phone calls come into our help desks around the world every day. We record and analyse that information, classify it, and take it down to a level of detail that we can translate into specific product improvements.

Once the problem area is quantified, and identified its impact on customers assessed, we set priorities for addressing and targeting the associated usability issues.

We conduct expert reviews with our team of ergonomists, human factors people, graphic designers, GUI evaluators, and so on, to get all perspectives. We recognise that customers are whole, complete people, so we treat their needs in a holistic way, by bringing together the skills of many disciplines.

User groups across the world provide an additional source of valuable information allowing us to establish what they think of our products and the support that they receive.

All of this work ensures that we have a reliable picture of our customers' needs. The research process is consistent across the globe, allowing us to collect and combine the reactions of customers, whether they happen to work in Japan or Europe, America or Asia. This process enables us to compare, consolidate and crystallise all that we do into a truly global perspective.

This valuable data transcends internal debate about what we think customers want, it makes assumptions irrelevant, it means that we are working from hard, indisputable fact, straight from the customer.

5.2 Customer Requirements

So, who are our customers? To get a real picture, we use a combination of powerful research techniques. We create customer profiles, identifying what specific customers actually do, and how they do it. People with direct customer contact like trainers and customer support teams, help us to get a clear picture of who individual customers are, what their marketplace is, what instruments they trade, and what would make a key difference to their performance.

We draw up usage scenarios, describing where, when and how customers use our products, and detailed descriptions of the tasks they carry out. We gather data on how long it takes to perform tasks and how often they do them. Another focus is on navigation: How do our customers access the data? In what order? How do they want to display it? Do they want to import that data into a spreadsheet or a graph? Where do they want to store it?

This deep understanding of our customers helps us to provide them with the most effective way to navigate through the system for their particular needs.

We combine qualitative and quantitative data from these many sources into a document that we call a usability requirements specification. This document sets the performance targets for the product and is presented to the development team, ensuring that usability is a core requirement, rather than a last minute bolt-on.

5.3 Design

Once we have this part of the puzzle completed, beginning to understand what our customers need, the next step is to map a design to meet those needs. Based on customer requirements, we define the scope of the product, the functions and customer activities it will support.

The design process is divided into two discrete stages: High level design and Visual design.

5.3.1 High Level Design

We develop a conceptual design to help organise the different objects customers need to see or control to carry out their work and a navigation model, showing how customers move around the system, and the actions they take.

We visualise this, and develop a low fidelity prototype. This is often a paper and pencil storyboard of how a customer operates. We use it to check and clarify with them that this is in fact how they would like to work in the future. It gives us the opportunity for quick customer evaluation of our concept, right at the earliest stages of a product's birth.

This iterative, high-level interface design cycle, continues until we are satisfied that customers are comfortable with the high-level architecture. So we avoid the danger of going too deeply into the design, committing ourselves before there's a clear understanding of what customers really want.

At the final stage of this first cycle, we carry out an impact assessment, prioritising tasks within the context of what we can do in a manageable and affordable time frame.

5.3.2 Visual Design

Once we have validated the initial design from the customer's view, we're ready to move on to detailed visual design. This stage helps ensure that the product's detailed layout, structure, terminology and interface are all consistent with our best practice design standards.

As another continuous loop of iterative design, we enhance our initial test prototype, creating a live, working high-fidelity Visual Basic model. This is vital to give a realistic simulation of the customer's interaction with the product.

5.4 Development and Usability Evaluation

By this stage of the process we have evaluated our high-fidelity prototype internally, with customers. But the evaluation has really just started. Now we are on firmer ground, we can move on to actual product development, constantly backed up by evaluation and review with customers.

Fig 3. Evaluating Usability with a Customer

As a result of this process, we have seen tremendous breakthroughs. Contrast this process with the old days: We would start by writing a functional specification, and to a certain extent that would be what was finally built. We wouldn't directly evaluate with customers, until the beta test just before launch by which time it was too late to make any radical changes to the product.

Now what we're seeing is thorough usability evaluation throughout the very earliest, and seminal stages of a product's life. We've seen as high as 40% improvement in usability, from the initial prototype through to the final product development. Those improvements run across the board in key metrics to measure factors such as task efficiency, task effectiveness, learnability, productivity and likeability.

The pressure to be first is extreme, but you've still got to be first with a working and usable product. Patches to stick over the bug-filled crevices in your software releases do little for your reputation and brand, but most of all do little for your customers. Because customers are now built into every stage of our product development process, the products evolve as they are built, keeping pace with the market place. By making product development's more intense, product launches can become less of a gamble. We're swapping the adrenaline buzz of premature launches for the excitement of creating the right product, right first time.

Why use unwilling and blind guinea pigs when you hit the market place, when you can plan ahead and perform usability evaluation with real and willing customers right up front, customers who are simply chafing to be listened to. Listening brings its own reward. Key customers are already engrained in the product from its earliest stage. They've seen its progress, more than that they've steered it, and helped conceive the product. There's no better ambassador or lobbyist for your product than a user who helped build it. People anticipate the launch, and market acceptance is better than instant.

6 Supporting the Customer Centred Design Process

So that's our Customer Centred Design Process. None of this is a black art. It's a systematic, scientific and doable process, involving hard data, and hard work. Now let's look at some of the things that we have done to make this process a living reality.

6.1 Usability Evaluation

A lot of hard work goes into evaluating products, getting a real picture of how they can boost the customer's performance.

We combine our findings from sources including usability evaluation, GUI reviews, and expert evaluations by ergonomists and human factors people. We get creative input from graphic designers to ensure that our user interfaces not only meet requirements, but deliver the sizzle along with the steak. Everything is done in the context of our consistent design standards and the aim of interoperability.

To do this, we approached the top consultancies working across all of the disciplines associated with usability, and pooled their expertise. This allowed us to set up and run our usability evaluation facilities, which we are told are among the most comprehensive and sophisticated in the industry.

But what do customers make of it all? In this case, numbers speak for themselves: Over five hundred customers have volunteered to take part in our evaluation programmes, they all feel excited to be involved in the design of products that will eventually use and form a clear commitment to the products during the evaluation.

In addition to our technology and people, the success of the evaluation programme results for the way that we run our Usability Laboratories. This is how they work.

We invite representative customers from target markets into the labs, explaining the process to them. The evaluation take place in a Laboratory where we simulate real-time, real working conditions. A tester prompts and interviews the customer through a carefully constructed session. A consistent approach is vital, allowing comparison of data over time and between countries.

We capture views of the customer and the screen, so that we can see and understand what they do, see what they see, and see their reactions. The evaluations are video recorded for further analysis and distribution to development groups. Often we use video-conferencing to link together customers and developers right across the world.

Fig 4. Analysing usability evaluations in the London laboratory

The fact is, we never really know how a customer will use a product, until we actually get them to do it. For reliable samples, we evaluate a product with many customers, up to twenty five people per week at our London laboratories.

And the results? Well, for example, usability evaluations threw up problems customers were facing in developing quote lists. We streamlined the process, and measured the impact. We found that we'd cut the average time for customers to create a quote from 90 to 11 seconds with zero training.

Usability evaluation has proved so successful that we are rapidly expanding our network of usability labs, with more coming on line in Milan and New York, and ones planned for the far east.

6.2 Reuter Customer Performance Support

One new development that all our research tells us customers want, is “Just In Time” electronic performance support. Support that is fully integrated into the system, offering them instant help, when, where and how they want it. After all, if our customers are at the centre of our business, so too should they be at the centre of our support philosophy.

Reuters has its own existing expensive, extensive, external infrastructure to support customers. It is comprehensive and very responsive ranging from help desk to customer relations, customer training to sales and marketing activity, and so on. We strive for synergy between all of these elements, providing a reliable infrastructure of support around the customer.

But in an industry where thirty seconds is history, you begin to see this uncomfortable gap between the customer and the support infrastructure, no matter how good it is. We decided to bridge this gap with an intelligent layer of electronic performance support systems by applying s diverse range innovative techniques.

The new field of electronic performance support offered a whole plethora of technological solutions in search of problems. Hyper text, hyper-media, CBT, wizards, cue cards. It could easily be a Pandora's box full of inconsistent, random elements of support tools. Instead, we needed to give customers a coherent package of support.

Following the fighter crew analogy we described at the start of this paper, we realised what we were offering was like the help offered to pilots. Screens of information to help them cope with rapidly changing conditions, in a mission-critical environment.

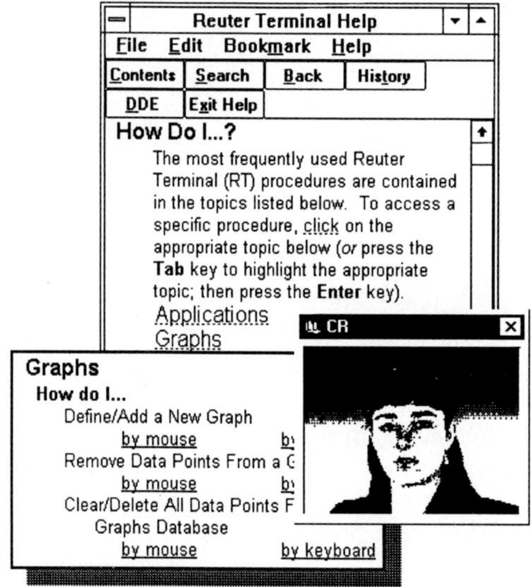

Fig 5: Combining Multi-Media and Task oriented performance support

What sort of on-line support do customers need? Accurate and detailed maps. Comprehensive and responsive instruments. A simulator, where they can try out ideas, or get a quick demonstration on how to perform a function, then switch back instantly to the action. Moving from training to trading at the flick of an icon.

Our customers need a navigator, sitting over their shoulder, giving expert guidance. And an autopilot to handle routine, or rare and complex tasks. Finally, they need the intuitive pilot mode, where they're trading with the full benefit of context-sensitive help.

Let us look at these tools in more detail. What are the components that make up each of these areas of support?

The customers' maps are database directories and effective query and hierarchical menu structures. The instruments are on-line user guides and help systems. The simulator offers CBT tutorials and demonstrations. For navigation, hyper-text and tip cards, our version of cue cards, provide on screen guidance and procedural support. The auto-pilot gives context-sensitive help and wizard technology, and finally, the full intuitive user interface is ready when the customer really wants to "fly" the system.

Together these mechanisms provide us with the model for our Electronic Performance Support System, taking customers beyond proficiency to mastery. It's just part of our comprehensive approach to user interfaces.

6.3 Supporting Developers

All this is only possible if we convince everyone involved in creating our products, right across the world, of the importance of usability. We have to market the approach to all parts of Reuters and to our third-party developers. We have to train and support them, and make the technical tools the developers need, easy to use too.

6.3.1 User Interface Design Guides

To give developers clear design standards to work to, we developed both corporate and product specific User Interface Design Guides. The guides are delivered in both on-line and paper formats providing developers with the flexibility that they need.

The guides take the Microsoft standards, and translate them to provide specific guidelines for user-interface design within the financial services community. By choosing to work with the best, we are able to set out best practice design standards.

We have also developed an interactive version of the guide, because as well as visual design, you need to model in real-time the action and performance of the user interface.

We use our electronic user interface design guide as a training tool for developers. We have broken our design standards down into logical and digestible modules. We distribute these to our developers and product managers, enabling us to track a cumulative improvement in the knowledge of user interface design throughout the company. From the first module on dialogue boxes, through modules on colour and icons, to typography and layout. The series builds up and is circulated every three months on a pressed CD-ROM. But it's not just for training, it's an active tool and includes source code ready for developers to capture and apply immediately.

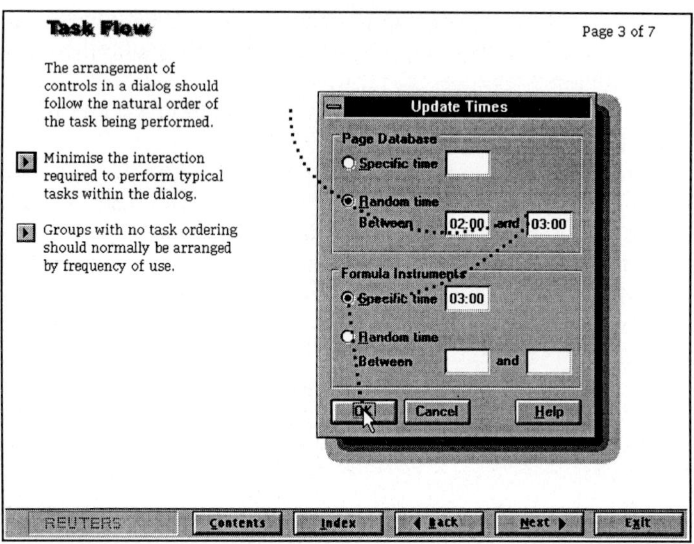

Fig 6. The Interactive Design Guide

6.3.2 Icon Library

We have developed an icon library which will play a key role in promoting a consistent approach across all of our products. A year and a half ago we had six different development groups scattered across the world. Each group was producing icons and toolbars for related products. The potential danger was of confusing customers by creating six different icons for quotes and graphs and tickers and news and so on. Our first step was to put all our existing products side by side in our user interface design lab. It lets us identify, and root out any inconsistencies.

Our next step has been to bring all the development teams together and create a class library of icons, evaluating and redesigning where necessary, with a high-calibre graphic design team. Above all, we would only use icons which we could prove worked with different customers, in different markets and in different locations, to ensure that these icon standards represent best practice in global usability, and ensure interoperability.

As we make the design of our products more consistent, they will be easier to link together. Customers will be able to use them instantly, mix and match applications, and transfer data between them. The energy and synergy released by bringing these products together will be the turbo charge to launch us into the future.

7 Breaking Free of the Past, Moving Towards the Future

The Customer Centred Design process takes us from slow linear development to customer-driven evolution. It helps us to create products which meet and grow in time with the needs of the market. The product life cycle pivots around its life-force, the customer. Everything that we do revolves around that centre of gravity set by the customer, product evolution is focused completely within the circle of service surrounding them.

The usability group will continue to be a catalyst for cultural change, promoting usability world-wide. The Customer Centred Design process continues to spread around Reuters. It is now at the heart of many key product groups, giving product managers the customer data they need for advanced planning and new product development, and acting towards our goal of product convergence. Our next big challenge is to move from a primarily centralised usability group to being totally embedded into the fabric of the way the company conducts it's day to day business.

All markets will be in a state of constant flux, calling on organisations to be ever more flexible constantly changing to meet the transient needs of their customers. This change is only possible if products evolve as they grow. This can only happen if customers are seamlessly integrated into the design process, giving instant and detailed feedback.

The future is building a new company that puts and keeps customers at the heart of the design process. A process that draws the entire company together around a common goal that of creating products that customers passionately want, not passively accept.

One thing is certain, in our quest for usability we will continue to work with customers and give them the products that they really want. Creating the spark that will release their creative energy and take us all beyond the final frontier.

The New Media Interface: a Case for Reappraisal

Patrick Purcell
Imperial College of Science & Technology
South Kensington, London SW7 2BT, United Kingdom

Abstract

In recent years the role of media technology as a mediating agency between the user and the user's complex information environment has had a significant impact on the design and format of the user interface. However, current plans for digital media in many aspects of entertainment, education and information indicate that the next generation of media technology will have an even more profound impact on future interface design. Individual exemplars from various media industries are presented below and compared. The comparison reveals a seemingly dichotomous situation, at once convergent in shared infrastructure between media, while, at the same time being so divergent in a proliferation of new applications in electronic publishing, telecoms services and broadcasting.

The source of the paradigm shift in many of these applications is the emergence of digital coding as the common language of communication. This common digital language offers a unique opportunity to leverage converging technologies such as television, computers and telecommunications into a global communications infrastructure offering a vastly augmented range of services to users. To exploit this potential, we will have to absorb new media concepts, such as fully interactive TV, "dial up movies", "broadcatching" rather than broadcasting. Such concepts will demand a radically new approach to the way, in which we may conceive, design and implement future multimedia interfaces.

1. Multimedia Contexts

From being a research topic, with its roots in raster graphics, multimedia has grown to become a major growth point in the information technology business, primarily in the workstation and personal computer industries. In the second half of the nineties, the pace of multimedia research and development has quickened, actively exploiting the best that current technology has to offer, in the form of high bandwidth, enormous computing and signal processing power, intelligent agents, object oriented software, and high fidelity presentation methods.

Concurrently, major developments in certain industries other than computing and electronics, seriously portend that the most significant advances for multimedia in this decade will be determined by new factors quite extraneous to multimedia, such as new forms of digital broadcasting and publishing.

2. Digital Television: aka "Bit Radiation"

Compared with, say, automotive design and certain areas of consumer electronics, the television receiver has not been the subject of significant electronic advance. However, the current trends in broadcasting research & development promise to change this situation significantly. The initial proposals for HDTV indicated linear projections of technical advance. Topics included increasing screen resolution and changing the aspect ratio of the screen. Traditionally, broadcasting has been based on the concept of a single transmitter radiating an identical video signal to a population of passive receivers, adjusted to its frequency. In this single mode of transmission, programme origination, transmission and reception are handled as a tightly coupled triad, all linked in real time operation.

Recently however, with the announcement of the national programmes for digital TV in Britain, other more radical proposals have been entering the arena of future HDTV. They are essentially predicated on the idea that the television industry should take more account of the widespread use of digital techniques, that have begun to affect so many applications in the fields of media, communications & information technology. As the technology of television moves away from its analogue antecedents towards its digital future, it finds a new alignment with those technologies whose digital infrastructure it shares. Given the view of future TV as an intensive digital processing technology, with much of that processing occurring in the TV receiver, it may be claimed that future television will introduce extensive information processing into our homes and daily lives.

Indeed, today's PC, with its high-definition graphics processing capability, may be perceived as the TV receiver of the future. Reciprocally, the future television receiver will have much of the functionality of a computer, leading to the existence on the market today, of new hybrid devices, that are part PC and equally part TV.

This specification of advanced TV provides it with a basis for convergence with other active developments, such as digital movies and multimedia information systems. Versatility is seen as the cardinal virtue of the open architecture structure.

The key features of digital TV and digital video include amenability to data compression, modularity, and scalability, resulting in a television video signal, with capacity for variable screen resolutions, frame rates and aspect ratios.

The progressive intersection of the new TV transmission media with other media, including computer and telecommunication networks is linking television with new forms of electronic publishing, for example, electronic yellow pages, on-line cartographic information, tele-shopping, multimedia information systems and ``dial up" movies. In this development, what we have come to know as "broadcasting", may in future (with a high degree of user selection) be redefined as "broadcatching". Broadcatching underlines interaction and selection based more on the user's choice and availability than on the broadcasters schedules. Significant advances in image processing research, have further reinforced the alignment of television delivery with these telecom services, for example in ``thin wire TV" on existing phone lines. The process of recording on the VCR, one's favourite television program for viewing at a more convenient time has become a very familiar process. Digital television will take the proactive viewer into a much enhanced level of choosing, down loading and browsing of favourite programmes. Future interactive digital TV sets will be able to respond to the command, " download for me last night's Panorama and last month's World in Action"!

Apart from the alignment of digital television with other new forms of entertainment and information technologies, we may expect progressive reduction in the need for live broadcast, to the point where newscasts and sportscasts may ultimately become the few regular transmissions, tied to the broadcasters schedule. Amongst the technical advantages that we may expect from the new digital television, include more efficient transmission, enhanced audio, ghost-free reception and the incorporation of a variety of multimedia communications interfaces. Cumulatively it seems clear that the new television will play much more extensive and varied roles in the living room of the future, going far beyond entertainment to have a major impact on our work and life styles generally.

3. Multimedia Information Systems

"A picture is worth a thousand words", an adage of long standing, is being given a fresh impetus by current developments in imaging technology. In recent years, visual collections, image libraries and museums embraced optical storage technology to provide better means for accessing the records of very large collections of images.

Advances in the technology of digital image collections as a major application area, have a special relevance to ongoing concurrent developments in electronic publishing, in high speed data networks and in advanced telecommunication services.

Today's electronic image libraries, linked to object oriented data bases and accessed by powerful, specially developed search languages, have created a new genre of electronic publishing, namely MMIS (Multimedia Information Systems). MMIS technology has evolved in those professions, industries and disciplines where the image has a singular significance, for example, in medicine, in advertising and the media, in design, in architecture, fine arts, advertising, graphic arts and photography. Art institutions, galleries, museums and image libraries have provided many of the pioneering applications, in the successive generations, through which multimedia information systems have been evolving. The most common mode of implementing visual referencing systems has been as a single-site station, with the image collection held on one or more optical storage devices. Institutions such as the Tate Gallery or the

National Gallery have pioneered applications in the UK. The Smithsonian, the Metropolitan and the Getty have pioneered similar systems in the USA.

Other important initiatives have taken the form of collaborative partnerships, which have included the Uffizi gallery in Florence, the Prado Museum in Madrid, the Musee d'Orsay in Paris, and the Ashmolean in Oxford. The membership of these consortia also represent national and multinational telecommunication organisations (such as BT, France Telecom, and Telefonica) to support the technical task of linking these organisations into a functioning international art and cultural network

A current example of the potential role of the electronic image library as a multimedia node in a distributed system, operating on a broadband data network, is France Telecom's Image Directe project. One may anticipate that these exemplars, will achieve for the world of images and visual information what has already been accomplished by the long established on-lineonline text data bases, for current affairs, business information and financial services.

4. Digital Cinema

In certain respects, the technology of digital HDTV and digital cinema share many corresponding technical features. They include, for example, the techniques of storing, processing, transmitting and receiving digital video. In the technology of digital movie processing, the issues of image scale, bandwidth, frame rate and screen resolution are all independent variables. Digital video is not just a versatile medium for the transmission of digital movies. Digital techniques are offering fresh approaches, for example, in shooting films. New techniques include the incorporation of range sensing cameras into movie making as a feature in the development of 3D movies and the consequent ability to manipulate real world scenes with the freedom usually associated with computer generated 3D models. The extensions to utilise direct 3D displays for replay are particularly exciting.

In due course however, when a new generation of directors and producers have gained full insight into, and understanding of the techniques of digital film and video, we may expect that the impact of digital techniques will have a profound effect on all aspects of film making, including scripting, shooting, editing, transmission, projection and most significantly how on we may experience movies both as an entertainment and as an educational medium in the future.

5. Multimedia and Virtual Presence

The art and technology of visualisation has been a long standing and prime motivation for research in advanced digital video and autostereo techniques. From its origin in monochromatic vector graphics, the impetus to depict both real and imagined objects and processes has been a major goal. Advances in colour, simulation of texture, stereoscopic display, complex digital modelling, specular reflection, translucency, transparency and image resolution, has each made its distinct contribution to the realistic depiction of complex objects, scenes and processes. Now computer graphic rendering techniques and computer animation have been conjoined with the physics and chemistry of holography to generate a new range of visually refined and iridescent imagery. The distinctive optical character of these new images reflect both the ultra precise fabrication techniques of holography and the power of modern computer graphic processing engines.

The artefacts, resulting from this conjunction of technologies generally play a role as objects of aesthetic interest in the art gallery or as a powerful medium of visualisation in the laboratory. The extension of this composite technology to applications in medicine and in systems for industrial design, architecture and engineering is providing the impetus for further research and development in this interdisciplinary field.

Current research includes full colour three dimensional portraits, medical visualisation of CAT and MRI scans, automotive design and architectural CAD data bases, large scale holograms, wide-angle holography & very recently the first holographic video. The ability to generate realistic full colour holographic images from digital models of proposed designs, represents a major advance in design communication, as a form of "design hardcopy". The development of the computer based hologram represents a distinct departure from the "true" hologram, which must be exposed in laser light to an object of nearly the same size as the desired image, size being no constriction for computer modelled objects. While holographic stereograms have been generated as a series of perspective images and synthesised as a form the "frozen" computer animation to achieve the "look around" effect, more recent research is directed to combining the role of computer animation with supercomputing, to produce moving or animated holographic video in real time. The new resources combine a supercomputer, and a custom built rotating display system. It may well be that the impact of current parallel processing techniques will be such as to take holographic imaging further away from the core of wave front reconstruction physics, such that computer generated 3D holography-type images will look to classical holography more as an inspiration, than as a source of operating techniques.

6. Conclusions: the venues for multimedia applications

The previous sections evidenced the role of multimedia in such diverse applications as multimedia information systems, advanced television, digital cinema and visualisation technology. The increasing involvement of multimedia is providing a common linking infrastructure to these former discrete areas of activity. While to the superficial eye, the operation of analogue video is comparable with a digital movie sequence, the difference in underlying technology presages a marked difference in terms of future modes of entertainment to be offered, and the provision of electronic information. Digital video information transmission is often discussed in terms of alternate delivery channels, either via computer networks, terrestrial broadcast, cable, satellite broadcast or telecommunication delivery. In fact, the future availability of digital video should result in a plurality of concurrent options, where the determinant for delivery of visual information will simply be the location and the convenience of the user, irrespective of whether the user is in the home, classroom or office. The aim of this statement has been to illustrate the current dynamic of change in communications, in broadcasting, in entertainment and information technologies and the role of multimedia therein. It is a pattern of change, that is simultaneously divergent in terms of the wide range of new applications being created, but equally convergent in terms of the increasing intersection of the channels of information delivery, in which our phone may deliver our television and our television may deliver (and process) our multimedia data. It is an exciting prospect, in which innovative interface design will play an important role.

Long Term Research on Intelligent Information Interfaces

Jakub Wejchert
Esprit Long Term Research
DG III, European Commission
Rue de la Loi 200
B-1049 Brussels, Belgium

Abstract

Intelligent Information Interfaces (i^3) is a new initiative of the ESPRIT Long Term Research. Its aim is to promote research and development of new interfaces and interaction paradigms for interacting with information. These new interfaces will provide comfortable access to information for the broad population (i.e. not restricted to few specialists). An i^3 home page *http://www.cordis.lu/esprit/src/eyehome.htm*, a Brokerage page *http://www.cordis.lu/esprit/src/eyelist.htm* and an i^3-NET page *http://www.i3net.org* provide information about i^3 activities.

1. Introduction

Intelligent Information Interfaces (i^3) is a new Esprit Long Term Research "pro-active" initiative, which aims at developing new human centred interface paradigms for interacting with information for the broad population. i^3 aims at a radical departure from present-day man-machine interface concepts and does so under the assumption that this must be guided by a long term vision for combining human and information society aspects with the technological development. Two main schemata support the principal aims of i^3, namely new forms of interaction, that will engage people as active participants in the creation and use of information, rather than simply being passive recipients. Both place the interplay of human, society and technological factors on as the key to the development of these interfaces. The first schemata, called *Connected Community*, places particular accent on the communication within a local geographical community. The second schemata, called *Inhabited Information Spaces*, addresses the creation of information spaces for people who are geographically dispersed. These schemata were introduced in order to provide a human-centred vision for interacting with information through a guiding master-plan for a set of related projects.

There was an open call for schemata in September 1995. Following an elaboration of the successful schema proposals, an open call for project proposals (September 1996) will result in a selection of projects that implement the main objectives. The projects should deliver new models, new techniques and new technologies that could, if successful, constitute the necessary building block for the interface development of tomorrow.

2. Objectives of i^3

The i^3 initiative aims at *developing* new human centred interfaces for interacting with information, suitable for the broad population.

2.1 Broad Population

The objectives of i^3 addresses many concepts. First let's look at the accent on the broad population. If the information society is to work then it must apply to all society - not just the select few specialists. A key to making this happen is ensuring accessibility, participation and ease of use for all. For this to happen, new approaches for interacting with information are needed that will leap beyond the present-day solutions. In the past the traditional approach has been to design interfaces that assume technically knowledgeable users, and hoping that this will extend outside of that sphere. In contrast, i^3 specifically targets the broad population and specifically excludes specialist use. For example, it excludes work on new interfaces for pilots, but would consider work on interfaces for pilots in their non-specialist role, for example in the home. To hope to arrive at new interaction paradigms for the broad population there must be a long term view that intertwines human, societal and technological factors in an iterative manner right from the start.

2.2 Interacting with Information

In the initiative, the term "information" is taken in the broad sense of the word, embracing information that is mediated through communication with people, through participation in entertainment, or through tele-services. It does not simply refer to the traditional interpretation of "a user getting information from a data-base". Also the term "human-centred" is employed and the term "user" is avoided. Specifically, this means that the future interfaces research and development should be based around the fundamental physical, cognitive and behavioural aspects of humans and will enable bi-directional interaction, allowing information to be given and received in natural and effective ways. In addition this means that the interfaces will be designed for people in their environments and will have a "look", "sound" and "feel" appropriate to their uses. All these aspects should contribute to future interfaces having the role of a mediating influence for human activity and interaction, rather than simply a tool that permits the passive consumption of information.

2.3 Human Centred Technological Development

"Human-centred" is not only a passive concept it is also a dynamic one: it encompasses the notion of empowering the lives of people. Empowerment is further reaching than simply enriching the individual - it also enables the individual to act and be able to do things that he or she could not do before. Examples of interfaces that empower an individual could include ones that can act as personal "guides" by offering a range of services such as real-time consultation or augmenting personal knowledge. To empower an individual, an interface has to adapt to the personal preference of the individual, for example, by pro-actively searching and filtering information in order to suit a personal profile, or by being easily customisable to suit fashion or personal image. It could also provide controllable degrees of privacy and security. In essence, the term human-centred aims to place the human, human values and human activities as the central driving force of technological development.

2.4 New Interfaces, New Paradigms

In order to try and bring about some of the changes mentioned above, the initiative aims at a radical departure from present-day man-machine interface concepts and does this under the assumption that this can only be done through a long term research effort guided by a long term vision. Although it is appreciated that some improvements can be made through incremental improvements to present-day interface scenarios - this will not lead to the "quantum leap" required for new interfaces of the information age. This will be an age in which both the value and quantity of information will have multiplied exponentially compared to our present day levels.

What do new paradigms mean in the context of interfaces? What is meant is a completely new way of interacting with information or people, mediated by technology. An example from the recent past illustrates this. Let's take an example from the evolution of human computer interface: consider the simple command line input that many of us have used. This consisted of a line at which a set of commands could be typed. We can take this as one paradigm for human-computer interaction. Now, "incremental approaches" would take and try and improve command line input as much as possible; various comments could be used to help editing on one line or perhaps editing on many lines could be possible. However, these improvements will not take us very far; what is needed is a "quantum leap" that takes us out of the command line paradigm into a new one: in our case, the "Windows/Desk Top" paradigm, which we can say is the current paradigm for human-computer interaction. Here, instead of forcing a human to use something close to a "machine language", it used the analogy of the Desk Top that is displayed, and can be interacted with on the screen using icons, a mouse, and so on. Moving from one paradigm to the next took a long term investment that was guided by a more user-centred vision of mapping the office Desk Top into the interface. By analogy, i^3 aims at developing the new interaction paradigms necessary for the information society of the future.

3. Approach

For such new paradigms to be given a chance of emerging, new guiding visions are necessary. For this reason, i^3 first calls for new human-centred visions and masterplans for future interfaces, and then calls for projects that will carry out the work guided by the very best of these visions. It principally consists of two stages: a call for schemata and a call for projects

1. Open call for schema proposals (September 1995).
   Evaluate and select a small number of schemata. (January/February 1996).
   The selected schemata are elaborated and finalised in agreement with the Commission. (March - June 1996).
2. Open calls for projects to carry out the tasks described by the schemata (September 1996).

This will result in long term research projects, covering areas such as computer science, cognitive psychology, engineering, art and design, that will be harnessed and guided by a long term human centred vision and masterplan. This description of a new vision as well as a master-plan of how to implement it is referred to as a schema. In fact there is a similar procedure used in architectural competitions for the execution of public buildings. In this case too, vision must precede implementation similarly.

The first stage is a competition for visions of a future building described by an outline sketch and overall costs. The best of these submissions are then asked for elaboration and refinement and the best chosen.

Then follows the second phase when there are calls to tender for the site contractors, which carry out all aspects of building, implementing the plans and vision. Needless to say, we would have little vision if all building were started by simply laying the bricks without an over-riding concept.

4. What will emerge from i^3 ?

Notable features of schemata will probably include: a genuine notion of a bi-directional approach to interfaces, in contrast to the asymmetrical "active service provider feeding information to the passive user" view; a strong influence of design cultures together with a non-linear plan for coupling technical innovation with citizen participation; as well as care to channel technological innovation within a human-centred vision, thereby setting the basis for discovering new interaction paradigms.

It is difficult to describe specifically what the initiative will provide until the schemata have been selected and elaborated on; however some general statements will hold. The projects that will implement the schemata will aim to deliver new models, new techniques and new technologies that could, if successful, constitute the necessary building blocks for the interface development of tomorrow. Clearly the initiative does not intend i^3 projects to immediately lead to interface products, but it will lead to results from which future product development could evolve; these "results" would typically take the form of demonstrators or research prototypes. Results from i^3 projects could thus feed into the downstream programmes of Esprit or ACTS, in the further development of such research. In addition the models, techniques and insights gained from i^3 projects could provide input for future telematics projects that might integrate, test and deploy future applications in the user context.

5. Further Information

This article presented gave some background on the i^3 initiative in an informal way. It presented the main ideas with illustrative examples and drew conclusions of what will be expected to emerge from the initiative as it evolves. Regularly updated information about this initiative is available on the i^3 home page, at the following address:

http://www.cordis.lu/esprit/src/eyehome.htm

Additionally, a Brokerage page was set up in order to facilitate proposers in the creation of project partnerships, at the following address:

http://www.cordis.lu/esprit/src/eyelist.htm

No single project will be expected to address all aspects of a schemata. Rather, it is expected that the work suggested by a schemata will be carried out by several projects with a degree of synergy among them. In this context a Network of Excellence (with the i^3-NET home page *http://www.i3net.org*) was set up with the primary goal of supporting cooperation between projects.

ETHICS: User led Requirements Analysis and Business Process Improvement

Enid Mumford
Emeritus Professor Manchester University
4 Windmill Close, Appelton, Warrington
Cheshire WA4 5JS, United Kingdom

Abstract

This paper discusses a participative design method called ETHICS. ETHICS focuses on the non-technical aspects of systems design, in particular a pre-change diagnosis of needs and an effective restructuring of the work situation. The front end of ETHICS, QUICKethics, is used to assist the definition of information needs prior to the acquisition of MIS.

1. Introduction

ETHICS stands for Effective Technical and Human Implementation of Computer based Systems. It is a systems design methodology that involves users in the specification of their information needs and in the design of the organizational context that surrounds the technical system. It is also called ETHICS because user involvement is perceived by its developer Professor Enid Mumford, as an ethical approach to systems design [1], [2], [4], [6].

ETHICS has three important design stages. First, the analysis and description of needs and problems. These are frequently information needs, but will also include other factors such as poor work processes and significant operational problems. Second, the setting of clear objectives for the design of the new system. These objectives will be both related to improving efficiency and to increasing the job satisfaction and quality of working life of the user group. Third, the redesign of the work organization. This is done, first, to improve the ability of the department or function to operate at high efficiency when achieving its business mission [5]. Ideally, this reorganization is carried out before the introduction of new technologies. Second, to enable the new technical system to operate as efficiently and effectively as possible. This further reorganization is established once the new technology is in use. In the past, both of these forms of reorganization have been called "*organizational design*". Today they are often called business process improvement or business process reengineering.

ETHICS will be described in detail later in this paper, but first it is important to discuss the advantages of user involvement, and to be clear about what participation means and requires.

2. What is Participation

Participation has many definitions. Here are two:

- "participation creates opportunities under suitable conditions for people to influence decisions which affect them", and
- "all members of a work group who are affected by a decision are involved in influencing it"

A definition that fits user involvement in systems design defines participation as: *"a process in which two or more parties influence each other in making plans, policies or decisions. It is restricted to decisions that have future effects on all those making the decisions or on those represented by them".*

All definitions recognize that participation involves more than one set of interests, and that it is concerned with decision taking. Any company or group using it to assist systems design must identify the interests involved, and the subjects with which the decision taking is or should be concerned. It is also necessary to consider in some detail how the participation is to be managed. This will include the structures and processes that will ensure it works effectively.

3. Why have Participation?

The arguments for participation today are many and varied. Managers may decide to try a participative approach because they believe that participation is morally right - people should be able to determine their own destinies. Or they may see participation as helping to produce an interested and committed group of staff and therefore assisting in the avoidance of morale and job satisfaction problems. They may believe that participation is a valuable educational experience and provides understanding and knowledge that can help an organization to realise its business objectives or, alternatively, that such knowledge will enable any negotiating that takes place to do so with all interest groups operating from an informed position.

A particularly significant argument today is that expensive systems may fail to work effectively or even to become operational if user participation is not a part of the design process.

There is now a high degree of risk in not involving users. Frequently users have knowledge that systems designers urgently need. The London Ambulance system failure was apparently influenced by a lack of user involvement.

Many of today's users are powerful groups who can be ambivalent about a new system if they are not involved. This is true of management groups, particularly senior management, many of whom were educated without having contact with computers. Most important, if users are not involved the new system may not be 'relevant' to their information needs. In the author's experience a bad fit between a new system and the requirements of the user is the most frequent cause of user dissatisfaction.

Employees are usually interested in participation for different reasons. If they are low down in the company hierarchy in the office or on the shop floor they can see it as a protective device that will enable them to prevent things that they believe to be undesirable from happening. They want to avoid being deskilled or forced to undertake tasks they regard as time consuming and irrelevant, or even made redundant. They also hope to have more interesting jobs, better opportunities to provide a good service and for promotion and an improved quality of working life. Participation may assist them to achieve these.

Managers often have to be persuaded to participate. They plead lack of time or claim it is the computer department's responsibility. Once they do get involved, however, they also become committed to a new system and appreciate that they can steer the design process in a direction that will enable them to do a more effective job. The most difficult group to persuade to participate are usually top management.

One of the problems, and also advantages of participation, is that it brings together individuals or groups who may have very different interests. Each interest group is likely to define the problem in a different way and to direct the participation process at different objectives. The challenge for any organization that decides to use participation as a strategy then becomes to create the kinds of structures and processes that will assist all the different stakeholders to obtain some gains from using this approach. These gains will not necessarily be all of the same kind but they should enable each group to say with conviction *"the new system will have clear benefits for us"*.

4. Participation Structure, Content and Process

Any company interested in user involvement in systems design must take decisions on the structure of participation, the content of participation and the process of participation. The structure of participation is concerned with the mechanisms for enabling participation to take place.

A company creating a participative structure will, for example, have to decide whether to choose direct or indirect forms of participation. Direct participation is when everyone with an interest in the new system wants to exert some influence. This is often true of management or specialist groups. Indirect participation is when influence is exerted through intermediaries. If an indirect approach such as a representative group is chosen as the vehicle for decision making, then attention has to be paid to such matters as ensuring that all interests are represented, to deciding how the members of the participative forum are selected or elected and whether a number of groups at different organizational levels are required.

When a structure for participation is being created decisions have also to be taken about the extent to which certain groups of participants will be allowed to influence decisions. There can be 'consultative' decision taking in which the participants give evidence to the decision makers, this evidence being taken into account when decisions are taken. There is also 'consensus' decision taking in which all participants have an equal voice in the decision making process, and "responsible" decision taking in which the participants are given full authority for making decisions in any way they see fit and are not constrained by any laid down procedures.

The author has used a number of different participative structures in the firms where she has contributed to systems design. She has used a "consultative" decision process in which employees contribute ideas to the design process, although the final decision is prepared by the specialist group. She has also used a *'"representative"'*approach in which design groups formed from selected or elected representatives of the various interest groups take design decisions and a 'consensus' approach in which members of a design group constantly discuss ideas and solutions with their constituents. They then prepare a number of alternative solutions, the final choice being made by the constituents and not the design group. These options of *"consultative"*, *"representative"* and *"consensus'* participation can also be used at different organizational levels.

The content of participation is the nature of the issues about which decisions are taken. But it is more than this. It involves a consideration of decision boundaries; that is, what subjects can be considered participatively and what subjects are outside the jurisdiction of the participative group and are seen as executive decisions which are not taken by the user design group.

The process of participation also involves the acquisition of knowledge so that decisions are taken from an informed position. It involves learning, the development of effective working relationships over time, the setting and achieving of goals, and the implementation of solutions.

5. Participation as a Contribution to Effective Systems Design

The design of new systems is very suitable for a participative approach for the following reasons:

- It usually involves a number of interest groups (management, systems designers, direct users, indirect users, suppliers, customers etc.).
- It requires knowledge and this knowledge is likely to be spread throughout the different interest groups and not be located solely in one.
- The design task is complex and takes time. Participation enables a shared learning process to take place in which each of the interest groups can contribute to the problem solving process.
- The various interest groups are likely to have different values, needs and objectives and these can be brought out into the open, discussed and attempts made to reconcile them as part of the participative process.

Participation involves a process over time and not merely the giving of an opinion at one moment in time. It requires a high commitment from users who may be associated with all aspects of systems development including analysis, design, construction, implementation and evaluation. Participation in the total design task for a new system would involve the following:

- Participating in the initiation of the project. Agreeing that it shall go ahead.
- Diagnosis and specification of existing problems and needs.
- Setting of organizational and technical objectives.
- Examination of alternative solutions.
- Selection of 'best fit' solution.
- Detailed design of organizational and technical work systems and procedures.
- Implementation of the system.
- Evaluation of the working system.
- Strategies for further development.

Systems design can occur at three different organizational levels. The top where it is concerned with strategic planning, the middle where it covers system definition for a number of processes, units, functions or departments and the bottom where it relates to the implementation of a technical and organizational subsystem for a single department or function. The participative approach can be used at all of these levels although it may take a different form depending on whether it is concerned with higher or lower level systems.

6. The ETHICS Approach

6.1 Starting with Organizational Redesign

Once clear objectives for change have been agreed then, ideally, the change process should begin with organizational redesign or business process improvement.

There are two reasons for starting here rather than with technical design. The first is that new technology needs to be associated with an effective, streamlined form of work organization and not with an old system often created to accommodate manual or early computer processes. The second is that it is important for a design group to be very clear about the business mission, objectives key tasks, critical success factors and major problems of the work area it is concerned with before making major investment decisions in technology.

Business process reengineering is being sold as today's management panacea but exhortations to try it are not usually associated with a clear description of how to do it. ETHICS contains such a methodology derived from socio-technical systems design [3]. Here is a brief description of how to proceed.

The methodological framework of ETHICS is influenced by a cybernetic model developed by Professor Stafford Beer, the Socio-technical design principles of the Tavistock Institute and the Total Quality programmes of W. Edwards Deming. The work of Beer provides a neat analytical model of a "viable system" and this, in turn, enables clear simple descriptions of work activities to be made (see figure 1). A firm, department, or work process can be described as a hierarchy of five levels of activity. Each of these levels must be recognised, designed and managed, and must interact smoothly with the others if work is to proceed at a high level of performance. The diagram below shows the five levels in the model.

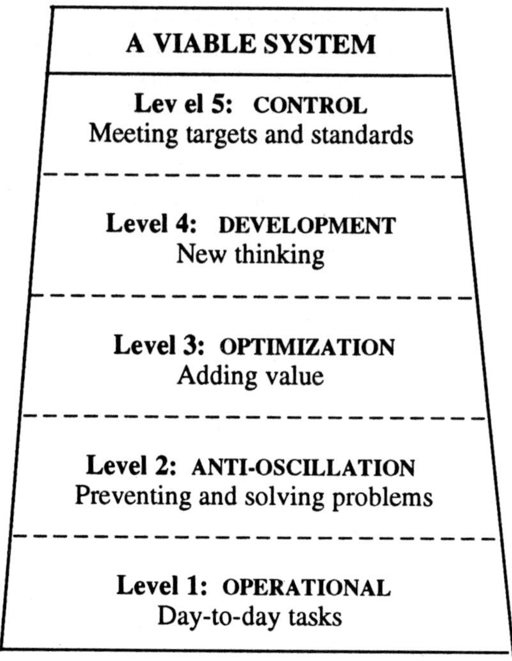

Fig.1: Levels of Cybernetic Model

This viable system model enables those responsible for redesign to examine existing work processes and to set out systematically and comprehensively ideas for an improved system. The contribution of socio-technical design to ETHICS is twofold. First, it provides a clear philosophy - that the aim of system design is to optimize both the use of people and technology. Technology should be designed to work as efficiently as possible but, at the same time, the activities of people should be designed so as to provide opportunities for learning and self-development. Second, it also provides a design logic that enables work processes to be analysed in a systematic step-by-step manner. A design group which must contain both users and technical specialists should proceed in the following way.

6.2 Designing the Organizational System

Diagnosing the problem is the first task in designing the organisational system, and consists of following 10 steps.

Step 1: Identifying the Process.

The system that is to be redesigned should first be identified. It may be a long work process stretching from the receipt of an order to the delivery of a product. This will cross many boundaries and have to be designed in stages. Or it may be a shorter process focusing on the work of a single department or function, for example a sales office.

Step 2: Define the mission, efficiency objectives, critical success factors and major problems (key variances). As any redesignn must be directed at enabling a system to achieve its business mission more effectively, this mission must be agreed and clearly stated. Once the mission is written down major efficiency objectives and critical success factors related to its achievement should be identified. The most serious problems that prevent or slow down its achievement should also be noted.

Step 3: Describe the environment in which the system is located.
This will include internal and external environments. These are other systems with which the selected system must interact, the office, departamental or other environments and the external supplier and customer markets.

Step 4: Describe the work process (unit operations).
Next, the design group should identify the different sets or networks of activities which progress the product along the route of the work process. These are groups of activities which help move the product into its finished state yet which are relatively self-contained. Usually there will be some kind of discontinuity between each stage - for example, the introduction of a new set of procedures, a new material or an elapse of time. They are called unit operations. This is level one of the Beer Viable System Model.

Step 5: Identification of variances.
The design group should now look in more detail at the system problems or "variances". A variance being defined as a weak link in the system where it becomes difficult to achieve required or desired norms or standards. A variance is considered 'key' if it affects the quantity or quality of output, or operating or social costs. Variances should be carefully documented. They are often to be found at the boundary between one unit operation and the next and at the boundary between the system and its environment. This is level two of the Viable System Model.

Step 6: Value adding activities
Activities which add value to the product as it moves through the system should also be noted. This is the 'value chain' and is part of level three.

Step 7: Work relationships - analysis of the social system.
Required individual and group work relationships should next be examined and documented. These would cover:

- Who needs to work with whom and how.
- A description of the relationships required between staff for the optimal production of the product.
- A note on the extent of required work flexibility. The knowledge each employee needs to have to carry out his or her work and to understand the work of others.

Step 8: Job satisfaction analysis. How staff see their roles.
The design group should also examine the extent to which staff think a new organisation of work and changes to their present roles could remove frustrations and increase job satisfaction. A questionnaire plus small group discussions can assist this analysis.

Step 9: Development activities.
An assessment should be made of how the systems of technical and business support in operation impact on, and affect, the process being investisated. Will these also need reorganization? The same should be done for systems that supply materials and services. This is level four of the viable system model.

Step 10: Strategy and the corporate environment.
Information should be obtained on how corporate development plans might affect the future operation of the process that is being redesigned. This is level five of the Viable System.

6.3 Arriving at a Solution

Arriving at a solution is the next task, and consists of following step:

Step 11: Proposals for change.
Finally, the design group should gather together all this information and, after discussions with the different interest groups associated with the system, should arrive at an action programme for change. Ideally, proposals for action must contribute both to the improvement of the business system and to the improvement of the social system. The latter requires change directed at improving job satisfaction and the quality of the work environment.

6.4 Proposals for Change

Proposals for change should fit into the Beer framework. There is a need to:

- Consider again the mission, efficiency objectives, critical success factors and strategies for overcoming major problems. (key variances). These must be reexamined with some care as subsequent design decisions will be evaluated in terms of their ability to contribute to their achievement.
- Specify the new flow and organization of the sets of work activities. (level one unit operations).
These are the day-to-day or regular activities related to the production of the primary product. Redesign should include the removal of redundant tasks and the speeding up of slow tasks. It is important to retain some slack in the new work process. Very tight systems place employees under stress and remove opportunities for use of initiative and creative thought and action.

- Note proposals for controlling potential new variance areas.
Even though the new system is an improvement, the old problems are still likely to be found at the interfaces between one unit operation and the next. Many of the old variances situated between the system and its environment will also still exist and need controlling more effectively than before.
- Note proposals for adding value.
Identify those activities that now contribute most to the development of the product and establish how they can be carried out most effectively.
- New development activities.
When redesigning a system the future must never be forgotten. Required new developments will come from an examination of the external environment and the changes that are likely to take place there. Think about introducing new activities, for example, new customer services, which can add value to the work process.
- New business strategies. Proposals for long term as well as short term change should be examined and documented.
- Required relationships.
All these proposed changes will lead to a requirement for new skills, roles and relationships. These must be identified and appropriate training programmes prepared.
- Required job satisfaction improvements.
Step eight of the diagnosis of needs will have shown the level of job satisfaction associated with the old process. Activities and conditions causing frustration and dissatisfaction must now be removed or improved without new problems being created.
- New measures of performance.
Lastly, wherever targets and goals can be set to measure improvement this should be done. An estimate of improvement often requires a knowledge of the pre-change situation. Whenever possible pre-change measures should be collected before changes take place.

In many situations the socio-technical concept of self-managing groups will be found to be an organizational solution that achieves both business and social objectives, although the degree of self-management permitted will depend on the views of staff and management. A degree of self-management is found to increase motivation and assist the better control of business problems, quality improvement and the achievement of production targets.

Each proposed change, as it is discussed, must be evaluated in terms of its ability to contribute to the achievement of the business mission and objectives, the critical success factors and the elimination or improved control of problems. These organizational changes should now be tested out with a pilot system. If they prove viable in the sense that they increase efficiency, reduce costs and improve job satisfaction then consideration can be given to technology. The next step is the identification and introduction of a new technical system that will fit into and enhance the new work organization.

7. Examples of Organizational Design

Early examples of organizational design or business process improvement include the removal of moving assembly lines by Philips in the Netherlands and the replacement of simple, routine tasks by a work system which enabled each worker to assemble a complete television set. The development of multi-skilled craftsmen by Norsk Hydro in their fertiliser plant and the well known experiments by Volvo in which the moving automobile assembly line was replaced by a dock system in which groups of workers assembled an entire car. It is interesting that although economic pressures caused Volvo to abandon this system in the eighties, they have now returned to it in one of their plants.

Projects with which the author has been involved include the redesign of a major bank's foreign exchange department so that clerks were given responsibility for all activities associated with a group of clients instead of single tasks. This required them to become multi-skilled. A similar system was introduced in an aircraft engine manufacturer with purchase invoice clerks being made responsible for all activities related to a group of suppliers. Similar projects have been carried out in an international chemical group and an American computer manufacturer. All of these projects were associated with the introduction of new computer systems and all tried to give employees more responsibility through multi-skilling and opportunities for problem solving and decision taking. All of these projects also led to greater efficiency and more Job satisfaction for staff.

Today, consultants in the Netherlands are using a version of ETHICS to facilitate organizational change in a number of major Dutch corporations.

8. QUICKethics: Requirements Analysis to assist Choice of Software

Once the new form of work organization has been thought through and piloted it becomes necessary to assess information requirements. The front end of ETHICS which is called QUICKethics (QUality Information from Considered Knowledge) is used to assist this. Increasingly, QUICKethics is used to guide the choice of appropriate software. Users have included air line managers, nurses selecting a ward management system and production managers investing in a material and capacity planning system.The Beer Viable System model can be used for specifying information needs in the way described in figure 2.

QUlCKethics offers a mix of activities all directed at the elicitation of accurate information. These include a questionnaire, group discussions and the visual build up of knowledge needs through placing individual items of wanted information on flip charts or a magnetic board.

The questionnaire is given to each manager in the group to complete before the meeting. It begins by asking the manager to describe his or her work mission, key tasks, critical success factors and major problems. These are seen as the essential elements of the manager's job. They are also almost certainly the most stable. They will only change fundamentally if the manager experiences major changes of role and function.

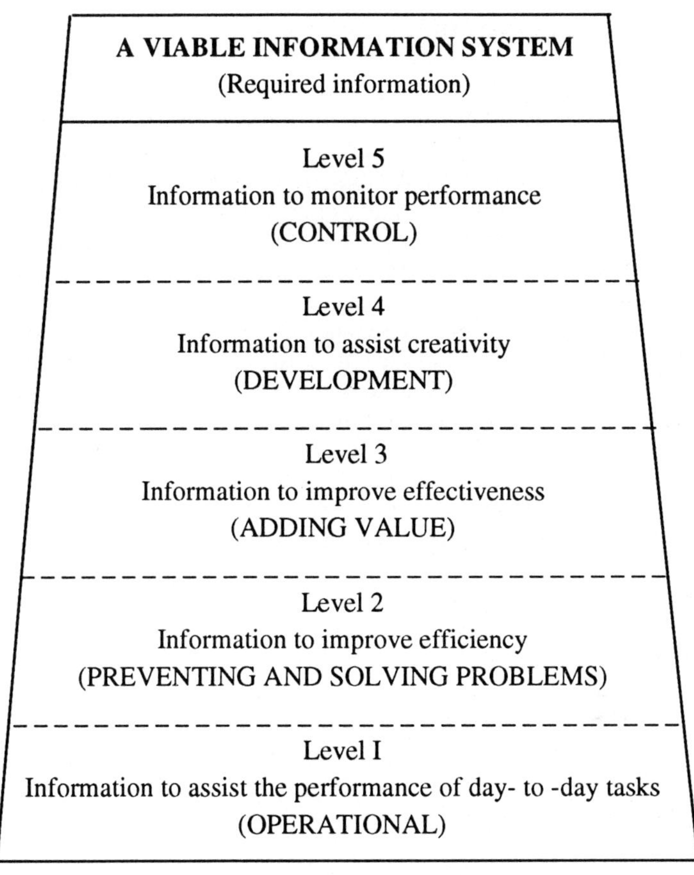

Fig.2: Information needs specified with Beer Viable System model

The manager is then asked to describe each of his or her key tasks in detail. This analysis covers the five level cybernetic model of Beer, shown above.
Each of these levels must be handled well individually and interact smoothly with the others, if the task is to be carried out at a high level of performance. Finally, the manager is asked to state the information needs associated with each level of each key task. He or she is then asked to separate these into quantitative and qualitative and to prioritise them into *"essential"*, *"desirable"*, and *"useful"*.

Some days after completing the questionnaire the managers meet together for two days, discuss their information needs as a group, document these and agree a core information structure that will act as a starting point for implementing the new system.

The author has recently used QUICKethics in a Dutch company manufacturing power tools which required computers for shop floor material and machine capacity planning. This will be used as a case study to illustrate the ETHICS approach.

9. A Case Study Example

The proposal was to abandon an old and unsatisfactory computer-based material planning system and to substitute more advanced software that would run on a new IBM AS 400 machine that had recently been acquired. Nine managers were involved in the project - two planning managers, three factory production managers, the finance manager, a quality manager and two managers from R&D.

The author went through the QUICKethics questionnaire with each manager individually, wrote the interview up and gave the report back to the individual manager so that he could check its accuracy. These interviews had a threefold purpose. First, to enable the manager to think clearly and systematically about his role and responsibilities before considering his information needs. Second, to enable him to obtain a clear picture of his information needs before meeting his colleagues in a group situation. Third, to arouse interest and a sense of ownership in the proposed new system.

One week after the interviews the managers met as a group. As nine is quite a large number for fast decision making, the author split them into four groups - Planning, Production, Quality and R&D. Each of these groups was asked to think back to their individual answers the week before, and to now agree and prioritise a set of essential information needs. Each list was described and explained by one of the sub-group who had produced it and was discussed by the group as a whole. During the meeting a Board level manager stated what senior management required. This included software that did not need more than 15% customising for the company; that could be implemented safely and without risk - there must be no possibility of plant stoppages, and that was supporting rather than controlling of users.

The last task for the group was to agree on a core information system that could act as a starting point for implementation. Everyone present agreed that this should cover three items. First, Bills of Material. These specified in detail the materials and production steps associated with each product. Second, material planning and machine capacity planning should have next priority. These were two critical activities which were essential to the running of the production system. Finally, it was agreed that the managers, reduced to six in number, should become the user design group for the project.

The author went away and produced a comprehensive report which detailed the core system, the essential information needs of Planning, Production, Quality and R&D, and the detailed information needs of each manager. This last would act as a development guide to be implemented over time, once the system became operational.

10. Benefits from ETHICS and QUICKethics

ETHICS is now being used in three ways. First, for the task for which it was originally designed - to help the future users of a system to play a major role in the design of that system by diagnosing their needs and problems, setting business and technical objectives for the system and, assisted by the professional systems designers, restructuring their work situation and the tasks contained in it so as to increase both business efficiency and the quality of working life. Second, ETHICS is being used to assist managers to define their information needs prior to the introduction of a management information system. Here a simplified form of ETHICS, called QUICKethics has been developed. Third, ETHICS is being used as a general problem solving tool to enable groups to analyse needs and problems systematically with a view to improving performance. This improvement does not necessarily incorporate new technology.

All of these provide benefits for users. They have the satisfaction of participating in an important development activity designed to improve their own work situation. This gives them a sense of control, a feeling of ownership and the satisfaction of involvement in a creative activity. Because they have carefully diagnosed their own needs and problems and contributed to the final technical and organizational solutions, the new system will be seen as both highly relevant to the users' present work situation and open to future change by them as circumstances alter. And they will have had an important learning experience which will assist them to become more effective in the management of their own change.

11. Results of ETHICS Application

One lesson learnt is that participation works and that groups at every level of the company find it useful, satisfying and enjoyable. It produces systems that have a high relevance to user needs and, in the author's experience an absence of perceived relevance is a frequent source of system failure.

A second lesson is that today's systems are so technically and organizationally complex that systems designers have difficulty designing them without help from users. This problem is exacerbated by today's trend to outsource the IT function.

A third lesson is that it is still very difficult to persuade firms to use a participative approach to systems design. There are a number of reasons for this. First, new systems have so much hype associated with them that managers are reluctant to believe there is any risk of system failure. Second, senior managers and systems specialists are often afraid that participation means handing over a degree of control to users. They are reluctant to do this.

A fourth lesson is that participation, like all innovations, requires skill and good management for it to succeed. Firms may not possess these attributes.

12. Future Developments

ETHICS and QUICKethics are well documented but still paper based. Although the formation of user design groups and participative discussions are an essential part of the method, these do not all necessarily need to take place in face-to-face situations. Research in the United States on the structure and management of electronic discussions can provide guidance on how the method could be developed to encompass groups who cannot physically meet. The author hopes to develop appropriate software to facilitate discussion processes over networks. ETHICS and QUICKethics work smoothly, are enjoyed as social processes and produce fast and excellent results. Nevertheless, they are not widely used. Their considerable use in the Netherlands is due to the author at one time being associated with a Dutch software company and to the interest and use of the approach by a Dutch Consultancy specialising in the management of change. There are now many books on ETHICS and a number of training courses provided by the author. The stimulation of a more general use appears to require more than this.

Relevant Books

1. Mumford E. "Systems design: ethical tools for ethical change", Macmillan, 1996.
2. Mumford E. "Effective systems design and requirements analysis", Macmillan, 1995.
3. Mumford E. and Beekman G.-J. "Tools for change: and progress: a socio-technical approach to business process reengineering", CSG Publications, 1994.
4. Mumford E. "Designing human systems for health care", Eight Associates, 1993.
5. Mumford E., MacDonald B. "XSEL's Progress: the continuing journey of an expert system", Wiley, 1989.
6. Mumford E. "Designing human systems for new technology", Manchester Business School, 1983.

Bridging Software Design and Usability Analysis through Task Modelling

Patrizia Marti
Italsoft
Corso del Rinascimento 52
I-00186 Rome, Italy

Veronique Normand
Thomson-CSF Laboratoire Central de Recherches
Computer Science Group, Advanced Human-Computer Interaction Laboratory
Domaine de Corbeville, F-91404 ORSAY, France

Abstract

A user-centred approach to systems design and evaluation is presented. In particular task modelling is proposed as a bridging technology for understanding users' needs, feeding this understanding into design and evaluating the usability of design choices. The approach is proposed as a general methodological framework for the design, the development and the evaluation of interactive systems. We discuss the beneficial bridging effects of task modelling throughout the development life cycle presenting the experience of the ESPRIT Project CHARADE, an integrated system for handling environmental emergencies. The main aspects of our experience are reported highlighting how the system life cycle has been characterized by an early and continual involvement of the final user, and how task analysis and modelling are shared resources for the entire development process.

1. Introduction

The concept of "User-Centred System Design" [14] was developped as a reaction to the classical function-directed design, around the simple key idea that placing the users at the centre of the design, and evaluation activities would ensure that the system is designed to meet their needs. User-centred system design is generally implemented through a iterative process model [5], characterised by an iterative design with many cycles of "design - test with users - redesign", based on a massive use of prototypes. Iterations aim at further refining and adjusting the evolving system design, in order to closely fit the users' needs. Our approach to the system development process is an iterative user-centred approach is based on two considerations: *(i)* the development processes is based on rapid prototyping and multiple design-test cycles would benefit from a more structured approach for reducing and better controlling the number of cycles and improving traceability of decisions.; *(ii)* the task analysis and modelling is widely acknowledged as a major human factors tool for user-centred system design ([7], [2]); its practice however suffers important criticisms, mainly: an imbalanced focus on analysis, Task Analysis failing to directly contribute to system design; the inadequate format of Task Analysis outputs, which hinders exploitation at design time. These considerations call for a structured development process involving a broader view of task analysis, and tools ensuring the effective exploitation of task analysis results throughout the process. Starting from different proposals in the research community [1] [9] we sketched a task-based development process as the instanciation of task analysis in an iterative process.

Our approach [15] [10] is characterized by the presence of task modelling at all process stages, the reuse of the output of initial task analysis activities transformed and improved along the successive stages of the process. This user centred and task-centred perspective on the design of the target system counter balances the traditional function-oriented approach, favouring a process where the user needs and task requirements identified in the early phases are fully supported in the final product. The continuum of task models supports the traceability of task constraints and related design decisions and ensures the effective exploitation of the human factors point of view all along the process.

The CHARADE project development process is an implementation of this approach. CHARADE (an acronym for "Combining Human Assessment and Reasoning Aids for Decision making in environmental Emergencies") is a project running in the 3rd Framework Program of the European Community with a consortium composed by seven organizations. The consortium is composed of five system developers: Alenia (Rome, Italy) as the project leader, Alcatel ISR (Paris, France), Ceselsa Inisel (Madrid, Spain), Italsoft (Rome, Italy), Thomson. The CHARADE project aims at building a software platform for the development of decision support systems in the field of environmental emergencies; its primary application domain is forest fire fighting [18].

In the following sections we report the main aspects of our experience highlighting how the system life cycle has been characterized from the initial phases by an early and continual involvement of the final user and how task analysis and modelling are shared resources for the entire development process.

2. Task-based Development Process

Figure 1 illustrates the main characteristics of our approach, highlighting the different task modelling topics (on the right-hand side of the diagramme) with respect to the general analysis, specification, design and evaluation stages. For clarity's sake, only the main resulting products are represented, leaving out actions and their dependencies.

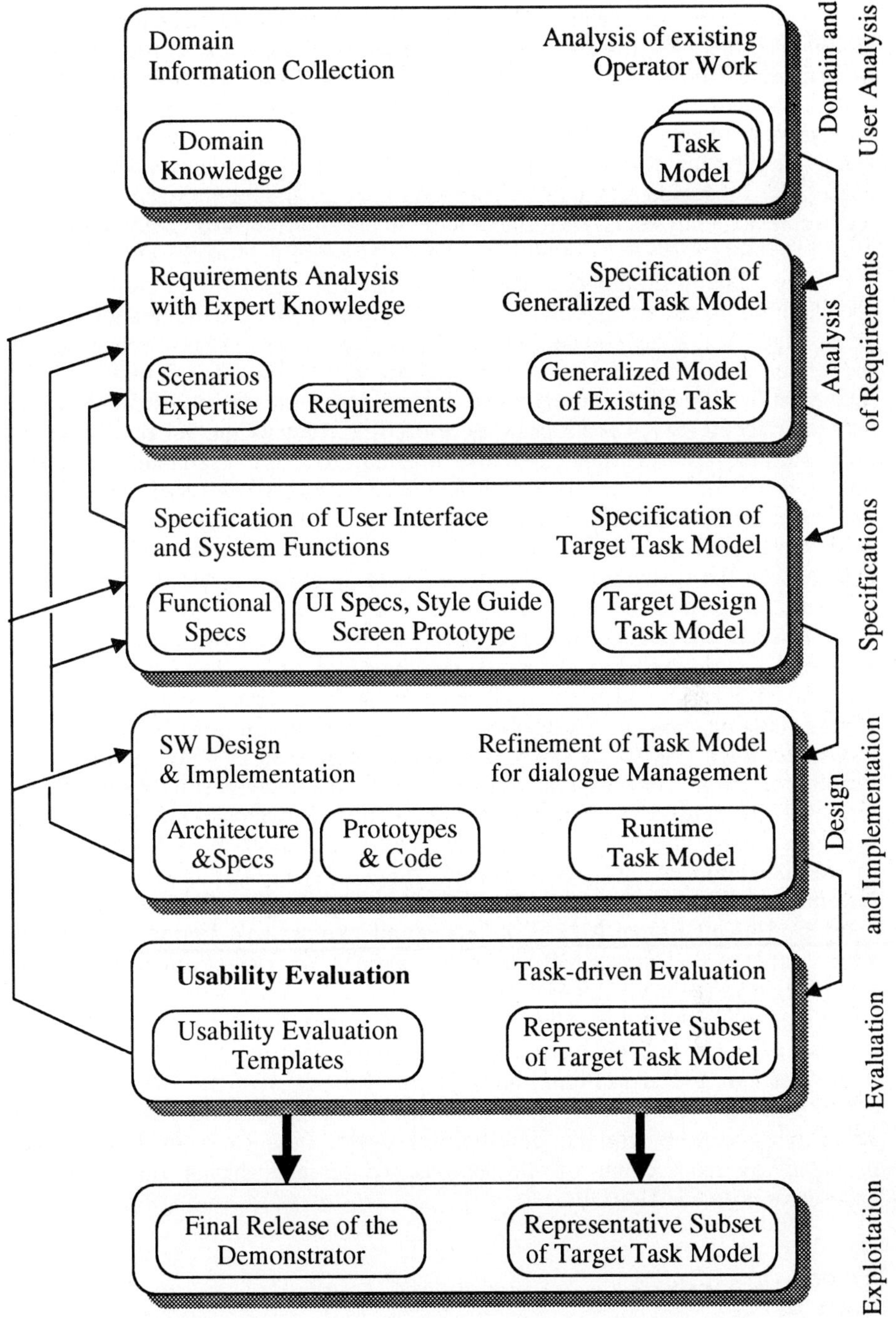

Fig. 1: System development cycle of CHARADE

Task analysis is usually performed at the analysis stage, along and in interrelationship with application domain analysis [11]. Here the existing work of users is studied and analyzed; the interview of different operators leads to the construction of different task models; a generalized model of existing tasks is built as a synthesis of the different task models. Expert knowledge acquisition leads to a refinement of the generalized task model. The generalized task model contributes to the identification of user requirements in terms of task constraints; requirements analysis is performed with the support of the generalized task model for identifying and delimiting potential system functionality.

The generalized model of the existing tasks is again an input to the system specification phase, along with the analyzed requirements and application domain knowledge. A new task model is built at this stage, the target task model, that is the model of the target system-operator activity. This model is defined in interrelationship with the functional specification and with the specification of the user interface; it serves as a repository of needs and constraints for functional and user interface specification; in return, it is adjusted and augmented as design decisions are made. The CHARADE Dialogue Manager is a generic component that takes as input an augmented task model; this runtime task model is used to drive the overall user-system dialogue and to provide the user with a level of feedback on the realization status of his/her tasks during a session. Finally, the evaluation stage uses the target task model as a support for usability analysis.

The CHARADE design process relied on the extensive use of a specifie notation for task modeling. Our task modeling notation is inspired from MAD [19] and TKS [8]; it consists in a graphieal notation to represent task graphs conveying task/sub-task decompositions, sequencing constraints between tasks, loops, etc. Each task in the graph is moreover described in a task template collecting functional, operational, pragmatic and relational characteristics of the task. A Task Editor tool supporting this notation was developped. The same basic task modelling notation was used throughout the process, with a growing concern for formalization: at the Analysis stage, template slots were only partially and informally filled; at the end of the design stage, template slots were fully completed using formal logical or procedural expressions. Formal expressions were written in the Alcatel-ISR Spoke™ language, our object-oriented programming language in the CHARADE project.

The remaining sections concentrate on the most characteristic aspects of the process: existing tasks analysis, target task model construction and exploitation, both at design and at run-time, prototyping cycle, evaluation. They clarify the contents of the evolving task models and show how the task modelling serves as an unifying concept for the development cycle. Practical considerations are provided, as an account of the lessons we learned during our three-year experience with CHARADE.

3. Task Analysis

Task analysis and its associated techniques provide a framework and methodological tools for data collection on the existing work of users in the application domain, and for the structuring of these data. As experienced in

CHARADE, such tools are mandatory when analysing and modelling the operator's work. The task analyses in CHARADE greatly contributed to an "in depth" characterization and formalization of the application domain. They led to a close examination of the fire control activities, and allowed to clarify and conceptualize our knowledge of these activities, with a direct impact on functional and interface design.

The impact of task analysis on system design can be assessed in particular by observing the consequences of holes/defects in the first task analyses. The evaluation with the end users revealed that part of the usability problems and functional defects of the first CHARADE Demonstrator were due to lack of information or incorrect interpretation during the task analysis.

A good example of this problem is the representation of the task of "sending allocated resources to the fire zone". During the task analysis there was a misunderstanding on the modalities of tasks execution. Resources are never sent individually, but normally in groups, i.e. a grouping of different types of equipment (e.g. a helicopter needs ground control for its activity to extinguish the fire) following the requirements of the intervention plan. This mistake in task analysis had an immediate follow-up in the interface commands associated with this task: the user could not identify his allocation plan in the list of resources to be sent, and committed errors in associating types of equipment to a particular action of the fire extinction.

Contrarily to our initial analyses, there was a low occurrence of a convoy composed of a single piece of equipment.

Task analysis and modelling are complex and time-consuming jobs. They require qualified interviewers, so as to e.g. avoid a functional orientation bias, as was experienced in CHARADE. It is moreover necessary to precisely identify the scope and the level of detail that needs to be addressed: the danger is to waste time modelling elements that will be skipped later on in system design.

However, it may be difficult to conduct an "in depth" task analysis in a real system situation. Additional effort and time is requested in order to conduct broad task analyses in cases in which the target system is not clearly delimited, i.e. if there is not just one target operator but several potential user organizations, possibly in different countries, as it is in CHARADE project. Scopes need to be carefully restrained to a set of general tasks, and the required level of detail needs to be precisely delimited.

4. Building the Target Task Model

The target task model allows a representation of the system from the operator (as task-performer) point of view, counter-balancing the traditional functional point of view.

The target task model is a structure maintained in parallel with the system functional specifications, and representing the task constraints and the task-related impact of the functional design decisions. Building the target task model and specifying the system functions are two closely dependent, mutually constrained processes.

The target task model takes as input the generalized task model stemming from the analysis stage; once the main functions of the target system have been identified (as a response to the requirements analysis), the generalized task model undergoes some major transformations, as follows. Tasks which are out of the target scope are removed, and new tasks are introduced, possibly deeply changing the existing structure. The availability of automated situation assessment and planning tools, as an example, may allow a planning task at the very beginning of the fire intervention, which was not so far from fire control centers; this naturally deeply affected the fire intervention task structure.

Other tasks are grouped or modified e.g. to integrate new modalities. The target task model is gradually built up, transformed and augmented as the system functions are clarified and refined; it serves as a repository for modelling the way these functions will be used, how action and control will be distributed between operator and system, how data and control flows will be organized, what constraints need to be verified. In return, the target task model holds constraints that need to be satisfied by functions; as a reference structure central to the system design, the task model also offers support for checking the coherency of the different design decisions.

The CHARADE resource allocation task has the post constraint (i.e. constraint on completion) that at least one resource is allocated to each action of the intervention plan.

Building the target task model and refining the system functions are both processes that also take as input elements from users through prototyping activities (see section 6). Sessions with users around scenarios and prototypes allow us to check, revise and refine decisions embedded in the target task model.

As experienced in CHARADE, the target task model appears a good tool for discussing and making decisions between all partners working on the project (i.e. the different function designers and the different user interface designers). Building and checking the target task model with the involvement of all partners allowed us to reach a common view of the Demonstrator functionality. We were able to clarify the details, e.g. how each task would be supported by the system, shedding light on many dark points. In CHARADE, the target task model really became central to discussions between partners in the last part of the project, when finalizing and assembling application functions, and user interfaces and dialogue manager.

At this stage of the project, the evolving task model is proved in as useful for identifying and repairing incoherencies (e.g. incoherencies experienced in CHARADE involved badly targeted functions, the impact of failing functions was overlooked, sequences of function calls were underspecified)

5. Target Task Model in MMI Subsystem

As a representation of the conceptual task structure of the system under design, the target task model conveys a large part of the constraints and features to be embodied in the system dialogue and user interface. This is therefore an important input to the user interface specification phase. We went even further in that direction implementing a runtime task-based dialogue manager.

5.1 User Interface Design

Basic choices as to the organization of the user interface presentation were grounded in the structure of the target task model: the identification and delimitation of the different 'workspaces' through a grouping of related general tasks, the grouping of the commands, the grouping and filtering of the data. The target task model was in particular used as a tool in order to check the validity and coherency of the presentation design: checking that all data necessary for performing a given task are provided in the presentation, that only pertinent elements are directly presented; that some tasks can be performed in "parallel', that some iterations or interruptions are allowed.

A particular issue that we had to handle is the level of multi-tasking which is offered to the user. The question remain: "Is it useful/necessary for the user to handle several tasks concurrently?". For several reasons, we decided to constrain the multi-tasking to a minimum requested by the task model; this minimum requires a specific organization of the user interface. Our aim is to reduce the need for multi-windowing, since window management operations are too time and attention consuming for our end-users.

A second main source of inspiration for the user interface designers naturally was provided by the users (as reported in section 6) and the discussions around prototypes provided invaluable input to the refinement of our design decisions.

5.2 Task-based Dialogue Management

The Man-Machine Interface (MMI) subsystem of CHARADE is organized around a generic two-level architecture, and distinguishes between the handling of local interaction, presentation details (in a standard mouse and keyboard environment), and the management of the global session. The main generic part of the MMI subsystem is the Dialogue Manager component, which provides functions mainly at global level. The target task model itself can be seen as the deep motivation for dialogue-level constraints [15], and the introduction of a runtime task model is a useful feature of the CHARADE.

In opposition to many dialogue managers, our Dialogue Manager uses the notions of "tasks" and "commands", rather than just "commands". The Dialogue Manager uses a declarative model of the user-system tasks in order to drive the overall dialogue, to control the user actions, to activate the system functions, and to provide the operator with a level of feedback on the realization status of his tasks. The runtime task model is closely derived from the target task model, the structure of the design task model is automatically translated into an object oriented representation, and further augmented with items specific to runtime needs. In particular, target task model elements under exploitation are the decompositional and sequencing relationships between tasks, as well as the constraints on the activation, termination, interruption, and cancellation of a task. A second declarative model is the Task Handling Model, which allows to specify the system behaviour (as tasks are performed) through a set of specific handlers.

These handlers contain procedures that will be executed prior to task activation, right after task completion, or as a part of task realization (e.g. calls to a supporting system function). Figure 2 illustrates the declarative models used by the dialogue manager; the example graph is extracted from the CHARADE Demonstrator Task Model.

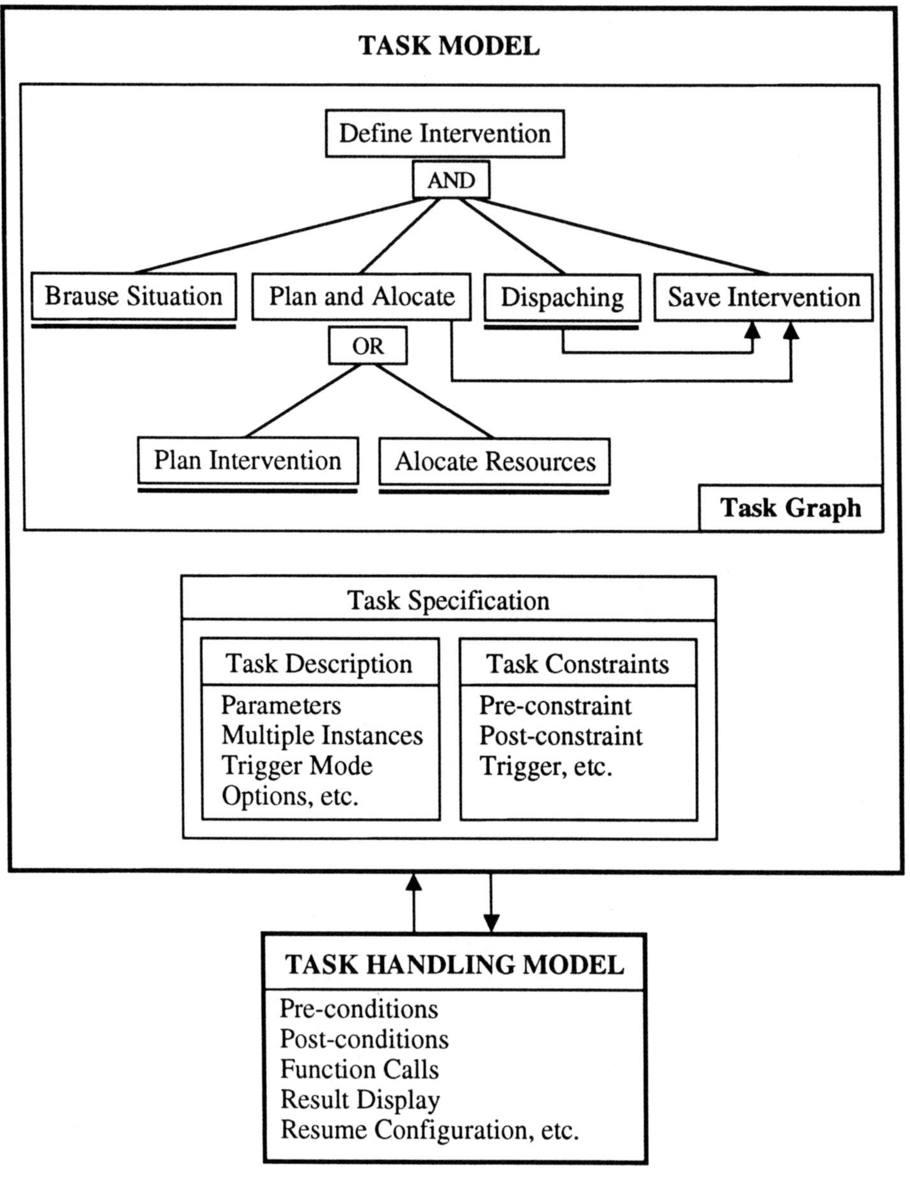

Fig. 2: Overview of the task model and task handling model

The user-system activity runs as a succession of task activations: user commands are translated into task requests, controlled by the task model constraints, and executed based on the task handling model. The task manager component of the dialogue manager maintains the task context at any point of a session, computing the activability and completion status of all tasks. The task coordinator component exploits the task knowledge. It performs the task handling functions through function calls to the modules, automatically triggers the task activation and adapts the user interface data according to the task context. These adaptations include a level of contextual feedback on task activability status, on task realization status, the suggestion of commands, warnings about unsatisfied task constraints (e.g. on the task completion), etc. In the context of the CHARADE Demonstrator, this feedback is implemented through graphical indicators (dynamic icons reflecting the status of the main tasks) and textual messages.

These mechanisms allow to closely check the coherency of the user actions, and provide elements for a level of feedback on the realization status of the user tasks. They allow, from the system design point of view, a flexible declaration of the user system activity constraints, supporting evolutions of the system design cycle, and in particular, the evolution from one prototype to the next one, as experienced in CHARADE.

6. Prototyping and Iteration

As discussed in section 2, basic concepts of the iterative and spiral development processes are prototypes and iteration. Prototyping allows the developers to deliver successive versions and obtain feedback before extensive resources have been committed to implementation. They provide benefits in easing the communication with the users; improving design through feedback and iteration; reducing risks associated to the production of unusable code; increasing the user acceptance [17].

In CHARADE several task scenarios [3] were used as testbeds for prototyping. The task models developed during the analysis and the design of the system provided the context for task scenarios. Each scenario could be represented by a description (text, picture or diagramme) of a task or a sequence of exemplar tasks of the designed prototype. The aim was to support user participation in design through the use of simple prototypes, based on the actual experience of the users when accomplishing their tasks.

This prototyping technique was utilized in CHARADE in different design phases of the development process, on different kinds of prototypes, as follows.

- "Horizontal" prototypes extensively integrating the system characteristics, without the implementation of all supporting functions. These kinds of prototypes were useful to verify the integration between the various modules of the system, and for testing the available operative sequences.
- "Vertical" prototypes that enable detailed demonstration of a few functions in a narrow domain of the system. These kinds of prototypes allowed in-depth testing of some functions and an evaluation of importance of the support given to the use.
- Paper or software mockups to define and evaluate the interface.

- Rapid prototyping environments as support to the direct user's involvement in the system design.

The scenario-based design technique was also successfully experienced in some sessions of interactive prototyping [12]. In other words this was an experience of on-line implementation of the user's suggestions, directly submitted to the "design/coding/evaluation/redesign" cycle. Obviously we didn't expect that the users were in the position of proposing a design from the starting point, but we assumed that they were able to react to concrete proposals of the designers. Our method used a rapid prototyping environment based on high level functionality provided by a GIS (Geographical Information System) and an object oriented language. From this environment a team composed of a designer, a user and a programmer worked to define an access model to the zone affected by fire, and also trying to implement on-line the users' suggestions. This technique was extremely efficient in obtaining positive results: in a few working sessions it was possible to design a model of how to access the zone threatened by fire judged favourably by the user in successive sessions concerning the evaluation. Moreover, the users involved in the design were extremely satisfied to see their suggestions implemented, while the designers saved time in producing source code before the model and its usability were tested. The knowledge captured by the task models was a vehicle to enable the communication between users and designers, since they could cooperate in developing prototypes on the basis of a common understanding of the application domain.

7. Evaluation

Beside on-going evaluations on prototypes, a formal evaluation was done at the end of the design process with usability objectives which were developed during task analysis and used as criteria. A task-driven approach [6], [16] was adopted for the evaluation of CHARADE. Following the approach, a set of representative tasks was selected, and a task was accepted as *representative* if it matched one of the following features:

- it could solve the potential usability problems with the system,
- it was composed by actions that are frequently done by the users,
- it was supported by new or modified functionality, and
- it was critical to system's operation.

Two cycles of evaluation were performed during the development process of the CHARADE. The first evaluation cycle aimed at assessing usability aspects and the functional design of the first version of the demonstrator. Two kinds of evaluation were performed in this phase, heuristic evaluation with endusers [13], and "walkthrough" [4] were performed by the different designers. The results were used to formulate the specification of the following version and to redesign those parts of the demonstrator that were not completely satisfactory.

The second cycle of evaluation was performed on the CHARADE Demonstrator. The users were involved in evaluating brand new or redesigned functions, and the user interface. This further cycle of evaluation was aimed at assessing the degree of acceptance of the demonstrator and what was still needed to overcome usability problems. Two intentions guided the experimental plan of the second cycle of the evaluation: *(i)* to confirm that a good percentage of the usability problems depicted during the first cycle of evaluation were solved in the second version, and *(ii)* to evaluate that the design choices made in the second version were compliant with the user requirements and recognised usability principles.

Nine main tasks were selected as representative for the system and the users' activity. The users were asked to evaluate each task and fill in evaluation reports, namely a user evaluation form for each task (post-task questionnaire) and a global evaluation form (post-test questionnaire). Test evaluation forms were filled also by the test team, reporting notes and comments related to the test.

A list of usability requirements was developed. It included nine parameters like: easiness to complete the task, acceptability of system performances, the appropriateness of information presentation, the reliability of system responses, the system flexibility and control etc. Pilot sessions were made in order to evaluate and refine the list. The evaluation of each task was formulated by the users checking values in structured rating associated to the questions.

A detailled discussion of the evaluation of the experimental usalibility results is not intended in this paper, some results in terms of benefits of our methodological approach are worth to be mentioned. The advantages of the task-driven approach to the evaluation can be summarized in the following considerations:

- it provides an easy way to select aspects to be evaluated that are likely to be really meaningful for the user, hence for assessing system usability;
- it allows the decomposition of the system evaluation into a number of task evaluations, with two benefits: (i) shortened sessions will result in more accurateuser's evaluations, and (ii) partial evaluations can be carried out on prototypes whichare not yet robust enough for full testing.
- it guides the definition of usability requirements for the system.

8. Conclusions

Task-based system design still is a research issue in the MMI and software engineering community. Our experience with task modelling in a real system design context was highly valuable in front of the relative immaturity of the domain; it allowed us to clarify the interests and limitations of task analysis, and to refine a task-based system development method.

The continuum built and used task models (an existing tasks model, a target task model, a runtime task model, an evaluation task subset) which served as vehicles for capturing human factors aspects and perspectives throughout the system design cycle. In particular, the task models supported the cognitive processes of the developer and users and allowed the development of appropriate design and evaluation tools. It is clear that the effective design approach in CHARADE is far from exemplary, especially the specification of the system (and with it the specification of the target task model) should have been frozen sooner in the project life, and the delay caused by the exploratory dimension of the project anticipated.

However, the CHARADE experience confirms the interest of the endusers in the task-based system design, and calls for more precise methodological steps.

References

1. Barthet M.F. "Logiciels interactifs et ergonomie", Dunod, Paris, 1988.
2. Browne D. "Structured User-Interface Design for Interaction Optimisation (STUDIO)", Prentice Hall, London, 1994.
3. Carroll J.M. "Scenario-based Design", Wiley & Sons, New York, 1995.
4. Clayton L., Rieman J. "Task-Centred User lnterface Design: A Practical Introduction" Boulder Colorado, University of Colorado, 1993. (ftp.cs.colorado.edu/pub/cs/distribs/clewis/HCI-Design-Book)
5. Collins, D., Designing Object-Oriented User Interfaces, Benjamin Cummings Publishing Company Inc., Redwood City, CA, 1995.
6. Dumas, J.S. Redish, J.C. "A practical guide to usability testing", Ablex Publishing Corporation, Norwood, 1994.
7. Johnson P. & H. "Designers-identified requirements for tools to support task analyses", in Proc. of INTERACT'90, pp.259-264., 1990.
8. Johnson P. & H. "Task knowledge structures: psychological basis and integration into system design", in Acta Psychologica 78, pp.3-26, 1991.
9. K. Y. Lim and J. B. Long, "Instantiation of Task Analysis in a Structured Method for User Interface Design", Proc. of Task Analysis in H-C-1, 11th Interdisciplinary Workshop on "Informatics and Psychology", Schärding, Austria, June 9-11 1992.
10. Marti P. "The interface design of an integrated system for handling environmental emergencies", Proc. of International Conference on Cognitive Ergonomics, Padua, Italy, 3-5 March, 1995.
11. Newman W.M., Lamming M.G. "Interactive System Design", Addison Wesley, Workingham, 1995.
12. Nielsen J. "Usability Engineering", Academic Press, Boston, MA, 1993.
13. Nielsen J. Mack R.L. (eds.) "Usability Inspetion Methods" Wiley, New York, 1994.
14. Norman D., Draper S.W. (eds.) "User Centered System design: New perspectives on Human-Computer Interaction" Hillsdale, Lawrence Erlbaum Associates, 1986.
15. Normand V. "Modelisation de la tâche: quelle place dans la conception et la mise en œuvre des systèmes interactifs?", Cinquièmes journées sur l'lngénierie des Interfaces Homme-Machine, IHM'93, Lyon, October 1993.
16. Ravden S. Johnson, G. Evaluating Usability of Human-Computer Interfaces, Ellis Horwood, New York, 1989.
17. Redmond-Pyle D., Moore A. "Graphical User Interface Design and Evaluation", Prentice Hall, London, 1995.
18. Ricci F., Mam S., Marti P., Normand V., Olmo P. "CHARADE: a platform for emergencies management systems", CHARADE Project, Public Report, 1994.
19. Scapin D., Pierret-Golbreich C. "Towards a method for task description: MAD", Proc. of Work with Display Units Conference, Montreal, Canada, September 1989.

MAPI:
MUSiC Assisted Process Improvement

Jurek Kirakowski
Human Factors Research Group, University College Cork, Ireland

Nigel Bevan
National Physical Laboratory, Teddington, Middx. TW11 0LW, UK

Abstract

The MAPI (MUSiC Assisted Process Improvement) project in the ESPRIT Human Comfort and Security area uses methods for usability measurement derived from the successful Framework III MUSiC project (Measuring the Usability of Systems in Context). These methods implement the principles of the draft ISO standard 9241, part 11, which defines usability as: "the extent to which a product can be used to achieve specified goals with effectiveness, efficiency and satisfaction in a specified context of use". The service providers of MAPI have identified a number of different configurations in which MUSiC methods can be delivered in order to satisfy the industrial objectives of the MAPI industrial partners. The objectives of the MAPI project are to show that MUSiC methods can assist companies to improve their processes, and to highlight ways in which the current MUSiC tools need to be developed and delivered in order to be cost-effective.

1. Introduction

The MAPI project is a set of trial applications of the use of MUSiC methods for usability evaluation. The acronym MAPI stands for *MUSiC Assisted Process Improvement.* MUSiC is a set of methods developed in ESPRIT for *Measuring the Usability of Systems in Context.* The MUSiC project ran from 1990 - 1993; MAPI began in the autumn of 1995 and will last approximately 15 months.

MUSiC contributed to the development of the draft ISO standard 9241, part 11 [7] which defines usability as: "the extent to which a product can be used to achieve specified goals with effectiveness, efficiency and satisfaction in a specified context of use". The MUSiC project developed methods for measuring usability based on this definition.

A major benefit of using *MUSiC methods* for usability measurement is that they provide a means of specifying usability goals and evaluating whether they have been achieved. The goals are expressed in terms of the purpose of business systems which is to enable users to achieve tasks effectively, efficiently and with satisfaction. MUSiC provides methods for measuring effectiveness and efficiency:

- whether, or what proportion of typical users can correctly complete the task,
- the efficiency (productivity) of typical users,
- how the efficiency of typical users compares with an expert user: this gives an indication of the point on the learning curve and may highlight a need to improve the user interface or to provide more training;
- the proportion of the time for which a user is productive: this may also highlight a need to improve the user interface or to provide more training.

But following the ISO 9241-11 definition, it can be seen that it is also important to measure *user satisfaction*, particularly as poor satisfaction is likely to lead to deterioration in performance, as well as low job satisfaction, which in turn leads to rapid staff turnover, absenteeism, and a host of other consequences of poor staff morale. A graphic recent account of the sometimes dire consequences of neglecting end-user satisfaction is given in [4]. Satisfaction can be measured with the SUMI questionnaire developed within the MUSiC project. In addition, measures of *cognitive workload* recommended by MUSiC can be used to assess mental effort. These may be useful indicators of situations where users have to expend excessive mental effort to achieve acceptable performance, and are particularly important in safety-critical applications.

Unless the evaluation can take place in conditions of actual use, it is necessary to decide which attributes of the actual or intended context of use are to be represented in the evaluation. When specifying or evaluating usability it is important that the context selected is representative of the important aspects of the actual or intended context of use. The *Usability Context Analysis Guide* provides a systematic method for describing the context of use and specifying the context to be used in an evaluation, and is a fundamental part of the MUSiC method. To get valid and reliable results, representative users should perform typical tasks in representative environments. The users and the tasks they perform are selected as a result of a context study assisted by the Usability Context Analysis Guide [14].

2. Performance Measurement Method

The Performance Measurement Method was developed at NPL as part of MUSiC. Observing how users interact with a system gives valuable information about usability, unobtainable by other means. Analysis of what is observed, with the help of a video recording, provides a highly effective means of evaluating usability. The method is fully documented in the Performance Measurement Handbook, and is supported by a software tool (DRUM) which greatly speeds up analysis of the video, and helps manage the evaluation. A description of DRUM is given in [10] .

The Performance Measurement Method gives reliable measures of the effectiveness and efficiency of system use, by evaluating the extent to which specific task goals are achieved, and the times taken to achieve those goals. It also gives measures of time spent unproductively (for example, overcoming problems and seeking help), plus valuable data about the source of such difficulties. These measures enable comparison of prototypes of alternative designs with earlier versions of a system, for example, or with competing products. The diagnostic information helps identify where specific problems are encountered and where improvements need to be made.

2.1 Video-assisted Usability Analysis

DRUM, the Diagnostic Recorder for Usability Measurement, is a software tool originally developed at NPL within the MUSiC Project. It supports the Performance Measurement Method, and also has wider applicability. Video clips of end-users working with a system provide convincing evidence for designers and developers of the usability of their system, and of specific problems. However, analysis is required to convey this information effectively, as an unanalysed interaction log contains too much low-level detail.

Video analysis has previously been very time-consuming, with analysis times of ten hours for every hour of video being typical. It can now be performed much more quickly using DRUM - one or two hours to analyse one hour of video. A first pass analysis can be performed in real time during recording. DRUM supports the management and analysis of usability evaluations, including the derivation of usability metrics, and the identification of evaluator-defined critical incidents for design feedback.

2.2 User Satisfaction: SUMI

Measures of satisfaction describe the perceived usability of the overall system by its users and the acceptability of the system to the people who use it. SUMI, the Software Usability Measurement Inventory, was developed by the Human Factors Research Group at University College Cork, to measure user satisfaction, and hence assess user perceived software quality. SUMI is an internationally standardised 50-item questionnaire, available in several languages. It takes a maximum of 10 minutes to complete and needs only small user sample sizes (SUMI is described in [8]).

The results that SUMI provides are based on an extensive standardisation database built from data on a full range of software products such as word processors, spreadsheets, CAD packages, communications programs etc. SUMI results have been shown to be reliable, and to discriminate between different kinds of software products in a valid manner. In particular, the SUMI database allows evaluation of a product against what is considered to be the prevailing market norm, and the statistical background to SUMI enables the analyst to pinpoint quite precisely the relative standing of the product being assessed to the market as a whole.

SUMI results are analysed by a computer program called SUMISCO, which produces a standard SUMI report that can be easily imported into a wider product evaluation report. SUMISCO relies on a summarised statistical database that is revised at least once a year to keep up with changes in the market. SUMISCO provides an overall assessment and a usability profile which breaks the overall assessment down into 5 sub-scales: Affect, Efficiency, Helpfulness, Control, and Learnability. These scales have been derived by an iterative process of factor analysis of large databases, and present a view of subjective usability for which there is a high level of solid empirical support. In addition, Item Consensual Analysis (ICA) can be used to list those items on which the software being rated was significantly better or worse than average. ICA is a technique developed specifically for the SUMI questionnaire, and it too has been proved in numerous industrial trials. ICA enables the analyst to pinpoint topics about the software product that are considered to be above or below the market standard. It can be used in conjunction with an interview method to focus in to those features of the product that are giving rise to user dissatisfaction.

The Human Factors Research Group, are, in the MAPI project, developing a number of different ways in which SUMI may be administered (by email, as a Web site, on a standalone computer) as well as a number of different ‚flavours' of SUMI, for instance and most importantly, a multi-media "edutainment" products version, and a version specifically for the evaluation of public-access terminals. These developments have been made in response to the demands of the industrial partners of MAPI.

2.3 Cognitive Workload

Cognitive workload relates to the mental effort required to perform tasks. The Technical University of Delft has developed a Guide to Cognitive Workload Measurement as part of the MUSiC project [6]. European health and safety regulations implementing the EC Display Screen Directive [5] specifically require evaluation to avoid problems of mental stress. Two specific measures for evaluation of Cognitive Workload, the SMEQ questionnaire and the NASA TLX questionnaire are recommended by this report. More detailed examination of cognitive workload can be achieved by taking physiological measures of change in heart rate but these are not always practical or necessary.

Mental stress can become a problem specifically in situations where the work of the end users is demand-paced (such as in ticket sales or process control applications). Bravo [4] reports an end user in this kind of application who was told to "take 10 minutes to pull (herself) together" The end user reportedly suffered a nervous breakdown and was in therapy for 8 months.

However, even in self-paced work, cognitive workload must be monitored as an increase in workload will indicate a nexus point in the application that may benefit from re-design in order to simplify or de-intensify the need for decision making on the part of the end user.

3. MAPI Project

The industrial partners in MAPI have identified processes and products that are critical for them with respect to end-user quality. These partners are: Lloyd's Bank PLC (lead partner, UK), Sogei SpA (Rome, Italy), State Museums (Berlin, Germany), Cyco Ltd.(the Netherlands), Ericsson (Stockholm, Sweden), AMPS (Stockholm, Sweden), and Inland Revenue (UK). These partners are in various degrees of sophistication with regard to the employment of usability technology, but all are agreed that the adoption of technology of the kind developed during the

MUSiC project is of potential benefit to them and indeed to the future of their businesses. Each organisation has nominated a trial application so that seen from an overview, the MAPI project targets a number of different sectors within the software industry, requiring usability engineering at different parts of the software lifecycle.

Each industrial partner is associated with one or more organisations which function as *service providers* in the project. The service providers are:

- National Physical Laboratory, Teddington, UK,
- Human Factors Research Group, Cork, Ireland,
- WIT-Lab, Delft, the Netherlands,
- Data Management SpA, Milan, Italy,
- NOMOS Management AB, Stockholm, Sweden.

The first three service providers have full ownership rights to the MUSiC project results being exploited in MAPI; Data Management was an industrial partner in MUSiC and is currently playing a leading role in disseminating MUSiC results in the FINSIEL group of companies in Italy, and NOMOS Management was the first organisation to develop links with the MUSiC project group in order to specifically exploit the project results in Scandinavia. NOMOS is also since May 1994 a Microsoft Solution Provider and Usability Partner.

3.1 Project Objectives in the Industrial Context

The MAPI project came about because of the need of the industrial partners for an effective integration of quality of use technology into their mainstream practices and products, and the need of the MUSiC service providers to identify modes of delivery of MUSiC technology that are industrially effective and cost-efficient.

The project objectives are to:

- Change the evaluation culture of the companies concerned, so that the companies take up MUSiC as a long term investment.
- Demonstrate the uptake of MUSiC technology successfully by companies involved in a broad range of software developments, thus showing the industrial applicability of MUSiC to other companies in the sector.
- Demonstrate the uptake of MUSiC in many parts of a development lifecycle, thus showing the broad applicability of MUSiC tools and techniques.

The MAPI project is therefore seen as an initial move leading to a strategic leveraging action to make an effective contribution to European practices with regard to quality of use engineering.

MUSiC technology allows organisations to quantify quality of use of products, and it enables them to specify targets and identify work that needs to be done to achieve these targets. This technology is applicable at all stages of the life cycle of an IT product: not only in those time critical phases where the product is being created, but also in prior market positioning and definitional phases and in post-release phases to support activities such as marketing, product support, and product enhancement.

MUSiC methods and associated technology stand as the leading edge technology in European quality of use engineering (see [1],[3],[9],[12],[13] to name but a few of the recent books and articles in which aspects of MUSiC are reviewed).

In comparison with the state of the industry in the USA, it can be seen that European technology is leading the market. Indeed, all the major international IT companies have now purchased and use parts of the MUSiC toolset, both in the USA and in Europe. However, it must be said that the way MUSiC technology is supplied at present is craft-like. For MUSiC service providers, the way of providing MUSiC must be improved, and the markets for MUSiC technology must be opened by means of trial applications and leveraging actions. Outside of MUSiC the current international situation is characterised by two major trends:

1. informal assessment and diagnostic activities that rely on a craft-like approach handled by individuals with often considerable personal expertise in the field but few standardised tools or procedures (cf for instance the excellent account by Nielsen, in his book *Usability Engineering*, 1993 [11]).
2. approaches that are qualitative and are therefore difficult to place in a management perspective with regard to cost justification and process improvement (cf the summary of the state of the art by Bias and Mayhew, 1994, in their aptly-named book *Cost Justifying Usability* [2]).

We see many companies which are starting to consider the incorporation of user-based quality of use assessment into their processes, but it is clear that for most, these are as yet uncharted waters.

In the more commercial end of the market place, we see that many popular magazines now incorporate usability reviews of software. The methods used by some are informal, to say the least, but an evaluation service provider to an influential group of magazines has recently purchased MUSiC tools and training and now is seen to regularly publish usability profiles based on this technology in *PC User* magazine.

3.2 Delivery of Usability Technology

The major phases of each sub-project depend on the particular circumstances of each of the industrial partners, and the delivery packages are explained in greater detail below. However, overall, each delivery package corresponds to the following stages:

- User training and problem definition
- Implementation of MUSiC in Trial Application
- Assessment of results and definition of future company strategy.

These stages are now explained in greater detail. MUSiC partners already have an informal network which allows one partner to be the co-ordinating ‚industry interface‘ with a company, but which nevertheless enables other MUSiC partners to contribute training or consultancy effort as needed. The key element of the service delivery is to provide MUSiC products and services in a seamless and integrated manner, allowing the participating industrial partners to feel that they ‚own‘ those parts of MUSiC they have chosen to integrate.

A phenomenon which happened early in the project was that many of the industrial partners began quite spontaneously to generate their own, internal ‚Usability Evaluation Guidelines‘. Although there appears to be much commonality between these guidelines, what is most interesting is the range of diversity between them as each organisation reflects on the most appropriate way to assimilate the technology on offer to improve their internal processes. There is quite clearly no single prescriptive ‚golden path' to the attainment of this objective just as there is no single software lifecycle model to which an organisation must subscribe if they wish to incorporate end-user involvement into their process.

MAPI therefore seeks to deliver MUSiC technology through a number of different "template packages". These are more in the spirit of hypotheses about what industrial partners want MUSiC to deliver than tested routes to application. As MAPI progresses, these template packages are subjected to a process of refinement and evolution.These packages, defined in consultation the industrial partners, are as follows:

- **Whole Life Cycle:** This package refers to applying MUSiC methods to the whole developmental lifecycle. After the initial activities of Process Analysis, Context of Use Analysis and Stakeholder identification, the Usability Test Plan is drawn up, and a Cost Estimate is issued. Thereafter the precise MUSiC measurements depend on the companies' activities within their lifecycle as specified in the Usability Test Plan. At the end of the process a Summative Evaluation report is compiled. Other elements of the MUSiC process may or may not be included in the Usability Test Plan, depending on the precise nature of the kind of process involved and the interactions between the identified stakeholders.
- **Partial Life Cycle:** This package refers to applying MUSiC methods to part of a lifecycle (although the MUSiC service supplier should be brought in at the start of the development process, their activity will be limited to certain phases as determined by the needs of the client). Process Analysis is therefore crucial, as is Context of Use Analysis and Stakeholder identification. The Usability Test Plan and Cost Estimates are issued. They are likely to be of smaller duration and cost less than if the service were for a Whole Life Cycle. A Baseline Usability measure may need to be made, in order to set targets against which improvement is to be measured. The overall evaluation will be Cumulative over the Baseline rather than Summative.
- **Version Improvement:** This package is applicable when a product exists as a previous release and a user base is established. It comprises of all the activities of the Whole Lifecycle package, as well as Goal Elicitation, Baseline Usability Measurement (on the basis of the current usage patterns; this may also form part of the Goal Elicitation procedure). Usability Bugs need to be identified for the Baseline version, and the evaluation is reported Cumulatively on the basis of improvement over the Baseline. Progressive Improvement reporting is relevant because the whole concept of version improvement implies re-working and adapting work practices if necessary.
- **Alpha Test:** This is the most traditional view of usability: a working alpha test version is in existence, and one or two quick improvements are envisaged. The Goal Elicitation and Stakeholders' meetings usually suffice to generate sufficient material for a Usability Test Plan and Cost Estimate since the Process is usually fixed by the time alpha testing is envisaged. Otherwise the package is similar to Version Improvement, only that the scale and cost of testing should be less than if a full Version improvement was

requested. Context of Use is important, because the user population may not have been identified by the Alpha Test stage whereas with a released product, a user population exists *de facto*. Usability bugs of the first alpha version are not usually considered worthy of a formal deliverable, since it is known that usability bugs will exist. They are treated within the Cumulative Evaluation report as part of the engineering process.

- **Workflow Analysis:** This package takes a product as implemented and used on a regular basis in one or two sites and uses MUSiC tools and methods to analyse the patterns of usage of the product and to present a report on what can be improved in the product or what kind of uses the product best lends itself to. Context of Use evaluation is important, the evaluation is Summative, and identification of Usability Bugs is of prime consideration for the company.

These packages were identified at the start of the project as an initial hypothesis on which to plan the intended work. The final shape of these delivery packages, and indeed an appreciation of whether all these different delivery packages are commercially viable, is an important end result of the MAPI project.

4. Results Assessment and Future Company Strategy

The major question is whether the industrial partners involved are willing to make a long-term investment in incorporating MUSiC technology into their future plans. All the industrial partners have already indicated a likely continuation scenario. Thus one yardstick with which to measure the effectiveness of the MAPI project is to examine how many of the industrial partners and associate partners undertake to carry on with MUSiC. In order to overcome a vague ‚wish list‘ approach to assessing this goal, each company proposes to frame quantitative future projections.

However, the benefit of the project is not only to the industrial participants directly. In order to benefit other industries in the software market, an assessment must be made of the kinds of delivery packages that have been successful, reasons for their success, and likely improvements to ensure greater effectiveness and cost benefit.

The MUSiC tools clearly, in the eyes of the present industry participants, present a useful initial working set. However, the need for additional tools has been noted, and there are moves within the service provider network to furnish such tools in the near future.

In addition, a more formal framework for co-operation among MUSiC service providers must be considered, as well as proposals for an accreditation scheme to which other service provider centres will be able to join. In effect, the process of creating such a scheme has already been started by a wider group of service providers, with the MUSiC partners as the nucleus, acting in concert independently with the service providers.

Acknowledgements and Further Information

MUSiC and MAPI are partly funded by the European Commission. NPL work on MUSiC was supported by the UK Department of Trade and Industry. Further information about the MUSiC project may in the first instance be obtained from either of the authors of this paper. Additional information regarding the MAPI project may be obtained from Mr K Bray, Project Manager, MAPI, Lloyds Bank PLC, 100 Pall Mall, London, SW1Y 5HP, UK.

References

1. Bevan N., Macleod M. "Usability measurement in context", Behaviour and Information Technology, vol.13, pp.132-145, 1994.
2. Bias R.G. and Mayhew D. "Cost justifying usability", Academic Press, Boston, 1994.
3. Bösser T. "Measures and methods for quality of use", Springer-Verlag, Berlin, 1995.
4. Bravo E. "The hazards of leaving out the users", in: D. Schuler and A Namikoka, (eds), Participatory Design: Principles and Practices, Earlbaum, Hillsdale NJ, 1993.
5. EC "Minimum safety and health requirements for work with display screen equipment", Directive (90/270/EEC) Official Journal of the European Communities No L 156, 21/6/90, 1990.
6. Houwing E.M., Wiethoff M., and Arnold A.G. "Introduction to cognitive workload measurement", Delft University of Technology, Laboratory for Work & Interaction Technology (WIT Lab), 1993.
7. ISO (International Standards Organisation DIS 9241-11: "Ergonomic requirements for office work with visual display terminals (VDTs)", Part 11: Guidance on Usability, 1995.
8. Kirakowski J. and Corbett M. "SUMI: the Software Usability Measurement Inventory", B J Ed Tech, vol.24.3, pp. 210-214, 1993.
9. Kirakowski, J. "Evaluating Usability of the Human-Computer Interface" in: Pfleger S. et al. (eds), Human Comfort and Security, pp.21-32, Springer-Verlag, Berlin, 1995.
10. Macleod M. and Rengger R. "The development of DRUM: a software tool for video-assisted usability evaluation" in: JL Alty et al. (eds.) People and Computers VIII (Proc. of HCI'93 Conf., Loughborough UK, September 1993). Cambridge, pp.293-309, 1993.
11. Nielsen J "Usability Engineering", Academic Press, 1993.
12. Preece J. et al. "Human-Computer Interaction", Prentice Hall International, 1994.
13. Redmond-Pyle D., and Moore A. "Graphical user interface design and evaluation: a practical process", Prentice Hall International, 1994.
14. Thomas C. and Bevan N. (eds). "Usability context analysis: a practical guide", Version 4. National Physical Laboratory, Teddington, UK, 1995.

Usability Evaluation of Software Applications

Reinhard Oppermann
HCI Research Division (FIT.MMK)
GMD- German National Research Center for Information Technology
D-53754 Sankt Augustin, Germany

Abstract

Providers and employers of information technology applications have to ensure the conformance with the requirements and recommendations given in ISO 9241 part 1 to 17 and ISO 9000, as far as concerned to define the demands of the EU Directive 90/270. However, no accepted methodology and instruments exist to operationalise the relevant standards. Therefore, a software based evaluation procedure, called ISO 9241-Evaluator, has been developed as a comprehensive combination of methods and instruments supporting a guideline-based expert judgement.

1. Motivation

The working live in the business and industrial environment and the daily live in the private sector is expected to be characterised by an increased introduction and use of information technology. Much more than by the performance of the hardware the benefit of the systems is restricted by inefficiency of the software. The interaction with information systems is no easy matter for the users. It can be ineffective and inefficient. It can frustrate users and reduce their motivation. No matter what kind of systems is considered, word processors, management information systems or telebanking systems for clients the understandability and usability of the user interface is an important bottleneck of benefit of the systems. Usability of information systems has gained both an increased importance and an increased attention with designers, providers and employers of technology. But the usability is far from being an integrated part of the software quality assurance in the production and maintenance cycle of software.

From the legal point of view applications of information technology have to be compatible with the outlines of the "Council Directive on the minimum safety and health requirements for the work with display screen equipment 90/270/EEC" [2]. The directive means that the employers should provide software tools that can productively and easily be used and learned by the users.

The council directive has been enforced on 1st January 1993 and is now being transferred in the European Union into national laws. Ergonomic requirements and recommendations are laid down in the multipart International Standard ISO 9241. The requirements and recommendations of ISO 9241 [6] represent the state of the art in ergonomics of the office work place environment. Compliance with this standard can serve as a means for providers and employers of information technology to show conformance with Council-Directive 90/270/EEC.

2. State of the Art

No accepted methodology and tools exist to implement the relevant standards into software design and evaluation. There are examples of approaches to measure the usability of software systems. For instance, in the MUSiC project [7] the context of use is operationalised in a handbook, guidelines and a questionnaire. In the ERGOguide project [5] a methodological framework was elaborated with the context of use, mental stress and methodological improvement strategies as the basis of a criterion-oriented evaluation strategy. But they both show deficiencies in the usability of the proposed methods in practice and in covering the demands of the current state of the ISO standards.

The heuristic evaluation approach of Nielsen [8] is a pragmatical one: based on a small group of typical users or experts a software application will be evaluated. This evaluation method is based on a set of human factors design principles that should be considered in software design. By integrating the support for the development of a usable software and the support for the evaluation of the resulting product the design aid facilities of IDA (see [10]) and the evaluation facilities of the proposed ISO 9241-EVALUATOR can iteratively be combined in the design process leading to an increased quality of the product.

3. ISO 9241-EVALUATOR: Quality Assurance of Software

The methodology of the ISO 9241-EVALUATOR is based on EVADIS, which stands for "Evaluation of Dialogue Systems" and was developed at the GMD in close co-operation with the Institute for Applied Computer Science and Information Systems at the University of Vienna and the consulting company Ernst & Young, Vienna. The first and second release of the methodology has been published as both a book by Walter de Gruyter, Berlin, New York in 1988 and 1992 and as a program. EVADIS II (see 19]) covers part 10 of ISO 9241, the most comprehensive standard for the design of dialogue systems, and the first software relevant part of the standard that has been finally accepted as an international standard.

Our methodology aimes at providing an efficient assessment guideline that covers the current state of the art in user interface design requirements as of ISO 9241/CEN 2 92 41.In part 11 the multi-part standard defines the concept of usability in terms of effectiveness, efficiency and satisfaction and describes the context of use in which the usability assessment has to be performed. Part 10 contains the general principles for the user dialogue (the dynamic aspect or the "feel" of the interface) explained by applications and examples of these principles. The principals for the presentation of information (the static aspect or the "look" of the interface) are described in part 12. Part 13 describes the requirements for the user guidance. The general principles will be concretised for the different dialogue techniques in part 14 to 17.

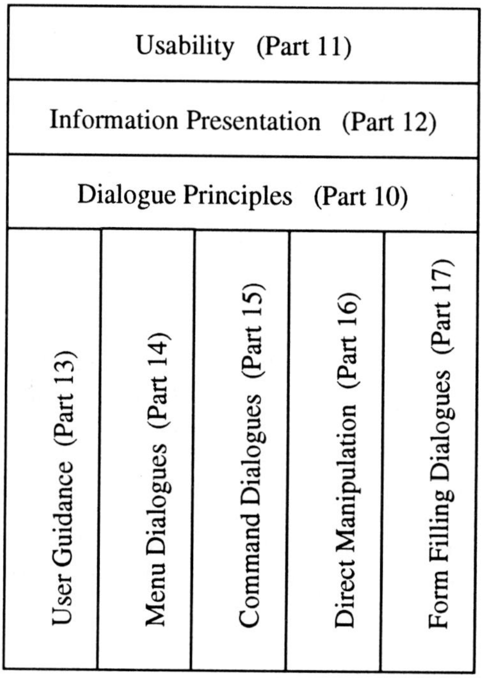

Usability (Part 11)				
Information Presentation (Part 12)				
Dialogue Principles (Part 10)				
User Guidance (Part 13)	Menu Dialogues (Part 14)	Command Dialogues (Part 15)	Direct Manipulation (Part 16)	Form Filling Dialogues (Part 17)

Fig. 1: Structure of the multi-part ISO 9241

Figure 1 (see [4]) shows the structure of the multi-part standard ISO 9241 with respect to software ergonomic requirements.

3.1 ISO 9241-EVALUATOR

The ISO 9241-EVALUATOR is a structured and comprehensive approach to assess the application of the recommendations of ISO 9241, part 10 to 17 consisting of a combination of methods forming a method based expert judgement:

- a guideline-oriented checklist of test items to evaluate the user interface of the software, and
- a simplified work place analysis to explore user characteristics and the context of use (typical users, typical tasks, typical equipment, etc.).

The evaluator is a human factors expert evaluating software usability and conformance with ISO 9241. The expert approach is based both on a task to be performed with the tested system and on questions asked by a software ergonomics expert. This method is subjective since the expert examines and answers questions according to his personal expertise. It is objective, because the ergonomic requirements [9] are precisely formulated to enable the evaluator to answer questions under traceable conditions. Advantages of a guideline-based evaluation method are: it is relatively fast, uses few resources, provides an integrated view, and can be addressed to a wide range of behaviour.

In the ISO 9241-EVALUATOR test instructions, examples and comments are provided to support the applicability of the method. The evaluation guide consists of three steps and includes a detailed tracking of the evaluation process with a clear notation and structure. Step 1 describes the context of use (users, tasks, and environment) and is supported by a questionnaire. Step 2 is the central step of the evaluation process. Here all selected test items (see example in figure 2) have to be evaluated considering the context of use as described in the first step of the procedure. The result of these activities is a test record that forms the basis for the result interpretation and for writing the test report in the step 3.

The evaluation procedure can be used for summative or formative evaluation purposes. Therefore it has to be embedded in the software engineering process at different stages [11]. Hix [3] discusses in more detail the incorporation of usability evaluation techniques into the software life cycle.

3.2 Context of Use

The software-ergonomic evaluation of usability has to be placed in the context of use consisting of the users, their jobs and tasks, the hardware and software, and the organisational, technical, and physical environment. Although usability is a property of the overall system, our focus of evaluation is the software product. It is possible to address properly the usability of the user interface only if the particular context of use has been identified. The investigation of the context of use is performed by considering the following characteristics ISO 9241 Part 11:

- *The user:* User types (e.g. user populations) based on information about users skills and knowledge (e.g. software experience, hardware experience, task experience, organisational experience, education, training), personal attributes (e.g. age, gender, physical capabilities, disabilities), cognitive attributes (e.g. intellectual abilities), motivation.
- *The software:* Descriptions of the functionality and main application areas of the software, available instructional items (e.g. handbooks, on-line tutorials).
- *The job and tasks:* Details about the job of the user as a whole, and the tasks for which the software will be used as an aid (e.g., task goal, task name, task frequency, task breakdown, task duration, task flexibility, task output, task dependencies).
- *Organisational environment:* Aspects of the structure of the organisation (e.g. hours of work, group working, job function, work practices, management structure, communication structure, interruptions) the attitudes

and culture (e.g., policy on use of computer, organisational aims, industrial relations), and the job design (e.g. job flexibility, performance monitoring, performance feedback, pacing, autonomy, discretion).

- *Technical environment:* Hardware and basic software which is necessary to use the examined software, reference material.
- *Physical environment:* Workplace conditions (e.g., humidity, temperature, noise), design of the workplace (e.g., space and furniture, user posture, location), workplace safety (e.g., health hazards, protective clothing and equipment).

The simplified work place analysis to explore user characteristics and the context of use is based on ISO 9241, part 11 and will refer to the test items. This relation between the evaluation of the software product and the context of use ensures that only necessary information will be gathered with these methods and helps to develop a highly practicable evaluation procedure.

3.3 Two-dimensional Framework

The test items for the software evaluation are embedded in a two-dimensional matrix. The first dimension consists of the technical system components, and is inspired by the IFIP model for user interfaces and adapted to the structure of the multi-part ISO standard. The second dimension consists of the software-ergonomic principles which arebased on the dialogue principles of ISO 9241, part 10 and extended by requirements for the I/O interface of a system. For a discussion of how usable usability principles are see [1].

Figure 2 shows the structure of a sample test item. To test a software product for conformance with ISO 9241 the standard requirements have to be applied regarding the criteria of usability that are derived from the product´s context of use [4]. In the example item the *"if-clause"* refers to the condition of application, the remaining sentence provides the guideline, i.e., recommendation according to the involved *"should"*. Therefore the conformance test is a two-stage process. First the application of the "if-clause" is to be proven. If so, product attributes will be compared with the criteria of usability. In this comparison the context of use has to be considered. The necessary context information has been gathered using the simplified work place analysis to explore user characteristics and the context of use. The test instruction gives the evaluator useful information how to test the specific attribute of the software product in a systematic way. Examples and comments suggest desirable ergonomic requirements. The evaluator can use this information during the evaluation process. For a specific aim of an evaluation or to evaluate a particular component of a system predefined "views" can be selected or new ones can be created by the evaluator. Views are subsets of test items representing specific issues, for instance, menu presentation, mouse navigation, speech input, window design, and so on. Typically a test item will be evaluated several times in different test situations i=1....n. Each test situation will be shortly characterised by the evaluator (e.g., menu structure of the main menu; menu structure of the customer window). For each test situation a new evaluation has to be performed.

Component: 2.1.5.1 Menu structure

Criterion: Conformity with user expectations

Keyword: Structuring into levels and menus: Conventional or logical categories or arbitrary grouping

Source: ISO 9241 Part 14.5.1.1 to 5.1.3 and Part 10.3.4.1

Item No.: 2151.04.01:

If options can be arranged into conventional or natural groups known to users, options should be organised into levels and menus consistent with that order.

Test instruction: Examine all menu items concerning a consistent order of the structure. Identify the criteria for the menu structure.

Comment: Menu structures should reflect users´ expectations and facilitate the users´ ability to find and to select menu options relevant for the task and should support the users´ flow of work. Task specific or user specific conventions are better then logical or arbitrary ones.

Note: The number of options placed in a given menu depends both on the display space available and the discriminability of the individual options.

Test situation (i=1.....n): to be filled in by the evaluator during the evaluation
Criteria of usability:

- o conventional categories ELSE / logical categories ELSE
- o arbitrary categories if conventional and logical categories are unavailable
- o not applicable

Explanation of the evaluation: ....

Fig. 2: Example of a test item

An assessment of each test item in different test situations is necessary for a systematic evaluation of a software product. Different answers in different situations can show a context sensitive response to a specific task situation but it can also be an indication for an inconsistent user interface. Analysing the evaluations of each item a final judgement determines whether or not the software fulfils the ergonomic requirements of ISO 9241.

3.4 Evaluation Software

The software for the ISO 9241-EVALUATOR runs on a PC under Windows, and was developed by W.-W. Strapetz, at the Ernst & Young Consulting GmbH Vienna, and University of Vienna. The software package supports the evaluator during the whole evaluation process and provides an assessment summary. The evaluator specifies and records the test situations for each test item, evaluates each test item for several test situations, and writes an explanation of his or her evaluation.

The software calculates an average score for each ergonomic criterion and for each technical component and sorts the results by components or ergonomic principles. Hier the evaluator is freed of administrative work and can concentrate on the evaluation process.

3.5 Application of the ISO 9241-EVALUATOR

EVADIS as the predecessor of the ISO 9241-EVALUATOR has been widely used for teaching and training students and practitioners at Universities (e.g. Vienna, Koblenz, Bonn, Dortmund, Bremen, Hamburg) and in commercial training courses (e.g. SEH´87 - SEH´93); it has also been used in commercial and industrial companies (e.g., Lufthansa Köln; Bundesamt für Post und Telekommunikation Berlin; Citybank AG Meerbusch; DATEV Nürnberg).

The ISO 9241-Evaluator can now be used for the conformance testing of products with ISO 9241. One of the first application being tested is the work flow management system of the assurance company Allianz Elementar.

The testing shows that the ISO 9241-Evaluator works and identifies conformance attributes and those features of the software that are in conflict with the ISO standard. In the given case it is interesting to see that the designers´ conscious deviations from the standard have been detected by the ISO 9241-Evaluator.

The test theoretical quality assurance (e.g. reliability and validity) of the ISO 9241-Evaluator is in preparation.

4. Conclusions

ISO 9241-EVALUATOR will contribute to the accessibility of software quality. The support of the evaluation is a pragmatic one by restricting the scope of the method to the given or forthcoming parts of the standard ISO 9241. The advantage of a guideline based evaluation method is that it is relatively fast, uses few resources, provides an integrated concept, and can be addressed to a wide range of products.

Acknowledgement

I would like to thank Marcin Sikorski (University of Gdansk) and the partners of the EVADIS team for their comments to an earlier version of this paper: Thomas Geis (TÜV Rheinland, Cologne), Manfred Koch (Ernst & Young GmbH Vienna), Jochen Prümper (Dr. Prümper & Partner, Munich), and Harald Reiterer (University of Vienna).

References

1. Ch. Bastien, D. Scapin "How usable are usability principles, criteria and standards?", in: D. L. Scapin (ed.): HCI Evaluation Methodologies, HCI International 1995, July 9-14, 1995.
2. "EEC: The minimum safety and health requirements for work with display screen equipment", Directive of the European Economic Community, 90/270/EEC.
3. D. Hix "Usability evaluation: how does it relate to Software Engineering?", in: D. L. Scapin (ed.): HCI evaluation methodologies, HCI International 1995, July 9-14, 1995.
4. W. Dzida "Standards for user-interfaces", Computer Standards & Interfaces, vol.17, pp.89 - 97, 1995.
5. W. Dzida, M. Wiethoff, A. G. Arnold: "ERGOguide - the quality assurance guide to ergonomic software", Delft University and GMD, 1993.
6. "ISO 9241: Ergonomic Requirements for Office Work with Visual Display Terminals", 1994.
7. M. Macleod: "Usability: practical methods for testing and improvement" Proceedings of the Norwegian Computer Society Software´94 Conference, Oslo, 1-4 February 1994.
8. J. Nielsen "Usability Engineering", Boston: Academic Press, 1993.
9. R. Oppermann, B. Murchner, H. Reiterer, M. Koch "Software ergonomische evaluation - Der Leitfaden EVADIS II", (German), Walter de Gruyter, Berlin, 1992.
10. H. Reiterer "User Interface evaluation and design", Oldenbourg, München, 1994.
11. H. Reiterer, R. Oppermann "Evaluation of user interfaces: EVADIS II - a comprehensive evaluation approach. behaviour & information technology", vol.12, nr. 3, pp.137 - 148, 1993.

Are You Sitting Comfortably ?

Heather Piper
Taylor Nelson AGB plc
Westgate, London W5 1UA, U.K.

Abstract

IT systems should be accurate, reliable, efficient and comfortable to use. The first three are essential, the last, *comfort*, a useful bonus. With some systems, however, "comfort/ease of use" is paramount: information gathering, for instance, where the users' view is restricted to their interaction with the input mechanism. In market research, respondents are involved via exposure to some form of interview. Their participation, and the quality of the information obtained, relies on their task being perceived as relevant, straightforward, well managed, comfortable. This paper illustrates Taylor Nelson approaches that ensure data quality through respondent comfort. Current surveys for TV audience, grocery measurement and quality of mail services are described; so too is recent development work using automated speech recognition to conduct telephone interviews without an interviewer.

1. Introduction

Market Research today is a fast growing international industry. From its early roots in Victorian social studies based on the innovative concept of statistical sampling it has evolved to become a multi-disciplinary profession whose work is used to help frame policy and track outcomes by business, government and social institutions. The industry was worth 3.2 billion ECUs across Europe in 1994. Currency fluctuations make growth estimates difficult, but UK revenues have grown by more than 5% in real terms in each of the last 3 years, ahead of the overall economy and ahead of advertising expenditure.

Research activity covers a wide variety of areas; food and grocery, media, opinion polling, product and service quality tracking, to name but a few. Irrespective of country or application, market research has four core disciplines:
data collection, data preparation and analysis, data interpretation, and information reporting and presentation. It was the researchers' need for efficient handling of large scale data entry, and the analysis of resulting large data sets that made us early and intensive users of computer technology. A culture of innovation in the use of IT is now reflected in all aspects of our work, often stretching back to the initial phase of data collection.

2. Data Collection

Data collection is arguably the most important part of the Market Research process. Once a survey is "in the field", data collection errors can be difficult to detect and difficult to correct. Producing reliable data means getting this right! And at this stage, we also have to deal with our most valuable asset: our respondents.

Although some surveys provide incentives to respondents (e.g. prize draws, or gift catalogue "points") it is often true to say that respondents have little to gain personally from participation. They take part because we have persuaded them to do so, convincing them of the relevance of the project, the seriousness of our intention and that the task is as simple and comfortable an experience for them as we can make it.

In return for their cooperation we must treat them well, for the sake of our survey, our company's reputation, and the industry as a whole. To that end, the public face we present to respondents is vital. Our interviews' conduct, our printed questionnaires, any technology that we expose them to, must all be geared towards ensuring a relevant, polite, well managed, comfortable experience.

An *IT approach* to data capture can be used to simplify the respondents' task, to allow more detailed information to be gathered, to speed up processing times, and to reduce costs. We would usually expect to see at least two of these benefits from any new technology development. Below we describe three long running Taylor Nelson surveys that use such approaches, and a fourth area of development currently under investigation.

3. Television Audience Measurement

Watching television is a popular pastime; selling TV advertising is a lucrative one. The trading currency used to buy and sell advertising slots is that of television audience ratings. Knowing the size and composition of audiences for different programmes and time slots assists in planning advertising campaigns that can best reach a productís target audience.

Our company's involvement with the British ratings data goes back to the late 1950's. Over the years, the methodology has changed, to encompass strong technological solutions for increasingly more complex markets and more detailed customer needs.

The original self completion diary required respondents to complete, for each 15 minute timeslot, details of which channel, if any, they were watching. Nowadays, in each panel home, a monitor attached to each television set automatically records the set's on/off and channel information to the nearest second. All individuals in the home simply record details of their *personal* viewing by pressing the button allocated to them on a remote control unit when they themselves start viewing, and again when they stop. The task for each respondent has been considerably simplified, from keeping a record of what they did and remembering to post it to us regularly, to merely button pressing when they view. These "AGB People Meters" record viewing times much more accurately than we could ever have expected a respondent to report their behaviour to us. And this is achieved within the context of a vastly more *complex TV scenario*, and the majority of homes now have more than one set. The number of channels continues to increase. There are terrestrial and satellite channels. Some people receive satellite *channels via dishes*, other through *cable systems*. People use their VCRs to record programs for watching at a later date. On some occasions they watch TV through their *video recorder*, either because they forgot to retune, or because the reception is better that way. The People Meter can decipher all of this automatically.

Then, during the night, our central computer makes contact by phone with each panel home, and - without allowing the telephone to ring - the viewing data is downloaded over the phone. Basic ratings information is available the following morning.

The equipment's style is as important as its functionality, to maximise acceptability by potential panel members. A brief description of the main features is given below.

- The *handset* has widely spaced buttons, clearly labelled with the person's name, ensuring that small children and the elderly find the system as convenient to use as do the more technologically adept.
- The meter itself is a *small black box* which sits on top of the TV set and does not look out of place in the living room. Its display gives constant, unambiguous indication of which panel members are registered as viewing, minimising the chances of error.
- Each *meter is wired* to its TV, and if present by that set, to a VCR and/or cable tuner. The meter is also plugged into an electric socket. No further cabling is required. The system as a whole transfers its data over the normal electrical wiring of the home, each set meter passing its information to one small Central Data Storage Unit (CDSU) which is situated at a convenient location for connection to a phone socket. The CDSU is then responsible for transferring the data to the central computer in the course of the nightly telephone contact.

The success of this technology is such, that apart from using it ourselves for the British ratings service (at 4,600 households, the largest national TV panel in the world) we license its use in a further 16 countries. Around 18,000 of our meters in total are deployed around the globe.

4. Grocery Market Measurement

The food and grocery industries have always been heavy users of market research. These were the earliest of branded mass markets, using consumer panels to discover exactly *who* was buying their products, and those of their competitors.

The original approach for data capture involved self-completion diaries. But as grocery products became more complex, with many brand/flavour variants, and some markets became more difficult to describe and designing an elegant, user friendly self completion document became a harder task.

An interviewer administered questionnaire helped, as interviewers could be trained to understand the market definitions, but the need for clustered samples, to accommodate regular interviewer visits, was a survey design restriction we wanted to remove. Furthermore, with more housewives working full or part time, it was becoming increasingly difficult to recruit and maintain panel members who would be available at home for those interviewer visits.

We needed a return to self completion, ensuring that we could achieve the required level of reporting detail from a workload that respondents would find acceptable.

The bar-codes on your groceries tell us what we need to know: the manufacturer, the brand, the variant, flavour, size and some special offer details.

We worked with MSI/Symbol to design a barcode scanner and modem suitable for installation in panel membersí homes and for use by the general public. Ten thousand homes now have this equipment. All household members use it to enter details of their bar-coded purchases, using the scannerís wand, its keypad and pre-printed bar-codes in a special codebook, to tell us: who did the shopping, which store they visited, total amount spent, and then for each item purchased its *barcode*, and its *price*. Telling us about the householdís main weekly shopping trip usually adds between 5 and 10 minutes to the time taken by the housewife to unpack the groceries.

As with the TV meters, data retrieval is via the telephone, using dial up/ring suppression techniques. It is then up to us to interpret the bar-codes, with reference to a file of almost 1.5 million live bar-codes and their descriptions. Some development work was requested, as follows:

- We tested various scanner/modem designs, and then we designed our own.
- We used a keypad in telephone layout, rather than calculator style.We slimmed down the scanner body to make it suitable for holding comfortably in a smaller hand. For similar reasons it is light weight.
- Usage tests by various age groups helped choose how pressure sensitive the keys should be. All redundant keys were dropped.
- We designed the scanner so that it could be used out of the modem, for maximum portability. But the modem was also designed to allow the scanner to function fully if the respondent preferred to leave it in place.

A light grey housing was chosen for the equipment, to maximise acceptability in the kitchen, the most commonly chosen site for its location. So successful was our redesign, that MSI have introduced it as an extension to their range of scanner/modem products.

5. Postal End to End Surveys

In the cases of TV research and grocery measurement mentioned previously, the research applications are so valuable and so consistent, that they merited the investment made in what are essentially bespoke solutions. This last example of an IT solution in use, is for a smaller scale project, using a general audiotext approach, for registering digit based data from touch tone phones.

On a continual basis, we perform quality checks on the time taken to deliver items of mail within Britain. This involves instructing a panel of 1,600 reporters, to post to others in the group, certain items supplied by us, on the dates we ask. When these items are received, they inform us by making a short, simple call to a FREEPHONE number, during which they register:

- their panel number,
- the letter/item number,
- the date received, and
- the date of postmark.

All of this can be expressed as digit strings, which are simple to enter on touch tone phone keypads. Check digits are used on panel numbers and item numbers; logic checks ensure no Sunday or Bank Holiday deliveries are claimed, and that postmark dates are never after apparent receipt dates.

The limitations to responses imposed by audiotext services are understood; but when audiotext does fulfil all the needs of the data collection, as in this example, it provides a neat and cost effective solution to handling large numbers of short data capture calls. We use it to handle around 15,000 calls per month.

6. Work in Progress on Automating Telephone Research

In this last section we will describe development work recently undertaken concerning the use of Automatic Speech Recognition for Telephone Market Research.

Telephone research is an area of growing importance to the industry world-wide, and for Taylor Nelson in particular.

Interviewers are being asked to work later at night to contact an increasingly mobile society. There is a perceived increase in personal risk involved in face to face interviewing, by both interviewer and respondent, as fears of crime increase. Much time is spent by interviewers in the field travelling between addresses. Telephone interviewing reduces the impact of these issues.

So long as the questions are suitable for asking over the phone, and so long as the restriction of the sample to the telephone owning population is acceptable, this is likely to be the approach adopted.

In terms of benefits, the possibility of replacing our interviewer with a Speech Recogniser does not simplify the respondentís task, nor does it allow us to gather more complex information. The respondent still has to understand the questions and respond as before, over the telephone. The benefits in this instance would be for the research company: reduced costs, possibly faster processing times, and opportunities for conducting international research to a consistent methodology from a single site, with reduced need for native speakers. But we could not make such a change unless we were sure the experience was no less comfortable for the respondent than the current human to human one.

We were intrigued by the technology and in a recent IEATP project ("Advanced Speech Recognition and Speaker Verification", partners GEC Marconi, Taylor Nelson) we explored the possibilities of conducting telephone interviews without an interviewer. We assessed the Speech Recognition requirements for market research interviewing. The problems of ASR dialogue design for interviewing can be illustrated in the following diagramme.

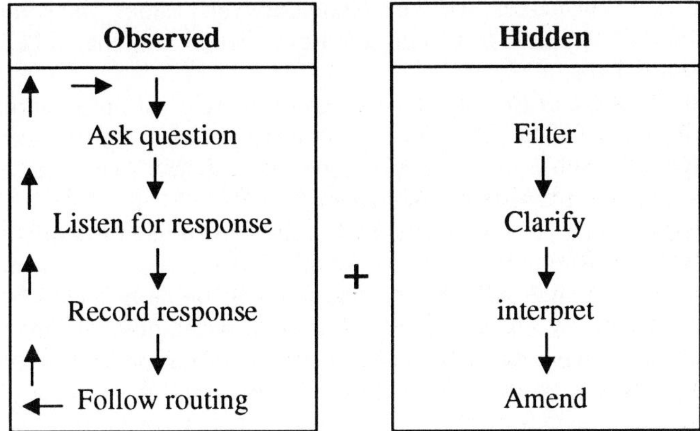

Fig.1: Observed and hidden acts carried out by an interviewer

The interviewer not only carries out the observed acts, but is continuously carrying out the hidden acts. Similarly our ASR technology and supporting software must do both. The pilot questions we employed in our demonstrator were straightforward. They concerned holiday taking during the current year. The questions can be summarised and paraphrased as follows.

1. Have you had a holiday so far this year?
2. Are you planning a holiday in the remainder of this year?
   IF NO HOLIDAY AT 1 AND 2 THEN **CLOSE**
3. Thinking of your most recent/next holiday:
   Where did/will you go?
4. Have you been before?
5. Was it/will it be a package?
6. How did/will you travel?
7. Length of holiday

CLOSE

Fig.2: Pilot questions

The full flowchart diagramme for this questionnaire runs to 10 pages of A4. A full specification of dialogue and recognition requirements runs to 90 pages. However, the questionnaire itself takes less than three minutes to complete.

All the questions, prompts and reiterations were recorded in the appropriate past and future tenses. Trips abroad were filtered sequentially; Europe, USA, rest of world. This reflects the incidence of holiday taking from the UK and also reduces the potential for recognition confusion. In addition to full/proper country names we also included the names of some popular destinations, e.g. Majorca, to capture data even when anticipated ëerrorsí were made by respondents.

However, one can't always have 100% foresight. In the method of travel question although we included "plane" and "aeroplane" we omitted "aircraft" from the list of eligible recognisable responses. Clearly over time experience builds up a lexicon of probable utterances.

In this particular pilot we wanted to let the flow go as smoothly as possible thus we went for minimum levels of confirmation, checking back only at key routing points in the dialogue, or if replies seemed "unlikely". Thus for example on the "which country visited" question answers were divided into those with high probability to visit and low probability. Confirmation within the dialogue was only sought for those low probability destinations. We have a particularly good recording of a journalist trying the system in a forthright manner being asked - "did you say Uzbekistan?" - yes she did!

We analysed 170 calls. Over 60% completed successfully, using just the basic features of isolated word/phrase recognition, and without any form of talkover. The single biggest problem involved respondents speaking too soon; not usually interrupting the prompt, but on simple questions, just answering faster than the system could contend with. If this one problem had been resolved, success rates would have reached the high 80's. We believe improved talkover facilities could be the answer here.

We have been encouraged by our progress so far, in that our design approach appears to be on the right track. Respondent reaction also has been favourable. But we know we need to extend our design approach to handle more complex speech technologies, e.g. talkover and word spotting. And the single biggest barrier to successful deployment of the technology is that building good systems takes too long.

We begin work in November 1995 on REWARD, a Framework IV Telematics project, led by Vocalis, that will address these issues. Our aim will be to combine the best in recognition technologies with the best in dialogue design skills, and package these items for general use. A Service Creation Toolkit will then bring good design within the reach of those, who although inexperienced in speech technologies, want to develop services in their own areas of interest.

Additionally trial services, developed in the 5 languages and market areas of the user partners, will give further scope for testing respondent/user reactions. Will Speech Recognition provide the next IT solution for market research, safely maintaining that all important respondent comfort ? We think it will.

Voice-based Dialogue in the Real World

Norman M. Fraser
Vocalis Ltd
Chaston House, Mill Court, Great Shelford
Cambridge CB2 5LD, U.K.

Abstract

Organisations which receive incoming telephone calls from customers are faced with a common set of problems. What is the best (fastest, cheapest, friendliest) way to identify what a customer wants and satisfy their requirement? What is the best way to manage variations in call volume? What is the best way to address the customer-led demand for increased quality and variety of telephone services in an increasingly competitive and cost-sensitive market? How can the process of creating new telephone services best be speeded up? The Language Engineering REWARD project addresses the needs of organisations (i) to create automatic teleservices using robust spoken language dialogue technology and (ii) to automate the process of creating such services. The project brings together five user organisations (from the PTO, Business Travel, Market Research, Telemarketing and Maintenance sectors) and two technology supplier organisations, along with a larger User Interest Group drawn from a variety of different European nations, and representing a wide range of languages and vertical market sectors.

1 Introduction

The telephone is one of the most important tools in business. Organisations which receive incoming telephone calls from customers are faced with a common set of problems. What is the best (fastest, cheapest, friendliest) way to identify what a customer wants and satisfy their requirement? What is the best way to manage variations in call volume (peaks and troughs) over time? What is the best way to address the customer-led demand for increased quality and variety of telephone services in an increasingly competitive and cost-sensitive market? How can the process of creating new telephone services best be speeded up?

The "REal World Applications of Robust Dialogue" project (EC Telematic Applications project LE-2632, REWARD) focuses on the needs of organisations with diverse interests in public telecommunication operators (PTOs) and ordinary businesses which offer different kinds of service over the public telecommunications network (we shall call the latter of these *telebusiness* organisations). The goal of PTOs is to increase the volume of traffic in the network. For telebusiness organisations, the telephone is simply a tool which enables them to do business. In spite of these different perspectives, organisations of both types have a number of features in common. In particular, both have customers who contact them by telephone to make enquiries, to buy goods and services, to settle accounts, to lodge complaints, to supply information, and so on.

The REWARD consortium consists of five user organisations and two technology supplier organisations. The users are the Swedish PTO Telia TeleRespons AB and the telebusinesses DanTransport Rejsebureau A/S (Denmark), Taylor Nelson AGB plc (UK), the Nederlands Instituut voor de Publieke Opinie en het Marktonderzoek BV (NIPO, Netherlands), and Manufacturing and Development S.A. (MADE, Spain). The technology suppliers are Vocalis Ltd. (UK) and the Center for Person Kommunikation, University of Aalborg (CPK, Denmark). The project co-ordinator is Vocalis. The REWARD project will begin in December 1995 and run for three years.

This paper is structured as follows. In section 2 we examine the business communication needs of these user partners. Section 3 identifies spoken language dialogue technology as an important solution to some of the more pressing user needs, and surveys progress in deploying such technology to date. The two main technical outputs of REWARD will be a service creation tool to support the rapid creation and modification of spoken language dialogue applications, and a number of trial applications to be demonstrated under realistic conditions. The service creation tool is discussed in section 4, and the planned innovative teleservices in section 5. Issues relating particularly to the multilingual European context are examined in section 6. Section 7 outlines the project lifecycle to be followed in the REWARD project, with particular emphasis on the crucial area of technology validation. The wider implications of REWARD are briefly identified in the concluding section.

2. User Requirements

Telia TeleRespons AB is the operating subsidiary of Telia AB (the government owned PTO in Sweden) responsible for providing Operator Assisted Services. Its business can be divided into areas of Information, Call services, Answering Services, and TeleMarketing Services. In all business areas there is a close relation between customers, operators and technical support systems. Telia TeleRespons (henceforth "Telia" will be used as an abbreviation for "Telia Tele-Respons") offers approximately 45 different services. Market research clearly indicates that PTO customers are demanding enhancements in all business areas. The evolution of the *Intelligent Network* and the increased availability of advanced telephone terminals will create a host of possibilities for customers. To support them through this explosion in services, it is vital that customers should be able to obtain assistance easily whenever they need it. This help should be efficient and *very user-friendly*. Telia itself needs to be able to respond rapidly to changing user demands by creating new or improved services in the shortest possible time and with the minimum of effort and risk.

DanTransport Rejsebureau is a business travel agency which conducts all its transactions by telephone. It has no high street travel shops. Competition is very keen in the travel sector, with profit margins being constantly squeezed lower. It is widely believed that travel organisations will have to find new ways of doing business in order to survive. The major component of the cost structure of the travel agencies consist of salaries and other personnel costs. Given the present percentage-based earnings structure, travel agencies will not be able to survive in the face of the forecast decrease in transport prices. The result is that travel agencies will have to apply the same methods as in the financial sector, i.e. to collect handling fees. If the airlines should decide not to collect the same fees, it will lead to a serious twist of competition. If the individual consumer contacts the airline directly, they will potentially be able to buy their ticket at a cheaper price. However, they will not receive neutral guidance, as they would through a travel agency. Business travel agencies thus have a very strong requirement to reduce the cost of delivering their services, without compromising the currently high standard of these services.

Taylor Nelson (whose core business has traditionally been in the area of market research) is aiming for vigorous expansion of its telemarketing business over the coming years. To do so successfully will require a mixture of increased operator staffing, improved facilities and efficient usage of resources. Handling inbound calls, particularly, requires that the problems of call volume fluctuation are managed efficiently.

Like Taylor Nelson, NIPO is a market research organisation, capable of offering customers qualitative research (in-depth interviews, group discussions) and quantitative research in order to provide them with practical information about their market, customers, attitudes, and opinions. The three main quantitative research methods are face-to-face, panel and telephone interviewing. of there three, telephone research is the most important in terms of number of interviews, number of interviewers and turnover. In a climate of intense competition, cost efficency is vitally important. Although improvements to the present data collection systems are constantly being made, further increases of speed and reductions of cost will be relatively small. To achieve a major step forward, the following are required:

- transfer of projects to interviewerless research instruments,
- reduced reliance on native speakers of particular languages,
- ability to survey in the global market independently of time (24 hour services),
- ability to conduct large numbers of interviews in parallel, and
- high rates of productivity in designing and programming new question-answer dialogues.

Manufacturing and Development S.A. (MADE) is an SME based in Barcelona with a second office in Madrid. Its activity is PC repair for both commercial and private users. Currently it provides customers with a telephone help line to provide information about quotations, reparability, planned collection dates, availability, etc. It is committed to improving the quality and flexibility of its customer care programme and in the last 18 months has developed a 24 hour help line using DTMF (touch tone) signalling. Whilst the system works well from a technical viewpoint, it has achieved limited usage amongst customers. Customer research has shown that this is due to either lack of DTMF telephones in customer homes/offices, or because of problems in the human factors design of the technology. A novel solution is required to deliver a higher level of service to customers in an efficient and cost-effective fashion.

There are thus two sets of competing requirements to be addressed in this project. First, there are the requirements of end users to access telephone services quickly, easily and with the minimum of stress. For many users, the helpful human agent delivers a standard of service quality which they will not easily give up. From the other side, providers of teleservices are faced with the high costs of staffing such services with skilled service agents. The economic arguments for automation are compelling.

The automatic solutions developed in the REWARD project must be sensitive to these competing requirements. The aim is to develop solutions which are both economically attractive (thus satisfying the service providers' requirements) and user-friendly (thus satisfying the end users). Spoken language technology is perhaps uniquely well placed to achieve this difficult balancing act, since it holds out the possibility of *replicative* automation (which provides a familiar service in a familiar way, but using a new underlying method) rather than *replacive* automation (which completely redesigns the service to meet the needs of the technology).

3. The REWARD Solution and the State of the Art

The REWARD project will directly address these needs. First, it will equip the user partners with an integrated tool to enable staff with a commercial orientation rather than a technical orientation to create new automatic telephone services based on spoken language dialogue technology (and/or DTMF). Second, it will result in the creation and extensive field testing of a number of trial automatic telephone services in realistic environments.

The technology suppliers, Vocalis Ltd. and the Center for PersonKommunikation, University of Aalborg (CPK), have considerable experience of developing telephone-based spoken language dialogue systems and supporting tools. However, it must be stressed that the object of the REWARD project is **not** to develop the core technology components; these already substantially exist in the suppliers' laboratories. Rather it is to *integrate* them in practical solutions and to *embed* these at the heart of live public telephone networks so as to deliver appreciable benefit to PTOs, telebusiness organisations and members of the public.

During the last few years, speech technology has begun to be deployed in real world telecommunications applications [13,18,19,20,21,22,23,24,25]. In 1989 Bell Northern Research began deploying "Automated Alternate Billing Services" through local telephone companies in the United States, with Ameritech being the first. The system simply rang customers, told them they had a collect call, and asked whether they would accept the call. Using a very small vocabulary (yes/no, plus some synonyms), the system successfully completed about 95% of the calls that were candidates for automation [6]. In 1992, AT&T introduced a service to automate the other end of the transaction, allowing customers to place collect calls, use a calling card, order a person-to-person call, or place bill-to-third-number calls. User trials were considered successful, not just from a technical standpoint, but also because customers were willing to use the service[10]. By the end of 1993, it was estimated that over 1 billion telephone calls each year were being automated by this service.

A key difference between the two systems is that the latter introduced word-spotting and barge in technologies. Word-spotting allows key words to be recognised in the midst of additional acoustic material. Barge in (also known as talkover or echo cancellation), allows users to speak and be recognised while the system is playing a message. A small but growing number of speech recognition-based services using these technologies have now been trialled by PTOs, mostly in the USA. These have focused on areas such as voice dialling, and directory assistance call completion. One of the most advanced systems currently in public use in Europe was introduced in 1994 by Telia (using Vocalis technology) to automate part of the directory enquiries task [11].

Publicly funded research has provided the major driving force for the technology advances exemplified by these systems. In the US, this has been co-ordinated by DARPA [8] (latterly ARPA [1]) through its competitive evaluations in large vocabulary speech recognition (Resource Management task) and spoken language understanding (ATIS task). European researchers have featured amongst the highest placed entrants in recent evaluations. There has been a clearer focus on the special issues associated with spoken language dialogue in Europe than in the USA. Projects such as SUNDIAL, the Danish national project on Spoken Dialogue Systems, the Phillips train timetable system, RAILTEL and VERBMOBIL have established a strong base of expertise in Europe in spoken language dialogue systems. In the field of market research, important initial investigation of speech recognition has been carried out by Taylor Nelson, with encouraging results [4,5].

A host of graphical service creation tools exist for designing DTMF-based telephone services [12]. However, very few tools have taken seriously the additional complexities inherent in designing services based on spoken language dialogue (see [7] for a notable exception). A related development has come from NIPO, which has developed a formal scripting language for market research interview dialogues [9].

It is still the case that no large-scale commercial "conversational" dialogue systems have yet been deployed in realistic telephone usage conditions. The REWARD project aims to prove conversational dialogue technology in such real world settings, and so hasten the approach of this technological landmark.

4. Service Creation Tool

Both Vocalis and CPK have invested considerable effort over the last few years in creating laboratory prototype graphical dialogue design tools. This was done by CPK as part of the SUNSTAR project [2,3,15] and subsequently as part of the Danish national project on Spoken Language Dialogue Systems. The Vocalis work was carried out with support from Vocalis' own R&D budget, building on the results and lessons of the SUNDIAL project. Though these systems emerged independently, there is a surprisingly high degree of similarity at both the conceptual and implementational levels.

CPK has used its tool to develop prototype spoken dialogue systems which have been publicly demonstrated at international conferences. Vocalis staff have used its tool to develop speech recognition-based telephone services which are currently being used by members of the public on a daily basis. However, neither system has been used by non-experts to develop systems, and it is clear that further integration and support work needs to be done to make this possible.

The existing tools will form the basis of a jointly developed teleservice creation tool in the REWARD project. A distinguishing feature of this tool will be its emphasis on supporting the creation of teleservice dialogues based on advanced spoken language understanding technology. This project will thus break new ground, in that there have so far been no realistic field trials of integrated graphical tools which support the complexities associated with natural language understanding.

The service creation tool will be implemented in C/C++ and will use the X-Windows graphical user interface system. It will be developed on workstations running the UNIX operating system, and will support the following features:

- a single point of entry to the tool; all features will be reachable from the top-level menu.
- a simple graphical user interface to all parts of the tool.
- on-line help available at every point in the system.
- active agents (otherwise known as 'wizards') to lead untrained users through the process of service creation, making suggestions and explaining the implications of different choices where necessary.
- a vocabulary building sub-system, which allows users to define application-specific speech recognition vocabularies using phoneme models. The underlying assumption is that users have no special knowledge of phonetics. The tool will also be supplied with a library of commonly-used words ('yes' and 'no', the digits, date words, time words, etc.).
- a grammar building sub-system, which allows grammatically naive users to define grammars for continuous speech understanding. Once again, libraries of commonly used phrase types will be provided.
- a dialogue building sub-system, which allows naive users to define the structure of service dialogues graphically, by means of a flowcharting system. In this case also, there will be a library of common sub-dialogues (e.g. for credit card number entry and confirmation) which will allow commonly used sub-dialogues to be defined once and then reused wherever needed.
- a facility to embed calls to external programs (such as databases) at any point in the dialogue.
- the ability to attach counters to any part of a dialogue, so as to generate customised call statistics.
- a set of default options, controlling such things as the phoneme model set to use in recognition, the number of times to ask the user to repeat an utterance before giving up, etc., will be provided. This will hide a large number of choices from the user. However, an options editor will make the default settings available to the user for adjustment where necessary.

- a verification facility which validates the well-formedness of new service dialogues and ensures that all error conditions are defined.
- an interactive debugging facility which allows users to step through a dialogue, one dialogue state at a time.
- a 'compile and link' feature, allowing users to create a runtime application based on what has been designed using the service creation tool. It will be impossible to compile a new service application unless it has been successfully verified.

5. Innovative Teleservices

The existing service delivery technology developed by Vocalis and CPK will be customised and ruggedised, and used to run large scale demonstrations of the teleservices created by each of the user partners. Telia will use the service creation tool to develop PTO helpdesk services (Swedish); DanTransport will develop an automated domestic flight ticket reservation service (Danish); Taylor Nelson will demonstrate a telemarketing service (English); NIPO will demonstrate a market research service (Dutch); and MADE will demonstrate a customer care service (Spanish).

The following examples illustrate the anticipated scale and complexity of the innovative teleservices to be implemented and demonstrated. The final detail of each service will be agreed during the requirements analysis activity in the early months of the project. Advanced spoken language understanding technology will be used in each innovative teleservice to interpret caller utterances, though, as the first example illustrates, limited DTMF input may be used where the context renders it natural and straightforward.

Telia will use the service creation tool to develop at least one PTO helpdesk service. Each service will be relatively simple, but very robust. Dialogues of more than a few turns are unlikely. For example, a call diversion service dialogue might proceed as follows:

System: Which service?
Caller: I want all my calls to be forwarded to another number.
System: Please use your telephone keypad to enter the number you wish to forward your calls to.
Caller: 0-1-2-2-3-8-4-6-1-7-7
System: Do you want call forwarding to take immediate effect?
Caller: Yes, but I don't want any calls to be forwarded after 10.00 pm.
System: OK. Between now and 10.00pm your calls will be forwarded to 01223-846177. Can I do anything else for you?
Caller: No thanks.

Towards the end of the project, the innovative service(s) will be fully integrated in Telia's normal service delivery environment in one of its central offices in Sweden, thereby testing access to live databases and modification of real customer profiles. Telia's demonstration services will be implemented for the Swedish language. DanTransport will develop an automated domestic flight ticket reservation service, also based on spoken language dialogue understanding.

Though the exact details of dialogues with such a system will be established during the user requirements and functional specification process, dialogues could be expected to resemble the following example:

System: Thank you for calling DanTransport Domestic Flight Booking Service. Do you want to book a domestic flight ticket?
Caller: Yes, please.
System: Where do you wish to fly from?
Caller: From Copenhagen to Aarhus.
System: Copenhagen?
Caller: Yes.
System: To Aarhus?
Caller: That's right.
System: When do you wish to travel?
Caller: In the morning of May the fifteenth.
etc...

This service will be demonstrated in DanTransport's offices in Denmark with integration to its on-line ticket booking system.

Taylor Nelson will develop and demonstrate in its normal work environment in London at least one telemarketing teleservice. The exact scope and details of the service will emerge during the preparation stage of the project. However, it can be expected to cover the sorts of issues outlined in the following example, for registering a magazine subscription:

System: Thank you for calling ABC magazine subscription line. Do you wish to take out a subscription?
Caller: Yes, please.
System: Which title would you like to subscribe to?
Caller: I'd like to start getting "Country Life", please.
System: And how would you like to pay?
Caller: By credit card.
System: What is your credit card number, please?
....
System: Is the subscription a gift for someone else?
Caller: No, it's for me.
System: Would you like it to be sent to your home address?
etc...

NIPO will implement at least one market research survey interviewing system, which will lead callers drawn from a research panel through structured opinion-seeking interactions. The user base can thus be characterised as "specialised" (but not "experienced"), since priming material will be sent to them telling them what to expect before they encounter the system.

System: Good morning, thank you for calling NIPO's automatic market research system. Please read out the identification number which appears at the top of the letter you received from NIPO.
Caller: The number is 57084.

System: Thank you. The questions I will ask you are about your most recent holiday. It will take about 10 minutes at the most. Did you take a holiday this year?
Caller: Yes, I did.
System: Did you go abroad?
Caller: Yes.
System: In which foreign country did you spend most of the time?
Caller: I went to Norway.
System: Now I will read out some statements. Can you tell me to what extent you agree with each statement? Please say if you entirely agree, agree, disagree or entirely disagree. The first statement is: I prefer beach holidays.
Caller: Totally agree.

MADE will specify and demonstrate a teleservice automating key aspects of its customer care service. The specific teleservice will be selected during the preparation phase of the project. It will be implemented in MADE's normal business environment in Barcelona and will operate in Spanish. An example reflecting the kind of performance foreseen for the demonstration service is shown below:

System: Good morning, thank you for calling MADE's customer care line. Could you please tell me your repair reference number, which appears at the top of your receipt.
Caller: Hold on...my number is 10145.
System: Okay, your equipment has been repaired at a cost of 12,500 Pts. Would you like to have it shipped to your address?
Caller: No thanks. I'll pick it up.
System: Okay, thank you for calling MADE.

These services need to be implemented on a service delivery platform which has the capability to support multiple simultaneous spoken language dialogues while interfacing with the public telephone network at one end and with an application database at the other. Both Vocalis and CPK have developed platforms offering these capabilities, which will require only modest customisation for the REWARD project.

6. Teleservices in a Multilingual Context

The European Union is characterised by linguistic plurality at every level. The official languages are complemented by a much larger number of other languages which are in daily use in minority language communities. In order for this plurality to be celebrated as a strength, it is necessary to design multilinguality in a new communications technology, rather than adding it on as an afterthought.

The innovative teleservices developed in the REWARD project will, in the first instance, be presented in the national languages of the user organisation responsible for developing and demonstrating them. Thus, Telia will use Swedish, DanTransport will use Danish, Taylor Nelson will use English, NIPO will use Dutch and MADE will use Spanish. The underlying speech recognition algorithms of Vocalis and CPK are language-independent. This has already been proven by Vocalis in real systems in the field, albeit with sub-REWARD functionality. The language-particular component necessary to instantiate a recogniser for any given language is the set of phoneme models. Ongoing work to collect and disseminate telephone quality speech data for a wide variety of languages (for example the EC SPEECHDAT project and the recently-created European Language Resources Association) will facilitate the process of migration to other languages.

The ability to demonstrate a teleservice in one's own language is an important first step, but all of the user partners in the project are keen to address transnational markets as part of their business strategies; in other words, they want to be able to work multilingually.

The service creation tool will provide service managers with a very useful structured tool for localising teleservices, thereby minimising the amount of time and effort needed for this important task. The service creation tool itself will be capable of being localised to each of the languages represented in the project, simply by the selection of the appropriate set-up option. It will also provide facilities for adding new localisation packages at minimal cost.

The REWARD project thus aims to provide a solid infrastructure for the design, delivery and localisation of advanced spoken language teleservices in five different languages in the first instance, with the possibility of adding extra languages downstream.

7. Project Lifecycle

REWARD is an *innovative application* project which follows the standard lifecycle for Telematic projects. It is divided into three stages: preparation, development and verification, and demonstration. Each stage is divided into approximately three workpackages, with additional project management and concertation and dissemination workpackages running throughout the entire project. Technology and applications developed in the project will be validated in two different ways. In Stage II they will be tested under controlled circumstances in the laboratory, first, in the premises of Vocalis and CPK, and subsequently in the premises of the user partners. Validation will be specification driven. That is, a series of structured tests will be carried out to ensure that the functional and technical specifications have been adequately implemented. Validation reports will be prepared, detailing the extent to which the items being tested conform to the specifications, and reporting on the consequences of any failures to conform. This activity will be carried out cyclically during Stage II, with as many test/debug iterations being carried out as time and/or needs dictate.

In Stage III (and assuming validation has proceeded with no major outstanding problems) the systems to be validated will be moved out of the laboratory and into realistic large scale service delivery environments in the premises of each of the user partners. The systems will run *live* for set periods of time, with detailed monitoring of usage patterns and, where possible, collection of user feedback. If necessary, the services may be adjusted and further iterations carried out. Detailed evaluation reports will be prepared following large scale demonstrations, and these will form an important part of the project's output.

8. Conclusions

REWARD can be expected to benefit European industry by facilitating the rapid creation of new kinds of teleservice, or the automation of routine parts of existing services. In this way, the cost of service provision can be reduced and economic growth stimulated. European citizens can also expect to benefit in the long term through access to user-friendly automated services and improved existing services, with skilled service agents being liberated to provide more detailed assistance to callers with non-routine requirements.

Though the kind of services foreseen in REWARD may negatively impact certain highly repetitive jobs, it is expected that the overall effects on employment will be positive, with cost savings obtained through automation in one area providing opportunities to finance a higher standard of person-to-person service where it really matters. The kinds of REWARD services will have a major impact on users, by providing simple and natural access to the growing wealth of information and services which are now emerging. The REWARD philosophy is to encourage human-computer interaction by means of the most human-friendly communication medium in existence: spoken natural language.

The fact that the REWARD prototypes are being developed for multiple languages will help to bring about equality of service provision across national boundaries, thus contributing to social cohesion in the linguistically diverse European context. By increasing the ease of use and accessibility of teleservices, REWARD will make an important contribution to the establishment of the Information Society.

References

1. "ARPA", Proceedings of the Speech and Natural Language Workshop. San Mateo, CA: Morgan Kaufmann, 1994.
2. Bækgaard A., Duhn J., Giannantoni A., Roman A. and Engelberg K.-J. "Dialogue Design, Dialogue Description Language", Deliverable IV.3-2, ESPRIT project 2094 SUNSTAR, 1990.
3. Bækgaard A., Roman A. and Wetzel P. "Advanced Dialogue Design, DDL-Tool and ICM", Deliverable IV.6-2, ESPRIT P2094 SUNSTAR, 1992.
4. Blyth B. and Piper H. "Speech recognition: a new dimension in survey research", Journal of the Market Research Soc., vol.36/3, pp.183-203, 1994.
5. Blyth B. and Piper H. "Developing speech recognition applications for market research", Proceedings of the 47th ESOMAR Marketing Research Congress, Davos, Switzerland, Sep. 1994.
6. Bossemeyer R.W. and Schwab E.C. "Automated alternate billing services at Ameritech: Speech recognition and the human interface", in Speech Technology Magazine, vol. 5/3, pp.24-30, 1991.

7. Dalsgaard P, Bækgaard A. "Spoken Language Dialogue Systems", CRIM/FORWISS Workshop on Progress and Prospects of Speech Research and Technology, Munich, Germany, Sep. 1994, in Proceedings in Artificial Intelligence, ISBN 3-929037-91-2, 1994.
8. "DARPA" Proceedings of the Speech and Natural Language Workshop, San Mateo, CA: Morgan Kaufmann, 1992.
9. Doorn van, L. and Hess T. "New research possibilities by computerised personal interviewing", Proceedings of the 41st ESOMAR Marketing Research Congress, 1988.
10. Franco V "Automation of operator services at AT&T", Proceedings of Voice'93, San Diego, 1993.
11. Forssten, B. "Speech technology: a one-shot possibility", Proceedings of Voice'94, London, Oct. 1994.
12. Grigonis R. "The graphic art of IVR", Comp. Telephony, pp.51-88, 1995.
13. Larsen L. B. "Development and evaluation of a spoken dialogue for a telephone-based transaction system", Eurospeech'95, pp.1973-1976, Madrid, Sep.1995.
14. Lennig M. et al "Flexible vocabulary recognition of speech", ICSLP'92, Banff, 93-96, Oct. 1992.
15. Lindberg B, Kristiansen J. and Andersen B. "SUNCAR Functional Description", STC WP-IV.008, ESPRIT project 2094 SUNSTAR, 1992.
16. Lindberg B. et al "An integrated dialogue design and continuous speech recognition system environment", ICSLP'92, pp.1553-1556, Oct. 1992.
17. Meisel W. (ed.) "Speech Recognition UPDATE", Encino, CA: TMA Associates, 1993.
18. Nakatsu R. "Anser: an application of speech technology to the Japanese banking industry" in Computer, vol.23/8, pp.43-48, 1990.
19. Nielsen P.B, Bækgaard A. "Experiences with a dialogue description formalism for realistic applications", ICSLP'92, pp.719-722, Banff, Oct. 1992.
20. Peckham J. "A new generation of spoken dialogue systems: results and lessons from the SUNDIAL project", Eurospeech'93, pp.33-40, Berlin 1993.
21. Peckham J. and Fraser N.M. "Spoken language dialogue over the telephone", H. Niemann, R. de Mori and G. Hanrieder (eds), in Progress and Prospects of Speech Research and Technology, Sankt Augustin, pp.192-203, 1994.
22. Peckham J. and Fraser N.M. "Speech Understanding and Dialogue", Cambridge, MIT Press (forthcoming).
23. Rohwer E. "An advanced multi-DSP platform for speech technology integration in computer telephony applications", Eurospeech'95, pp.59-62, Madrid, Sep. 1995.
24. Wilpon J.G. "Applications of coice processing technology in telecommunications", D. B. Roe and J. G. Wilpon (eds) in Voice communication between humans and machines, Washington, DC: National Academy of Sciences, 1994.
25. Young S.J. et al "The use of syntax and multiple alternatives in the VODIS Voice Operated Database Enquiry System" in Computer Speech and Language, vol. 5, pp.65-80, 1991.

MASK:
Multimedia Multimodal Service Kiosk

Eang Sour Chhor
MORS
Centre d'Affaires Paris-Nord
Tour Continental, BP 200
F-93153 Le Blanc Mesnil, France

Abstract

The rigidity of touch-screen based, and menu-driven user interfaces for public services prevents users from transacting tasks as fluently as when communicating with another person. The objective of the MASK project is to pave the way for more advanced public service applications by employing multimodal and multimedia input-output. The project will produce a demonstrator implemented in a real public service context (railway traveller services). The development of the project demonstrator and its experimental application in the automated kiosk services will provide realistic guidelines for better integrating multimodal and multimedia interface technologies in the public service applications.

1. Introduction

Nowadays, more and more automated machines are used in several domains like delivering goods, bank notes, transport tickets, information etc. Although these machines are more and more sophisticated, most of the time they are not quite user friendly and the man-machine interface is often complicated and ambiguous for the user. Even if significant efforts were made, in terms of integrating new technologies in the user interface, like touch screen and multimedia, the user still has to operate according to the machine demands. One of the MASK project goals is to adapt the machine to the user by combining speech recognition with touch screen and multimedia technologies [1, 2, 3, 4, 5]. The MASK service kiosk will be able to "understand" natural language taking into account user hesitations, and will also be able to recognize different speakers (i.e. multimodality capability). The MASK project analysis technological requirements in the context of users and the tasks they perform, and conducts simulation-based studies using a Wizard of Oz technique in order to support these analyses.

The MASK project should make technological advances in three main areas, as follows:

- in the development of robust flexible user-computer dialogues
- in the real-time interpretation of concurrent user data entries via multiple input modalities in realistic public service contexts
- in real-time integration of multimedia feedback to guide users in realistic public service transactions.

The design of the enhanced kiosk will be implemented and evaluated in the context of representative tasks and users, and improvements in effectiveness are expected over current systems. The results of the work will be exploited within the project by the industrial partner (MORS). It is expected that the advances made in the context of the demonstrator will be exploitable by other systems in other applications, thus increasing the general competitiveness of Europe in the world-wide market for public service systems.

2. MASK Consortium

The development of this project is 50 % funded by DG III of the European Commission under the ESPRIT programme. The consortium consists of five different companies in three separate countries: France, UK and Spain:

- MORS, a French Industrial company, acts as the leader of the project. MORS is also responsible for the kiosk integration (software and hardware) and the exploitation plan of the MASK project.
- The SNCF (Société des Chemins de Fer), French Railway Research Department, is responsible for the needs definition.
- LIMSI (Laboratoire d'Informatique pour la Mécanique et les Sciences de l'Ingénieur), one of the CNRS (Centre National de Recherche Scientifique) laboratory (French), is responsible for the spoken language system.
- UCL (University College London), Ergonomics' unit of the University College London, is responsible for the ergonomics aspect of the user interface.
- GCI (Grupo de Consultores en Informatica), Spanish company, is responsible for the multimedia development.

3. Project Overview

There is a close relationship between the size of a town and the complexity of its urban transport; the bigger the town, the more complex the urban transport. In big cities, it is sometimes a real obstacle course for people to find out their routes. In order to give travelers more efficient information (available 24 hours a day), many transport organisms have installed information kiosks in their network. In fact we can transpose this information problem to several public organisms, for example public administration.

Many information kiosks and many ticket dispenser machines were developed in order to solve the problem. Actually, these machines are based on engraved buttons or touch screen. These kiosks are able to give train or bus timetables, routes etc., and can give the route information with the optimization of the duration. Even though touch screen dialogue interface has improved the user interface, the rigidity of touch-screen based, menu-driven user interfaces for public systems prevents users from transacting tasks as fluently as when communicating with another person.

The main objective of the MASK project is to pave the way for more advanced public service applications by employing multimodal and multimedia input/output. The project will produce a demonstrator implemented in a real public service context (rail traveler services). The research and development of the MASK demonstrator will provide valuable information to developers of other public service systems, and also guidelines for better integrating multi-modal multi-media interface technology with the aim of making a man-machine dialogue as simple as a natural dialogue.

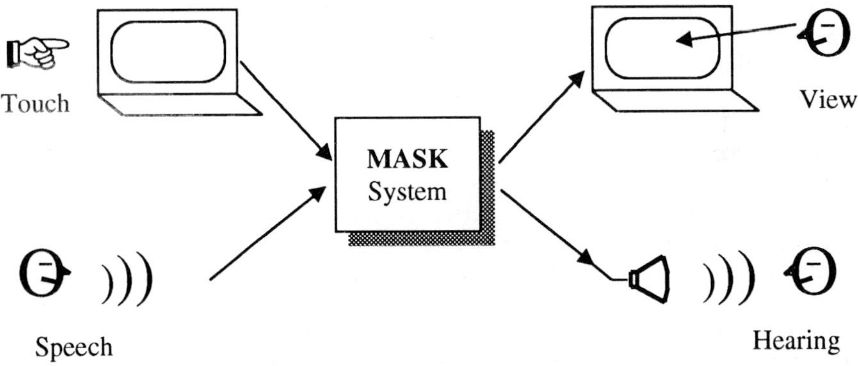

Fig. 1: User Interfaces of the MASK system

The MASK user interface uses four of the human senses: the *touch* (touch screen), and the *voice* (spoken language) in order to explain the user needs by appropriate inputs to MASK system, and the sense of *hearing* (voice synthesis), and the *view* (multimedia display) in order to obtain the answers in form of outputs (see figure 1) of the MASK system. However, the success of the user interface heavily depends on the management of the inputs and outputs based on a good and efficient analysis of the user behaviour.

4. User Requirements

The University College London has developed early prototypes of the final system using the Wizard of Oz (WOz) techniques. WOz prototypes utilize a hidden human 'Wizard' to perform speech understanding and other aspects of the prototype. The major WOz studies of the project have just been completed. The studies involved testing 115 subjects in Gare St Lazare in Paris during a one month period. The data is currently being analyzed but informal observations concerning the studies may be summarized as follows:

- Push to Talk is a feasible speech entry system for MASK
- MASK users did not attempt low level integration of Input Modalities.
- Delay of the speech output was used in guiding user behaviour.
- MASK users were able to cope with speech understanding errors.

One of the key studies conducted in Paris compared a 'Push to Talk' system, to a system where users' speech was detected automatically. For the *'Push to Talk'* system, users pressed a dedicated on-screen button whenever they wanted to input information using speech. The automatic speech detection version was implemented through the intervention of the human wizard, creating a very much idealized system, far in excess of the capabilities of existing technology. In general, as might be expected, users preferred the automatic speech detection system. However, the loss of performance with push to talk was not drastic and the vast majority of users had no problems using this technology when guided by the spoken output messages of the system. This indicates that for the near future, 'Push to Talk' can be an effective method for controlling speech entry in public access multi-modal, multi-media systems.

During the empirical studies, the vast majority of the users of the MASK system did not attempt to *integrate the Speech and Touch* Screen input modalities at a low level. An example of a low level interaction would consist of the user saying "I want to go there" while touching a destination displayed on the screen. Much of the early design activity of the project involved the issues of how to implement responses to relative reference queries. The empirical studies have demonstrated that for public access systems, multi-media, multi modal systems, with simple purchase and information tasks, users will either use speech or touch to enter information and not attempt to integrate the modalities.

The MASK system is designed to be a 'walk up and use' system for which users require no previous training. The spoken output system is designed to guide users throughout their use of the machine. The spoken output must assist users who are having difficulties, without being intrusive for experienced users. For the MASK system, spoken output may be used to report some user error, provide a specific prompt for user entry or issue more general help for the user. Error messages, indicating for example that the user had not held the 'push to talk' button down while talking, were issued immediately. Specific prompts and more general help messages were issued after a time delay. In general, this approach seemed to provide an effective system for both naive and experienced users. It is believed that this approach would be generally applicable to systems of a similar type. The detailed data analysis, which is still to be conducted, will tell us far more about the effects of different lengths of time delay on system effectiveness.

5. Effects of Errors

When human beings understand speech they sometimes make errors. The same is true for computerized speech understanding systems. A study was conducted to see the likely effects of understanding errors on users interaction with the machines. Many of the results from this study will not be available until after the detailed analysis of the data. However, informal observations indicate that for the MASK system, perhaps because of alternative modalities and the nature of the multimedia display, small errors in speech understanding did not present users with major problems in carrying out their tasks. This is a positive observation for systems similar to MASK, indicating that it is still possible to develop systems with speech understanding technology, even though that technology is not always 100% effective.

6. System Design Implications

One final observation concerns the Wizard of Oz technique that was used to carry out the studies. The technique was very valuable at providing an early version of the system upon which studies could be conducted with target users. However, the system was developed independently from the software and hardware components of the final demonstrator. Also, this was the first known attempt to conduct these types of studies on this scale. Consequently, the cost of running these studies for a commercial organization may be prohibitive. This indicates that in order to make the WOz approach to early prototyping a common component of the commercial development of multi-modal systems, improved methods and tools are required to integrate the techniques more fully with conventional system development.

The ergonomic study of MASK is very important for the specification of the user interface in order to take into account the user behaviour and to make the man-machine dialogue as natural as a human dialogue.

The MASK speech recognition system is able to understand, in natural language, more than ten thousand queries and more than one thousand words.

The MASK kiosk is speaker independent, this means that no speaker specific enrollment data is needed for new users. The MASK kiosk is able to understand a large number of speakers and covers a wide variety of accents and voice qualities. The MASK kiosk is also able to manage user hesitations. Queries are semantically analysed in order to deliver the requested information. The speech processing system was tested in a wide range of scenarios with more or less complex demand, for instance: 'I want to go to Marseille with the departure from Paris on Monday at 13h30, second class, no smoking'. If some data are missed the MASK kiosk will help the user by asking him (synthesis voice) dedicated questions in order to fulfil all the database information related to his trip. The MASK kiosk is able to adapt its process according to the user expertise. Even though the speech recognition system needs a 'powerful computer' at this stage of the MASK development, the increase of computers' calculation power at low cost allows real improvement to the multimedia technology (including speech recognition).

Multimedia technology makes software applications attractive (more generally electronic machines with their software) and more user friendly. We should also consider the current social side where the use of a computer will be a commonplace for an increasing number of people. According to these two points, we strongly believe that the future MASK kiosk, with speech recognition, which will be more user friendly, will increase the numbers of users for automated kiosks. For the MASK project, the speech recognition language is restricted to the "SNCF domain" and the French language. At the end of the project a MASK demonstrator kiosk will be provided and tested on site. The results of the work will be exploited within the project by the developer of the current service kiosks.

The extension of the application to other domains and foreign languages is important for a commercial view point, but requires new software developments. The industrialization phase is also very important because we have primarily to validate that it has to comply with the market price, and secondly to validate the industrial product technical feasibility in a harsh environment. It is expected that the advances made in the context of the demonstrator will be exploited by other system developers in other applications, thus increasing the general competitiveness of Europe in the world-wide market for public service systems.

7. Conclusions

The MASK project with the integration of speech recognition and multimodal interface technologies is aiming to improve user interface for information kiosks and ticketing machines with ollowing benefits: provide new services to the clients, improvement of user interface using multimedia multimodal technology., decrease of transactions time at automated service kiosks, reduce load on the ticket window sales staff at peak times, accumulate experience in client acceptance topics and new technologies, enhance the ergonomics and the flexibility of man-machine dialogues based on ergonomic studies.

The project results are relevant in the *development* of robust and flexible user-computer dialogues, in the real-time *interpretation* of concurrent user data entries (via multiple input modalities) in a realistic context of public services, and in the real-time *integration* of multimedia in public services.

References

1. Lamel L. et al. "Recent Developments in Spoken Language Sytems for Information Retrieval", ESCA ETRW Spoken Dialogue Systems, May 1995, Visgo, Denmark.
2. Lamel L. et al. "Development of Spoken Language Corpora for Travel Information", Eurospeech'95 Madrid, Sep. 1995.
3. Dowell J., Life A. and Salter I. "The design space for a multimodal multimedia travel facility", Proceedings of 7th Annual Conference of the European Society fo Cognitive Ergonomics, (ECCE7), 1994.
4. Dowell J., et al. "Designing the multimodal speech interface to a public travel facility", Proceedings of the International Ergonomics Association World Conference 1995, Rio de Janeiro, October 16-20, 1995.
5. Dowell J., Shmueli Y. and Salter I. "Applying a cognitive model of the user to the design of a multimodal speech interface", Proceedings of IMMI Conference 1995.

Spoken Language Component of the MASK Kiosk

J.L. Gauvain, S. Bennacef, L. Devillers, L.F. Lamel, S. Rosset
LIMSI-CNRS, BP 133
91403 Orsay cedex, France

Abstract

The aim of the Multimodal-Multimedia Automated Service Kiosk (MASK) project is to pave the way for more advanced public service applications by user interfaces employing multimodal, multimedia input and output. The project has analyzed the technological requirements in the context of users and the tasks they perform in carrying out travel enquiries, and developed a prototype information kiosk that will be installed in the Gare St. Lazare in Paris. The kiosk will improve the effectiveness of such services by enabling interaction through the coordinated use of multimodal inputs (speech and touch) and multimedia output (sound, video, text, and graphics) and in doing so create the opportunity for new public services. Vocal input is managed by a spoken language system, which aims to provide a natural interface between the user and the computer through the use of simple and natural dialogues. In this paper the architecture and the capabilities of the spoken language system are described, with emphasis on the speaker-independent, large vocabulary continuous speech recognizer, the natural language component (including semantic analysis and dialogue management), and the response generator. We also describe our data collection and evaluation activities which are crucial to system development.

1. Introduction

Information technology has the potential to improve information and services for the general public. However, often such services fail to realize their potential and are frequently under-used. The problems with public service provision are exemplified in the kiosks currently available for rail travellers to obtain information about train services and local facilities, and to purchase tickets. The average transaction time at such kiosks is four times as long as with service staff. As a consequence, the kiosks are under-utilised, being used primarily at night when no agent is present, or when there are long lines for human service.

Evidently, the technology being used does not meet the particular needs of intended users in the context of the tasks they want to perform. Specifically, the rigidity of touch-screen-based, menu-driven user-interfaces prevents users transacting tasks fluently, as when communicating with another person.

The goal of the ESPRIT project MASK (Multimodal-Multimedia Automated Service Kiosk) is to develop an advanced interface employing both multimodal and multimedia inputs/outputs in order to pave the way for more advanced public services. In the context of the project, the technological requirements of users carrying out travel enquiry tasks have been analyzed and a prototype information kiosk has been developed. The kiosk, which will be installed in the Gare St. Lazare in Paris for evaluation with real users, should improve the effectiveness of such services by enabling interaction through the coordinated use of multimodal inputs (speech and touch) and multimedia output (sound, video, text, and graphics) and in doing so create the opportunity for new public services. The partners in the MASK project are MORS (coordinator, F), SNCF (F), LIMSI-CNRS (F), and UCL (UK).

The role of LIMSI in the project is to develop the spoken language component of the MASK kiosk. Spoken language systems aim to provide a natural interface between a user and a computer by using simple and natural dialogues to enable the user to access stored information. The main information provided by the MASK kiosk is access to rail travel information such as timetables, tickets and reservations, as well as services offered on the trains, and fare-related restrictions and supplements. Other important travel information such as up-to-date departure and arrival time and track information will also be provided.

Eventual extensions to the system will enable the user to obtain additional information about the train station and local tourist information, such as restaurants, hotels, and attractions in the surrounding area. In the next section an overview of the architecture of the MASK spoken language component is given, followed by sections detailing the subcomponents of the overall system. This is followed Section 3 concerned with our data collection activities, which represent a significant portion of the effort in system development. In Section 4 we describe the objective and subjective evalutation measures used to assess progress.

2. System Overview

An overview of the spoken language system for information retrieval is shown in figure 1 (x is the input speech signal, w is the word sequence output by the speech recognizer).

The main components of the spoken language system are the speech recognizer [7, 8], the natural language component [2, 3] which includes a semantic analyzer and a dialogue manager [2], and an information retrieval component that includes database access and response generation. While our goal is to develop underlying technology that is speaker, task and language independent, any spoken language system will necessarily have some dependence of the chosen task and on the languages known to the system in order to achieve the best possible performance.

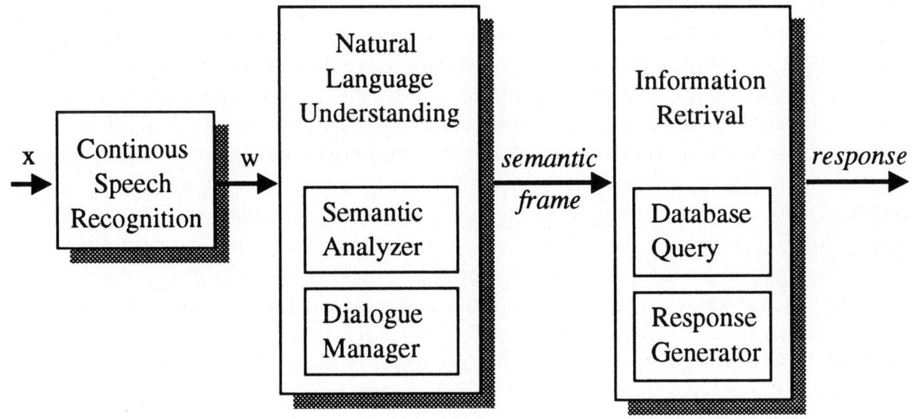

Fig. 1: Overview of the spoken language information retrieval system

2.1 Speech Recognizer

Speech recognition is concerned with the problem of transcribing the speech signal as a sequence of words. Today's most performant systems are mainly based on a statistical modelisation of the talker. From this point of view, message generation is represented by a language model which provides estimates of for all word strings w . The acoustic channel encoding the message w in the signal x is represented by a probability density function $f(x/w)$. The speech decoding problem consists then of maximizing the a posteriori probability of w, or equivalently, maximizing the product $Pr(w) \cdot f(x/w)$.

This formulation highlights the main problems to resolve: that of estimating the language model $Pr(w)$, and the acoustic encoding $f(x/w)$. Language modeling entails incorporating constraints on the allowable sequences of words which form a sentence. Statistical "*n-gram models*" attempt to capture the syntactic and semantic constraints by estimating the frequencies of sequences of n words. A backoff mechanism [9] is used to smooth the estimates of the probabilities of rare n-grams by relying on a lower order n-gram when there is insufficient training data, and to provide a means of modeling unobserved n-grams. The n-gram statistics are estimated on the orthographic transcriptions of the training set of spoken queries. Word classes are used for lexical items such as the cities, days, months, are used to provide more robust estimates of the n-gram probabilities, when there is no reason to believe that differences in their frequencies in the training data are significant or representative.

Sub-language models are being developed for use with system directed dialogues. These sub-languages will allow the search space to be reduced, improving the accuracy and reducing the computational needs. The recognition lexicon has on the order of 1500 entries, including 500 station/city names, and is represented phonemically with a set of 35 phonemes.

Acoustic modeling makes use of continuous density hidden Markov models (HMM) with Gaussian mixture. Context-dependent phone models are used to account for allophonic variation observed in different contextual environments.

The speech recognizer is a software-only system (written in ANSI C) that runs in what is close enough to be perceived as real-time on a standard Risc processor. The system is speaker-independent, so that no speaker-specific enrollment data is needed for a new user. Speaker independence is achieved by using acoustic models which have been trained on speech data from a large number of representative speakers, covering a wide variety of accents and voice qualities.

Two types of acoustic compensation are used in the recognizer to account for the background acoustic noise and acoustic channel variability.The first compensates for the typical noise present in the acoustic environment of the train station by explicitly modeling different typical noise levels. Between user transactions, the system periodically assesses the level of the background noise and chooses the most appropriate acoustic model set. The second type accounts for differences in the particular acoustic channel for the current utterance by the user. These differences which arise from the differences in the speakers' heights, distance and orientation relative to the microphone, as well as speaker-specific vocal characteristics are minimized by use of incremental cepstral mean removal.

The output of the recognizer is passed to the natural language component. In our current implementation the output of the speech recognizer is the best word sequence, however, the recognizer is also able to provide a word lattice.

2.2 Natural Language Understanding

The natural language component is concerned with understanding the meaning of the spoken query. This component has two subcomponents - semantic analysis and dialogue management. The semantic analyzer carries out a caseframe analysis [4,5] to determine the meaning of the query [1,3], and builds an appropriate semantic frame representation. In this analysis, keywords are used to select an appropriate case structure for the sentence without attempting to carry out a complete syntactic analysis. The major work in developing the understanding component is defining the concepts that are meaningful for the task and the appropriate keywords. This undertaking, which is quite important (and difficult), is obviously task-dependent but hopefully language independent. However, in transfering to another task in a related domain (such as for air travel information and reservation) many of the same concepts and keywords are conserved [11]. The concepts for the MASK task as shown in figure 2 are train-time, fare, change, type, reserve, service and reduction and have been determined by analysis of queries taken from the training corpora to augment the a priori task knowledge.

The caseframe parser has been implemented in C++. The caseframe grammar is described in a declarative file so as to allow for easy modification of the cases. Casemarkers are surface indicators designating a case and provide syntactic constraints necessary to extract the meaning of the request. For example, in "de Paris à Lyon", the preposition *de* designates Paris as the departure city, and the preposition *à* designates Lyon as the arrival city.

Semantic Category	*Example*
train-time	Quels sont les *horaires* des trains allant de Paris à Lyon ?
	What are the *times* of trains from Paris to Lyon ?
fare	Quel est le *prix* du billet ?
	How *much* is the ticket ?
change	Quels sont les changements ?
	What are the correspondences ?
type	Quel est le type du train qui arrive a 20 heures 5 ?
	What type of traill is the one arriving at 8:05 pm ?
reserve	Je veux reserver une place dans le train de 8 heures 10.
	I want to reserve a seat on the 8:10 am train.
service	Quelles sont les prestations offertes dans ces trains ?
	What services are available on these trains ?

Fig. 2 : MASK concepts

In the phrase "à 20 heures 5" is an example of a postmarker, designating 8:05 pm to be a time. Since the understanding of numbers is very relevant to the travel information task (appearing in times, dates and train numbers), a restricted local grammar is used to extract the corresponding values.

Figure 3 shows the resulting semantic frame for an example utterance. The keyword *aller* triggers the caseframe *train-time*, and the parser constructs the complete semantic frame by instanciating the slots *from, to* and *stop* with the corresponding words *Paris, Marseille* and *Lyon* respectively. The analysis is driven by the order in which the cases appear in the caseframe *train-time*. The query *"Je veux aller demain matin de Paris à Marseille en passant par Lyon"* (I would like to go from Paris to Marseille via Lyon tomorrow morning.) will result in the same caseframe.

Je veux aller demain matin de Paris à Marseille en passant par Lyon
(I would like to go from Paris to Marseille via Lyon tomorrow morning)

< train-time >	
from:	paris
to:	marseille
stop:	lyon
relative-day:	tomorrow (demain)
morning-afternoon:	morning (matin)

Fig. 3 : Example of semantic frame

The dialogue manager ensures the smooth interface between the user and the computer. The dialogue process formally consists of transitions between five dialogue states: opening formalities, information, stagnation, confirmation subdialogues and closing formalities [2]. The dialogue history is used to complete missing information in the semantic frame and the dialogue context may be used to provide default values for required slots.

2.3 Information Retrieval

The response generator uses the semantic frame to generate a database request to the database management system. The retrieved information is reformatted for presentation to the user along with an accompanying natural language response. A vocal response is optionally provided along with the written and tabular information. The generation of responses is complex bacause if toomuch information is given, it may be difficult for the user to extract the important part. If not enough information is returned, the interaction will take longer, as the user will need to ask for more detailed or additional information. In the MASK project we are experimenting with different forms of response - text strings, tables, and ticket images, so as to facillitate the transfer of information to the user.

When vocal feedback is provided the speech must be very natural and intelligible, as the average user cannot be expected to have previously heard synthetic speech, nor to be tolerant of poor quality output.Therefore simple playback of pre-recorded speech is used for fixed messages that are unlikely to be changed. However, since is not possible to present variable information using direct playback of pre-recoreded speech, we make use of a speech concatenation approach [10] where the automatically generated response text is used to locate dictionary units for concatenation. This will be completed with a diphone dictionary constructed with speech from the same talker, so that in the event that the necessary dictionary units are not located, diphone synthesis can serve as a back-off mechanism. This capability can also enable the extension to new words.

3. Data Collection

In order to develop a spoken language system, task-specific data must be available to train the acoustic and language models. Collection of such spoken language data represents a significant portion of the work in system development. The use of additional acoustic and language model training data has been shown to almost systematically improve performance in continuous speech recognition [6]. Similarly, progress in understanding is closely linked to the availability of spoken language corpora.

Using the MASK spoken language system, we have recorded over 10,000 queries from over 150 speakers [12]. The recordings are made at LIMSI in office environement, simultaneously with a close-talking, noise cancelling Shure SM10 and a table-top Crown PCC160 microphone. Each subject participates in a 2 hour recording session, during which time they solve at least 10 MASK scenarios with a range of complexities. Two example scenarios are given in figure 4. The scenarios are periodically modified to ellicit a wider variety of vocabulary items, such as city names, dates and times of travel. We also include specific scenarios in which users need to find out information about concepts not yet handled by the system, to see how they react in order to help us develop ways to detect such situations and to guide the user accordingly. To help assess our progress in system development, at the end of the recording session each subject completes a questionnaire addressing the user-friendliness,

(S1) You want to go from Grenoble to Paris next Friday, as late as possible. You want to take a direct TGV and to pay a reduced fare. Reserve a non-smoking place.

(S2) You are traveling from Bordeaux to Avignon next Sunday. You have a reduction *Carissimo*. Your dog is traveling with you. Reserve an aisle seat in a second class, smoking car. Will you need to change trains ?

Fig. 4: Example of scenarios used for data collection

The cumulative number of subjects and queries recorded are shown in Table 1. The average sentence length is 8 words. Each query is transcribed and classified as "answerable without context" (13%), "answerable given context" (67%), `"politeness forms" (<1%), "out of domain" (<1%), and "temporarily out of domain" (19%). This latter category refers to queries which were not treated in the version of the system used to collect the data, but will be treated in future versions. Politeness forms also occur in about 3% of the sentences: please (1.5%), hello (1.5%), thank you (0.5%).

Month	Jan	Feb	Mar	Apr	May	Jun	Jul
# speakers	12	42	78	106	113	143	153
# queries	208	1603	3825	6219	6853	9587	10368
total # words	1.6k	12.3k	29.1k	44.5k	48.6k	69.6k	77.8k
# distinct words	273	737	975	1120	1168	1349	1444
# new words	-	420	211	113	34	-	68

Table 1: MASK data collection status

Other interjections such as then, well, and okay occur in about 3% of the utterances. Spontaneous speech phenomena such as hesitations, false starts and reparations occur in about 25% of the queries. The filler word euh occurs in 9.4% of the queries, and breath noises (inspiration and expiration) were marked in about 11% of the transcriptions.

The MASK spoken language system uses a mixed-initiative dialogue strategy [2], where the user is free to ask any question, at any time. However, in order to aid the user to obtain a reservation, the system prompts the user for any missing information needed for database access. There are on average 14 queries to solve a scenario. Approximately one-third of the system responses are direct requests asking the user to provide specific information. These direct requests involve the class of travel (27%), date (23%), departure city (16%), time (15 %), smoking (13%), and arrival city (6 %).

A nmumber of 650 dialogues were analyzed to see how subjects respond to system initiatives. Subjects provided a direct response to these requests over 60% of the time, however they frequently also provided additional information. For example, when asked for the departure city, the user often also specified the arrival city and/or the time of travel. In collaboration with the SNCF, we have recently carried out recordings at the Gare St. Lazare in Paris in order to have access to a more realistic potential user population. More than 120 subjects solved during a 10 day period an average of 2.5 scenarios by using the current prototype system. We are in the process of transcribing and classifying the queries, and analyzing the dialogues.

4. Evaluation

The development of a spoken language system is incremental, where errors are analysed and the system is refined. The link between development and evaluation is so tight that we consider evaluation to be part of the development process. Periodic evaluation on specified test sets allows us to continually monitor progress through objective performance measures.

4.1 Objective Evaluation Measures

The speech recognizer is evaluated in terms of speed and recognition accuracy (word and sentence error). An analysis of the recognition errors is carried out to determine their effect on the understanding performance. The understanding component is evaluated using typed versions of the exact transcriptions of spoken queries including all spontaneous speech effects, such as hesitations or repetitions, (so as to evaluate the understanding component without intrusion of errors made by the speech recognizer) and on the recognized word string. A semi-automatic method is used which compares the resulting semantic frame to reference semantic frames for each test query.

Corpus	#Sets	WAcc	NL	SLS
MASK Jan95	205	78%	85%	60%
MASK Apr95	205	85%	93%	79%
MASK Aug95	205	90%	93%	85%

Table 2: Evaluation of the MASK spoken language system

In Table 2 gives evaluation results of the MASK data collection system on a set of 205 queries from 10 speakers. The word accuracy (WAcc) is has improved from 78 in Jan95 to 85 in Apr95, to 90 in Aug95. Natural language (NL) understanding of the exact transcriptions of the same set of spoken queries, without removing spontaneous speech effects such as hesitations or repetitions, is 93%. The complete spoken language system (SLS) has an understanding rate of 85%.

A frequent understanding error is due to sentences that include 2 queries such as *"Je voudrais réserver, remontrez-moi les tarifs"* (I would like to make a reservation, show me the fares again.). While we instantiate correctly the 2 caseframes, we are not yet able to treat this at the dialogue level. Another common error arises when the user makes an implicit reference to a previous response given by the system. For example, the user may ask for an earlier departure time *"Je veux partir plus tôt"*, without ever having specified a departure time. To treat this, we need to interpret the previous response(s) given by the system.

We are currently working on improving the maintenance of the dialogue history so as to be able to relax previously specified constraints, so as to be able to handle requests such as *"Montrez-moi tous les trains"* (show me all the trains) after having specified a departure time.

4.2 User Evaluation

It is also important to assess the overall performance of the system from the point of view of the subjects. Since March'95 all subjects have completed a questionnaire (see figure 5). The results of the analysis of the responses are in a scale of 10, and address the user-friendliness (1-3), reliability (4-6), ease-of-use (7-9) of the MASK system.

1. Is it easy to speak to the system?
2. Is the system easy to understand?
3. Does the system respond fast enough?
4. Are you confident in the information given by the system?
5. Did you get the information you wanted?
6. Are you satisfied with the information?
7. Did the system recognize what you said?
8. Did the system understand what you said?
9. If the system did not understand you, was it easy to reformulate your question?

Fig. 5: User questionnaire

Subjects are also asked what are the good aspects of the system, how it should be improved, and if they would use such a potential system. Information about the subject includes how often they travel by train, how they obtain their tickets, and their computer experience. The results of the analysis of the responses of 61 speakers are shown in figure 6 an a scale of 10.

	Questions	Ease of Use 1, 2, 3	Reliability 4,5,6	Friendliness 7,8,9
a	Experience: Expert (17)	7.7	7.5	7.1
b	Experience: Novice (44)	7.2	6.5	5.7
c	Age < 24 (31)	8.3	6.9	6.6
d	Age 24 - 50 (25)	7.3	6.7	6.0
e	Age > 50 (5)	63	6.9	5.8
f	Travel: Frequent (36)	6.9	5.9	6.1
g	Travel: Infrquent (25)	7.5	7.0	6.1

Fig. 6 : User evaluation of the performances of the spoken language system

The results of the analysis of the responses of 61 speakers are shown in figure 6 an a scale of 10. In (a) and (b) the responses are divided based on the comfort of users with the system, independent of their age and their travel habits. Users were classed as novices if they had difficulties speaking with the system or using the computer. In general "expert" users (no difficulty speaking with the system and used to working with computers) were more at ease with the system, and judged it to be more user-friendly, easier to use, and more reliable than the novices. The novices were more likely to critique the reliability of information obtained from the system, whereas the experts criticized problems in understanding or dialogue. In(c), (d) and (f) the responses are subdivided by the age of the subjects, where there is a clear tendancy of younger subjects to assess the system more favorably than the older subjects. As shown in (f) and (g) for the naive subjects, frequent train travelers are slightly more sceptical and dissatisfied with the system than infrequent travelers In general, users express an interest in using such types of systems, and often ask to come back to participate in future experiments.

5. Conclusions

This paper has described the spoken language component of the MASK kiosk. A prototype spoken language system has been used to collect data at LIMSI and at the SNCF, and this data has been used for system development. On a test set of 205 queries from 10 speakers, the speech recognition word accuracy is 90%. Natural language understanding of typed transcriptions of the same queries is 93%. The complete spoken language system has an understanding rate of 85%. We expect that as more data is collected the understanding rate will improve, as we previously observed for our L'Atis system [11]. Analysis of the understanding errors on new data enables us to incrementally improve the understanding component. Our experience with data collection is that as the system performance is improved, subjects speak more easily and use longer and more varied sentences. They are also more likely to perceive that errors are their own fault, rather than the system's. As a result they continue to speak relatively naturally to the system, enabling us to record more representative spontaneous speech. We have recently collected data from 120 subjects at the Gare St. Lazare in Paris. In early 1996, the MASK kiosk will be installed in the Gare St. Lazare. Data collected on-site will be used to further improve the system, better matching the system's capabilities to the user's needs.

References

[1] Bennacef S.K., H. Bonneau-Maynard, J.L. Gauvain, L. Lamel, W. Minker "A Spoken Language System For Information Retrieval", Proc. ICSLP’94 Yokohama, Japan, Sept. 1994.

[2] Bennacef S.K., F. Néel, H. Bonneau-Maynard "An Oral Dialogue Model based on Speech Acts Categorization'", Proc. ESCA Workshop on Spoken dialogue Systems, Vigso, Denmark, Spring 1995.

[3] Bonneau-Maynard H. , J.L. Gauvain, D. Goodine, L. Lamel, J. Polifroni, S. Seneff "A French Version of the MIT-ATIS System: Portability Issues", Proc. Eurospeech'93 , Berlin, Germany, Sept. 1994.

[4] Bruce B. "Case Systems for Natural Language", Artificial Intelligence, vol.6, 1975.

[5] Fillmore Ch.J. "The case for case", in Universals in Linguistic Theory, Emmon Bach & Robert T. Harms (eds.), Holt, Rinehart and Winston, Inc., 1968.

[6] Gauvain J.L., L.F. Lamel, G. Adda, M. Adda-Decker, "The LIMSI Continuous Speech Dictation System: Evaluation on the ARPA Wall Street Journal Task", Proc. IEEE ICASSP-94, Adelaide, Australia, April 1994.

[7] Gauvain J.L., L.F. Lamel, G. Adda, M. Adda-Decker, "Continuous Speech Dictation in French", ICSLP-94, Yokohama, Japan, Sept. 1994.

[8] Gauvain J.L., L.F. Lamel, G. Adda, M. Adda-Decker, "Speaker-Independent Continuous Speech Dictation", Speech Communication, vol.15, pp. 21-37, Sept. 1994.

[9] Katz S.M., "Estimation of Probabilities from Sparse Data for the Language Model Component of a Speech Recognizer", IEEE Trans. ASSP, Vol.35/3, 1987.

[10] Lamel L., J.L. Gauvain, B. Prouts, C. Bouhier, R. Boesch, "Generation and Synthesis of Broadcast Messages", Proc. ESCA Workshop on Applications of Speech Technology, Lautrach, Germany, Sept. 1993.

[11] Lamel L., S. Bennacef, H. Bonneau-Maynard, S. Rosset, J.L. Gauvain, "Recent Developments in Spoken Language Sytems for Information Retrieval", Proc. ESCA Workshop on Spoken Dialogue Systems,Vigso, Denmark, Spring 1995.

[12] Lamel L., S. Rosset, S. Bennacef, H. Bonneau-Maynard, L. Devillers, J.L. Gauvain, "Development of Spoken Language Corpora for Travel Information", Eurospeech'95, Madrid, Spain, Sept. 1995.

Designing Co-operativity in Spoken Human-Machine Dialogues

Laila Dybkjær, Niels Ole Bernsen, Hans Dybkjær
Centre for Cognitive Science, Roskilde University
PO Box 260, DK-4000 Roskilde, Denmark

Abstract

Dialogue model design for Spoken Language Dialogue Systems (SLDSs) is still based mainly on common sense, experience and intuition, and "trial and error" strategies, rather than on established design principles. Co-operativity in dialogue systems is crucial to comfortable human-machine spoken dialogues. This paper presents a set of principles of co-operative user-system dialogues which have been derived from a corpus of task oriented spoken human-machine dialogues. The set of principles is shown to include as a sub-set an established body of principles of co-operative human-human dialogues. Analysis of results from a user test of an implemented SLDS prototype shows that the set of principles is adequate to account for the dialogue problems identified in the test corpus. Both empirical and theoretical grounds indicate that the principles presented in this paper may constitute a comprehensive set of guidelines for the design of co-operative human-machine dialogues.

1. Introduction

Current task-oriented spoken language dialogue systems (SLDSs) technologies are based on the assumption of a co-operative user dialogue behaviour. This fact does not, however, pose to many problems for dialogue designers because the penalty for non-co-operativity is that users fail to get their task done. There is no point in designing the dialogue for non-cooperative users who want to make the system fail. Indeed, this design goal is impossible to achieve. However, comfortable user-system dialogue interfaces requires that also the system's dialogue behaviour be co-operative. If this is not the case, penalties can be severe, ranging from users having to repeatedly initiate clarification and repair meta-communication with the system, up to failing to get the task done or abandoning SLDSs technologies altogether. Meta communication is communication on the dialogue itself rather than on the task domain of the dialogue, and is typically initiated for purposes of clarification and re pair. In particular the speech recognition capabilities of current SLDSs are still fragile [8]. Sophisticated meta-communication functionality is needed to overcome the effects of system misrecognitions [17]. Thus, to the extent possible, the user's needs to initiate clarification and repair meta-communication should not be compounded by non-cooperative system behaviour. At any stage during dialogue, the co-operative user should know what to do and how to do it, without having been led astray by a non-cooperative system. A crucial dialogue design goal, therefore, is to optimise system dialogue co-operativity in order to prevent user-initiated clarification and repair meta-communication. Such meta-communication tends to increase to a level beyond what is currently technically feasible, the demands on the system's language comprehension and dialogue management capabilities and decrease the user's satisfaction in communicating with the system. The practical problem therefore becomes: how do dialogue designers design co-operative system dialogue behaviour? To our knowledge, whereas there is agreement in the literature that current, task-oriented SLDSs require co-operative user dialogue behaviour [7, 13], the question of how to design co-operative system dialogue has not been addressed in any systematic way. There is a clear need to do so, particularly if the result would be a set of guidelines for co-operative system dialogue design for effective and systematic use as development and evaluation tools during early design. This might significantly reduce development time by reducing the need for lengthy Wizard of Oz experimentation, controlled user testing, and field trial cycles, thereby reducing overall development costs.

In the course of developing, implementing and testing an SLDS prototype in the Danish Dialogue project, we have developed a set of principles of co-operative system dialogue. Given the way these principles were developed, compared to well-established theoretical results from the analysis of co-operativity in human-human dialogue, and subsequently tested in a user test of the implemented system, we believe that the principles deserve consideration by the SLDS dialogue design and evaluation community. It seems likely that the principles cover most, if not all, aspects of co-operative system dialogue design and hence might be useful to the design and evaluation of the many SLDSs which are now making their way from research laboratories through field testing to product development. The most advanced among these systems have system-directed dialogue which means that system co-operativity is a main design goal.

The Danish SLDS prototype addresses the domain of domestic flight ticket reservation and has been developed in collaboration with the Center for Person Kommunikation at Aalborg University and the Centre for Language Technology in Copenhagen. The system runs on a PC with a DSP board and is accessed over the telephone. It is a walk-up-and-use application. It understands speaker-independent continuous spoken Danish with a vocabulary of about 500 words and uses system-directed dialogue. The prototype runs in close-to-real-time. It has the following main modules: a speech recogniser, a parser, a dialogue module, a database, and an output module with pre-recorded speech. The system is a representative example of advanced state-of-the-art systems. Comparable SLDSs are found in [1, 9, 14].

In what follows, Section 2 provides an account of the development of our principles of co-operative system dialogue leading to an expression of the principles themselves. The principles were derived from a corpus of simulated human-machine dialogue which was recorded during the design of a dialogue model for the Danish dialogue system. The purpose of the principles is to prevent users from having to initiate clarification and repair meta-communication because of non-cooperative dialogue design. Section 3 compares the principles with Grice's maxims of co-operativity in human-human dialogue. We had developed our principles independently of Grice's work and only subsequently became aware of the close relationship between that work and our own efforts. It turned out that Grice's maxims could be mapped onto a sub-set of our principles of co-operativity, which suggested that our efforts at principle development were on the right track. The theoretical efforts of articulating the principles and comparing them with Grice's maxims took place in parallel with the implementation of the Danish dialogue system and after the Wizard of Oz experiments preceding implementation. Thus, the principles were *not* used as design guidelines during implementation. This meant that the test, with naive users, of the implemented system could be considered a test of the completeness of the principles. Section 4 describes the results of that test. The results indicate that the application, during early dialogue design, of co-operative dialogue design principles can help SLDSs designers prevent user-initiated clarification and repair meta-communication and thereby increase the habitability of their products. Section 5 concludes and discusses how the principles of co-operative system dialogue behaviour may be developed into low-cost guidelines for use in SLDS design practice as well as in SLDS evaluation.

2. Developing Principles of Co-Operative System Dialogue

Dialogue design for SLDSs consists in defining and refining a set of design requirements or constraints which are traded off against one another in an iterative development process until an acceptable result has been achieved. No matter what methods are used during this phase, the central point of dialogue development is to observe and analyse the user-system interaction to assess whether the dialogue model satisfies the design requirements and is adequate in terms of functionality and usability. User and system dialogue problems should be identified and analysed, and results used to change the dialogue model before performing a new iteration of observation and analysis.

2.1 The Wizard of Oz Experiments

Dialogue models for SLDSs are often designed by using the Wizard of Oz method (WOZ). WOZ is an iterative simulation technique which is well suited for the development and testing of dialogue models prior to implementation. During each iteration a human (the ‘wizard’) simulates the system or parts thereof in dialogue with users who should be made to believe that they are speaking to a real system [15]. The dialogues are recorded, transcribed and analysed, and the results used to improve the dialogue model. This iterative process continues until a dialogue model has been achieved that satisfies the design requirements. The model is then implemented and tested on representative samples of the intended user population. The advantage of using the WOZ method is that user and system problems can be removed prior to the implementation of the dialogue model. Given the state of current SLDS development environments, the extra cost of performing WOZ experiments will often be less than the cost of making changes to the implemented system in the light of results of controlled user testing or field testing of the system. However, even if the WOZ method is being used, it remains true that today's dialogue model design for SLDSs is based primarily on common sense, the individual designer's experience and intuition, and trial and error, rather than on established dialogue design principles. This means that if, during WOZ, the dialogue designers are not very careful in addition to being lucky, many user and system problems may still remain to be discovered during implementation and subsequent tests of the system.

Seven WOZ iterations were performed to produce the dialogue model for the Danish dialogue system [12]. Since the application is accessed over the telephone, real-time performance was considered a constraint which had to be satisfied by a usable system. In the context of the chosen hardware and software including the speech recogniser, the real-time constraint gave rise to additional constraints:

- At most 100 words can be active in memory at a time to enable real-time performance.
- The average user utterance length should not exceed 3-4 words.
- The maximum user utterance length should not exceed 10 words.

The two last-mentioned constraints served the additional purpose of maintaining the recogniser error rate at an acceptable level. Furthermore, because of limited project resources the system vocabulary size was set to about 500 words.

Apart from real-time performance, the main usability constraints were: sufficient task domain coverage, robustness, natural forms of language and dialogue, and dialogue flexibility. These usability constraints had to be traded off against the above-mentioned resource constraints and technological constraints. It was the task of the WOZ experiments to optimise the trade-offs [10].

The first five WOZ iterations served to train the wizard and produce an outline dialogue model. Each iteration generated only a few dialogues. The dialogue model was initially represented as a loosely ordered set of predefined phrases but was soon turned into a graph structure (a state transition network) in order to facilitate the wizard's job (cf. Figure 1). The graph has predefined system phrases in the nodes and expected user input contents along the edges. Users (subjects) were exclusively system designers and colleagues. The last two WOZ iterations were considerably larger than the first ones and aimed at defining the dialogue model to be implemented. Each iteration involved 12 subjects mostly from outside the lab. None of the (9) external subjects had tried the system prior to the WOZ experiment. External subjects were selected so that half of them had a background as secretaries and the other half were computer scientists. The expected end-user group is mainly secretaries. The computer scientists were included in order to study the reactions of people who had general system knowledge.

Throughout the experiments, interaction with the system was based on scenarios, i.e. domain relevant tasks. The first four WOZ iterations were based on a set of ten scenarios which were simply considered a set of cases for which the system should work and which were mainly used for domain and task exploration. Most decisions on precise reservation details such as date of departure were left to the subjects. In the last three WOZ iterations a new set of 28 scenarios was used. The scenarios were designed on the basis of the dialogue structure that emerged from the fourth WOZ iteration. By then the scenarios could be designed in a more systematic way, as most of the domain and task structure had been uncovered.

Each subject in the fifth, sixth and seventh iterations received (i) a letter which briefly introduced the system and informed on the experiment, (ii) four scenarios and (iii) a questionnaire to be filled in and returned immediately after the subject's interaction with the system. Subjects were not told in advance that the system was simulated. In a debriefing telephone interview after the session subjects were asked in WOZ7 whether they believed that they had interacted with a real system. The majority of external subjects believed that the system was real. Each of the two last WOZ iterations produced a corpus of 47 dialogues. From the seven iterations a total of 125 dialogues were transcribed amounting to about seven hours of spoken language dialogue. 24 different subjects were involved in the seven iterations.

After each iteration the transcribed dialogues were analysed and evaluated with respect to the extent to which the design constraints had been satisfied. Evaluation results were used as a basis for improving the dialogue model before the next WOZ iteration. In the first iterations it was easy to find suggestions for improvement by merely listening to the dialogues or looking through the transcriptions. However, as the dialogue model improved, more sophisticated and systematic methods of dialogue analysis became necessary. We began to match the scenarios to be used in the following iteration against the current dialogue graph structure in order to discover and, as far as possible, remove potential user problems. *Potential user problems* are problems discovered analytically by the designers when putting themselves in the place of the actual users. By contrast, *actual user problems* are problems which actually occurred during user-system dialogue. Many problems were discovered analytically through the scenario-based walkthroughs of the dialogue model.

In the last two WOZ iterations, we also matched the latest version of the system's dialogue model against the transcribed WOZ corpus in order to systematically assess improvements in system co-operativity and discover actual user problems. The dialogue model representation was split into a number of sub-graphs corresponding to different sub-tasks. Each transcribed dialogue was plotted onto the dialogue sub-graphs. Deviations from the sub-graphs indicated unexpected user or system behaviour. The deviations were marked and the reason(s) for the deviations analysed. This plotting of the transcribed dialogues onto the dialogue structure is very similar to the scenario-based walkthroughs but aims at discovering actual user problems. Figure 1 shows an annotated sub-graph from WOZ6. The annotation shows that the subject expected confirmation from the system. When it became clear that the system was not going to provide the confirmation, the subject asked for it.

The following dialogue fragment provides the background for the subject's deviation from the dialogue model. The subject has made a change to a flight reservation. After the user has indicated the change, the conversation continues:

E7: Do you want to make other changes to this reservation?
S7: No, I don't.
E8: Do you want anything else?
S8: Ah no ...I mean is it okay then?
E9: [Produces an improvised confirmation of the change made.]
S9: Yes, that's fine.
E10: Do you want anything else?

From this point onwards the dialogue finishes as expected. Analysis convinced us that the dialogue model had to be revised in order to prevent the user-initiated clarification meta-communication observed in S8, which the implemented system would be incapable of understanding. In fact, the WOZ6 dialogue model can be seen to have violated the following dialogue design principle: *Be fully explicit in communicating to users the commitments they have made.* As a result, system confirmation of changes of reservation was added to the WOZ7 sub-graph on change of reservation.

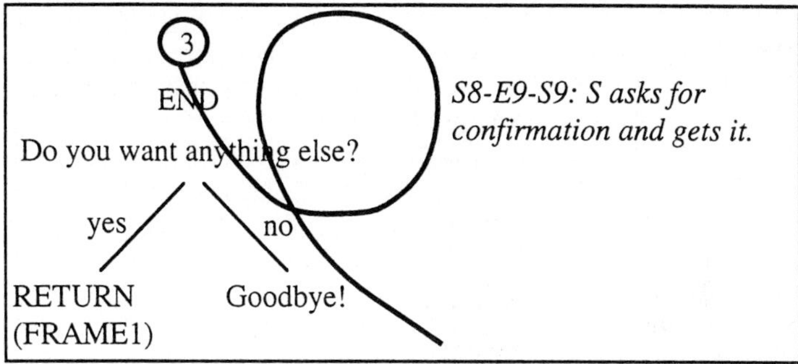

Figure 1: A plotted END sub-graph from WOZ6. The boldfaced loop deviating from the graph path shows unexpected user dialogue behaviour which may reveal a dialogue design problem. The encircled number (3) refers to the point in the previously traversed graph from which the subject jumped to the END sub-graph. The deviation is annotated with numbered reference (in italics) to the relevant transcribed utterances and a description of the deviation. E refers to the experimenter and S to the subject.

2.2 Developing Design Principles for Co-Operative System Dialogue

At the end of the WOZ design phase, we began a more theoretical, forward-looking exercise of categorising identified dialogue design problems and expressing the corresponding dialogue design principles. To this end, we plotted all the transcribed user-system dialogues from WOZ3 onwards onto their corresponding graphs. In addition, we compared each dialogue model graph pair (WOZn and WOZn+1) in order to identify and analyse all changes made to the dialogue model from WOZ3 through to WOZ7. To illustrate the latter process, Figures 2 and 3 allow comparison of part of the TIME sub-graphs in WOZ5 and in WOZ6, respectively. Some of the main differences between the two sub-graphs are: WOZ5 does not include the discount option, which reveals a flaw in task domain coverage. The 'fully booked' message does exist in WOZ5 but is represented in a separate sub-graph. When following the 'wrong time' and 'time' edges of the WOZ5 sub-graph, users are never allowed to state a precise hour of departure. Having provided information on the closest departure times, the system will go on to address a new topic. In doing so the system's dialogue contribution is not relevant, i.e. is not appropriate to the immediate needs at this stage of the transaction. This problem has been repaired in WOZ6.

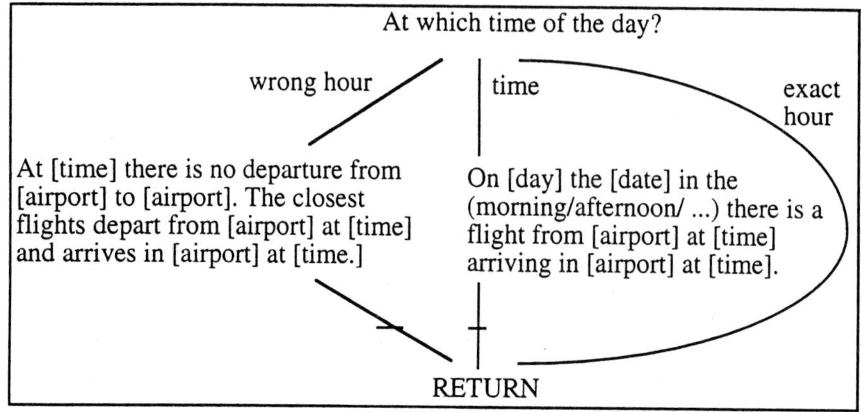

Figure 2: Part of the TIME sub-graph from WOZ5.

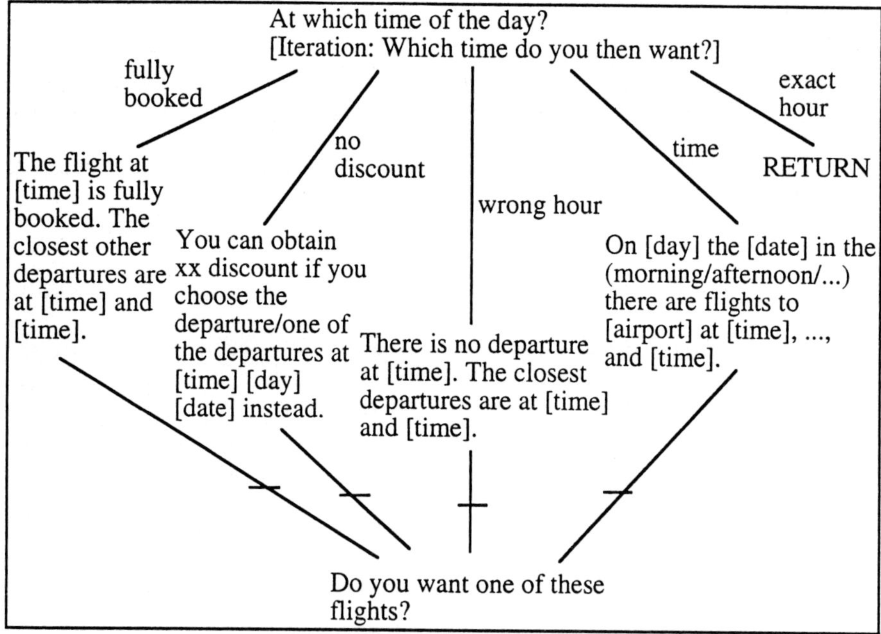

Figure 3: Part of the TIME sub-graph from WOZ6.

Based on the material illustrated above, the actual and potential user problems identified in the WOZ experiments were analysed, classified and represented as violations, made by the dialogue system, of principles of co-operative dialogue. Each problem was considered a case in which the system in addressing the user had violated a principle of co-operative dialogue. The principles of co-operative dialogue were made explicit, based on the problems analysis. In addition, we analysed how the system's utterances had been, or sometimes should be, improved to minimise user-initiated clarification and repair meta-communication [2, 6]. To illustrate the WOZ corpus analysis, we present below an example of an identified user problem type (a) and the co-operative principle (termed 'design commitment') which has been violated (b). A justification of the principle is provided (c), followed by examples of how the principle was found to be violated (d). Under (d) we note whether a particular example was discovered empirically (i.e. from actual user problems) or analytically (i.e. through design analysis revealing a potential user problem). Finally, a solution to each particular problem is proposed and sometimes discussed (e). This template (a-e) was applied to each problem that was identified [2]. In the original report on the data [2], the principles were illustrated by 36 concrete examples of their violation, but the total number of examples in the corpus were +100.

(a) *Problem:* Non-separation between novice users who need introductory information about what the system can and cannot do and intermediate and expert users who do not need such information and for whom listening to it would only delay task performance.

(b) *Violation* of design commitment: Separate whenever possible between the needs of novice and expert users (user-adaptive dialogue).

(c) *Justification:* There are major differences between the needs of novice and expert users, one such difference being that expert users already possess the information needed to understand system functionality.

(d) *Examples:* Introduction (WOZ7): A new question was added: "Do you know this system?" First-time users may obtain additional information about the functionality of the system and about how to communicate with it. Other users may proceed directly with their task. This problem was discovered from user problems. Users complained that the system talked too much. Consideration of this complaint led to the described design improvement.

(e) *Solution:* In WOZ7 it was made optional for users to listen to the introduction to the system. However, there were other situations in which shortcuts would have been desirable as well. The need for shortcuts perhaps could be met by allowing the use of keywords at certain points in the dialogue. This might work with expert users. For non-expert users, however, large numbers of keywords represent a non-optimal solution and would probably require access to a written system manual.

2.3 Design Principles for Co-Operative System Dialogue

The WOZ corpus analysis led to the identification of 14 principles of co-operative human-machine dialogue (see Table 1). The table includes a justification of each principle, which serves the additional purpose of clarifying the meaning and scope of the principle. Although not explicitly stated in each justification, we take it to be straightforward that violations of any of the principles may lead users to initiate repair or clarification meta-communication, because this is the strategy naturally adopted in human-human conversation in such cases.

Principles	Justification
P1. Provide clear and comprehensible communication of what the system can and cannot do.	Risk of communication failure in case of lacking knowledge about what the system can and cannot do. Violation of this principle leads users to have exaggerated expectations about the system's abilities, which may lead to frustration during use of the system.
P2. Provide sufficient task domain coverage.	Risk of communication failure in case of lacking task domain information. Full task domain coverage within specified limits is necessary in order to satisfy all relevant user needs in context. Otherwise, users will become frustrated when using the system.
P3. Provide same formulation of the same question (or address) to users everywhere in the system's dialogue turns.	Need for unambiguous system response (consistency in system task performance). The principle is meant to reduce the possibility of communication error caused by users' understanding a new formulation of a question as constituting a different question from one encountered earlier.
P4. Take users' relevant background knowledge into account.	Need for adjustment of system responses to users' relevant background knowledge and inferences based thereupon. This is to prevent that the user does not understand the system's utterances or makes unpredicted remarks such as, e.g., questions of clarification, which the system cannot understand or answer.
P5. Avoid 'semantical noise' in addressing users.	Need for unambiguous system response. The design commitment is to reduce the possibilities of evoking wrong associations in users, which in their turn may cause the users to adopt wrong courses of action or ask questions which the system cannot understand.
P6. It should be possible for users to fully exploit the system's task domain knowledge when they need it.	Risk of communication failure in case of inaccessible (or not easily accessible) task domain information. In such cases, users may pose questions which the system is unable to understand.
P7. Take into account possible (and possibly erroneous) user inferences by analogy from related task domains.	Need for adjustment to users' background knowledge and inferences based thereupon. Users may otherwise fail to understand the system.

Principles (continued)	**Justification** (continued)
P8. Provide clear and sufficient instructions to users on how to interact with the system.	Risk of communication failure in case of unclear or insufficient instructions to users on how to interact with the system. Users may become confused about the functionality of the system.
P9. Separate whenever possible between the needs of novice and expert users (user-adaptive dialogue).	There are major differences between the needs of novice and expert users, one such difference being that expert users already possess the information needed to understand system functionality.
P10. Avoid superfluous or redundant interactions with users (relative to their contextual needs).	Need for non-superfluous interaction with the system.
P11. Be fully explicit in communicating to users the commitments they have made.	Users need feedback from the system on the commitments made.
P12. Reduce system talk as much as possible during individual dialogue turns.	Users get bored and inattentive from too much uninterrupted system talk.
P13. Provide feedback on each piece of information provided by the user.	Immediate feedback on user commitments serves to remove users' uncertainty as to what the system has understood and done in response to their utterances.
P14. Provide ability to initiate repair if system understanding has failed.	When system understanding fails, the system should initiate repair meta-communication and not leave the initiative with the user.

Table 1: The co-operative SLDS dialogue design principles (left-hand column) and their justifications (right-hand column).

3. Principles of Co-operative System Dialogue

The work described in the previous section led to the development of general principles of co-operative human-machine dialogue. Most of the 14 principles aimed at improving system co-operativity. Only two principles (P1 and P8, see Table 1) were aimed at improving user co-operativity. Having developed these principles we became aware of a link between our work and Grice's Co-operative Principle and maxims [16]. Grice's Co-operative Principle (CP) says that, to act co-operatively in conversation, one should make one's "conversational contribution such as is required, at the stage at which it occurs, by the accepted purpose or direction of the talk exchange in which one is engaged". Grice proposes that the CP can be explicated in terms of four groups of simple maxims which are not claimed to be jointly exhaustive nor to have been generated on a principled theoretical basis other than the CP itself. The maxims are shown in Table 2.

Dialogue aspect	**M No.**	**Maxim**	**Grice's comments**
Group 1: **Quantity**	M1	Make your contribution as informative as is required (for the current purposes of the exchange).	
	M2	Do not make your contribution more informative than is required.	Grice observes that M2 is closely related to M5. In other words, maxims, as stated by Grice, are not mutually exclusive but may overlap.
Group 2: **Quality**	M3	Do not say what you believe to be false.	Grice notes that M3 and M4 seem presupposed by the other maxims. He nevertheless refrains from putting them in a different category from the rest.
	M4	Do not say that for which you lack adequate evidence.	
Group 3: **Relation**	M5	Be relevant, i.e. be appropriate to the immediate needs at each stage of the transaction.	Grice points out that the concept of relevance is in need of further explication (see, e.g. [18]).
Group 4: **Manner**	M6	Avoid obscurity of expression.	Grice notes that there may well be more maxims in Group 4.
	M7	Avoid ambiguity.	
	M8	Be brief (avoid unnecessary prolixity).	
	M9	Be orderly.	

Table 2: Grice's maxims and comments [16]. The left-hand column presents a higher-level grouping of the maxims proposed by Grice. We view the groups as addressing different aspects of dialogue.

Grice focuses on dialogues in which the interlocutors want to achieve a shared goal. In such dialogues, he claims, adherence to the CP and the maxims is rational because this ensures that the interlocutors pursue the shared goal most efficiently. Task-oriented dialogue, such as that for which our SLDS has been designed, would seem to be a prototypical case of shared-goal dialogue. However, Grice did not develop the maxims for the specific purposes of preventing communication failure and avoiding interlocutor-initiated clarification and repair meta-communication in shared-goal dialogue. Rather, his interest lies in the inferences which an interlocutor is able to make when the speaker deliberately does not adhere to one of the maxims. He calls such deliberate messages 'conversational implicatures'. In SLDS design we are obviously not interested in including such messages in the system's utterances. Grice's maxims, although having been conceived with a different purpose in mind, nevertheless serve the same objective as do our principles, namely that of preventing interlocutor-initiated clarification and repair meta-communication. It is exactly when a human or, for that matter, an SLDS, *non-deliberately* fails to adhere to a maxim, that the interlocutor is likely to initiate repair or clarification meta-communication. Thus, the main difference between Grice's work and ours seems to be that the maxims were developed to account for co-operativity in human-human dialogue, whereas our principles were developed to account for co-operativity in human-machine dialogue.

3.1 Principles which are Reducible to Maxims

Having discovered the link between our principles and Grice's maxims we made a detailed analysis of the relationship between principles and maxims [4]. At least superficially, our set of principles is considerably larger than Grice's set of maxims. The analysis demonstrates that a sub-set of our principles can be reduced to, and replaced by, the maxims. Briefly, referring to Tables 1 and 2 above, P5 may be replaced by M6 and M7, P6 by M1 and M9, P10 by M2 and M5, and P12 by M8 [4]. These maxims are capable of performing the same job as do the corresponding principles, in guiding the design of co-operative human-machine dialogue. In fact, the maxims perform the better job in view of the facts that (i) M6 and M7 spell out the intended contents of the infelicitously expressed P5, and (ii) M1 and M9 replace P6. The only maxims which have no corresponding principles are the maxims of quality M3 and M4. The reason is that one does not design an SLDS which provides false or unfounded information to users. The maxims of truth and evidence are so important to the design of SLDSs, that they are unlikely to emerge during dialogue design problem-solving. Truth and evidence form a major concern during system implementation, as it cannot be allowed, for example, that the system confirms information which has not been checked with the database and which might be false or impossible. Grice observes that the maxims of quality in general, and M3 in particular, have the special status of being presupposed by the rest of the maxims.

Another result of analysing the relationship between principles and maxims is the distinction between *generic* and *specific* principles. Grice's maxims are all generic. A generic principle may subsume one or more specific principles which specialise the generic principle such as to deal with certain classes of situations. Specific principles are important in SLDS design. The following three principles are specific and can be subsumed by one of Grice's maxims:

> P3. Provide same formulation of the same question (or address) to users everywhere in the system's dialogue turns.

P3 represents a precaution against the occurrence of ambiguity in machine speech and can be viewed as a specific principle subsumed by M7 (ambiguity).

P11. Be fully explicit in communicating to users the commitments they have made.

P13. Provide feedback on each piece of information provided by the user.

P11 and P13 are closely related, specific principles. Feedback is a special type of co-operative dialogue contribution in which the speaker explicitly expresses an interpretation of the interlocutor's previous dialogue contribution(s). We propose that P11 and P13 are subsumed by M1 (informativeness).

The fact that a sub-set of our principles of co-operative human-machine dialogue is near-equivalent to the Gricean maxims suggests that Grice's maxims are valid not only for shared-goal human-human dialogue but also for human-machine dialogue.

3.2 Principles which are not Reducible to Maxims

The remaining principles appear irreducible to maxims. Of these principles some are generic whereas others are specific. Moreover, the new generic principles express three new dialogue aspects in addition to the four aspects identified by Grice, i.e. 'quantity', 'quality', 'relation' and 'manner' (cf. Table 2). The new aspects are: dialogue partner asymmetry, background knowledge, and repair and clarification.

Dialogue partner asymmetry exists, roughly, when one or more of the dialogue partners is not in a normal condition or situation, such as having impaired hearing or being located in a particularly noisy environment. The non-normal dialogue partner should inform the dialogue partner(s) about the particular non-normal characteristics which they should take into account in order to behave co-operatively. In such cases, dialogue co-operativity depends on the interlocutor(s) taking into account the non-normal participant's special characteristics. Since, obviously, SLDSs are non-normal dialogue partners, their designers should make users aware of their non-normal characteristics if clarification and repair meta-communication is to be avoided. The following two principles address partner asymmetry.

P1. Provide clear and comprehensible communication of what the system can and cannot do.

P8. Provide clear and sufficient instructions to users on how to interact with the system.

Since our SLDS has limited task capabilities and is intended for walk-up-and-use application, it must provide users with an up-front mental model of what it can and cannot do, as expressed in P1. P8 has an analogous role. P1 and P8 introduce two new properties of dialogue co-operativity, namely partner asymmetry and speaker's obligation to inform the interlocutor(s) of any non-normal speaker characteristics. P1 and P8, therefore, cannot be subsumed under any other principle or maxim. We propose a new generic principle (P15-NEW) which subsumes P1 and P8.

P15-NEW. Inform the dialogue partners of important non-normal characteristics which they should take into account in order to behave co-operatively in dialogue.

Background knowledge and differences in background knowledge is an important aspect of dialogue. Interlocutors have different background knowledge. Such differences often have to be taken into account in order to maintain co-operative dialogue. Human speakers either have built in advance, or adaptively build during dialogue, a model of the interlocutor which serves to guide co-operative dialogue behaviour. Increased user adaptivity in this sense is an important goal in SLDS design [5, 11].

P4. Take users' relevant background knowledge into account.

P4 cannot be reduced to M1 (informativeness), since M1 does not include the notions of background knowledge and differences in background knowledge among interlocutors. Moreover, a speaker may adhere perfectly to 'exchange purpose' while ignoring important elements of the interlocutor's background knowledge. For similar reasons, M5 (relevance) cannot replace P4. In fact, P4 appears to be presupposed by maxims M1, M2 and M5 to M9 in the sense that it is not possible to adhere to any of these maxims without adhering to P4.

P7 and P9 are two specific principles which may both be subsumed by P4.

P7. Take into account possible (and possibly erroneous) user inferences by analogy from related task domains.

P9. Separate whenever possible between the needs of novice and expert users (user-adaptive dialogue).

In their proper domains, SLDSs should behave as experts towards their users. They should therefore have sufficient task domain knowledge as stated in P2.

P2. Provide sufficient task domain coverage.

P2 is a specific principle. However, because it deals with speaker's knowledge, it cannot be subsumed under P4 above. We propose to introduce a new generic principle which mirrors P4 and subsumes P2:

P16-NEW. Take into account legitimate partner expectations as to your own background knowledge.

Even if an SLDS is able to conduct a perfectly co-operative dialogue, it will need to initiate *repair and clarification meta-communication* whenever it has failed to understand its human user, for instance because of speech recognition or language understanding failure:

P14. Provide ability to initiate repair if system understanding has failed.

P14 states what the co-operative speaker should do in case of communication failure. P14 is a generic principle and cannot be subsumed under M1 (informativeness) which does not address issues of meta-communication. P14 may be replaced by the slightly revised P14*:

> P14*. Initiate repair or clarification meta-communication in case of communication failure.

3.3 The Final Set of Principles

It may be concluded that there are more principles of co-operativity in human-machine dialogue than those identified by Grice. Three groups of principles reveal aspects of co-operative dialogue which were not addressed by the maxims. This yields a total of seven dialogue aspects, each of which is addressed by one or more generic principles (see Table 3). Some of the generic principles subsume one or more specific principles (see Table 4). Specific principles SP10 and SP11 in Table 4 were developed as a result of the user test of the Danish SLDS (see Section 4).

4. Testing the Principles of Co-Operative System Dialogue

A user test of the implemented system was carried out with a simulated speech recogniser [3]. The recognition accuracy would be 100% as long as users expressed themselves in accordance with the vocabulary and grammars known to the system. Otherwise, the simulated recogniser would turn the user input into a string which only contained words and grammatical constructions from the recogniser's vocabulary and rules of grammar. The test was carried out in a way similar to the two last WOZ experiments (cf. Section 2). It involved 12 external subjects who had never tried the system. Each subject received four scenarios. Subjects conducted the dialogues over the telephone in their normal work environments in order to make the situation as realistic as possible. Each dialogue between a subject and the dialogue system was recorded. All transactions between the individual system modules were logged.

A total of 57 dialogues were recorded. Some subjects repeated a task if they failed to achieve their goals in the first dialogue attempt. The recorded dialogues were transcribed and analysed. In order to test our principles of co-operative dialogue design and obtain a detailed overview of user and system problems in the user test, we identified all such problems in the transcribed corpus. The dialogue being system-directed, we could specify the system's questions in a fixed tabular format. For each scenario and system question we then specified the key contents of the expected user answer. This provided a normative model of the completion of each scenario used in the test. After transcription of the test corpus, the key contents of the actual user answers were added to a table representing the relevant scenario. Each deviation from the expected user input indicated a potential problem and was carefully analysed. This analysis often required use of the transcribed dialogue itself as well as the logged transactions between the system modules during the dialogue.

Dialogue aspect	GP No.	Generic principle
Group 1: **Informativeness**	GP1	*Make your contribution as informative as is required (for the current purposes of the exchange).
	GP2	*Do not make your contribution more informative than is required.
Group 2: **Truth and evidence**	GP3	*Do not say what you believe to be false.
	GP4	*Do not say that for which you lack adequate evidence.
Group 3: **Relevance**	GP5	*Be relevant, i.e. be appropriate to the immediate needs at each stage of the transaction.
Group 4: **Manner**	GP6	*Avoid obscurity of expression.
	GP7	*Avoid ambiguity.
	GP8	*Be brief (avoid unnecessary prolixity).
	GP9	*Be orderly.
Group 5: **Partner asymmetry**	GP10	Inform the dialogue partners of important non-normal characteristics which they should take into account in order to behave co-operatively in dialogue.
Group 6: **Background knowledge**	GP11	Take partners' relevant background knowledge into account.
	GP12	Take into account legitimate partner expectations as to your own background knowledge.
Group 7: **Repair and clarification**	GP13	Initiate repair or clarification meta-communication in case of communication failure.

Table 3: Generic principles of co-operative spoken dialogue. Generic principles are expressed at the same level of abstraction as are the Gricean maxims (marked with an *). The left-hand column characterises the aspect of dialogue addressed by each principle. Comparison with Table 2 shows that the three first dialogue aspects have been re-named.

Table 5 shows a scenario table in which two problems were identified: (i) under-supported user navigation and (ii) answering several questions at a time. The user wants a roundtrip ticket. In the tested version of our SLDS, roundtrip tickets can only be booked as two one-way tickets. Not having been informed about this, the user attempts to book a return ticket. The first problem (i) lies in the lack of information to users on how to navigate the system in order to book roundtrip tickets. The second problem (ii) probably occurs because the user found no other way of telling the system that the departure airport for the home journey is different from the destination of the out journey. In the system's opening instructions to users, these are told to answer the system's questions one at a time.

After a first iteration of describing the identified problems, these were seen to belong to one of two broad types, i.e. *system problems* and *user errors*. System problems demonstrate flaws in, i.a., the design of the system's language processing or dialogue design components. User errors were of many types, ranging from misreading of the scenarios and initiating repair through questions which the system was unable to understand, through to non-co-operative dialogue behaviour. A detailed analysis is in preparation. We shall focus on the dialogue design problems in what follows. For each instance of a dialogue design problem type we made a diagnosis and proposed a cure. Figure 4 shows an example in which the user has asked both to depart at 7.20 (am) and to have discount. The diagnosis shows that the system imposes an unjustified priority among these two goals. The cure proposes how to revise the system's handling of inconsistent user input.

Dialogue aspect	**GP No.**	**SP No.**	**Specific principle**
Group 1: **Informativeness**	GP1	SP1	Be fully explicit in communicating to users the commitments they have made.
	GP1	SP2	Provide feedback on each piece of information provided by the user.
Group 2: **Truth and evidence**			
Group 3: **Relevance**			
Group 4: **Manner**	GP7	SP3	Provide same formulation of the same question (or address) to users everywhere in the system's dialogue turns.
Group 5: **Partner asymmetry**	GP10	SP4	Provide clear and comprehensible communication of what the system can and cannot do.
	GP10	SP5	Provide clear and sufficient instructions to users on how to interact with the system.
Group 6: **Background knowledge**	GP11	SP6	Take into account possible (and possibly erroneous) user inferences by analogy from related task domains.
	GP11	SP7	Separate whenever possible between the needs of novice and expert users (user-adaptive dialogue).
	GP12	SP8	Provide sufficient task domain coverage.
Group 7: **Repair and clarification**	GP13	SP9	Provide ability to initiate repair if system understanding has failed.
	GP13	SP10	Initiate clarification meta-communication in case of inconsistent input.
	GP13		Initiate clarification meta-communication in case of ambiguous user input.

Table 4: Specific principles of co-operative spoken dialogue. Each specific principle is subsumed under a generic principle.

Scenario: G-5-4-a-1 User: 10 Date: January 25 1995			
System questions	**Normative user answers**	**Actual user answers**	**Problems**
System already known	no / yes / -	-	
Customer number	2	yes (2)	
Number of travellers	1	1	
ID-numbers	4	4	
Departure airport	Copenhagen	Copenhagen	
Arrival airport	Karup	Karup	
Return journey	no	yes	Under-supported user navigation
Interested in discount	-	no	
Day of departure (out)	January 31	January 31	
Hour of departure (out)	around 7:30 / around 19:30	16:50	
Day of departure (home)	-	February 1	
Hour of departure (home)	-	18:10 (no departure) no [does not want one from list] 15:45 from Esbjerg (no departure [from Karup]) yes [wants one from list] 16:20	Answering several questions at a time
Delivery	airport / send	send	
More	yes	no	

Table 5: The table shows the system's questions, expected key contents of user answers, actual key contents of user answers, and problems identified in a subject's completion of Scenario G-5-4-a-1. Contents in brackets (third column) indicate key contents of the system's next utterance. Comments in square brackets are explanatory. One system problem type (undersupported user navigation) and one user error type (answering several questions at a time) were identified.

Table 6 shows the identified dialogue design problem types. Further analysis showed that each problem corresponded to the violation of one or more principles of co-operative system dialogue design. Table 6 shows that no new generic principles of co-operative system dialogue design were found in the analysis of the user test corpus. However, two new specific principles, SP10 and SP11, were found which both address the issue of meta-communication (see Table 4). This is not surprising. System misunderstandings were not simulated in the WOZ experiments which is why the WOZ corpus contains very few examples of meta-communication. As a result, there was little material from which to develop the specific principles of repair and clarification presented in Table 4.

S: U: red discount + out departure time at 7:20; S: no departure at 7:20. However 7:20 does exist, but without discount.
D: S gives priority to discount over time without reason.
C: S should ask U about priority: 7:20 is not a discount departure. Red discount can be obtained on the departures at x, y and z. Which departure do you want. [If U provides a new departure time: S: Do you still want discount? If U: No; S: List non-discount departures].

Figure 4: Example of the dialogue design problem: inconsistent user input. **S** (boldface) means symptom, **D** means diagnosis and **C** means cure. S (normal) means system and U means user.

Dialogue design problem type	**Principle(s) violated**
Ambiguous user input	SP11
Inference problem	SP8
Inconsistent user input	SP10
Insufficient instructions to users about the use of 'correct'	SP5
Misleading system utterance	GP1 and GP6
Undersupported user navigation	SP5
Incomplete, grammatically incorrect, or irrelevant response	GP1, GP6, and GP5
Missing feedback	SP2
Ambiguous system output	GP7
Database error	GP3

Table 6: Dialogue design problem types identified during the user test. The right-hand column shows the principles of co-operative dialogue design whose violation produced the problems.

5. Conclusion

We have described how a set of principles of co-operative system dialogue were developed from a relatively large corpus of simulated human-machine spoken dialogue. The principles were then shown to include as a sub-set a well-established body of maxims of co-operative human-human dialogue. Moreover, the set of principles has a considerably wider scope than that of the body of maxims. Thus, at the generic level, the principles address three aspects of co-operative dialogue which are not covered by the maxims. In addition, a sub-set of the principles are specific rather than generic principles. The specific principles have no counterparts among the maxims. Analysis of the dialogue corpus that was produced from the user test of the implemented system has shown that the set of generic principles is adequate for, that is, able to subsume, the identified dialogue problems. The corpus analysis did, however, increase the number of specific principles by two principles which both address dialogue issues that were not prominent in the original corpus of simulated human-machine spoken dialogue. These results suggest, we believe, that the principles of co-operative system dialogue discussed above represent a step towards a more or less complete and practically applicable set of guidelines for the design of co-operative SLDS dialogue.

At least two further steps are needed in order to turn the principles into a set of well-tested guidelines for the design of co-operative SLDS dialogue. The first step is to investigate how the principles actually work as guidelines in dialogue design: how comprehensible are they to SLDS designers? How adequate are they for the development of systems different from out own? How can they be used to reveal potential user problems during early design? Does their use have measurable effects? How should the principles be "packaged" to achieve maximum effect? Based on the answers to questions such as these on comprehensibility, adequacy, methodology, effectiveness and communication, respectively, the second step will be to attempt to provide the necessary support for the principles to become of maximum benefit to dialogue design practice.

References

1. Aust, H. and Oerder, M. "Dialogue control in automatic inquiry systems", Proceedings of the ESCA Workshop on Spoken Dialogue Systems, Vigsø, 30 May to 2 June, pp.121-124, 1995.
2. Bernsen, N.O. "Types of user problems in design. A study of knowledge acquisition using the Wizard of Oz", Esprit Basic Research project AMODEUS-2 Working Paper RP2-UM-WP14. In Deliverable D2: Extending the User Modelling Techniques. June, 1993.
3. Bernsen, N.O., Dybkjær, H. and Dybkjær, L. "Exploring the limits of system-directed dialogue. Dialogue evaluation of the Danish dialogue system", Proceedings of Eurospeech '95, Madrid, September, pp.1457-60, 1995.
4. Bernsen, N.O., Dybkjær, H. and Dybkjær, L. "Co-operativity in human-machine and human-human spoken dialogue", To appear in Discourse Processes, 1996.
5. Bernsen, N.O., Dybkjær, L. and Dybkjær, H. "A dedicated task-oriented dialogue theory in support of spoken language dialogue systems design", Proceedings of ICSLP '94, Yokohama, September, pp.875-878, 1994.
6. Bernsen, N.O., Dybkjær, L. and Dybkjær, H. "Task-oriented spoken human-computer dialogue", Report 6a, Spoken Language Dialogue Systems, Roskilde University, February, 1994.
7. Bilange, E. "A task independent oral dialogue model", Proceedings of the 5th EACL, Berlin, April, pp.83-88, 1991.
8. Bourlard, H. "Towards increasing speech recognition error rates", Proceedings of Eurospeech '95, Madrid, September, pp.883-894, 1995.
9. Cole, R., Novick, D.G., Fanty, M., Vermeulen, P., Sutton, S., Burnett, D. and Schalkwyk, J. "A prototype voice-response questionnaire for the US

Census", Proceedings of the ICSLP '94, Yokohama, September, pp.683-686, 1994.

10. Dybkjær, H., Bernsen, N.O. and Dybkjær, L. "Wizard-of-Oz and the trade-off between naturalness and recogniser constraints", Proceedings of Eurospeech '93, Berlin, September, pp.947-950, 1993.
11. Dybkjær, L., Bernsen, N.O. and Dybkjær, H. "Different spoken language dialogues for different tasks. A task-oriented dialogue theory", Human Comfort and Security, Springer Research Report, Springer Verlag, 1995.
12. Dybkjær, L. and Dybkjær, H. "Wizard of Oz experiments in the development of a dialogue model for P1", Report 3, Spoken Language Dialogue Systems, Roskilde University, February, 1993.
13. Eckert, W. and McGlashan, S. "Managing spoken dialogues for information services", Proceedings of Eurospeech '93, Berlin, September, pp.1653-1656, 1993.
14. Eckert, W., Nöth, E., Niemann, H. and Schukat-Talamazzini, E. "Real users behave weird - Experiences made collecting large human-machine-dialog corpora", Proceedings of the ESCA Workshop on Spoken Dialogue Systems, Vigsø, 30 May to 2 June, pp.193-196, 1995.
15. Fraser, N.M. and Gilbert, G.N. "Simulating speech systems", Computer Speech and Language 5, pp.81-99, 1991.
16. Grice, P. "Logic and conversation", In Syntax and Semantics, (eds.) Cole, P. and Morgan J.L., Vol. 3, Speech Acts, pp.41-58, New York, Academic Press, 1975. Reprinted in Grice, P. Studies in the Way of Words. Cambridge, MA: Harvard University Press, 1989.
17. Heisterkamp, P. "Ambiguity and uncertainty in spoken dialogue", Proceedings of Eurospeech '93, Berlin, September, pp.1657-1660, 1993.
18. Sperber, D. and Wilson, D. "Relevance, communication and cognition", Oxford, Basil Blackwell, 1986.

Usability Analysis of Spoken Dialogues for Automated Telephone Banking Services (OVID)

Mervyn A. Jack
CCIR, University of Edinburgh
80, South Bridge
Edinburgh EH1 1HN, UK

Jean-Paul Lefèvre
Agora Conseil
185, Hameau du Château
38360 Sassenage, France

Abstract

This paper describes the methodology in use on research project OVID to investigate the design, implementation and evaluation of spoken dialogues for automated telephone banking services. The project involves a series of large-scale field experiments using both Wizard of Oz (WOZ) schemes and real time speech recognition technology for the investigation of the perceived usability of such banking services which have voice response capability. The system possesses a fully integrated dialogue component which can be independently modified to suit different experimental objectives. The set-up for experiments using the WOZ scheme is described with details of the user evaluation measures employed in the research.

1. Introduction

Speech input and output software capabilities are now at a point where the implementation of a conversational speech interface can begin to be contemplated. Speaker independent recognition of telephone speech has been demonstrated for limited vocabularies, in isolated word and connected word systems. Much of these recent state of the art developments have been carried out as part of previous EC funded projects. Commercial pressure to incorporate such technologies within dialogue applications has resulted in the appearance of dialogue systems in automated network based telephone services. Although these developments allow spoken words to be recognised automatically (and spoken responses to be produced), in ways which will be able to support a future conversational interface, present dialogue software engineering methods are still far from being able to produce a scheme which can accommodate the full range of utterances which a user might use in communicating with an automated telephone banking service. The first fruits of this degree of flexibility are visible today in some limited applications while development of a full conversational interface is beginning. Present dialogues are system-driven with the dialogue being used primarily to correct recognition errors, using confirmation or repetition strategies for error recovery as the system takes the user through the transaction. A requirement exists for user-driven dialogues where the user will dominate the transaction and the dialogue will take care of the content, as opposed to the form, of the transaction. For banking applications the dialogue will focus on transaction details which the caller may have omitted to define (such as money amounts or day of the week) in addition to correction of recognition errors. Similarly, in this context, a need exists to allow the caller to talk in a normal speech style, as opposed to limiting replies to legal isolated digits or other limited vocabulary words only. Proof of the capabilities of voice processing software in this type of automated banking application could have far reaching effects in the introduction of voice processing in Europe and it is anticipated that a large number of banks could learn from the experience of the project and begin to use the technology proposed in their own operations. The benefits to the banks from widespread commercial roll-out of this service will be to reduce administration costs for banking operations and to reduce training costs of staff.

In the absence of the type of detailed trial application proposed here, applications developers will continue to offer 'best-fit' systems within the restrictions of existing technology. For example, systems based on isolated digit recognition technology have been introduced over recent months as a result of market-pull to automate telephone services. Time-to-market for technology enhancements in this specialised industry is of the order of six months, a timing trend which is expected to continue for the next few years as consumer demand for such systems continues to grow. This trial application offers a market-driven and application-driven opportunity to build confidence in the technology to a broad community of users and other players and to reduce concerns that a piecemeal development of services will be self-limiting.

Carrying out the trial application discussed here with access to public funding, will allow definition of the banking service requirements for voice technology to the advantage of technology suppliers, the banks, and most importantly the bank customers. Such work is outside the financial scope of any single commercial organisation and is also incompatible with the nature of research funding available to academic institutions. Access to EU funds for this trial application therefore represents one of the key elements to preparing the design of banking services in the creation of a range of viable telephone based services which will be both revenue generating to the banking service providers, and of social relevance to lifestyles in the 21st Century.

Previous work of the authors has revolved around the concept of dialogue space and is introduced as an aid to depicting the various components involved in the proposed trial work. The user is a key influence on the content of dialogue space. Included here are the user's cognitive processes as they are involved in hearing and understanding the dialogue prompt and in generation of the speech to be transmitted and recognised. Also included within the user component is the user's attitude since it is the user's response (and subsequent behaviour) to the overall performance of the automated service in allowing the user to complete the desired task which is of key interest in establishing the effectiveness of standards and features in the user interface and overall profitability of the service. A need exists to derive ways of measuring user attitude and response to the automated banking service. Any specific user interaction (call) with the automated service will result in a dialogue path or trace through the dialogue space. Allowable dialogue paths will be governed by the overall arrangement and inter-relationship of a network of nodes called dialogue building blocks, whose interconnection topology is specified by the dialogue structure. Any given user interaction will produce a dialogue trace which will pass through many or all of the dialogue building blocks, in a sequence governed by the specific conditions active at the time of that user interaction. These may include the ability of the user to read and/or say the required words at the correct time, as well as the ability of the automatic speech recognition system to correctly recognise correctly enunciated words.

Variables available to the work in exploring this dialogue space include the performance of the speech recognition system in terms of hypotheses and accept or query or reject outputs for each vocabulary word, the possible configuration of the contents of each dialogue building block and the interconnection of dialogue building blocks in a given dialogue structure. In addition, the definition of dialogue space in the context of a supporting visual representation such as a screenphone or PC screen integrated into the banking service will be of interest. The concept of dialogue space allows identification of two sets of evaluation metrics. Firstly it is possible to analyse how efficiently each user interaction actually traverses the dialogue space to achieve the final task goal, investigating such aspects as local inefficiencies within a dialogue building block. This will allow a detailed objective analysis of performance of the automated banking service to be carried out. Secondly it is possible to evaluate the user's (subjective) attitude to the problem of navigating through this dialogue space.

Usability can be defined as 'a concept comprising the effectiveness, efficiency and satisfaction with which specified users can achieve specified goals in a particular environment' [1]. Increasingly, in the development of a new technology such as automated voice services, the attitudes and perceptions of potential users are regarded as important considerations which have to be taken into account in the design of systems and services. Evidence suggests that there is a wide range of diverse approaches for measuring usability. However, in [2] Poulson argues for a general purpose measuring tool (a questionnaire) which can be used to assess the perceived quality of different systems in different settings. The methods adopted here employ a questionnaire in an approach based on field experiments over the telephone network. The experimental programme consists of a series of experiments in which the characteristics of the speech interface (including a speech recogniser) are manipulated and the dependent variables of user attitude and perceived usability are measured by a postal questionnaire and interview.

Modification of the speech interface involves changing the characteristics of the recognition system and/or changing the dialogue. Of particular interest in this work is the investigation of users' attitudes to speech interfaces using recognition system capabilities which are extrapolated beyond the current state-of-the-art. One of the major features of the work is that it is based on a parametric simulation of an existing speech recognition technology allowing experimentation with both current recognition performance levels and recognition performance levels extrapolated beyond those currently achievable. It is possible then to address, among other key issues, the shape of the usability function for automated telephone services for different levels of recognition performance. Modifying the speech interface can also involve changing the dialogue used in the telephone service. This allows important user interface and human factors issues to be addressed such as the impact of voice quality on users' perceptions of the telephone service; the degree to which conventional prompts influence the user's navigation through the dialogue; and the impact of dialogue structure and the specific wording of prompts on users' attitudes to the service.

2. Participant Population

One of the key experimental factors underpinning the work has been the availability of a pool of volunteer participants. These are recruited on a statistical basis by a professional market research company to a detailed specification based on geographical and demographical criteria. All such participants are assumed to be naive users of such a system and matched pairs or matched sets are employed in experiments, matched in terms of age group and sex (not geographical location). The participants are contacted by letter giving details of the banking task they are to perform. Immediately before each experiment, the operator reads out a defined pre-amble to the participant and activates the WOZ software to carry out the experiment

3. WOZ Experimental Configuration

The WOZ system includes the user/subject, the experimental operator, the speech recogniser software, a dialogue manager and a speech generator. The WOZ software handles all aspects of the experiments including the initiation of telephone contact at the volunteer subject's home or workplace; the delivery of dialogue prompts to the subject; the registering of keystrokes from the experimental operator made in response to spoken input from the subject; the on-line generation of recognition 'errors' when these are specified in the experiment; and the recording of all statistical data on keystrokes and timing of responses. The WOZ software runs in real time on an IBM-compatible PC with a plug-in circuit card providing connection to the telephone line.

In addition to simulating the speech recogniser, the software controls the archival recording of all interactions between the subject and the operator. The advantages of this WOZ scheme include full control over the experimental conditions; constraints imposed on the operators who key in the subject's spoken responses; and the fact that all other experimental conditions, such as the introduction of speech recognition errors, are entirely under software control. An important distinction is made between off-line and on-line simulations of recognition errors.

Because the experiments use a simulated recogniser and finite-state dialogue networks, it is possible to run new dialogue designs fully automatically with simulated user input. This is the off-line mode of operation. In this way results can be obtained which are characteristic of the particular setting of the simulated recogniser with the specific dialogue design under the strict assumption that the 'user' has supplied consistently perfect input. If the dialogue specification is considered as defining a dialogue space, the off-line mode selects particular paths through that space. These are the paths (i.e. dialogues which are transferred for use in the actual experiments. In other words, subjects are guided through the dialogue space along characterised dialogue paths referred to as scripts.

The main emphasis of this work will be to collect as much relevant information as possible on the human factors issues which are involved in automated telephone dialogues for banking applications. The work will involve an on-going series of experiments designed with a view to testing various hypotheses concerning speech software interfaces between humans and automated telephone banking services. The issues to be addressed will be defined by the partners on an on-going basis. These issues will include a whole list of important facets such as :

- dialogue designs for speaker authentication with digit recognition for PIN numbers,
- alphabet or keyword recognition for password recognition,
- user ability in memorising different system inspired passwords,
- user ability in memorising different user inspired passwords,
- lengths of digit strings and alphanumeric strings for account numbers,
- formats for money amounts,
- formats for dates and days,
- choice of voice for the speech synthesis,
- levels of formality for the system voice.

It is proposed to address the dialogue definition of these issues through an extensive series of Wizard of Oz (WOZ) experiments. These experiments will be carried out by taking telephone calls from bank users who will be asked to use a prototype automated service under the control of a spoken dialogue interface. Users will subsequently be asked to respond to a telephone questionnaire and written questionnaire. Users' spoken responses and experimental operators' speech will be recorded using high quality recording equipment and all relevant experimental data will be collected and filled under software control. These Wizard of Oz experiments will be carried out to test various approaches to human computer dialogue modelling for the banking application in order to achieve the efficient and effective information exchanges. It is expected that users will not react in a uniform manner; one of the interesting features is therefore to identify areas of common user behaviour and, if possible, to attempt to lead as many users as possible to produce similar responses. However, since it cannot be assumed that all users will respond in the same manner to machine interactions, the key issues will be isolated as specific to each particular application. In the simulations, a hidden human controller (Wizard) will simulate the behaviour of the computer in various ways, testing user reactions.

An important decision with respect to these studies will be the choice of experimental design to be employed. Generally, repeated measures designs are likely to provide the most useful results since they involve repeated use of the same users for different values of the independent variables thereby guaranteeing a very high degree of control over variables not under experimental control.

However, this experimental strategy will only be viable in conjunction with habituation studies undertaken to explore learning effects in the simulated environment. Since there are expected to be learning effects, two alternative approaches are open. Firstly, either matched pairs (or, more likely, independent subject) designs will be used with the relevant statistical tests of significance determining the number of users for each sample drawn from the population. Secondly, the habituation effects might be reduced by taking relevant measurements from users previously exposed to a large number of dialogues, thereby reducing any habituation effects to a statistically insignificant level. This strategy would allow for repeated measures experiments to be carried out but at the cost of requiring that all users be exposed to a large number of training dialogues. This will put a special burden on the recruiting of users and may be unrealistic if the number of training exposures exceeds more than three or four. Investigation of habituation effects and, in particular the suitability of given dialogue interface designs in assisting a user to change between several different services with a common dialogue 'feel', will form one of the primary activities for experiments and interviews with the local user panel.

A general definition of usability has been proposed by the International Standards Organisation (1990) as being

> 'a concept comprising the effectiveness, efficiency and satisfaction with which specified users can achieve specified goals in a particular environment'.

The ISO introduces the concept of 'usability attributes' which are those specific features and characteristics of a telephone service that influence the effectiveness, efficiency and satisfaction with which individual users can achieve specified goals in a particular environment. A point of departure for this project is an existing questionnaire which is based on a group of salient attributes which have been identified and proven by users. It consists of 22 Likert-type proposal statements and responses. Previous results have shown that the attributes which users find most salient in determining the usability of automated telephone services and applications are :

- ease of use
- reliability
- clear instructions
- clarity of voice

In designing an attitude measurement tool such as a questionnaire there are several important issues which must be addressed. In an attitude scale there should be an equal number of positive and negative items relating to the service and these items should cover a wide range of user attitudes. Such balance overcomes the danger that the overall score could reflect the users' tendency to agree rather than disagree with the questionnaire statements (an effect known as 'response acquiescence set') instead of providing valid information on usability. Furthermore the attitude scales should allow computation of an overall score for usability. However, in addition to estimating the statistical significance of the overall score, it is important to examine the score for individual items, since these may well highlight specific aspects relating to the usability of a specific service design. There should also be a set of open-ended questions and a general comments section included in the questionnaire to allow users to express opinions and perception not covered by the attitude scales. Including this provides a rich source of qualitative data which can augment the quantitative data provided by the attitude scales. For the particular usability measurement tool needed here, a seven-point Lickert scale with a mid-neutral point will be used. In such a design, questions of the proposing type are used, such as :

"The automated telephone system was easy to use".....

The intention is that the user will respond to each question using a 7-point Likert response scale ranging through the options

- ...strongly agree...
- ...agree...
- ...slightly agree...
- ...neutral...
- ...slightly disagree...
- ...disagree...
- ...strongly disagree.

Preliminary tests of the questionnaire will identify in detail the actual salient attributes that bank users assign to the type of automated service to be trialed on the project. For the questionnaire design it will be necessary to try different presentation formats for each country and to test questionnaire accuracy and questionnaire reliability. In addition a split in terms of telephone questionnaires and written questionnaires will be need to be considered.

Objective performance and assessment measures will also be possible in terms of timings for each response or section of the banking service functionality as well as hesitations by the user, confusions and repetitions. All of these can serve to offer an objective measure of the trial application performance. Although comparison between the type of automated service being trialed and a similar service as offered by a human may be beyond the scope of the project, it will be important to derive some assessment method to measure the 'insult rate' which might be experienced by a customer who is connected unexpectedly to the automated service without prior warning.

4. Dialogue Design and Evaluation

Effective dialogues are the key to the development of usable telephone services. Experiments have highlighted the range of difficulty that users can experience with such services and have suggested a variety of possible solutions. Users do not always response with words from the active vocabulary. Part of the user learning process involved in using an automated service is to know what can legally be said at each request for input by the service. Of course, this is a general problem in the design of human computer interfaces. In similar experiments carried out by the authors (256 subjects) there were 49 examples of unexpected responses to the service. The variety of responses included, very commonly, answering with a digit as well as 'yes' or 'no' in reply to confirmational prompt. For example in reply to 'Did you say six', the user might say 'No, five' or 'Yes, six' rather than simply 'yes' or 'no' as prescribed. One strategy found useful in minimising this problem is to remind users whenever possible of the active vocabulary, by including reference to it in prompts. For example, in recovery or confirmational prompts, where the active vocabulary is 'yes' and 'no' phrasing such as 'answering yes or no, did you say....' was used. Interestingly, when at the end of the dialogue interaction, the number was read back to the user, for confirmation using a prompt which did not contain such a reminder, 11% of subjects gave an inappropriate response, suggesting that learning how to use services of this type is something that needs continual reinforcement.

A further problem was identified in terms of inappropriately timed responses, spoken outside the time window in which the speech recogniser is active. One common type of inappropriately timed response is speaking during a pause in a syntactically complex prompt consisting of either a sequence of independent sentences or a single sentence having a main clause plus subordinate clause structure. In both these cases, there tends to be a short pause between the relevant parts of the prompt message and if the first part is semantically interrogative or alternatively is fully understood by the user, a response is made at that time. Again this is an important issue for automated telephone service interface design, requiring intelligent strategies for either avoiding the situation or for curtailing the delivery of the prompt if the user is detected as having spoken an input.

Silence by the user in response to a request for input is generally a sign of serious dialogue failure coincident with loss of navigation by the user. In a few cases this may be due simply to the user being distracted locally but in the great majority of cases it has been found to be due to the fact that the user does not know how to respond. Careful study of the contexts in which silences occurred in experiments has identified specific dialogue structural configurations reponsible for causing silence. These correspond to contexts where an unexpected transition occurs in the dialogue following a series of spoken prompts each of which is followed by a 'beep', to a stand-alone 'beep' prompt used without the support of a spoken prompt. This latter style of prompt is often used in rapid-entry or fast-track dialogues. The confusion apparently arises because the users are not able to interpret the significance of the isolated 'beep'. In experiments, 14.5% of subjects were silent at least once during a task, mostly attributable to this effect. Consistency of style of prompts is therefore judged as an essential element in maintaining user confidence and navigation during interactions with automated telephone services.

5. Conclusions

An approach to developing usable telephone dialogues has been described based on parametric simulation of a speech recogniser. The mean attitude scores for all settings of the simulated recogniser are high. Overall the results obtained to date, using the Lickert response scales and usability profile methods have successfully demonstrated the applicability of telephone and postal questionnaires in evaluating the usability of automated telephone services allowing the development of intelligent dialogue management schemes for such systems.

References

[1] ISO Ergonomic Requirements for Office and Visual Display Terminals (VDTs), Part 11: Usability Statements, International Standards Organisation, ISO-CD9241-11, vers. 2.5, 1990.

[2] D. Poulson, "Towards Simple Indices of the Perceived Quality of Software Interfaces", IEE Colloquium Digest Evaluation Techniques for Interactive System Design, Digest No. 1987/76, pp. 4.1-4.4, 1987.

Hypermedia-based Telecooperation Support for Marketing Software Products

Jörg M. Haake
GMD, IPSI
Dolivostr. 15, D-64293 Darmstadt, Germany

Manfred Thüring
BIFOA
Universitätsstr.45, D-50931 Köln, Germany

Caterina Rehm-Berbenni
FUTUREtec
Schützenstr. 14, D-51465 Bergisch Gladbach, Germany

Abstract

The development, distribution, quality assurance and maintenance of software products increasingly takes place in international markets and requires the intensive collaboration of several parties. To facilitate the different kinds of asynchronous and synchronous collaboration between remote users in different European countries hypermedia-based telecooperation support is a key component: Hypermedia enables the integration of heterogeneous information entities created by different partners as well as the structuring of such a multi-organizational knowledge base. Telecooperation technology enables not only asynchronous sharing of distributed knowledge but also tightly-coupled collaboration on synchronously shared workspaces. These facilities can be used to support communication and cooperation in the later stages of the software lifecycle, especially the market introduction of commercial software products.

This paper summarizes the requirements resulting from this application domain and outlines the design of a cooperative telecooperation system which is capable of meeting these requirements. An initial prototype of SEPIA has been adapted to the requirements of supporting the market introduction of software products. This prototype provides all necessary workspaces and the kernel of related cooperation facilities. For testing purposes, this version is currently installed in a LAN environment. Future development will expand this version to WANs, with the aim of supporting the introduction of specific software in several national branches of the European market.

1. Introduction

While technical support for software design and development has been making considerable progress within the last decade, support for the market introduction of software products has been widely neglected. This is quite surprising since it is well known that distribution, adaptation of systems to national markets (e.g., in terms of the language), maintenance and updating are very time consuming and expensive activities. Support for this domain of marketing is therefore likely to significantly reduce costs, to improve the usability of software products and to increase quality of services after delivery. In order to reach these goals, there is an urgent need for efficient cooperation between various stakeholders involved in the software life cycle, such as developers, distributors and customers.

Due to the globalisation of markets and the shift from single, independently acting corporations to virtual organisations operating as dynamic networks, communication between these stakeholders must cut across organisational and national boundaries. This is a particular challenge for European small and medium enterprises (SMEs) who must strive to defend their market share against multinational enterprises. To cope with this challenge, improved and enhanced communication facilities are needed to support coordination and cooperation between European SMEs who are active in the software market - a requirement which can only be fulfilled by means of modern telecooperation and Wide Area Networks (WANs). To facilitate the different kinds of asynchronous and synchronous collaboration between remote users in different European countries hypermedia-based telecooperation support is a key component:

Hypermedia enables the integration of heterogeneous information entities created by different partners as well as the structuring of such a multi-organizational knowledge base. Telecooperation technology enables not only asynchronous sharing of distributed knowledge but also tightly coupled collaboration on synchronously shared workspaces. These facilities can be used to support communication and cooperation at the later stages of the software lifecycle including procedures of quality assessments. It is quite clear, that the development of these facilities requires task specific interfaces based on cognitive task analysis, a user-centered approach and sophisticated navigational and collaboration concepts.

In the next section, the market introduction of software products will be examined as an example application domain and the requirements it places on coordination and cooperation support will be analysed. Section three introduces two emerging key technologies which can be used to address these requirements. Section four discusses how hypermedia and telecooperation technology can be combined to support the market introduction. The paper finishes with some conclusions and open issues.

2. Application Domain

The example application domain used in this paper is the introduction of software products into the European market. This implies co-operation bettween several companies, e.g. the company (A) performs the activities of releasing the product for different European countries, the companies (B), (C), and (D) ensure the adapting tasks to national particularities and regulations ("localisation"), and the company (E) performs development and maintenance tasks. To fulfil these activities, a close collaboration is needed between different partners playing different roles. In each target country, usually at least one partner introduces the software product into the market. Product development may either be centralised or distributed.

The formation of such a multi-party organisation can be regarded as the creation of a virtual organisation operating as a dynamic network of partners with different responsibilities and tasks. Today, such organisations may often take the form of joint ventures, but new forms of business organisations are currently being discussed (e.g. virtual corporations). The establishment of such a European distribution network draws together partners from various countries to form a "virtual enterprise" that sets out to conquer a promising market in a joint venture.

The most crucial factor for ensuring the success of this venture is the fast, fluent and flawless communication across organisational and national boundaries empowering the participating corporations to efficiently cooperate and coordinate their activities. Interviews with key personnel from software producers and distributors identified communication bottlenecks for three major activities of introducing software in a local or national (sub-) market: *testing*, *adaptation* of software and product documentation to different regions, *identification* of side problems and their solution. Traditional communication facilities, such as phone, fax and teleconferences do not support these activities efficiently, but cause a number of well known problems:

- high costs for communication and travel,
- insufficient speed to market due to the spatial distribution of partners which slows down the translation of technical documentation, the adaptation of the user interface to national particularities and the establishment of coordinated and comprehensive support service for customers,
- impediment of user feedback during customisation and usage of software products,
- communication breaks and misunderstandings between the developer, the main distributor and the national distributors leading to errors and overhead for their correction.

The interviews also revealed some of the requirements that must be fulfilled by advanced communication and cooperation facilities that aim to cope with these problems. An adequate support system should enable user organisations:

- to share the running and viewing of the software product as well as other standard applications,
- to switch control for the application sharing from one user to another,
- to jointly view documentation and training manuals,
- to create, view and manipulate shared and distributed information spaces that contain all pieces of information of potential interest for other partners (e.g. plans, documentation, task lists, status information), in a synchronous and asynchronous manner,
- to support informal communication with an audio channel and an electronic whiteboard, as well as formal communication via shared and interrelated documents (see above),

- to use telepointers in "What You See Is What I See"(WYSIWIS) situations,
- to make use of task oriented system support (such as specific document types and relations between documents, specific operations and procedures), and
- to use other cooperative facilities, e.g. annotations and checklists, during joint sessions.

These requirements can only be met by innovative telecommunication and telecooperation systems which connect nationally distributed organisations via Wide Area Networks (WANs) and also support the creation of a knowledge base in which test results, problems, solutions and related technical information are represented. There are a number of commercially available telecooperation systems, but none of these fulfils all requirements, nor can these systems be easily adapted to the particularities of the application domain. What is needed is an advanced telecooperation environment that supports all the activities listed above and enables its users to work in a problem oriented and task centered mode by providing adequate data objects and functionalities. In the next section, a combination of two key technologies will be discussed that fulfil the requirements listed above.

3. Key Technologies: Hypermedia and Telecooperation

Over the last 15 years, the rapid development and deployment of computer technology and communication networks has enabled the development of two new key technologies: hypermedia and telecooperation.

Hypermedia denotes the combination of hypertext and multi media. A hypertext consists of chunks of information (called nodes) interconnected by links. Links [2] are machine supported associations between nodes. Readers of a hypertext can open a node, read its content and reach related nodes by traversing links starting in the current node. This traversal (usually triggered by clicking on a link icon embedded in the node content) leads to a display of the destination node's content. From there, the reader can follow other links etc. A well known example of this kind of system is the World Wide Web (WWW) [1]. In general, nodes and links can be typed to communicate certain semantics to the user as well as enable the hypertext system to maintain constraints associated with the types. The resulting (potentially non-linear) network of information is called a hyperdocument.

Hypermedia documents are hypertext structures which allow nodes to contain not only text but also graphics, images, sound, video and animations. Hypermedia documents are well suited for representing strongly interconnected sources of information (e.g. traditional electronic documents) because they provide a uniform representation of multiple connections between information entities, they support reuse of information in different contexts, and they allow for task specific node and link types and operations.

Telecooperation technology comprises support for asynchronous as well as synchronous cooperation. Asynchronous cooperation support systems include E-mail, bulletin boards, group calendars and scheduling systems. Synchronous cooperation support systems include desktop teleconferencing applications, shared whiteboards and texteditors. Telecooperation systems (also known as "groupware") are generally intended to enable distributed users to work together on a common task [3]. Therefore, they provide a means for communication and coordination. However, many of today's telecooperation applications do not provide task specific support. In addition, the relationships between shared information and collaborating user groups are widely neglected.

The combination of hypermedia and telecooperation technology in terms of hypermedia based telecooperation systems is a promising direction to enable more comprehensive cooperation support as is required in many real world settings. In the next section, the possible use of hypermedia-based telecooperation support for the market introduction of software products is discussed.

4. Supporting Product Marketing

At GMD-IPSI, the SEPIA cooperative hypermedia authoring environment has been developed over the past 5 years (see [4]). SEPIA can be regarded as a prototypical hypermedia-based telecooperation support system. It is an open, tailorable, cooperative hypermedia system running on both Unix workstations and on PCs (under Windows).

Due to its tailorability, SEPIA can be customised to meet the requirements of a wide range of application domains in which remote users cooperate with each other. Different user activities are supported by dedicated "activity spaces". Each activity space provides task specific objects and operations to facilitate the user's activities when working on a task. Due to its high customisability, SEPIA can be adapted to new application domains, e.g. new activity spaces, hypermedia node and link types, and new operations can be built easily from existing ones. For each space, a number of dedicated hypermedia objects (nodes and links) of different types are defined. They are the building blocks used to create networks of interrelated pieces of information. The various node types are subdivided into atomic and composite nodes. A composite node allows for the aggregation of a subnet of information. Within a composite node it is again possible to instantiate objects from a predefined set of available node and link types. At the user interface level, activity spaces and the contents of composite nodes are presented within graph browsers. In such a browser, the user can view and rearrange the displayed network, create new nodes and links, inspect and edit node contents, and open composite nodes which then again display their subnet within a graph browser. A roaming box in each browser serves as a navigation aid in order to provide an overview of the displayed (sub)net.

Beyond its capabilities for structuring at the network level, SEPIA supports multimedia contents within nodes. All atomic nodes may carry multimedia information. In addition to "conventional" media, such as text, graphics, and audio, SEPIA can be customised to allow atomic nodes to contain other media or to refine existing types (e.g. subdivision of "text" into "documentation", "installation guide, "tutorial" etc.). Due to SEPIA's openness, any external application can be integrated in order to present or edit the contents of SEPIA's atomic nodes. The first step towards the integration of external tools is the differentiation between nodes and node contents. All nodes are handled by the user in a uniform manner. Each different type of node content is associated with its corresponding external application. When the user accesses a particular type of node content via a pop-up menu, the associated external application is started. The interface to the external tool is realised by the mapping of abstract functions (e.g. "open", "play", "execute") onto the specific functions of the application (e.g. call syntax).

Co-operative SEPIA supports cooperation of multiple, distributed users who are connected via a communication network. It provides group awareness ("who is working on which objects") in order to support coordination and spontaneous collaboration. Changes made by one user are reflected immediately at every other user's SEPIA installation. It is possible to provide all users with a shared view of the same part of the activity space (wysiwis - What You See Is What I See). A distinct telepointer is provided for each user in order to improve metacommunication on the contents of the activity spaces.

Within the application domain, SEPIA can serve as the integrating environment for different activities of the later phases of the software life cycle, i.e. system introduction, quality assurance, maintenance and user consulting. The following material specifically focuses on how SEPIA could be used to support the market introduction of software products. Illustrative results have been taken from a design study and initial prototype developed at IPSI. For the intended application domain, SEPIA will provide three different activity spaces to cope with the communication bottlenecks, as described in section two, a *testing* space, a *case collection* space, and a *documentation* space.

In the *testing space*, a check list can be created and maintained for verifying the behavior of the software product and testing its usability. The check list consists of a series of test items structured via a "followed-by" relationship. Each item node may contain a detailed description of its purpose (see figure 1). The procedure required to carry out the test for each item is specified in a separate node. It is a composite node containing the detailed steps to be performed during the testing phase to achieve meaningful results.

The *case collection space* provides access to the documentation of problems (and their solution) encountered in previous sessions within the introduction or maintenance phases (see figure 2). If a problem is, for instance, identified during a test procedure the person testing the software can contact the developer of the software package. Together they can open the case collection space and search for reports on previous occurrences of the same or a similar problem. This accumulated knowledge help them to find or quickly develop a solution for this problem. Whenever a new problem is solved, the test engineer can create a case report by copying the results documented in the testing space to the case collection space. This documentation may contain a description of the conditions which caused the problem and of the solution that was found.

In the *documentation space*, the technical documentation, the user manual and training materials are made accessible. They serve as a source of information during the testing and introduction phase. At the same time they are subject to changes reflecting the customization process of the software product. The expert performing the software testing can annotate these documents and may cooperate with a technical writer who is responsible for the professional changes of texts and graphics.

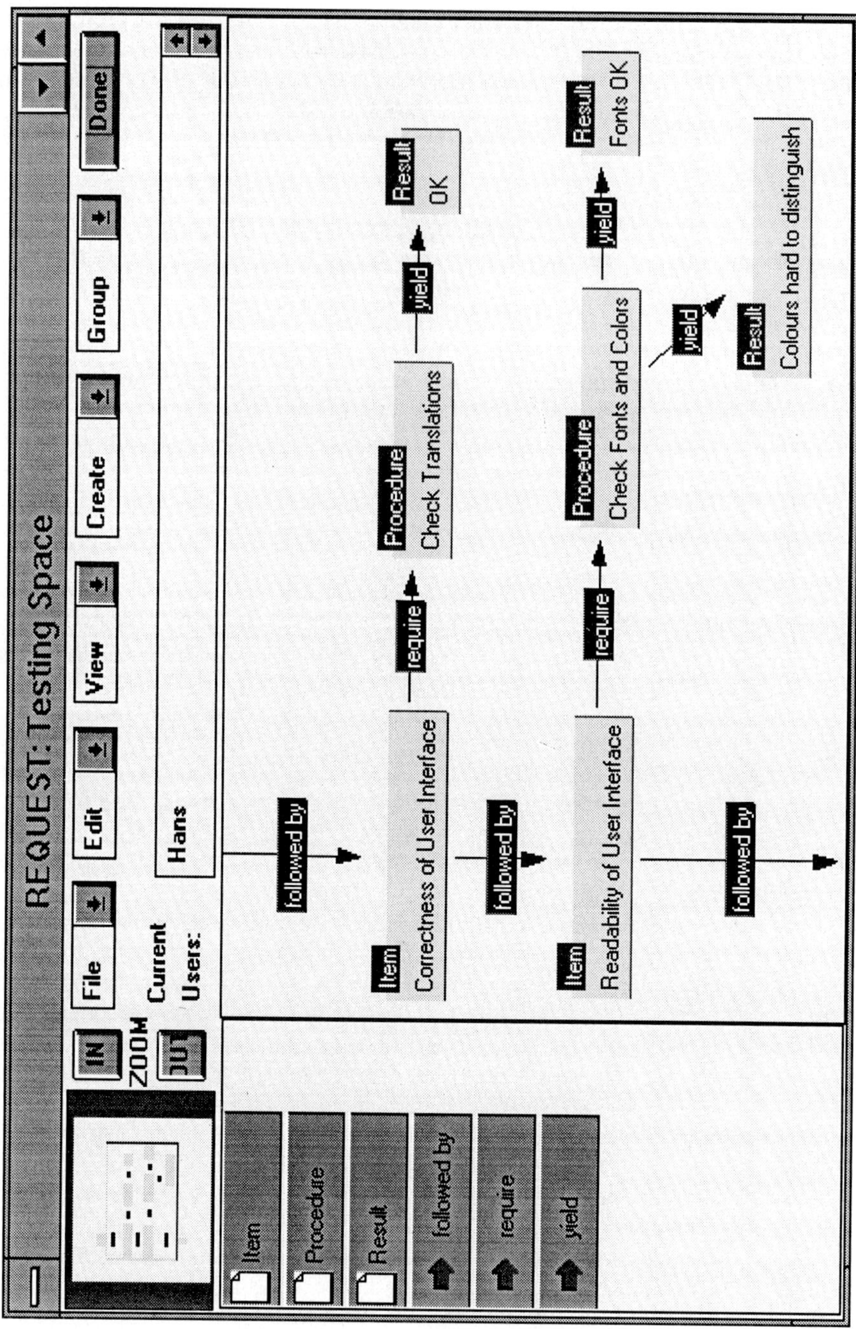

Fig. 1: Testing Space: test items, test procedures and results

The three spaces are complemented by an audio communication channel and by a sharing component which enables the users to share external standard applications. This makes it possible to jointly run, view and discuss the software to be tested simultaneously at different locations (e.g. in Germany and Italy).

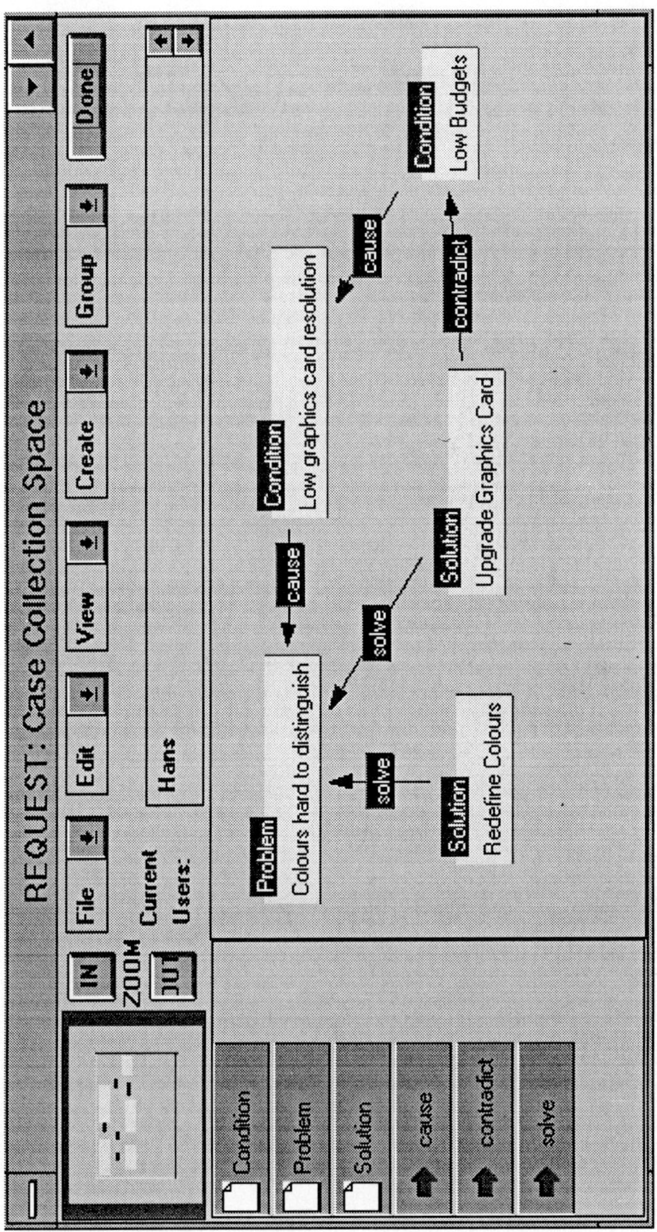

Fig. 2: Case Collection Space: problems and solutions

The component shares the user interfaces (windows) of the applications running on one user machine with all other participants of the cooperation.

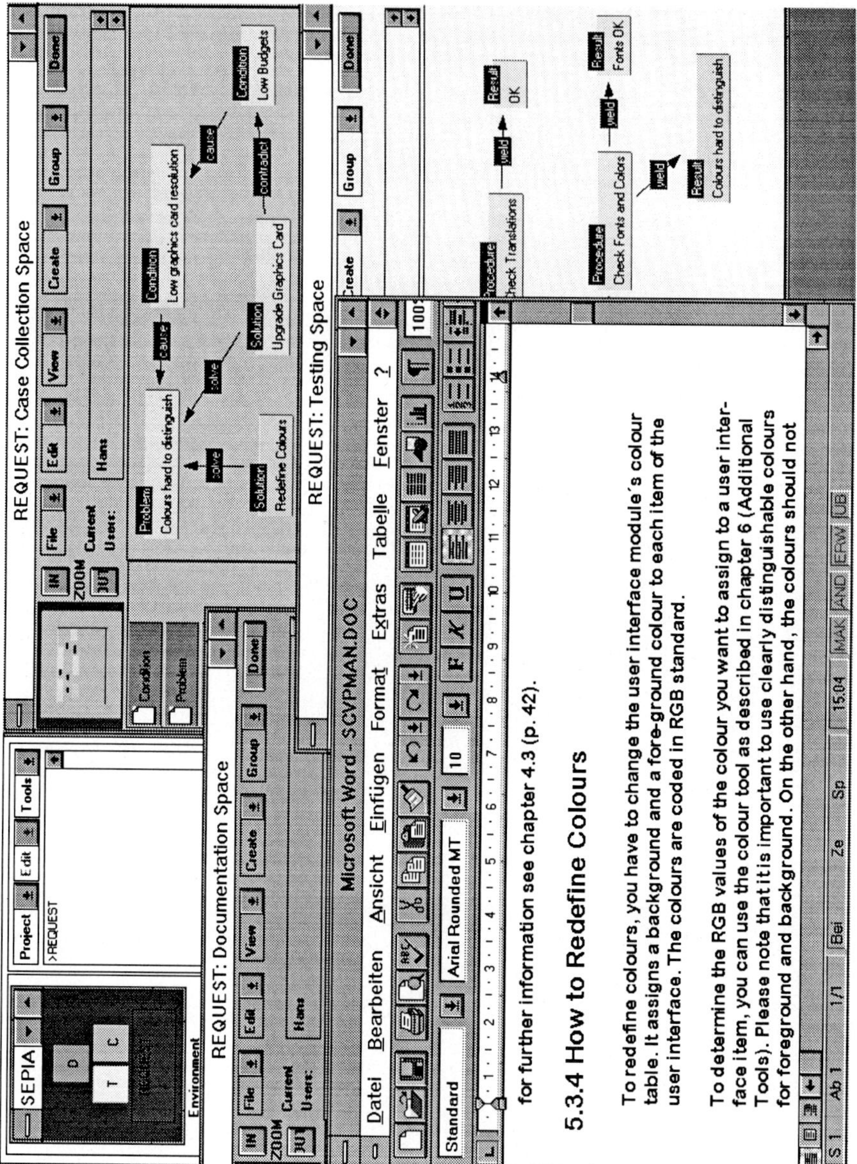

Fig. 3: Help desk environment with an external application

Figure 3 gives an example of the help desk environment with an external application consisting of three activity spaces and a window in which a Microsoft Word document is shared.

A TCP/IP connection via ISDN is used (socket communication) for the communication between the instances of cooperative SEPIA, running at different locations. This WAN is also the communication channel of the sharing component.

5. Future Research

SEPIA's functionality addresses all requirements that result from our interviews with software producers and distributors. Moreover, the system provides task specific support for those activities of software introduction for which communication bottlenecks were identified, i.e. testing, adaption and problem handling. The main bebefits of aour system are as follows:

- increases the marketing speed,
- decreases the effort and overheads of time intensive activities, such as translation, localizing, testing, training and user support,
- reduce errors due to communication breaks and misunderstandings,
- minimize costs by reducing expenses for travelling,
- avoid wrong design decisions due to lack of "local feedback",
- improve partner and customer satisfaction with respect to both the product and the provided services.

These benefits are particularly relevant for SMEs who strive to survive in a highly competitive market and have to cope with severe constraints on manpower and budget. An initial prototype of SEPIA has been adapted to the requirements of supporting the market introduction of software products. This prototype provides all necessary workspaces and the kernel of related cooperation facilities. For testing purposes, this version is currently installed in a LAN environment. Future development will expand this version to WANs. We also intend to use the full functionality in a pilot project in order to support the introduction of specific software in several national branches of the European market.

References

[1] Berners-Lee T. "Hypertext Transfer Protocol (HTTP), CERN, December 1991 (see <ftp://info.cern.ch/pub/www/doc/http-spec.txt>)

[2] Conklin J. "Hypertext: An Introduction and Survey", Computer Magazine, September, pp.17-40, 1987.

[3] Ellis C.A., Gibbs S. J., Rein G.L. "Groupware - Some Issues and Experiences", Communications of the ACM , vol.34/1, pp.38-58, Jan. 1991.

[4] Streitz N., Haake J., Hannemann J., Lemke A., Schütt H., Schuler W., Thüring M. "SEPIA: A cooperative hypermedia authoring environment", In D. Lucarella, J. Nanard, M. Nanard, P. Paolini (Eds.), Proceedings of the 4 th ACM Conference on Hypertext (ECHT '92), Milano, Italy, November 30 to. December 4, 1992, ACM Press, pp.11-22, New York, 1992.

GNOSIS Tool for Computer-based Training

C.T. Davarakis, A.V. Harissis
Systema Informatics
Aisopou 22A, G-15122 Maroussi, Greece

Abstract

This work describes the GNOSIS tool, developed within the scope of an national initiative, with financial support of the European Commission (Telematique-2). The purpose of the developed tool was primarily to provide the necessary environment for a distance learning process, utilising both a stand alone computer-based training environment, and a concrete interface over a VBI (Vertical Blank Interval) TV channel transmission of incremental educational data. The ultimate target of the developed product is to provide the necessary environment for Computer-based Training, either at a supervised training mode or at an autonomous standalone mode or at a distance learning mode.

1. Introduction

The avoidance of the general purpose tools (e.g. Authorware, Toolbook etc.) introduce additional overheads (in execution time, hardware requirements, user training) and are not mandatary for developing exclusively educational software.

The implemention of an efficient (Computer-Based Training) package without using general purpose tools was for us a major challenge Very important, at this point, was the distiction between *educational, learning and training* environments. We advocate the approach of a largely informative environment under the educational scope (holding an entire field of interest), consequently a learning environment comprising specific chunks of information and a methodology appropriate for using this information to the audience or users.

Finally, a training environment exhibits a participative learning process, determined by the increased involvement of the users and by the easy learning, proof of learning and validation of learning mechanisms.

The GNOSIS tool is a training environment which accompanied by the necessary information in terms of an approved field of interest, proliferates an educational profile. Moreover, the GNOSIS tool enables the creative trainer to design and develop an Edutainment Application (i.e. education through entertainment). The version 1.0 of the GNOSIS tool was the end-product of a Telematique-2 (TAMESIS) project, and consists of two parts: *(i) the teachers' module* for implementation or modification of multimedia courses, and *(ii) the students´ module* for running the multimedia courses. Following basic guidelines were here used:

- "minimise the teacher's required knowledge on computers",
- "follow a natural teaching model, i.e. present educational material to the student, let him study it, and then train him on this material"
- "minimise hardware requirements for the student's computer (the student is here the end-user of the package).

Taking these guidelines into consideration, we decided to use Microsoft Windows (version 3.1 or above) as *operating system*, since it provided sufficient support for multimedia applications and it is also widely spread. The basic concept should be:*"A «teacher» creates a «lesson» which the «student» «plays»"*. There should be two programmes, the *Authoring Tool* (AT) to create the lessons and the *Run-Time* (RT) to play the lessons. The AT is used by the teacher and the RT by the student. The *CBT* (Computer-based Training) package should support static image data (using bitmaps - BMPs), sound data (using wave form files - WAVs) and text data (using text files - TXTs) in order to present information to the student. But, the design should also be able to incorporate other data types, mainly video data (AVIs), if needed. There should be of various types of exercises available in order to check that the student understood the material presented. These exercises are easily described in TXT files.

2. Conceptual Design

The generic concept for building GNOSIS modules consists of:

- A *Linking Interface* to the operating system MS-Windows (3.1, win95, winNT). The Windows platforms constituted a strategic priority due to the overwhelming target market, therefore all three modes (Supervised training (S), Autonomous standalone (AE) and Distance Learning (DL), will be supported by MS-Windows.
- An *Authoring Environment*, mainly used by the instructors for the creation of a suitable course holding with the necessary material either for S or for AE or for DL training.
- A *Student Run Time Environment* either for S or for AE or for DL lectures.
- A *Multimedia Distributed Object Base Management* system catering for a modular approach; towards the build-up of a dynamic Educational Information Repository. In version 1.0, this repository manages static image data (bitmaps, BMPs) sound data (wave form files - WAVs), textdata (text files - TXTs) and video data (AVIs). Furthermore, the new version is being build to handle Windows 95 information and Virtual Reality Worlds (Superscape VR and DXF files).
- An *estimation and validation mechanism*, evaluating the performance of the students either on-line (S, DL) or through log files (AE), and also giving statistics of the assimilation percentages.

The kernel design comprised of the creation, development and execution of training stages. Each lesson was divided into Stages. Each stage was further divided in two parts, an "Introduction" (used to present data to the student) and an

"Exercise" which should be compleated by students. The students' response should be checked and results presented back to the students, so they could see how well they replied and why. We allowed only one introduction or only one exercise in a stage. Each stage should also contains "execution options" in order to control the flow of each lesson.

A general flow outline will be (see figure 1).

- Initial multimedia information is communicated to the students. Show an image, play a sound recording, display some text.
- Let the student do some exercise
- Proceed to next stage.

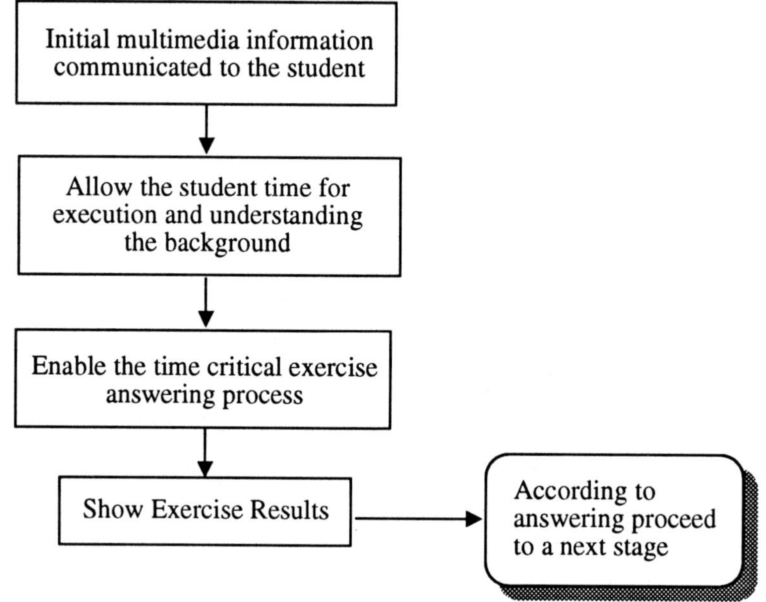

Fig. 1: Conceptual Model

The efficient packing of the data is an interesting problem. Text data and exercise data have been embedded in the lesson file, since these are different in each lesson. But video, image and sound data could be reused in various lessons on a CBT course [1]. We opted for enabling the teacher to decide whether to embed these data or to «refer» to them (as external files). Obviously, these external files should be given to the student, periodically (in case of S or DL modes) or on the installation phase (in case for S or AE modes).

2.1 GNOSIS Authoring Tool

The Authoring Tool of GNOSIS is a creative tool, enabling the instructor to activate his expertise and knowledge by using the *cohesion of presentations* (which may be in multimedial form), *of experimentation* (via hypermedia information access) and *of exercise tests* (via a set of exercise styles stored in the library, which also has the ability to store new exercises). Ultimately the instructor may either want to create new lessons or edit existing ones. The main Authoring console contains the following active areas:

- Main Information Space,.
- Stage Information Space,
- Stage Controls Space, and
- Help Space.

As the Authoring Tool is primarily used by the Instructors, when he prepares the training material for each lesson. Text files, image files, sound and video files can be incorporated in the prepared lesson. Standard text editors, image editors, video editors etc., can be freely used for the manipulation of each file before their integration in a new lesson. Special facilities are available for team work (i.e. for several persons working together in order to create a common lesson) which allow grouping, overviewing and finally selection and adjustment of the material. After performing the installation and execution, the authoring tool provides a set of possible selections. In the process of creating a new lesson, a set of Library Stored Lesson modes may be used, instead of one creating new Lesson modes.

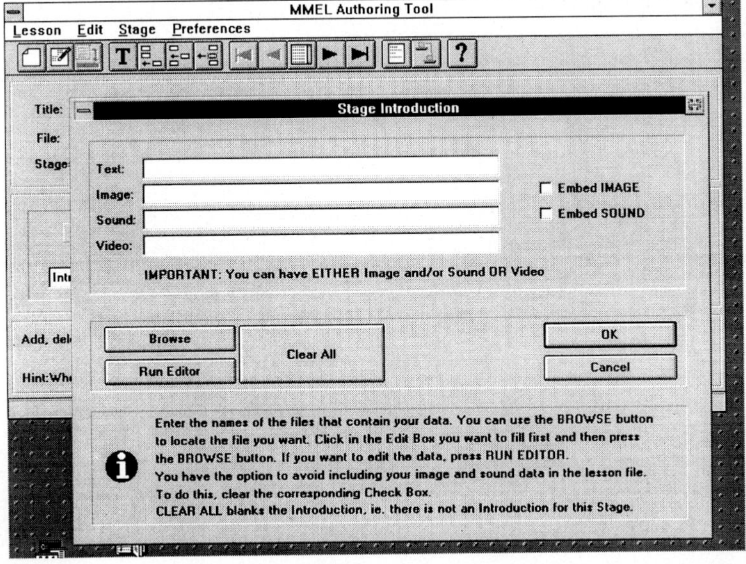

Fig.2: Authoring Tool of GNOSIS

In the first GNOSIS version, the following files are supported, while we are in the process of building cross-file filtering options:

- Text Files (of type .TXT)
- Image Files (of type .BMP)
- Sound Files (of type .WAV), and
- Video Files (of type .AVI).

In the process of creating new lessons and courses one can estimate the time which is needed in order to complete a process step. Below is a list of Archived Lesson modes:

1. Multiple Choice,
2. Matrix Selection,
3. Pair Selection,
4. Text Entry,
5. Right/ Wrong,
6. Hypertext, non linear information access, and
7. Accent Test (Mainly for Foreign Languages).

2.2 GNOSIS Run Time Programme

The Run Time, aiming to activate the student environment, has itself developers (Instructors) options. In the last version, the user may advance certain stages or go directly to a particular stage. It is a possibility given only to instructors, to be able to see «what they have created».

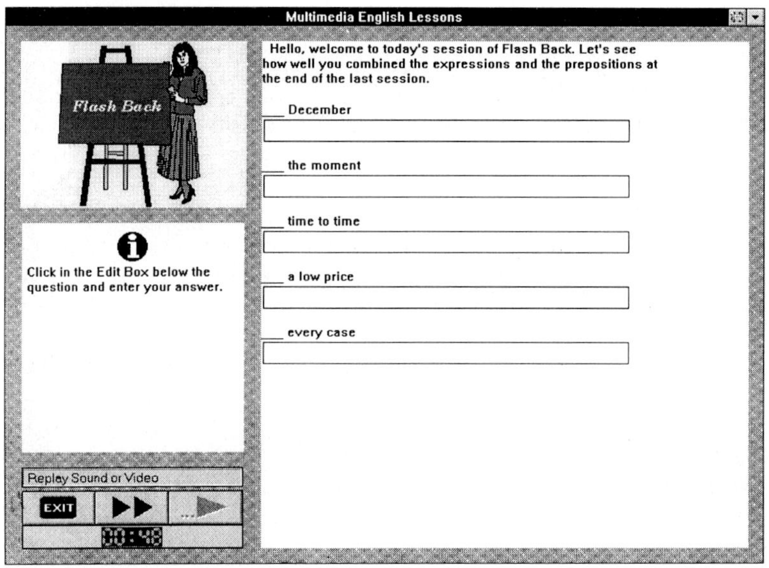

Fig.3: Run Time Programme of GNOSIS

All students should drive through the Lesson (or Course of Lessons) navigated by the route/routes that their teacher creates. It is, of course, very important to state that each student drives through the lessons on their own, the only limit being the speed of their PC. The main differences, in terms of design issues are as follows. *(1)* The button ADVANCE enables the Instructor option. *(2)* The file search is effected using full paths at the real address of files.of the various files. *(3)* Paths are given implicitly in the Student mode, via a relative address indirection. The Run Time enables the selection of Today's Lesson, according to the individual needs of each student. A limited number of control functions are available in the Student mode (e.g. EXIT, REPLAY, SOUND, VIDEO)

3. Performance and Usability

A very important aspect in the development process of any multimedia application is the check of its usability. This is normally done when the product has already been developed. However, aspects of usability should be considered from the beginning of the development, and this is what we did in the GNOSIS tool. Moreover, the performance of the developed product must be carefully considered as it has to do with the acceptability by several classes of users within a large market.

3.1 Usability Framework

By the term usability one may refer to the extend to which an end-user is able to carry out required tasks successfully and without difficulties, using the computer application system. According to Nielson [4], usability is traditionally associated with five *usability parameters*, which can also be applied for multimedia applications: *easy to learn, efficient to use, easy to remember, few errors, and pleasant to use.*

A framework for evaluating user-computer interaction is described by Sweeney, Maguire and Shackel [5]. It classifies usability evaluations in terms of three dimensions: the approach to evaluation, the type of evaluation and the time of evaluation in context of the product lifecycle. The approaches described are user-based, theory-based, and expert-based. Usability testing is defined as trying out the design of a piece of software or hardware in its development stages, before you have gone so far in finalising it that you can't backup and make changes [6l. Usability professionals gather, clarify and describe the viewpoint of the users, so that developers see it clearly and can also apply it effectively during the development process.. Usability tests are designed to identify difficulties and also to recommend solutions, with the aim of producing a «sit down and use it easily> product.

3.2 Performance Aspects

The performance of the GNOSIS tool was investigated by running several tests related to following capabilities:

1. *accessibility* of the various subenvironments and functions,
2. *responsiveness* to the user requested commands
3. *efficiency* for the resulting percentage of conveyed information over the creation complexity, and
4. *comprehensibility* with respect to various procedures and functions.

We have run the tests at a very early stage, and with the help of the end-user teachers and students, and the agreed opinion of the developers. As a result the GNOSIS tool has achieved an increased usability rate.

More accurately, with respect to efficiency tests we have estimated the Creation over Understanding Ratio (*CUR*). CUR can be estimated when for a particular information chunk, we enable an instructor to create an electronic lesson. Additionally, we have to evaluate at the students' side, via computing, the time and percentage of understanding for the particular chunk of information. This is a crude way of benchmarking educational software. It is crude because in order to be able to cross examination of different products you need to have a common evaluation information chunk, a common set of instructors and respectively a common set of students.

An open problem is the fact that even in these conditions you could not make a golden precision checking, due to the fact of latent training. The latter occurs when a student or teacher is faced with the same problem under different umbrellas (products). Only his/her first (under the first product exposure) solution attempts are genuine, the rest have an inherent rate of latent training. From the literature we found an average 24 hours to 1 minute CUR for products in 1994, but we were not able to find similar measures for 1995 products.

For a one hour lesson developed by the GNOSIS tool, and concerning English as a foreign language, we estimated an average of 16 hours hours of creation time for an "one minute" execution. Pre-requisites for this estimate were the existing information material and the teachers' exact knowledge of the exercises. Also the one hour execution was estimated for the worst case which is when the «student» directly answers the correct questions and opts for the right solutions (i.e. Instructor monitoring mode, in the GNOSIS run time). Also, possible image and video observations where kept to a minimum, or estimated as null for the computing of CUR.

For purposes of mounting the created course of lessons on a CD ROM, we have considered utilising the encouraging CUR estimate to attract education information providers towards this target. Afterall, on a CD-ROM we will have to find the relative merits between putting increased video time (up to possibly 90 minutes, e.g. CNN's Yearly CD-ROM), or increased number of images (maximum of about 6000 half screen 16 colour images). It is primary a question of pedagogues and technology constraint, and this is our concern when we try to utilise GNOSIS to produce educational CD ROM titles.

4. Transmission over TV VBI

In the case of the Telematique-2 (TAMESIS project), the GNOSIS environment was interfaced to a Modem for the periodic transmission of lessons to the TV headquarters (Antenna channel), for the consequent broadcast to the potential students. To that end the GNOSIS environment was augmented by a Transmit Lesson routine within the Authoring programme. In the receiving side of students, the Run Time environment was also enhanced to interface a VBI interface box, which enabled the students to transparently receive new Lessons. This interface is capable of activating a receive lesson routine, to hold and store the new lessons, especially to archive directories for further utilisation. In this case the students may execute the received lessons at their own learning steps. The television channel transmits the new lessons at pre-defined time intervals, and the students only have to keep their PC turned on (not even their TV set). The receiver routine caters for faulty and duplicate archiving. Therefore, in the undertaken project the demonstration carried out was done both for an autonomous mode (AE) and for a distance learning (DL) mode. Estimation of ratios of the time and effort to produce an electronic lesson over the execution time, and over the volume of training information as well as the apprehension percentage by the students are here expected.

Hence on the brink of enabling thousands of people to enjoy the services offered by large, distributed multimedia systems in their own homes through Interactive Television Systems [2], we have attempted to exploit existing pseudo interactive possibilities. It is obvious that conventional television systems and architectures must be re-designed to support new services (e.g. home shopping, interactive entertainment, financial transactions etc.). Exploitation of the VBI zone can only serve at this initial stage, for testing challenging multimedia environments.

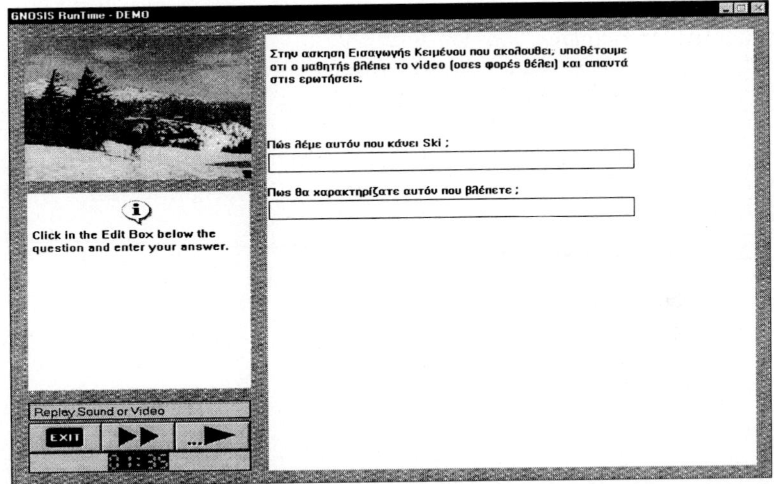

Fig. 4: A video clip in GNOSIS environment

5. Conclusions

The tools, products and applications related to the GNOSIS environment are numerous. Audio-visual material can provide valuable aids for teaching systems. However, a system is only useful if the learner remains active and motivated [3]. GNOSIS attempts to use intelligent simulation (e.g. Accent Tests), dynamic links (on-line generation of links based on student behaviour), and multimedia composition and creation.

The GNOSIS conceptual model enables user change of the parameters of a database or simulation of system knowledge about components in the environment (through semantic representations, scripts and formulae); and system reasoning about user actions, and also immediate response.

All already mentioned user requirements turned into system requirements and through usability tests have been proved as correct, consistent and complete. The implementation of a Course of Lessons on "English as a Foreign Language" confirm our real test bed and the market-oriented approach of GNOSIS.. The main effort at this moment concentrates in optimising the usability and performance issues.

Finally, and as more than 50 million CD-ROM drivers will be installed, world-wide, before the end of 1995, according to market researcher Dataquest in San Jose California [7]; we are now in the process of creating a complete CD-ROM edutainment (i.e. education through entertainment) title by utilising the GNOSIS environment.

References

1. Harissis A.V. "Developing a CBT package: «GNOSIS» a functional approach", International Foundation for Computer based Education, in Banking and Finance Journal, July 1995.
2. Furht B. et. al. "Design issues for Interactive Television Systems", IEEE Computer, Vol.28, No.5, May 1995.
3. Woolf B.P. and Hall W. "Multimedia Pedagogues: Interactive Systems for Teaching and Learning", Computer, Vol.28, No.5, pp.74-80, May 1995.
4. Nielsen J. "Hypertext and Hypermedia", Academic Press, San Diego, 1990.
5. Sweeney M., Maguire M., Shackel B. "Evaluating user-computer interaction: a framework", Int. Journal Man Machine Studies, Vol.38, pp.689-711, 1993.
6. Abelow D. "Wake up! You have entered the transition zone", Computer Language, pp.41-49, March 1993.
7. Bournellis C. "CD-ROM technology takes off", IEEE Computer, pp.11-14, July 1995.

Information Navigation in Teaching with DATABOOK

S. Pfleger
Expertise Information Systems
Budapesterstr.21, D-81669 Munich

P. Krauß
Technische Universität München
Arcisstr.21, D-80333 Munich

Abstract

Computer-based information navigation, a Virtual Reality approach, provides the technological platform for accessing large and complex data in an interactive way in administrative and industrial areas, technical documentation, teaching, control and maintenance. This paper presents the computer-supported information navigation system DATABOOK which is used in teaching at the Technical University of Munich. It runs on PC, and uses a relational inversion technique with true immersion in order to ensure efficient user interaction. The hardware development is based on the Siemens microcontroller SAB-80C166, and has been performed in co-operation with the company Siemens.

Efficient access to knowledge with substantial cost reductions are expected in industrial development and testing, if large and complex documentations on "written paper" are replaced by modern information navigation systems. Information navigation in complex maintenance areas (e.g. maintenance of airplanes and industrial installations) is another interesting application area of Information Navigation, since it ensures direct access to expert knowledge all over the word in critical situations.

1. Introduction

Information Navigation, a new achievement of the Virtual Reality technology, is based on *(i) an immersive technique* which ensures the "feeling of presence", of being in the real space, and surrounded by real objects, and also of being capable to interact with all available objects, *(ii)* an appropriate set of *tools* for providing efficient information processing during immersion, and *(iii)* comfortable input-output devices for the interaction with the user.

The use of information navigation facilities in teaching permits a student to be an actor [8] rather than a spectator, and his active role allows him to choose his own pace of learning, and to interact freely with the system (e.g. to ask questions, explore functionality, test and validate) with the aim of consolidating learning. The student can choose the most appropriate level of detail, considering his position in the knowledge acquisition process, and dynamically access multimodal data (text, images, graphics, flow charts, source code).

The Information Navigation System DATABOOK was developed with the aim of providing computer-aided teaching of microprocessor architecture and microprogamming in the "real" processing environment of a microprocessor, at the Technical University of Munich.

The software facilities use a relational inversion technique and provide both true immersion and interaction to the user in the PC environment. The hardware development was performed in co-operation with Siemens, and uses a microcontroller chip of Siemens with the CPU-core of the type SAB-80C166. Adaption to different levels of difficulty during the training process, and the customization to other microprocessor applications areas are future research topics which will ensure the development of cost-effective and highly qualitative technological platforms for computer-based information navigation in education, training, and Information Systems in medical areas [9].

This paper is structured as follows:

- the information navigation ontology is briefly presented in section 2,
- the topics of interactive teaching are addressed in section 3,
- an example of the real application of the DATABOOK system in microprocessing programming is presented in section 4, and
- the merits and limitations of our work are discussed in section 5 together with future developments.

2. Information Navigation Ontology

Ontology is here an explicit specification of an abstract and simplified view of the world, that we wish to represent for information navigation. Formally, the ontology of information navigation is a statement of a logical theory, and can be described by the set of entities (object, their concepts, their behaviour in execution environment, their constituent parts, and other entities) together with their relationships.

The set of objects build the domain of discourse, and their different instantiations build the agents. We associate the names of the entities in the universe of discourse (e.g. classes, relations, functions, or other objects) with human-readable text, describing what the names mean, and formal axioms that constrain the interpretation and the well-formed use of these terms.

The communication of a set of agents about a domain of discourse is performed in accordance with ontological commitments. Knowledge is attributed to agents by observing their actions; an agent is assumed to know something, if it acts correctly in order to achieve its goals. The actions of agents are based on a "*tell and ask*" functional interface, where a client interacts with an agent by making logical assertions (*tell*) and asking questions (*ask*).

Progmatically, the navigation ontology defines the vocabulary with which queries and assertions are exchanged among agents, together with the agreements to use the shared vocabulary in a coherent and consistent way.

However, consistency doesn´t imply completeness, and an agent is not required to answer all queries that can be formulated in the shared vocabulary. This means that not all questions can be answered in an information navigation application like an interactive teaching system. *Knowledge acquisition tools* play an important role in Information Navigation system efficiency. A hierarchical structure of the interface ontology for knowledge acquisition tools is illustrated in figure 1, and is expressed by four classes:

- dialogue class,
- parts class,
- presentation class, and
- knowledge representation class.

The *dialogue* class defines the user commands. The dialogue is here expressed by dialogue operations (see DASH [1]) and their effects that can take place in an interface discourse with an user. The user-tool dialogue consists of one or many dialogue structures for determining the way in which a user can navigate through the dialogue elements (e.g. windows, browsers, text fields). They also include fixed and variable sequences of commands. Each command processes one or many inputs, and can be activated in accordance with a set of preconditions. Command execution implies processing of actions. The correctness of an input, a command or an output is investigated by validators.

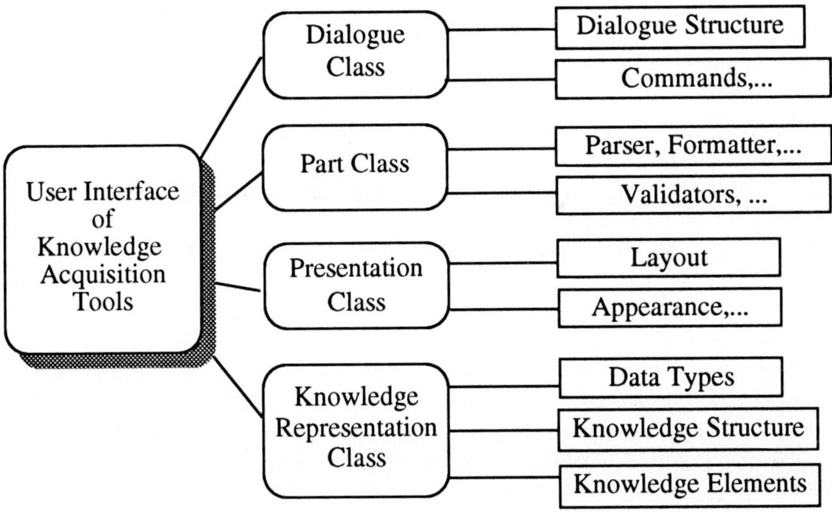

Fig.1: Interface Ontology of Knowledge Acquisition Tools

Several dialogue tools perform knowledge acquisition, allowing information manipulation and visualisation (e.g. by menues) and knowledge representation.
The *presentation class* is expressed by element layout (e.g. hight and width) and appearance objects (e.g. with slots like colour and font (see Interface Builder Tool supplied by the NeXT environment), and are implementation dependent (see the run-time system MART, as presented by Mecano [5]).

The *knowledge representation* class defines the types (data types, knowledge structure) and elements of the knowledge.

Neches [3] pointed out a number of problems that a knowledge acquisition tool should address: *identification* of the domain knowledge that will be formally encoded, *mapping* that knowledge into the encoding utilized by the computer, *validation* of the encoding (i.e. that the encoding accurately reflects the knowledge), and *knowledge validation* (i.e. that the knowledge is appropriate for a given task). Several developed tools based on PROTÉGÉ-II [5], Mecano [5], DOTS [2], SHELTER [3], HUMANOID [4] give the conviction that a common ontology for *knowledge acquisition tools* is useful and necessary, but the question of "how to achieve it by low costs?" remains.

The main *capabilities* of DATABOOK knowledge acquisition tools were implemented at low costs, and are as follows:

- *Visualisation and browsing* of existing knowledge, with the ability to see various hierarchical structures of knowledge and different clusters of related information types.
- *Editing and review* of knowledge, and *entry* of new knowledge.
- *Search and retrieval* of specific parts of the knowledge base.
- *Sequencing* of knowledge entry and *annotation.*

3. Interactive Teaching

The challenge of building good interactive systems [7] for teaching imposes the use of modern Virtual Reality technologies in order to make sure that they do not distract the student's attention from the subject to be learned, and that he can use images and computer graphics. These systems deal with a large amount of information, and therefore require advanced approaches in designing the information navigation ontology.

The replacement of usual books (written on papers) by teaching systems on computer imposes the existence of an easy access to information, and should also permit that the user to work his own way, and in his familiar working environment. In contrast to documents on paper, the teaching systems with graphics on screen have the advantage of allowing interactive access to the knowledge; they also allow to navigate information in different ways, since a book on the screen can be accessed by many paths in various ways.

The classical approach of functional decomposition is not appropriate for constructing a manageable system with a realistic effort. A better alternative is provided by *Object Oriented Design* techniques [6], which require a data decomposition approach in the presentation layer with a inference from the behaviour of the total system to the behaviour of its constituent parts. The main advantage of object oriented programming is the fact that less code is here needed, and therefore less development and debugging time and costs.

A new development system for teaching interactively microprocessor programming at the Technical University of Munich was started in 1994. This was an opportunity to try advanced approaches in designing an appropriate information navigation ontology, and to develop an efficient and easy to use system, taking into account following contraints:

- *Customisation*: adaption to the individual user (i.e. with no computer experience) which should maintain the user's usual working environment.
- *Screen splitting* facilities should allow parallel display of several types of execution information and source code documentations (flow charts, source code statements, etc.)
- The user should *interact intuitively* with the development system without distracting his attention from his work. He should not be obliged to think about complex commands or sophisticated syntax related to the computer platform.

Open questions were:

"Is such a system practicable?"
"What is the expected development effort ?"

The selection of the most appropriate technology was an important task during the development of the DATABOOK Information Navigation System. The Seeheim model, i.e. the standard architecture of interactive systems, leads to large procedural programs. The user interface was expected to become overcrowded with buttons and menus due to the requested user fuctions, no doubt a common practice in many interactive systems.

The *object oriented design* was one of the most encouraging techniques, and we used it in the design of our system The availability of standard user-interface toolkits in the computer platform allowed a substancial reduction to the expected development and maintenance costs. We also used the standard event handler and communication between the objects by message passing, which ensured that the operating system controls the user actions, and no effort was spent for specific control facilities.

The usual practice in developing and programming microprocessors is dictated by the existence of documentation in printed paper format. The user normally uses a book with the microprocessor's description and also detailed description of the used microcontroller (i.e. the manufactor's data book for a specific chip type), the information about the source code of his program, and some documentation of the dynamic system (block diagrams, flow charts, etc.). All these documents are normally available on paper.

The replacement of the paper by a computer screen has the advantage of allowing us to interact in another way with these documents. For example, in the book the pictures of memory cells are passive elements. On the screen it is possible also to show the actual values of each cell. Additionally computer-based interaction allows interactive testing, and on-line programme improvement.

The static information of a book "on paper" has been replaced by interactive information navigation on the screen (see figure 2). The multimodal developer's documents are activated in the same way. Selected tracing points in the flowcharts are used for testing the programmes during virtual execution in the real execution environment. Together with the memory cells and registers in the active databook the developer can visualise programme execution, due to the dynamic access to the memory and register data. All information displayed on screen belongs to a world which is familiar to the developer, and also easy to use since no a priori knowledge about the interface syntax (e.g. system's commands) is requested.

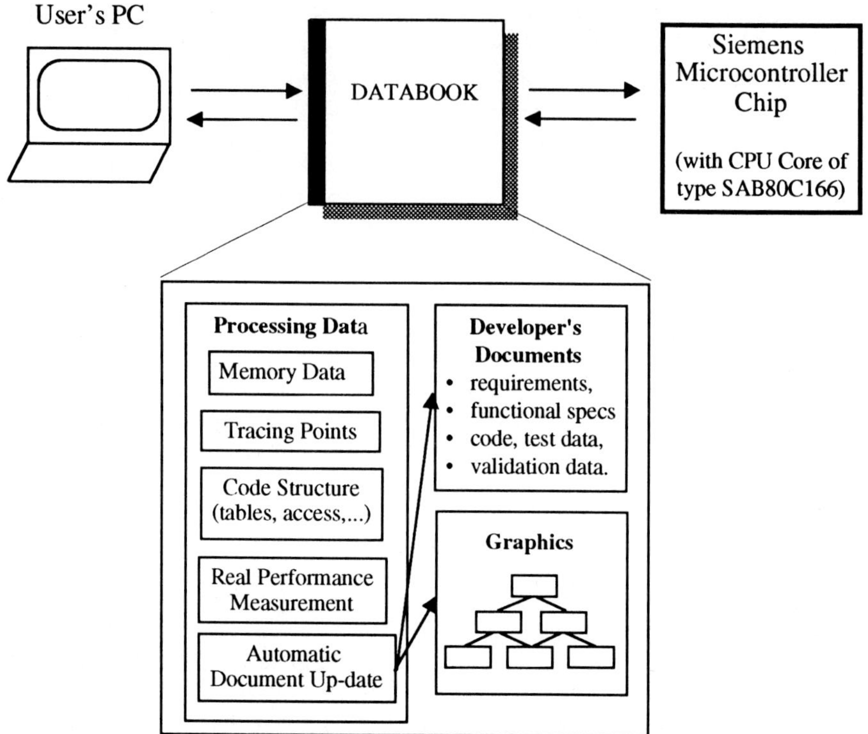

Fig.2: Application of the DATABOOK in teaching microprocessor architecture and microprogramming

The system provides text and graphics inside the windows. Our ontology is as simple as working with a book on paper, with the main advantage of having selective access to dynamic data in the real execution environment, and parallel display of connected data and descriptions.

4. Moving the Dialogue Control to the User

A very simple example of the real application of the DATABOOK system in microprocessor programming is given below. Screen splitting allow the students to obtain simultaneous access to the documentation stored on various levels of abstraction, and also to real execution data.

Each student can "access" the microcontroller directly, and can gradually learn, starting with simple tasks for beginners, until he becomes an expert. He can start with a simple view of the Siemens Microcontroller Chip architecture (see figure3).

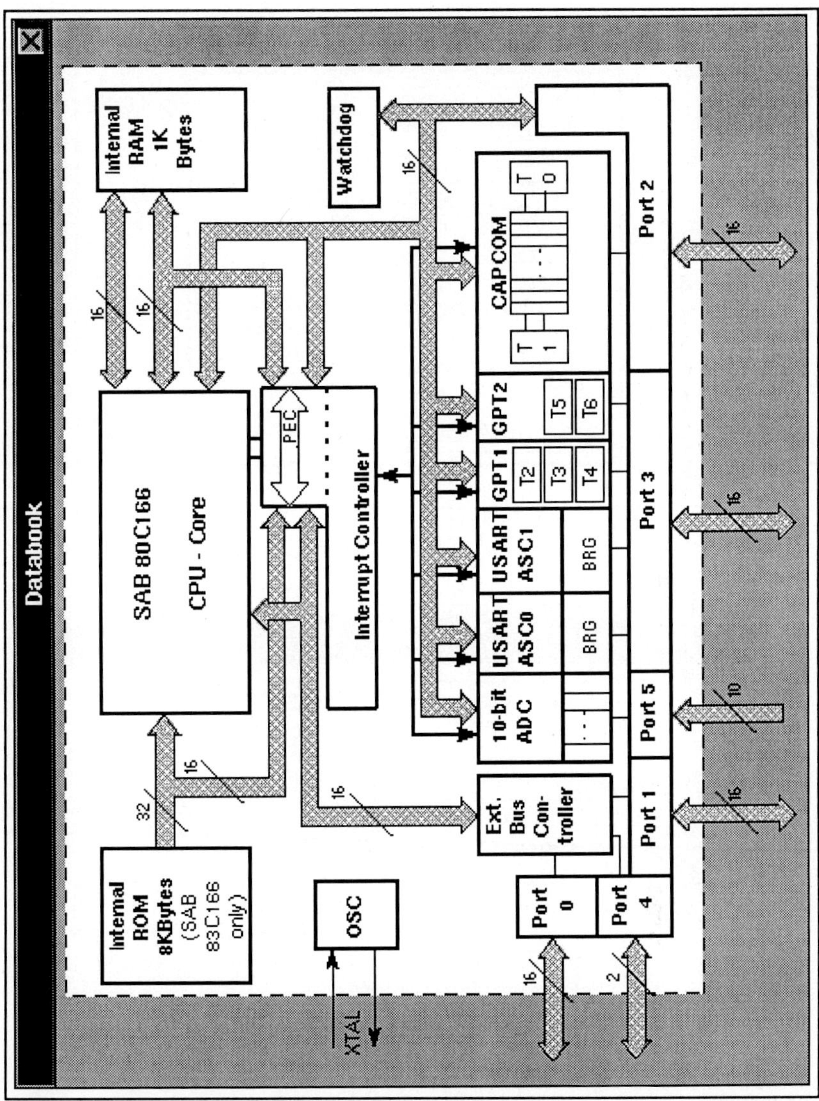

Fig.3: DATABOOK view of the Siemens Microcontroller Chip

In the next learning step a detailed description the CPU-Core component of the type SAB-80C166 can be accessed (see figure 4). The stepwise refinement is a well known design technique in industrial development, and several levels of specification detail can be accessed for programming microprocessor applications. Application testing is also supported, e.g. by programme tracing points, as illustrated in figure 5. Screen splitting facilities allow parallel display of several types of execution information and documentation (flow charts, instructions, etc.), together with their interconnection information.

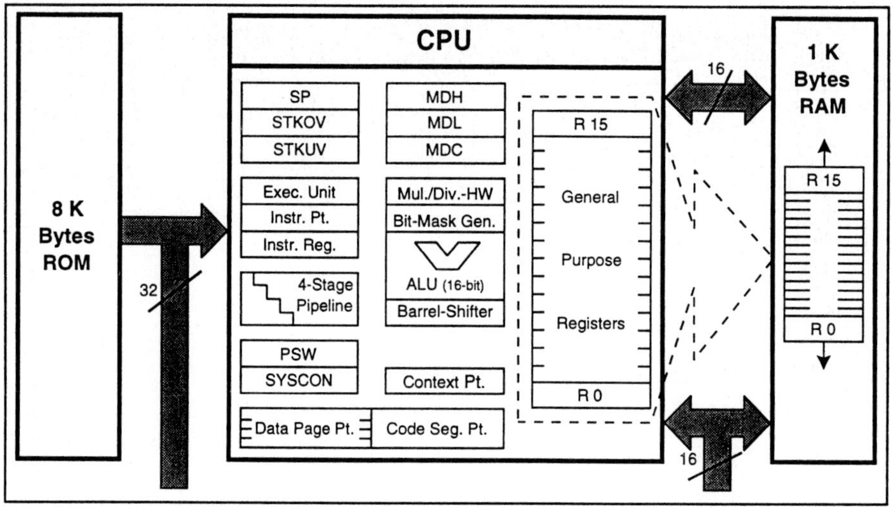

Fig.4: DATABOOK view of the CPU-Core of the type SAB-80C166

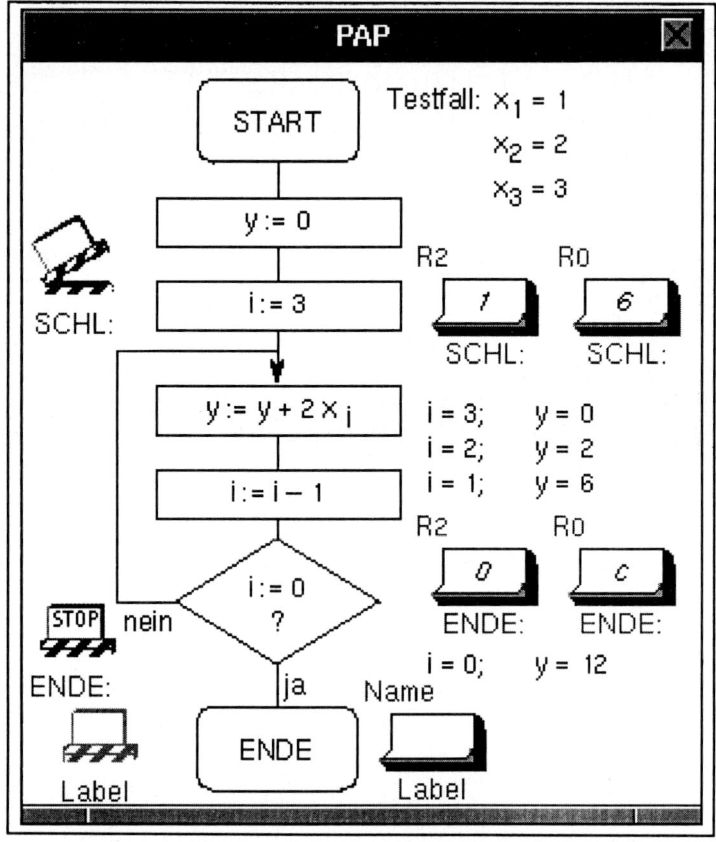

Fig.5: DATABOOK view of tracing points in flowcharts

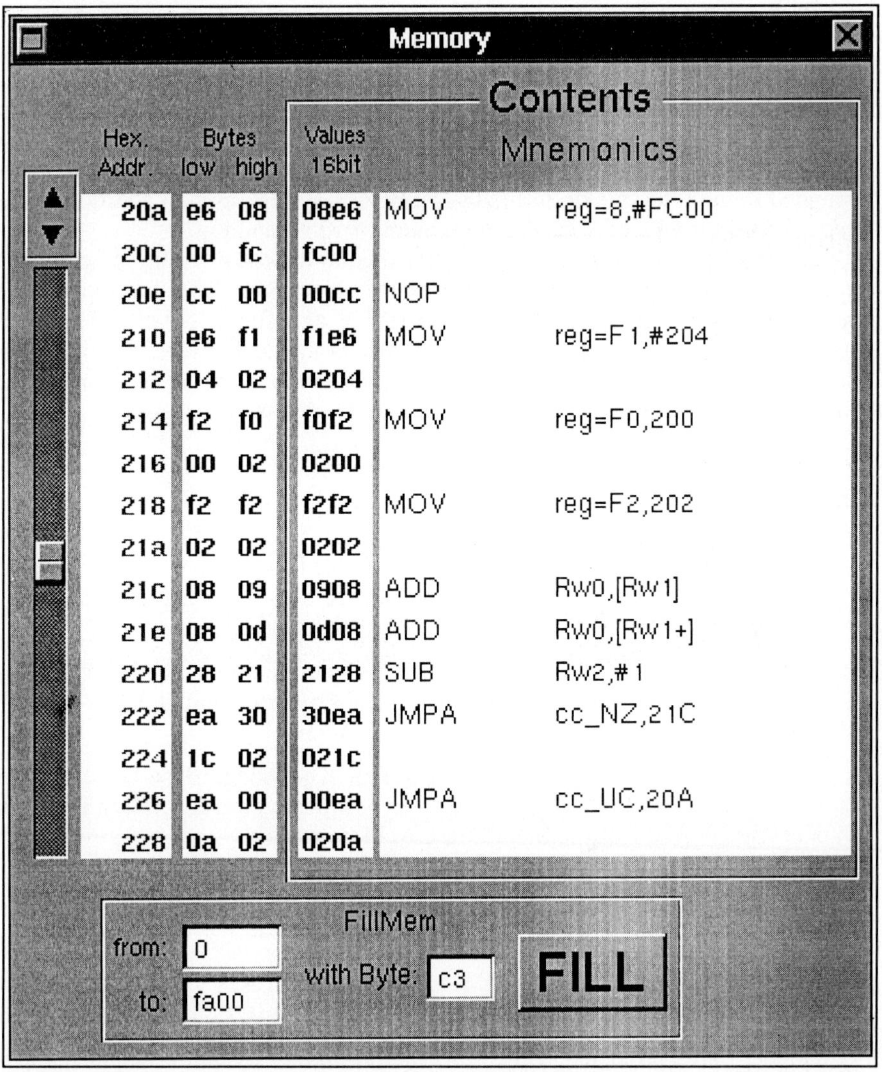

Memory

Contents

Hex. Addr.	Bytes low	Bytes high	Values 16bit	Mnemonics	
20a	e6	08	08e6	MOV	reg=8,#FC00
20c	00	fc	fc00		
20e	cc	00	00cc	NOP	
210	e6	f1	f1e6	MOV	reg=F1,#204
212	04	02	0204		
214	f2	f0	f0f2	MOV	reg=F0,200
216	00	02	0200		
218	f2	f2	f2f2	MOV	reg=F2,202
21a	02	02	0202		
21c	08	09	0908	ADD	Rw0,[Rw1]
21e	08	0d	0d08	ADD	Rw0,[Rw1+]
220	28	21	2128	SUB	Rw2,#1
222	ea	30	30ea	JMPA	cc_NZ,21C
224	1c	02	021c		
226	ea	00	00ea	JMPA	cc_UC,20A
228	0a	02	020a		

FillMem

from: 0 to: fa00 with Byte: c3 **FILL**

Fig.6: DATABOOK view of the memory adresses and the stored data in both hexadecimal and source code formats

Due to our ontology, both the microprocessor developer and the student can interact with elements of the presentation, e.g. memory cells. When the user changes the contents of a cell, the internal organization must provide the transfer of the new value into the corresponding memory cell of the microcontroller. A data transfer in the other direction must be supported when he edits the memory address. The content of the memory cell with this new address must be displayed in the image of the memory on screen (see figure 6).

5. Conclusions

The DATABOOK system is now in daily use at the Technical University of Munich. The system was developed in co-operation with Siemens at a reasonable development time of 6 months and with an effort of 12 man-month. An user-action interpretation with respect to the meaning of the data acces type was implemented in the first version of the DATABOOK system, and an additional dialogue control component is needed for dynamic event handling.

The implemented screen splitting allows simultaneous display of graphics, but this facility is limited very soon by the PC screen size. The development of context-dependent help facilities is in progress, and future development of a spoken-language interface for the help facilities is intended. However, the development of interactive 3D-graphics and computer animation facilities remains a challenge, due to their extremly high development efforts.

References

1. Erickson H. "Specification and Generation of Custom-tailored Knowledge Acquisition Tools" in Proc. of IJCAI'93, pp.510-515, Chambéry, France, August 1993.
2. Erickson H., Puerta A.R., Musen M.A. "Generation of Knowledge-Acquisition Tools from Domain Ontologies" in Proc. of Annual Workshop on Knowledge Acquisition, Banff, Canada, February 1994.
3. Neches R. "Cognitive Issues in SHELTER Knowledge Base Development Environment" in Proc. of AAAI Spring Symposium on Cognitive Issues in Knowledge Acquisition, Standfort, CA, March 1992.
4. Szekely P., Luo P., Neches R. "Facilitating the Exploration of Interface Design Alternatives: the HUMANOID Model of Interface Design" in Proc. CHI'92, pp.507-515, Monterey, CA, May 1992.
5. Puerta A.R., Tu S.W., Musen M.A. "Modelling Tasks with Mechanisms", Int. Journal of Intelligent Systems, Vol. 8, No. 1, pp.129-152, 1993.
6. Gobbetti E., Turner R. "Object-oriented design of dynamic graphics applications", in Thalmann D. and Magnenat-Thalmann N. (eds.), New Trends in Animation and Visualisation, John Wiley, London 1992.
7. Norman D.A. "Why Interfaces Don't Work" in Laurel B. and Mountford S. (eds.), The Art of Human-Computer Interface Design, Addison-Wesley, Reading 1990.
8. Krauß P. "Aktives Buch in der Lehre", Proc. of SIWORK'96, Zurich, in C.Cap (ed.), Workstations und Ihre Anwendungen, pp.143-154, v/d/f Hochschulverlag ETH Zurich, 1996.
9. Keller M., Weiss A., Krauß P., Hoch G., Quintern J. "Design of Multi-Sensor Closed-Loop Neurosimulation", in Pedotti A. et al. (eds.), Neuroprosthetics from Basic Research to Clinical Application, Springer-Verlag, 1996.

GeoSol: Decision Support in Monitoring Water Quality and Crisis Management

S. Pfleger
Expertise Information Systems GmbH
Budapester Str. 21, D-81669 Munich, Germany

R. Klebe, M. Rabels
Siemens Nixdorf
D-81730 Munich, Germany

A. Pöhlmann, H. Schießl
Technische Universität München
D-80290 Munich, Germany

I. Mirel, M. Giurconiu, D. Chivereanu, A. Carabet
Polytechnical University of Timisoara
Bd. Mihai Viteazul 1, R-1900 Timisoara, Romania

Abstract

Along with starvation, sickness and war, pollution is considered as a problem of the twentieth century. Besides the toxic substances and the phenols, other extremely dangerous contaminators e.g. detergents, pesticides, hydrocarbons, oil products and radioactive wastes affect the quality of drinking water.

Monitoring and control of the pollution of the surface water courses allows the supervision of the natural processes of dilution and self-purification, and also to take appropriate purification actions for re-establishing the equilibrium between self-purification and pollution processes. Continuous evaluation of the environmental monitoring data and support of the human operator in emergency situations are the main objectives of computer-based Decision Support Tools.

This paper presents the advanced decision support tool GeoSol (Geographical Solution) together with its experimental application in monitoring water quality of the Rhine river in Germany, and its benefits in solving environmental crisis situations. Running on PC (Personal Computer, MS-Windows, INFORMIX database facilities) and with access to GIS (Geographical Information System) it allows the continuous interpretation of water analysis data in the temporal and spatial domains. The technical solution of the GeoSol prototype adopted the principles of the client-server architecture, based on the requirements generated within two European projects developed by Siemens Nixdorf and its project partners, ESPRIT 7522/6339 GeoWorks and ENS project E2008 ENVIRONET.

1. Introduction

Among various uses in the field of water drainage, surface water courses located near the heavy populated urban areas play an important role in collecting and transporting used water and wastes, decomposition of organic substances, dilution and even decomposition of chemical or physical impurities. Taking into consideration the potential and degree of usage of each water course, the most difficult situation with regard to the degree of contamination is encountered in the case of small and medium-sized rivers which run near important industrial and administrative centres. The self-purification capacity of natural water courses is surpassed by excessive contamination with organic substances; this is usually prohibited by the existing legislation because it may render a source of drinking water useless and, in extreme cases, a water treatment is necessary in a natural or modified user environment.

The origin of the wastes transported by surface water courses, wastes which contribute to their contamination and pollution, come mainly from the used waters which are being discharged by the sewer systems of urban and industrial areas. The process of urbanizing and industrializing leads to the augmentation in time of the used water discharge flow, but also to an increase in mineral and organic substances and the harmful micro-organisms contained by them, while the surface water flow used as the source remains the same or is even reduced. Industry has undoubtedly a lot of advantages, but there are also numerous negative aspects: the water sources are being used up; the ecological equilibrium is being destroyed and the natural qualities of air, soil and water are being altered.

We will mention in the following lines some of the extremely dangerous effects of surface water course pollution : *(1)* altered organoleptic characteristics of the water, that is, anaerobic fermentation of organic substances leads to a taste and smell that are not allowed; *(2)* altered physical characteristics of the water: *(3)* changed turbidity, colour, temperature and electrical conductibility; floating substances turn up at the surface and deposits are formed at the bottom, which consume the oxygen dissolved in the water; *(4)* altered radioactivity, *(5)* altered chemical characteristics, i.e. changed reaction and hardness, a smaller quantity of oxygen dissolved in the water, toxic substances turn up; *(6)* a larger number of pathogenic bacteria; *(7)* extinction of the flora and fauna, especially of the fish culture, due to the decrease in dissolved oxygen; *(8)* ruining the scenery and harming the hygiene of the human settlements.

In order to avoid that these natural goods degrade, we have to fight both the pollution and the causes of pollution.

The natural means to fight against pollution are the effects of dilution as well as the phenomenon of self-purification, which take place or begin at the same time that the polluting substances are introduced. During the self-purification process, the water characteristics of surface courses are brought back to the initial qualitative levels, regaining the equilibrium lost during the pollution process; the animal and plant micro- and macro-organisms in the natural water course tend to regain their initial natural condition through the biocoenotic effect.

Several processes take place in natural waters in order to reduce the harmful effects of the polluting elements introduced in used waters; these processes are dilution, dispersion, deposits, neutralization, reduction, oxidation, etc., and they act mainly upon suspensions and organic substances. The capacity of self-purification depends on the types of polluting substances, and is expressed by the *quantity of polluting substance* per volume of the water which can be discharged in the time unit (e.g. in mg/ m^3/ hour)

In the water systems there are also processes which are opposed to the one of self purification, such as concentration and *accumulation of persisting harmful* substances, the interaction of different polluting substances, when even more harmful pollutants are formed. Self-purification does not affect some categories of *toxic substances or viruses* and due to the continuous developing of new organic substances, the number of processes which resist self-purification and classical purification has increased. Nature regenerates only a small part of very polluted waters and new problems arise when they are used as supplies because classical treating procedures are no longer sufficient; the adaptation of new measures and technologies is, therefore, necessary.

When the self-purification capacity of a water course is no longer sufficient, the flow of discharged polluting substances must be reduced through *purificatios* together with the degree of pollution caused by the used water.

Monitoring the water quality is a non-stop job, and computer systems are here needed since they are capable of permanently recording and evaluating the water quality, and also support the decision process of water control authorities in environmental crisis situation caused by pollution accidents.

2. Environmental Monitoring

Until recently, environmental issues in Europe have largely been handled as isolated national or regional problems with limited or no exchange of information across country, or national borders. The need for communication and the exchange of environmental data has long been recognised, but due to lack of administrative and technical tools for cooperation only minor tasks have been handled on a transboundary level. Environmental monitoring in the presence of complex sensorial information is a difficult task due to a "non-stop" stream of information and the request for continuous information evaluation. Adequate data acquisition and interpretation software in form of decision support tools are needed for monitoring of large geographical areas.

Computer-based environmental monitoring and interpretation ensure immediate and continuous detection of pollution states and propagation of information about the type of event, urgency level, local or global affected areas, event location. The location of the reported event ensures an automatic selection of the thematic and geographic maps containing this location, and visualization of the affected areas. Decision support has the significant advantage of providing, and verifying efficient solutions in environmental crisis situations, before implementing the best strategy.

The technical solution of the GeoSol (Geographical Solution) prototype adopted the principles of the client-server architecture, based on the requirements generated within two European projects developed by Siemens Nixdorf and its project partners, ESPRIT projects 7522/6339 GeoWorks and ENS project E2008 ENVIRONET. GeoWorks aims at producing a multimedia and geo-referenced information delivery system for local authorities [1]. GeoWorks is a user driven project that will be pilot tested by municipalities (Bologna, Lille) and the National Environmental Research Institute (NERI, Denmark). Decision support for spatial and temporal problem domains is a major field of investigation and service development within the GW project. Among the decision support interests of local authorities the environmental problem domains were chosen to focus the DSS (Decision Support Systems) development [7].

ENVIRONET, a project in the framework of the EU programme ENS, developed a trans-European telematics architecture and customised solutions for environmental alarming, crisis management, situation assessment, monitoring, and daily data exchange for public administrations [2]. Three pilot scenarios (River, Air and Coast) demonstrated the transboundary co-operation of environmental institutions and authorities on different regional and hierarchical levels. ENVIRONET aims at establishing a user-friendly technical platform for exchanging mail, alarm messages and relevant data within the field of environment in its broadest sense. Intended is the efficiency increase and also the decrease of the expenses of the environmental administration. Additionally, this project intends to stimulate the standardisation in administrative routines, technical methods and formats.

Three pilot scenarios, called ECASE (Emergency Control and Alarm Systems based on Environet) have been chosen to demonstrate technical feasibility and applicability:

ECASE AIR to demonstrate alarming and event handling in case of an incident with substances concerning air pollution as well as the standard requirements for periodical and ad-hoc data exchange. Several user administrations contributed to the definition of the demonstrator, that shows their cooperation in both accidental situation and daily work. The area of Saarland (Germany) and Lorraine (France) has been chosen to demonstrate ECASE AIR.

ECASE RIVER demonstrates the alarming, reporting and decision support for authorities involved in a river alarm caused by pollution. The project has been carried out in close cooperation with the relevant administrations on the river Rhine and with the International Commission for the Protection of the Rhine against pollution (ICPR). The demonstration showed the transnational cooperation and communication of authorities involved in river pollution and water management.

ECASE COAST shows the alarming and event handling in case of a pollution of coastal water. The Mediterranean area between Greece and Italy has been chosen for the demonstration and user administrations in both countries contributed to this ECASE demonstrator. When simulating the emergency, French authorities collaborated as remote experts in the scenario. All scenarios put particular emphasis on the transnational communication and cooperation between involved member states. Therefore, the requirements for electronic data exchange between heterogeneous authorities have been identified in the project. In order to develop the prototypes for the demonstration, necessary investigations and specifications for Decision Support Systems and for the identification of knowledge and data requirements have been made.

The ENVIRONET project started at the beginning of 1992. In a first phase an analysis of the needs led to a detailed specification of requirements. In the next step, the generic ENVIRONET network concept was defined, and customized solutions for the three pilot applications were elaborated on this generic network. Three life demonstrations for the pilot were held in autumn 1993 demonstrating simultaneously in different EU Member states the potential and the added value reached through ENVIRONET. These demonstrators also showed the support of the specific requirements for each individual work place (e.g. decision maker, analyst, warning post, etc.) in crisis and standards situations. A detailed user evaluation together with several test installations after this demonstration phase led to a consolidation of the ENVIRONET concept in 1994. Full ENVIRONET systems can be implemented on both national and international levels.

3. Decision Support

The basic requirements for the DSS (Decision Support System) prototype GeoSol came from the ENS project ENVIRONET. Although the ENS project ENVIRONET is mainly aimed at the development of a European telematics architecture, decision support services play an important role within the project, due to the abundance of environmental tasks the common users of this system are conducting. During the whole ENVIRONET project, requirements concerning the system architecture and applications were collected, reviewed and integrated in the overall system.

Because of the openness of the ENVIRONET system, the usage of data standards and user-friendly data access methods, the overall usage of the system is not only restricted to the pilot implementations within ENVIRONET, but is useful for the specification of DSS for general environmental management tasks and in other application fields. Due to the large user involvement, requirements for a future implementation of DSS in the area of environmental management were also established. [3] According to several interview sessions with users held in the ENVIRONET project, the typical problems concerning DSS are as follows:

- Lack of administrative routines for transnational co-operation.
- Lack of knowledge about available decision support information and data.
- Lack of knowledge about how to access and extract this data.
- Diversity in local IT technology (hardware, software and networks).
- Lack of network facilities for the exchange of mail and data.
- Lack of facilities for handling emergency situations (alarming and event handling).
- Lack of standardised formats for the exchange of relevant data.

Many of these deficiencies were also stated by the GeoWorks users. The most important general requirements for the establishment of DSS were as follows:

- Openness of system architecture.
- User defined DS interface.
- High capability for the integration of DS tools and standard applications.

The design of an integrated decision support environment (DSE) is an important basis for DSS. It enables the integration of various data bases, DSS tools and other standard applications that are in use at the pilot sites. These services should be available from one user workstation out of one interface.

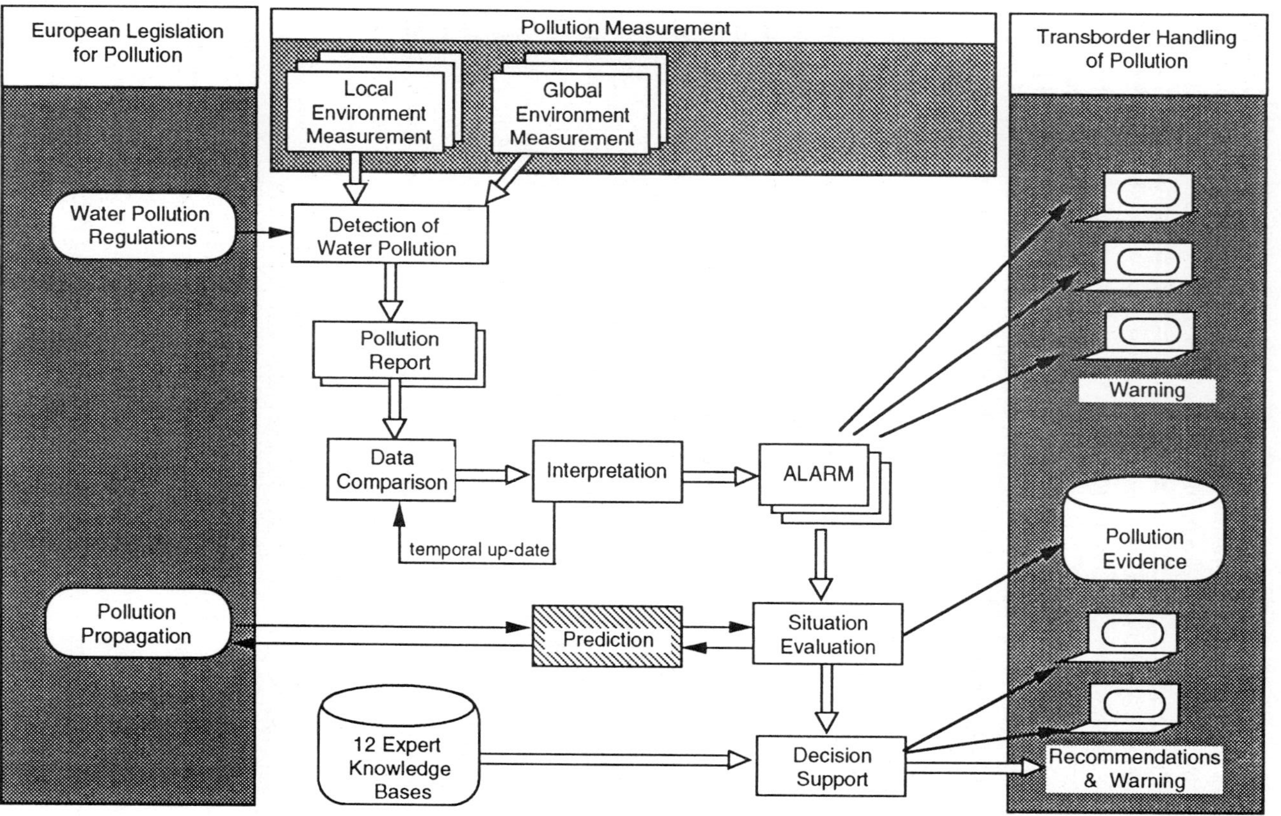

Fig. 1: User interface of the GeoSol decision support system

Nevertheless, there are additional requirements stated by the users, that are necessary for the handling of complex decision processes, and that are needed for the support of state of the art in DSS. These are as follows:

- *Linkages between various DS tools:* Often the DSS consists of mainly separated applications, that are not linked together.
- *Task oriented work flow:* Interconnectivity of decision support tools should be oriented on the work flow of a certain user task. Extensive knowledge about all the useful DSS would be no longer necessary, because the problem oriented application will offer all the necessary linkages to other decision support tools.
- *Usage of new technologies.* A major role for better and transparent decision making processes will be the usage of new technologies for the preparation and analysis of complex structured problems. The usage of multimedia techniques would offer new possibilities, e.g. in the area of environmental crisis management: *(i)* new media for situation analysis due to the usage of video and photographs within the decision support application, and *(ii)* better acceptance and understanding of decisions due to more sophisticated ways of problem presentation.
- *DSS application generator:* Each application generator should support this specification in order to create an application in according to the work flow and tool requirements of the users.
- *Creation and integration of Knowledge Bases* on methodologies (thematic and decision support oriented), experts, laws and regulations, technical and scientific literature.

4. GeoSol Prototype

The GeoSol prototype is an approach which demonstrates the capabilities of DSS (Decision Support Systems) in an integrated workflow oriented manner [4,5,6]. Various data sources and applications of the ENVIRONET project were used as a basis for this demonstration. This includes alarm forms, standard documents, measurement data, geographical data and substance data. To improve the work with various DSS tools and to facilitate the decision making process for the user, the tools were integrated within one user interface. This interface (see figure 1) enforces the workflow oriented decision procedures to improve environmental crisis management.

The GeoSol prototype demonstrates the functionality that should be available for the decision making user and it provides a concept how data from various data bases can be combined in a decision oriented application.

Environmental monitoring in the presence of complex sensorial information is a difficult task due to the stream of information and the request for continuous information evaluation. Adequate data acquisition and interpretation software in form of decision support tools needed for the water monitoring of large geographical areas. Computer-based environmental monitoring and interpretation ensure immediate detection of pollution states and propagation of information about the type of event, urgency level, local or global affected areas, and event location.

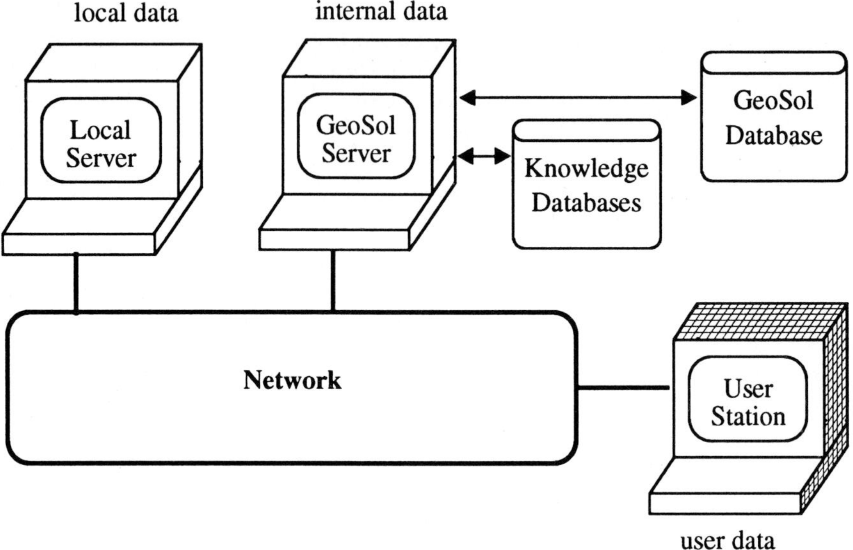

Fig. 2: GeoSol architecture

The location of the reported event ensures an automatic selection of the thematic and geographic maps containing this location, and visualization of the areas. Knowledge-based evaluation of the situation is here provided together with the long-term prediction of the water quality evolution in the context of dynamic event occurrence and causal event propagation in accordance with an *a priori* specified environmental model. Appropriate actions are generated, starting with the suggestion of an appropriate human expert (specialised in a specific type of pollution) up to the indication of the way in which past similar situations have been solved.

GeoSol uses a client-server architecture (see figure 2). This architecture takes into consideration that the user of DSS is connected with his workplace to a local server or a decentralised GeoSol server. Data within one user domain is stored on the workplace or the local server. For the distribution of data to other user domains or to access the various databases for the decision preparation, the services on the GeoSol server are used. This configuration allows the user to work locally (e.g. for training purposes) or globally to handle real time situations. The prototype of GeoSol runs on MS-DOS 6.2 with MS-Windows 3.1. The RDBMS INFORMIX Version 4.1 and INFORMIX ESQL Version 4.1 were used. The programming was done in C++ with MS Visual C Version 1.0. The GeoSol application provides following main functions:

- Registering or updating of an incident in predefined forms.
- Data fusion of several forms to one decision document.
- Transparent decision document history.
- Integration of new knowledge in the decision document.
- Information about databases available for the application.

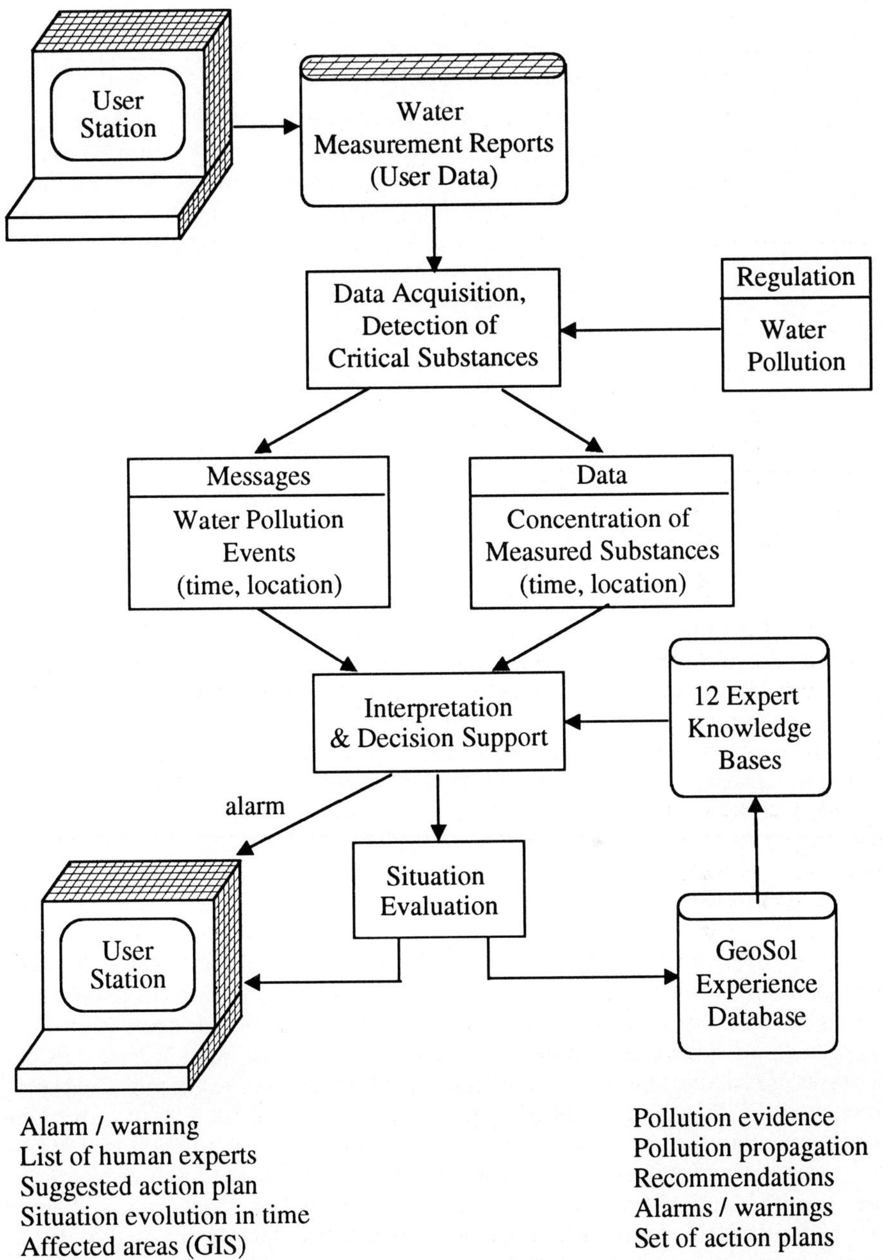

Fig. 3: GeoSol data flow

- Visualisation of affected geographical areas in crisis situations.
- Simulation, training and real time mode.
- User administration and access control.

These functions enable the user to get coordinated information and actions in emergency situations, relevant information about pollutants, information on incident history, decision support for possible counter actions, visualisation of situations with geo-related data and multimedia information about available experts and knowledge bases. The GeoSol tools are integrated in the MS-Windows user interface in order to allow the user to acces all available tools.

The data flow of GeoSol is illustrated in figure 3. Water Measurement Reports are continuously stored, and water pollution events are raised as soon as a high concentration of the critical substances is detected. Data acquisition records continously user data and is followed by a timestamp procedure in order to obtain the "age" of the stored information.

The concentration of critical substances in water is matter of national and transboarder reglementations for handling water pollution. The list of critical substances is specific to the measurement environment (water speed, surface and depth, etc.). Data fusion and interpretationis is performed with the aim of obtaining a global view of the water quality, and of the water pollution scenarios. Using this information, the knowledge accumulated in 12 Expert Databases (available for monitoring the water quality of the Rhine river in Germany) the Decision Support facilities provide hypoteses of the pollution situation, which are evaluated. The evaluation results are provided to the users in form of

- a list of human experts which could be contacted,
- an appropriate action plan in order to deal with pollution situations,
- GIS access to geographical and thematic maps,
- situation evaluation in time.

5. Conclusions

The configuration demonstrated by GeoSol shows an example of how complex information from different data sources can be integrated in one DS application, that is suitable for efficient crisis management. The user does not need deep knowledge of databases and data formats, since the application provides the necessary services to integrate the different DSS tools in a user friendly and work flow oriented manner. The GeoSol prototype will serve as a basis for future development and enhancement of decision support in environmental monitoring and crisis management. The core system will be customized to the problem- and area-specific applications required by the users. As an important improvement of the ENVIRONET pilot the usage of multimedia has been analysed and demonstrated in the ENS project MUMED [8]. The multimedia technologies of images, videos, video-conferencing, geographic visualisation, and automatic georeferencing through the ground positioning systems (GPS) have been shown to be most fruitful in the environmental domain. These technologies may well be integrated in a future DSS application that extends the GeoSol model.

References

1. GeoWorks EP-6339 & EP-7522, "Multimedia and Geo-Referenced Information Delivery Systems", Technical Annex (V2.0), Paris, 21 July 1992.
2. Sistemich F., et al "Environet ENS-E2008,.", Final Project Report, München, 1994.
3. Siemens Nixdorf, DSL, CMSU; GeoWorks EP-6339 & EP-7522, Deliverable 4.1: Specification of special Features for Decision Support Services, pp.17-21, Paris, 26.12.95.
4. Pöhlmann A. "Data Fusion in Decision Support Systems for Environmental Monitoring" (in German), Diploma supervised by S. Pfleger, Technical University of Munich, Munich, 1994.
5. Schießl H. "Man-Machine Interaction in Decision Support Systems for Environmental Monitoring" (in German), Diploma supervised by S. Pfleger, Technical University of Munich, Munich, 1994.
6. Pfleger S., Pöhlmann A., Schießl H. "User Manual of Decision Support System GeoSol" (in German), Technical University of Munich, Munich, 1994.
7. Augerinos E, Klebe, R., Nagle, J., Rabels, M., Kristensen, P.: A decision support system for distributed AM/FM-related data management. In: Proceedings of AM/FM Conference, Heidelberg, 1994.
8. MUMED ENS-E2308, Klebe R., Siemens Nixdorf: Multimedia Technologies for Telematic Services for Administrations, Study of Needs in the Environet Area, München, 1994.

User Support for Estimating the Passenger Flow in Airport Terminals

T. Heyde, J. Behne
AGIPLAN AG
P.O. Box 100151
D-45470 Mülheim a.d. Ruhr

G. Dettweiler, F. Neumann
Flughafen München GmbH
P.O. Box 231755
D-86326 Munich

Abstract

Appropriate techniques and prototype simulation tools which help the airport services to predict and optimize the passenger traffic flow have been developed for the new Munich Airport, with the aim of ensuring the technical base for analysing and predicting terminal efficiency, and to allow the optimization of the terminal capacity. The performed preliminary simulation tasks at the Munich Airport are here presented and the functionality of the simulation tools discussed, together with *generic interfaces* of the tools which will allow the adaption of the simulation package to the IT-systems used in airport operations.

1. Introduction

With the opening of borders markets are growing together and becoming more and more international. As one aspect of these developments traffic volume is growing in every mode of transport. Especially the air traffic has increased continuously from year to year and forecasts of various organisations as well as the air transport industry predict a steady growth of about 5 % p.a. for the passenger volume in the future. For example, at Munich Airport this means a permanent annual increase, and 700.000 up to 1 million passengers at the end of the century. Furthermore, a variety of influences complicate the operation of an airport, as follows:

- change of aircraft types which alter passenger volumes especially in peak hour situations,
- seasonal modifications of the flight schedule which vary the daily operation profile,
- increase in complex functions, efficiency and comfort under the constraint of increasing economy and security, and
- modification of operating conditions affected by new regulations.

A recent example for the last point is the complex modification of airport terminal operations which were necessary to meet the requirements of the Schengen Agreement following the unification of Europe. With these frame conditions there is a steady task for the airport authorities to keep the terminal facilities in an adequate shape to meet the demands of capacity and high level services at any time, and always in balance with economical actions.

Moreover these airport services guarantee their customers, primarily the airlines, best suppositions for efficient passenger handling. Permanent increase in passenger traffic and the complex integration of the European airports impose *non-stop adaption* of the airport services to a variety of changing conditions.

2. User Support for Estimating the Passenger Flow in Airport Terminals

Adequate support of airport administration services is requested for continuously modelling the dynamic passenger flow within the complex terminal areas, and for optimizing the terminal services in accordance with the real time constraints. However, *no suitable simulation platform* for modelling, evaluating and optimising the passenger traffic flow is available from the European companies.

Computer simulation allows to investigate the dynamic passenger flow in terminals under various frame conditions for present and future demands, in order to ensure necessary model expansions and adaptions which will help to avoid future traffic congestions.

As a special requirement for an appropriate simulation tool it was defined that the application could be used by the airport specialists themselves to achieve the highest possible level of flexibility.

Until now no suitable tool was available on the market, because all known offers (primarily from US-Companies) were bounded as a service, delivering solutions of evaluated constellations but not the tool itself.

Appropriate simulation tools, which have been available on the European market were evaluated and as a result AGIPLAN received the order to develop the special airport application based on our multi-purpose simulation technique.

During joint meetings between the Munich Airport and AGIPLAN an appropriate simulation tool for investigating the passenger flow in terminals was designed and calibrated.

The input for the terminal simulation model are market research parameters, flight plans and time tables and external scheduling or controlling software which lead to an output information about actual loads, waiting periods, existing capacities and also animation. Since the simulation of passenger terminals is a very complex area a precise definition on how to get the best approach to a simulation tool is necessary. Thus the proceedings for the build-up of a terminal simulation system are separated into four steps:

- determination of basic passenger data,
- determination of basic flight data,
- determination of the operational environment, and
- modelling of the simulation system.

In principle, the simulation tool of a a modular design to allow the modeling of the existing facilities as well as the remodeling of configurations for future extensions. In a first step the existing terminal building is realised within the tool. Thereby the terminal-layout was modelled with the primary functional elements, such as: passenger areas, arrival areas, departure areas, check-in counters, security control, passport control, boarding pass control, and customs control.

All the functional elements are connected by time-over-distance relations, taking into account the time-consumption for necessary procedures requested by each functional element.

The results of the simulation runs should explicitly be shown in an efficient manner, together with the fact that the effects of different strategies and different parameter settings can be analysed in a simple way. For this reason an analysis tool was programmed which performs user support in dealing with estimation of the traffic flow in airport terminals, and provides following information: *(i)* the level of service, *(ii)* the contents of workload buffers, *(iii)* expected bottlenecks, and *(iv)* the optimal capacity of each functional element. Due to its modular design the simulation programme has the ability to be expanded later on. These expansions will allow:

- to investigate the function of new terminal buildings in all aspects of function and economics to support the planning of the construction,
- to investigate the operational correlation between different terminals, and
- to ensure for all passengers a short transit time, which is an important measure of today's airports comfort level.

The simulation tool is an instrument that helps the airport operator to guarantee the full function of his terminal facilities, especially for future demands related to the activities of keeping a terminal in best performance conditions in order to meet the demands for optimal capacity, efficiency and passenger convenience at any time. The simulation ensures in this way the steady optimisation of the terminal facilities. Special objectives are here the evaluation of data outputs for:

- optimisation of passenger flows and elimination of bottlenecks
- resources re-distribution with the aim of increasing the existing capacity
- generation additional resources
- optimization and preservation of optimal terminal access quality by appropriate terminal re-construction activities with the aim of maintaining a high level standard of passenger services.

The obtained evaluation results were used at the airport of Munich for performance improvement of following terminal capabilities: *utilisation* of the modular terminal *space-units*, especially in front of passenger handling facilities, available *space per passenger*, *length of queues* at each functional element, *waiting time* at each functional element, *processing capacity* of each functional element, the *level of service*, and the cumulative waiting time.

The developed simulation model was validated in comparison with a real day operation, as a preliminary simulation run. A typical day of the running season flight-schedule was prepared for this validation. Staff members of the Munich airport measured the real situation in the terminals, which had been selected for the main "busy hour" operations. The validation showed as a first result, that few of the parameter assumptions, which have been estimated, were not applicable.

A complex process of iterative corrections of the assumptions was started, and the obtained results indicated that the functionality of the simulation platform was in accordance with the real needs and successfully validated. Furthermore, the obtained results demonstrated the complexity of airport terminal operations, which could hardly be described exactly without an appropriate simulation tool.

3. Conclusions

Sooner or later many European airports will be confronted with capacity, efficiency and optimization problems. There are many different airports all over the world, and therefore the simulation tool needs adaptions to the specific conditions of different terminal structures. Generic interfaces of the tool and the equivalence of the passenger handling elements himself allow the adaptation of the simulation packet to the terminal environment of each airport. This is a challenging task which requires team work between the airport staff, airport experts and computer specialists in order to solve the "simulation adaption problem" in changed airport conditions, with the goal of re-using the existing simulation platform for the traffic optimisation at other nodes of the Trans-European Network of Airports.

Acknowledgement

The authors acknowledge the assistance provided by H. Lenke (AGIPLAN AG) in editing this paper.

DIADEM: A Method for User Interface Development

Philippe Boutruche
Thomson-CSF, RCC
160 Bd de Valmy, BP82, F-92704 Colombes Cedex, France

Michael Kärcher
ISA Informationssysteme GmbH
Azenbergstrasse 35, D-70174 Stuttgart, Germany

Abstract

The paper describes the major industrial stakes related to user interface development that the providers of information systems have to face. The DIADEM method is then presented. This method provides an appropriate way for domain experts to express their needs, for software developers to express their constraints, and for human factors specialists to express their knowledge, giving them all the possibility to integrate their analysis with a common understanding, which is supported by simple formalisms and early prototyping. The method is widely used internally in the Thomson Group.

The goal of the ESPRIT project DIAMANTA is to validate the DIADEM approach in a wider range of application domains and contexts before performing a full integration of this method in the partners' development process. Furthermore, a framework for the deployment of the method in new projects and organisations is prepared. Finally, one of the applications developed in the scope of the DIAMANTA project is described together with its expected benefits. This application was developed by ISA, and provides both graphical and telephone-based user interfaces. It will use and customise the DIADEM method in order to generally define the dialogues for both parts of the user interface.

1. Introduction

The development of the modern Information Society can only be achieved if the applications providers are able to produce easy to use and to learn User Interfaces (UI), for more and more complex systems, and at reasonable costs. So the User Interface development becomes a major concern for information systems development, both from an end user satisfaction point of view, and from an economical and industrial point of view.

1.1 Industrial Stake

The two major stakes for companies developing User Interface (UI) software are quality and productivity. Quality directly concerns human appropriation of the system, while productivity concerns the industrial development process. Both aspects are considered as tightly related, and nobody would now release a system without taking into account human factors as essential to customer satisfaction and thus guaranteeing sales. The recent launching of a new version of a well known operating system shows an irreversible trend in this matter.
User satisfaction covers first human factors aspects related to utility and usability of the system. Utility concerns functional capacities of the system and the resulting activity for the end user. Usability concerns access to the functional capacities, and their ease of use through the UI. Everybody knows examples where a good functional system is rejected because of lack of usability. The difficulty of access and manipulation is also one reason why a lot of applications are used 20% to 30% of their real capacities.
On the other hand, the part of UI development has been measured to be between 20 to 50% of the total cost of a system, and these costs are still increasing. These increasing costs follow the new possibilities of machines to build more complex systems. Furthermore, UI themselves become more complex by the use of new techniques like multimedia and hypermedia data and openness to networks. The counterpart of this context is that UI development becomes more expensive.

1.2 Current Practices

Current practices concerning user interfaces are generally not well formalised, even if three approaches can be considered: production tools, methodology and software design, and user-centered approaches. The current UI *production tools* are providing powerful environments. They are widely spread, and allow a good level of productivity in the coding phases. They increase quality in the sense they improve global harmonisation of produced code and global layout. Nevertheless, having the right tool is not enough to produce a correct UI. The main reason is that they cover more the last phases of UI life cycle.

Methodologies are functional analysis and industrial process oriented, and remain poor concerning UI specificities. More generally, methodologies do not take into account the role and place of human factors in the system development. When, where and how do we need to define the user point of view. Common sense and experience are essential to succeed in making a good UI.

As we explained before, the main difficulty of tool or methodology approach resides in the impossibility to formalise a user centred view of the system. Top-down *user centred approaches* begin to leave the human factors laboratories towards industry. The proposed models analyse the user activity and propose methods and formalisms to define it (MAD, GOMS, PAC). The integration to a methodology remains difficult because they cover different phases of the life cycle, and do not give indications on how to relate this model to functional analysis and to software design and coding.

2. DIADEM Method

The goal of the DIADEM method is to provide a UI development approach which is integrated in an industrial development process. It defines activities from early requirements analysis to coding phases. DIADEM activities may be associated to classical software and system development methodologies. The concepts and associated formalisms are coming from top-down user centred approaches (tasks graph) and from software tools and bottom-up approach (components, presentations). Each activity is characterised by: the *result* of the activity, the *actors*, the *role of actors*, and the *concepts and formalisms* used to express the results of an activity. Before describing the steps proposed by the method, we first describe the concepts it defines to support the activities. We explain then how they are used in DIADEM activities. Each concept is not dedicated to one activity or one actor, but on the contrary, may be used by successive steps to serve as communication between teams and traceability between definition level. This is an essential role of the method.

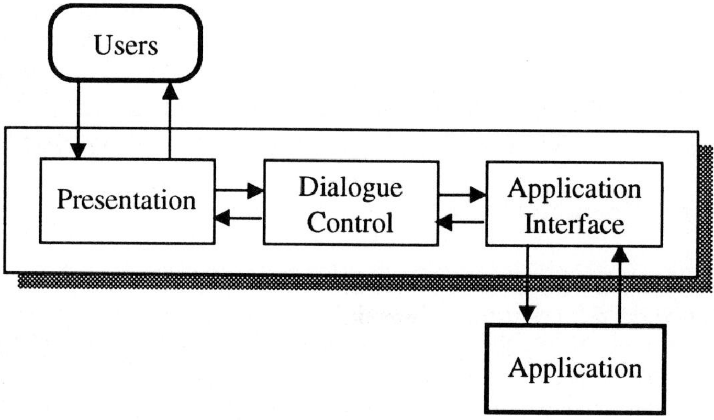

Fig. l.: Seeheim model

From a model point of view, DIADEM is based on the Seeheim model. The presentation part is in charge of the management and the interpretation of data sent to/by the physical user interaction devices. The dialogue control component manages the dynamics between the operator and the application interface while the application interface part deals with exchanges between the UI and the application (see figure 1).

2.1 Concepts of the Method

The concepts of DIADEM are expressed by: the task graph, the strategies, user objects, technical sheets, presentation hierarchy, UI handbook, and components. The *task graph* describes user activity in terms of goals. It expresses just hierarchical "use" relations, i.e. a task uses sub-tasks. The graph describes the user's point of view about system's functions (not logical or temporal relations).

The *strategy* of each task describes the "dialogue" definition, the sequences of interaction between the user and the system. The technical sheet expresses requirements on presentations (layout, information needs, etc.) and on applicative kernel of the system. Tasks are user actions on user objects, user objects are real world objects of the user's domain, the user will have to manipulate representations through the UI.

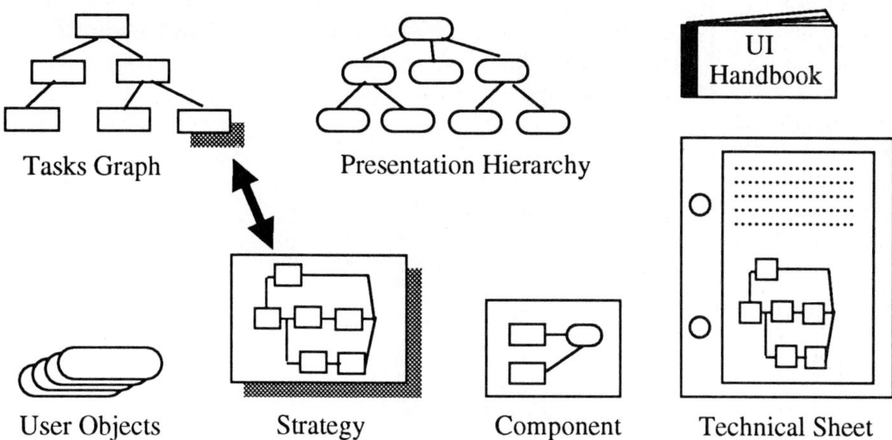

Fig 2: Main concepts of DIADEM method

When defining requirements on tasks, objects and presentations hierarchy, general choices have to be made to assure the overall coherence and homogeneity of the UI. The role of UI handbook is to register these choices of global interest, as well concerning the layout (look) as concerning the dialogue (feel). Software components are defined starting from technical sheets and tasks graph. Precise software interfaces are requested in order to ensure correct communication between these modules and other modules of the application.

2.2 Activities

Figure 3 describes how DIADEM activities are generally organised through a system development life cycle. Each project will adapt them depending on the size and context of the application.

The *system requirements activities* are generally performed by operational experts together with system architects and human factor specialists. The techniques used are "traditional" observation and analysis. The observation of existing systems can help in the new system definition by the observation of users at work. Starting from the general operational task definition, these activities will refine towards allocation of more precise requirements of the system to be "allocated" to an end user. These requirements become tasks and can be organised in a graph. This very first version of the task graph is the input to the next activities.

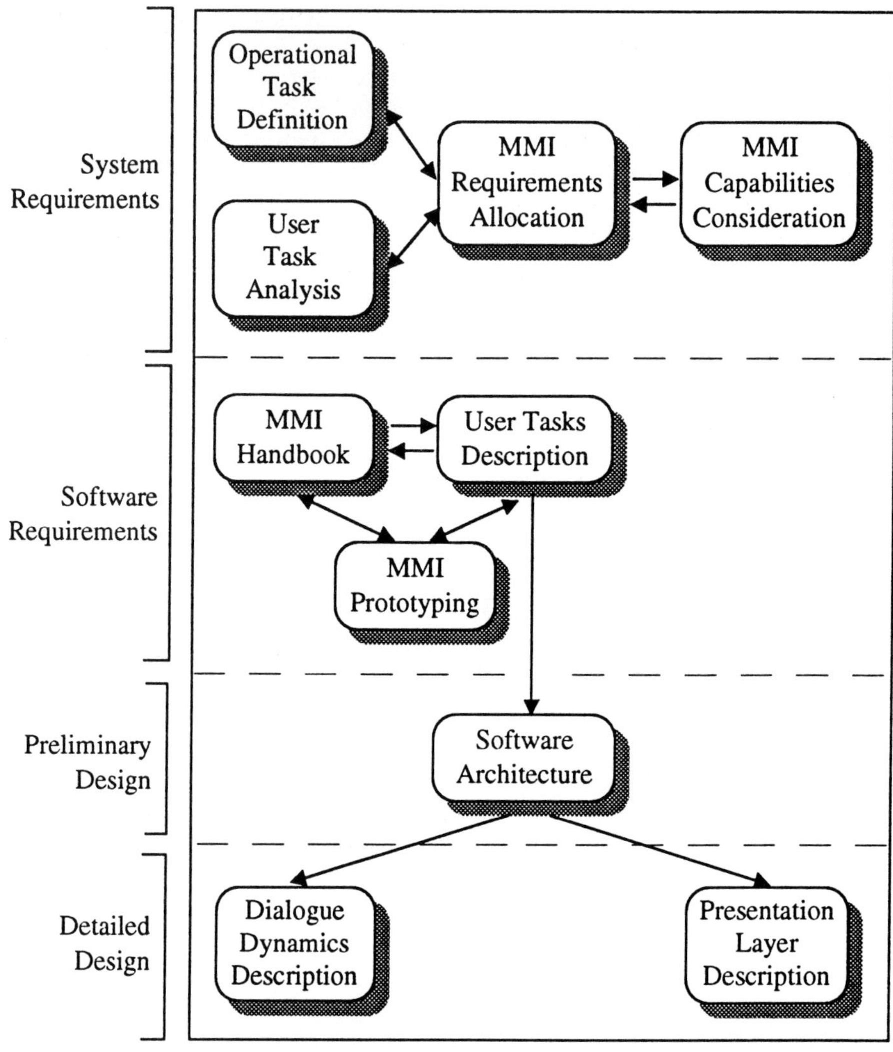

Fig. 3: DIADEM activities and project phases

2.3 Tasks Description

This activity is twofold: first the user's activity (task graph) is defined, and then dethe requirements on the dynamic of presentations and dialogue (technical sheets). The definition of the user's activity consists of identifying the tasks and organising them. The first levels of the graph are generally easy to define, then an iterative process is initialised where the actors define user objects, global recommendations and layout principles, and interaction principles and sequences, and then go back to the tasks organisation and so on.

Once a stable version of the tasks graph has been elaborated and agreed upon, each task is completely described in its technical sheet. A technical sheet is made of five main sections:

- The name made of a verb of action and an object.
- The description of the task, in terms of intention of the user.
- The dialogue requirements generally made of the graphical description of the strategy completed by textual explanation, when required.
  The DIADEM formalism describes "interactions", "applicative calls" and "transitions" .
- The presentation requirements define the layout constraints for a task
- The applicative requirements define the capabilities of the applicative part in order to support a task.

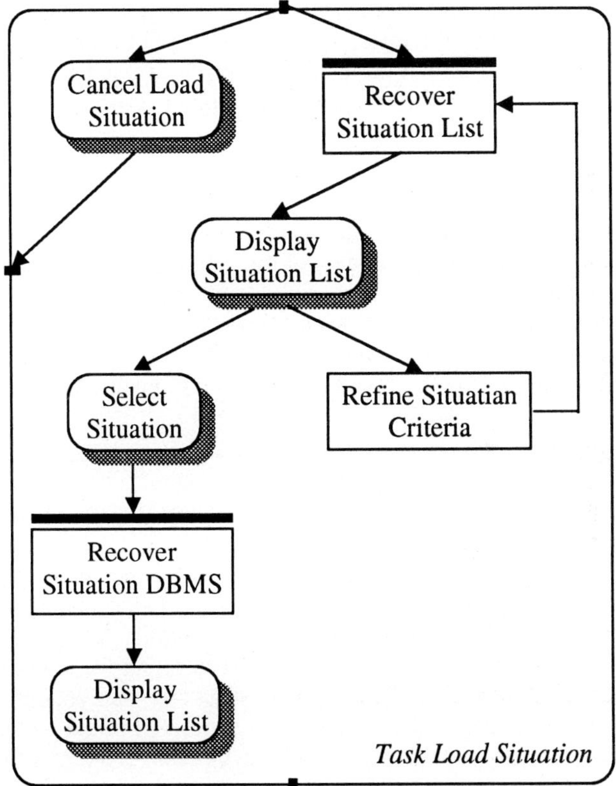

Fig. 4: Strategy example

The UI handbook is elaborated in parallel with the task description and prototyping activities. It is based on the Ul handbook writer guide. This book registers all choices and recommendations made during the definition phase, in a structured way. It is expected that experience is re-used for next applications, and can be viewed as a memory of UI principles of the company.

DIADEM Prototyping

DIADEM prototyping is an animation of all, or part of the specifications. It starts from the tasks described in the technical sheets and from the presentation description. A direct link exists between each element shown in the prototype and the specification in progress. Several different prototypes can be achieved together, each one intends to validate one aspect or another.

DIADEM prototype activities start with prototype objectives definition, and scenarios definition. The scenarios are made of couples {action, result}. The steps are defined by selecting the tasks to prototype in the graph, then to follow the corresponding strategies. Screens and navigation between screens are then coded with tools allowing fast and easy modifications (e.g. SPIRITS, TeleUSE, Windows4GL, VisualBasic). During the evaluation sessions, all the remarks feed back either tasks (operational remarks), or a paragraph of the UI handbook (remarks on the dialogue principles or layout etc.). This work is made easier because of the scenario is directly related to tasks described in the specification. Few iterations are generally observed before getting an agreement.

Presentation Description

The presentation description activity defines the windows, graphics, menus etc. It is based on the presentation requirements of the technical sheets and the UI handbook, and produces a tree of presentations (containers and UI objects). This activity is finalised at the end of design. Nevertheless, it starts earlier in the process by proposing rough versions in order to take into account the human way of thinking which goes from one level of abstraction to another.

Software Design

The UI definition activities present enough refinement topics to justify an adapted approach. When speaking about software design, refinement become less important. This is the reason why DIADEM does not define a very deep software design method. Starting from this point, all used software design methods are valid, especially object oriented design methods like OMT.

The first step of software design consists of defining the software modules and the general architecture. Then each software component is refined accordingly to the strategies and the requirements defined in the technical sheets. Traceability can be assumed between each task, each element (interaction or applicative call) of the strategy, and each requirement and the software components.

The method was designed to be generic, and has been used in the domain of traditional information systems. Even if it looks promising, it needs further experiments, and formal evaluation before being widely deployed. This is why the DIAMANTA project was born.

3. DIAMANTA Trial Application

Thc DIAMANTA ESPRIT Project 20507 started in September 1995, with a duration of 14 months. The consortium consists of Thomson-CSF/RCC (the "technology provider" and co-ordinator of the project), the Spanish partners STISA and ICB ("technology users" for a multimedia tourism application development), the German partner ISA (a "technology user" for sales support systems for second hand cars, using both graphical and telephone-based UI), and the German partner MMS laboratory of University of Kassel (a "method user" for the supervisory control of chemical processes, which co-operates with Bayer AG). MMS will also manage the performance evaluation and measurement tasks of the project.

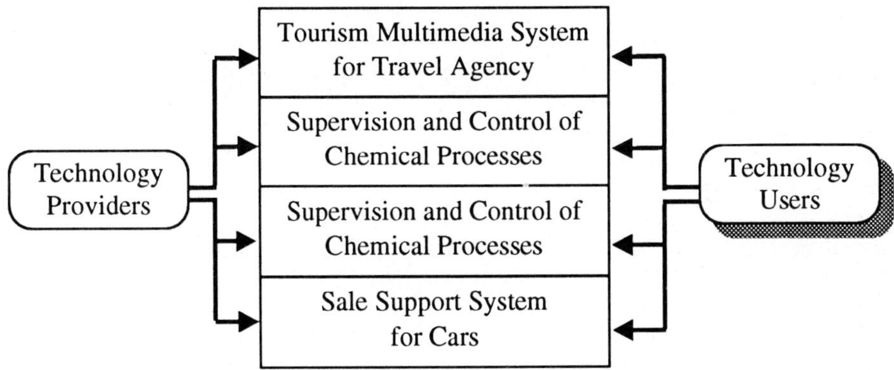

Fig. 5: Trial applications of the DIAMANTA project

3.1 Project Overview

The project addresses both industrial users of the method and end users of the applications. The main objectives of the project are as follows:

- Introduce the DIADEM method in new application domains and new contexts in order to validate the genericity, suitability and viability of the approach through three real life applications.
- Evaluate, analyse and measure the gain brought by the use of the method.
- Prepare the dissemination of the project results by providing a framework for introduction of the method in other projects and organisations.

3.2 Project Phases

The trial applications development consists of four main phases:

- technology transfer and adjustments,
- development phase
- evaluation and measurement, and
- dissemination of the project results.

Technology Transfer and Adjustments

The technology transfer phase aims to provide the industrial users with the required knowledge to apply the method to their project. As the method is to be used in existing applications which already have their own workplans and methods, the project plans and method need to be harmonised. This phase will result in trained development teams, revised plans of the trial applications and customisation of the method for each application.

Development Phase

The application development is not funded by the project, there are real applications under progress. After the technology transfer phase, all industrial users should be able to work by themselves to define and develop their application. But, as the method has not yet been widely deployed, it is necessary to follow and support the use of the method by early users. This is the role of the support activity of the technology transfer.
This support will work in two ways. The first one will be a "hot-line" provided by the technology provider, the second one will be workshops organised to make all trial applications communicate about their experience and give feedback on the use of the method to the evaluator and the technology provider.

Evaluation and Measurement

The evaluation and measurement phase provides the project with quantitative and qualitative data on the suitability of the method for the application domains and on its viability in the industrial context it has been applied. This phase will measure the cost and benefits of using the method against the objectives and expected results in terms of improvement of the UI development process.

The early experiments made by the technology provider gave some indication on the significant quantitative elements expected from the use of the method. The project will refine and synthesise the observed results in order to give more elements to prepare good re-deployment after the project ends.

The evaluation and measurement phase will be conducted in three steps: the establishment of a common evaluation and measurement procedure, followed by the evaluation and measurement of applications, then resulting in a synthesis.

Both subjective and objective measurements are applied, involving measurement of the development process, of software quality engineering and of human factors of the resulting UI. The objective measurements contain the data that can be precisely quantified not influenced by personal judgement of the industrial users or end users. Considering existing comments, this sort of data will, among others, consist of number of user tasks, number of screens, absolute number of code lines, number of possible user interactions, total time spent for each stage of the life cycle. The subjective measurement represents the attitudes of the different people involved in the software life cycle. It contains qualitative data, like user satisfaction, ease of assimilation of the method, workload measurement, and overall usability and utility ratings.

Dissemination of the Project Results

This is the conclusion of the project, and, the reason for doing the project. Assuming that the applications show the cost/benefit of the method, the phase aims at preparing DIADEM's re-deployment outside the consortium.
This phase will result in material required to help a new project in using the method. The material will be prepared on the basis of DIADEM's documentation and training course, the experience gained and on the conclusion of the evaluation. It will, in particular, present the experiences of partners, explaining the difficulties met and how they were solved, the process followed to introduce the technology in their project, and the impact the introduction of the DIADEM method had on the project organisation and progress. It will stress the main items to take into account so that the process (started in the applications) will be reproducible for other applications.

4. Two Trial Experiments of the DIAMANTA Project

The main trial applications of the DIADEM project are a *Tourism Multimedia System*, a *Supervisory Control of Chemical Processes*, and a *Sale Support System for Cars*. The last experiment is presented in section 5.

A *Tourism Multimedia System* for travel agencies will be developed by STISA, whose end users are travel agencies. ICB Travel, a travel agency located in Madrid, have asked STISA to develop their information management applications and Database Management Systems (DBMS). The multimedia application being developed for ICB Travel in the scope of DIAMANTA is called MIRANDA.

The aim of this application is to create a multimedia interactive system which can be used by the travel agent to show the tourists and business travellers information on travel possibilities, hotels at the destination, places to visit, and other tourism subjects.

Intuitive user interfaces, easy to use and guiding the user are fundamental for travel agencies, because travel agencies' personnel do not currently have computer knowledge and require a system they can use with little or no previous learning. In addition, and given that the objective is that customers can operate the system by themselves if they want more detailed information, the better the interface is, the more attraction it will have for the customers.

The system must be able to store, select and retrieve multimedia information and present it on the screen according to the user requests. To achieve this an appropriate user interface is to be developed. DIADEM will be used for this purpose. ICB Travel will participate in the project to express needs and validate the results.

MMS is developing a new generation of Man-Machine Interfaces for *Supervisory Control of Chemical Processes*. The project is called PBG: Participatory Design for Man-Machine Interfaces for Process Control Systems. The DFG (German Research Foundation) and the Dormagen site of the Bayer AG company both support this project.

Increasing demands on the quality of products as well as of industrial processes themselves have lead to more complex chains of processes, and thus to highly complex strategies for process control and for process automation. At the same time, the UI becomes increasingly intricate to represent all the necessary information from a given process. Operators must respond quickly and effectively in case of a plant malfunction. Incorporating the operators throughout the design process improves the task-orientation of the users and is likely to defeat problems like reduced vigilance and de-qualification.

DIADEM will be used during design of an actions oriented interface, supporting operation of the plant on the skill-based level in Rassmussen's model. In this context, it is expected that the introduction of DIADEM will improve software productivity and the quality of this UI. The method will first be customised for integration into the existing PBG project process, including early prototyping for supporting user requirements acquisition. The use of the DIADEM formalisms should in particular enhance the traceability between the evaluation scenarios and the UI requirements, and prepare the software development.

5. Third Trial Experiment of the DIAMANTA Project

This part describes ISA's application in the DIAMANTA project. The application is based on Computer Telephone Integration (CTI). This technique provides users with the capability to access information from the computer by means of only a telephone. We first describe the CTI context, then a short description of the applications is given. Rationale for and expected benefits from using DIADEM and future plans are also described.

5.1 Computer Telephone Integration (CTI)

Computer Telephone Integration (CTI) can be separated into two very different areas. The first area, which is widely understood as the essence of CTI, can be characterised as Computer Assisted Telephoning. It concentrates on assisting employees whose work includes many tasks carried out via telephone, e.g. in telephone marketing. Employees are assisted in routine tasks such as retrieving and dialing numbers, maintaining calling lists and, e.g. logbooks of outgoing calls. This area alone has a huge future market since it is believed to result in substantial productivity gains at comparably low cost.

However, our focus in integrating telephones with computers is rather the remote access to computers via telephones, i.e. substituting the telephone for screen-based and keyboard-based access to computers. This is what the term CTI will stand for in the following.

One would certainly wonder why the phone interface as a rather restricted very low-bandwidth is considered superior to modern graphical screen-based interfaces. Taking into account that phones are available nearly everywhere, that this technology is highly standardised, and that everybody is familiar with their operation, this type of interface seems adequate for a variety of applications.

The Application of CTI

Early applications of CTI were built as rather closed, very much voice-centred systems, e.g. Speech Mailboxes ('computerised answering machines'), call distribution systems, fax-back services, or simple information provision systems based on pre-defined ('canned') messages/texts. Such applications are in widespread use today and the market is considerably large but mostly occupied by the manufacturers of private branch exchanges (PABX).

Emerging systems in CTI extend towards accessing existing application systems or their data. While prior voice-based systems stored their data locally only, these newer systems are able to use data stored in other systems and thus of realising an actual integration of computers and telephones. Some examples of CTI applications are: home banking, order processing, stock inquiry, ticketing, and travel information (municipal transport, railways, airlines, hotel availability).

Benefits from CTI

Although the usability of phone-based user interfaces (UIs) is inferior to graphical ones, there are areas in which phone-based UIs yield significant advantages and benefits. The following is a list of the most prominent advantages: *availability, familiarity, initial cost, and automation.*

Telephones are *available* virtually anytime and anywhere, i.e. in nearly all households, companies, public places, and even on the road, considering the fast growing number of portable and car phones. Phone-based interfaces provide a feasible access point to information at any place any time, e.g.: for the business-person to query airline schedule, for inhabitants of flood-endangered areas to access high-water forecasts, and for query item availability in shops.

Virtually everybody knows how to operate a telephone and can be *easily* guided by spoken instructions. In contrast, fewer people are well versed in the use of personal computers or public access systems such as Minitel, CompuServe, or Datex-J.

Very low *initial investments* in hardware, software, and customer training is a convincing selling point. Consider for instance large publishing companies which intend to provide fully computerised order processing (e.g., in order to cut costs). Larger book stores will probably invest in the hardware and software for screen-based access; the small book stores, however, might prefer to use their existing means of communication - the telephone.

Automation of routine tasks: Companies providing services by phone can improve their quality of service by automating routine tasks, thus freeing up phone-operators to concentrate on exceptional cases and to provide better personal services.

5.2 CTI Pilot Applications in DIAMANTA

Our application experiment will be conducted in the design of an information system for customers of used car dealerships. The application will be equipped with both a graphical screen-based and a phone-based user interface.

System Architecture

The hardware platform used for the CTI pilot applications is an industry standard PC. For the telephone line interface one or more line boards serving three, eight, or 32 phone lines are used. The board uses Digital Signal Processors (DSPs) that support CCITT compliant ll-law ADPCM. A FAX-back service is also available. The operating system employed is IBM's OS/2.

The user interface for both the screen-based and the phone-based access modes will be implemented using the ISA Dialog Manager (IDM). IDM is a leading User Interface Management System (UIMS). It covers the dialogue and application interface parts. The dialogues are implemented in IDM's scripting language; the application interfaces support a variety of languages (e.g. C/C++, Cobol, SQL) and techniques (e.g. local calls, RPC via TCP/IP, LU6.2, UPIC). The standard product supports Microsoft Windows, OS/2 Presentation Manager, and the X Window System with OSF/Motif in the presentation layer. A variant has been implemented recently which supports phone-based interfaces on the presentation layer; this product is called ISA Telephone Dialogue Manager (ITDM).

Application: Dealers of Used Cars

The Sales Support System for Used Car Dealerships acts as an information exchange between car dealers and their customers. Customers can inquire about specific models in certain pricing categories either remotely via telephone or in the dealer's show-room through PCs equipped with graphical user interfaces. The customer has to specify the make, model, and (optionally) the colour and desired options (e.g. sunroof, air-conditioning, anti-lock braking system, automatic transmission). He can also indicate specific production years and the possible price range. After having entered part or all of this information, appropriate candidates are selected from the database and the results are presented. This dialogue is available in two primary modes of interaction:

1. The phone-based, remote access is achieved by means of (preferably DTMF equipped) telephones. The results are returned either by phone (spoken text), by paper-mail (in which case the customer has to leave his address as voice mail), or by means of the fax-back service.
2. The screen-based, local access is currently only planned on the dealer's premises by means of an MS Windows-based user interface with very similar functionality. This system is accessed either directly by the customer or by the salesperson, if the customer feels uncomfortable using the PC himself.

The system addresses a wide spectrum of car dealers ranging from those specialising in used cars to those who mainly deal in new cars but who also market trade-ins. Furthermore, independent car brokers who merely mediate between private sellers and purchasers will use this software. The development project is sponsored by a medium-sized used car dealership and by a telecommunication service provider.

The benefit for the car dealer in introducing this solution is reduced advertising cost since only a small excerpt from the current stock need be published. Furthermore, the customer will always receive the most recent information about current offers. An interesting side-effect for the car dealers is the possibility to analyse the customers' queries for the purpose of adjusting their offers and stock levels to the customers' demands.

5.3 Why Use DIADEM for CTI-Dialogue Design?

There are several reasons why DIADEM was considered an appropriate method for the design of phone-based user interfaces, and especially for systems equipped with both screen-based and phone-based interfaces:

- *Focus on Interaction* (instead of Presentation): Today's graphical screen based interfaces offer very rich presentation displaying screens packed with pictures, guiding descriptions, and the like. The design is often centred around the presentation instead of the interaction or dialogue flow. Phone based interfaces, however, lack the extra two spatial dimensions provided by screens and therefore have to focus on the dialogue flow in the interface design. This philosophy is one of DIADEM's cornerstones.
- *Consistent interaction* techniques: In order to be efficient, phone-based dialogues have to apply techniques that guide the novice user adequately while not slowing down or even annoying the expert user. In graphical interfaces, the expert can easily pick the relevant pieces from the screen surface and thus work efficiently. We expect DIADEM's charting technique to assist the designer in both establishing 'dialogue flow templates' to be applied throughout the system and to recognise easily any deviations from these standard mechanisms. The result should be consistent interaction techniques which are rapidly recognised and learned by the user.
- *Reduced effort* in the design of bi-modal interfaces and their quality improvement: These particular applications have been chosen in order to study how DIADEM influences the concurrent design of screen-based and phone-based user interfaces, and especially how DLADEM can reduce the effort by combining what used to be two different tasks in the user interface design. In addition, we expect better harmonisation between screen-based and phone-based interfaces so that an end-user who is already familiar with one type of interface can transfer this knowledge to the other type of interface.
- *Best Practice* in UI design: So far, phone-based user interfaces have not been designed in accordance with a formal method. Usually, state transition diagrams, flow charts, and several prototyping steps were employed in the creation of the user interface part. Using DIADEM, we also expect to have a better means of communicating the dialogue's structure to all people involved in the design process, e.g. the dialogue designer and programmer, the application designer/programmer, the system supplier's management, and representative end-users. We also expect to achieve a higher quality for the initial definition of dialogue structure and thus to reduce both the number of prototypes built during the design and the number of changes after the design is completed.

6. Future Plans

The DIAMANTA application experiment will provide ISA with further know-how about the DIADEM method and, given that the results of the trials prove advantageous, ISA will deploy DIADEM for numerous further projects currently being prepared. Projects for consideration are expected in the following areas of customer information systems: reservation systems for the travel industry, stock inventory by salesmen, and order processing.

Currently, non-screen-based interfaces are built in a turn-key fashion by ISA for its customers. In the future, we expect that customers will build or adapt the user interfaces themselves as has been seen in the area of (screen-based) GUIs in the last five years. Our co-operation with CASE manufacturers has also shown that large customers ask for formal methods to support the design of their own user interfaces. We expect a parallel development in the area of non-screen based interfaces over the next years, too, and thus want to be prepared for future customer demand.

The DIADEM method is, as of today, still a paper-and-pencil method. The method needs to be supported by computer-based tools in the future in order to foster its widespread application in industrial software development projects. Therefore, we would like to implement a CASE-tool that employs the DIADEM method within the framework of our UIMS product, the ISA Dialog Manager. The approach for implementing such a tool requires an upper-CASE tool that implements the DIADEM method. This tool shall be designed as an open tool in order to easily accommodate changes/ enhancements to the DIADEM method itself or variations to the method required by the customer. The upper-CASE tool shall be based on our Open Repository Access Technology in order to facilitate easy integration with a variety of Repositories and thus with a number of well-established CASE systems.

A configurable generator transforms the results of the DIADEM design tool into code for a variety of lower-CASE UIMS products. Producing a generator that can also be configured by the customer is vital for the commercial success of the tool, since the market for lower-CASE UIMS tools is rather broad (of several hundred products). Many customers have adopted an enterprise-wide strategy for specific tools and will thus reject the DIADEM method and the upper-CASE DIADEM design tool, if they are not able to support their choice of lower-CASE tool.

Acknowledegements

The authors would like to thank all the participants to the DIAMANTA project who contributed directly or indirectly to this paper, A. Martinez from STISA, P.G. Johannsen and B.B. Borys from MMS laboratory of the University of Kassel, Philippe Aknin from Thomson-CSF/SCTF and C. A. Poirier from Thomson-CSF/RCC who is the project manager. The ESPRIT project 20507 (DIAMANTA) is partially financed by the CEC DGIII-F4, with K.C. Varghese as Project Officer. The authors also wish to express their gratitude to the DIADEM team, and particularly to C. Boutillier for her significant contribution to the project definition.

Transferring Research Results from the Laboratory to the Market by Means of Intelligent Decision Support

John Darzentas, Jenny Darzentas and Thomas Spyrou
Department of Mathematics, University of Aegean
GR-83200 Karlovassi, Samos, Greece

Abstract

This paper describes a system that was built as a proof-of-concept demonstrator for Amodeus 2. The project researched ways and means of developing tools and techniques to aid the interface designer from the point of view of system, user and design considerations. As these products were the results of upstream research, it was also part of the project to find ways of transferring these results to the design community. One way was the DDAS (Designers' Decision Aiding System) whose purpose was to enable designers with specific interface problems to find which technique(s) would be the most appropriate for them to use. The system was designed using an approach based on Soft Systems Methodology (SSM) and fuzzy reasoning, and Intelligent Decision Support Systems (Intelligent DSS).

The usefulness of the system is that it provides a means of transfer of the modelling techniques in direct relation to the concern of the designer. In addition, a beneficial feature of the system is that it encourages designers to think about their problems and to understand them better. It is also a great advantage that the problem descriptions are expressed in natural language which allows the user more degrees of freedom, while at the same time the evaluation procedures are not constructed around quantifying processes thus ensuring that the initial freedom is retained to a large extent until the end of the decision making process. Finally, the system is generalisable to other situations where problems exist, where tools and methodologies exist to help out in those problems, but where a means of helping the problem owner decide what is appropriate for him is lacking. The work described below was carried out as part of the ESPRIT Basic Research Action Project 7040, Amodeus 2.

1. Introduction

Of the problems which arise when dealing with the products of today's technological world, two which are increasingly apparent to policy makers and users alike are those of usability and of transfer of research results [4,16]. The problem of the transfer of research results, especially where these results relate to usability of computer systems, is the subject of this paper. Thus in this case, the results of research, when successfully transferred to their intended end users, designers of computer systems, can substantially affect the usability of the system design and implementation.

The problem of making computer systems more "user friendly" has received much attention, and no one can deny that computers are now being used by users from all kinds of backgrounds, rather than the "initiated" as was once the case

However, in many systems in use or being designed presently, particularly safety critical systems, such as those in use in defence or in air traffic control systems, usability, - the ability to use a system and not make mistakes or be misled by the system -, goes far beyond the concept of "user- friendliness" and has repercussions on safety and security. While technology may leap ahead in bounds producing, for instance, images at faster and faster speeds, when humans interact with the systems, human computer interaction (HCI) research is needed to make sure that those systems take into account the limitations of human capabilities in terms of vision, memory and comprehension, learning new skills and so forth. And unless such research is moved out of the laboratories and exploited in the real world, the knowledge of how to use information and communication technologies (ICT) will continue to lag far behind the knowledge to produce it.

Generally, the problem of moving research results into the market place is a familiar one and driving force behind such European Union funded efforts such as the VALUE programme [18] and initiatives such as ISPO [17]. Typically, funded research takes place in academic or even industrial research centres and their upstream results are often subject to very slow take-up by industry, for a whole range of reasons: for example, "downstream" companies are wary of being "guinea pigs" or simply they are not aware of the potential of the results, and/or if they are, they are not able to envision how these results could be incorporated into their workplace or perhaps do not have the resources to investigate how they might be. It is worth noting that this is sometimes still the case even with specially commissioned research. Of the RACE programme it has been noted by the Commission itself that despite its many successes in advancing communication technologies, they are still far from being in widespread use [19].

The researchers, for their part, are often not equipped in terms of organisation and personnel to transfer their results into industry. Furthermore, their research results are rarely in a form that is easily translatable into a package that can be picked up and utilised by the intended end user.

This paper reports on an actual example of this transfer problem and moreover one where the research results to be transferred related to advances in human computer interaction. The paper describes a methodology which resulted in an active intelligent decision support system (DSS) which was designed to help users. In this case, designers of computer systems decide which tools and techniques, out of an array produced by HCI researchers, would be most useful for them. The methodology and the resulting DSS is of a generic nature and could be used for other situations where research results are available, but the end user needs a means of helping him decide which is best for him in his specific set of circumstances. Furthermore, these results were of the type that are difficult to transfer because they are not easily packaged for the user.

The methodology [11,12] was influenced by systems thinking and more specifically Soft Systems Methodology (SSM) [8,9], and also by most recent trends in Expert and Decision Support Systems, which require the user to participate "actively" in the process of decision making. In the case reported here, where qualitative rather than quantitative knowledge was represented in the knowledge base, a reasoning mechanism was designed based on and thus offering the power of fuzzy logic to evaluate non-crisply defined options [15].

The next section gives a brief background of the transfer of results problem as it occurred in the context of an HCI ESPRIT Basic Research project [2]. Section 3 discusses how the concept of an active intelligent decision aiding system, designed using an SSM based approach incorporating fuzzy logic was used as a vehicle for transfer. Section 4 describes the system, its architecture and how to use it, while in the concluding section, the contribution of this work to the problem areas of usability and transfer of results is discussed.

2. Transfer Problems

The Amodeus 2 [2] project researched ways and means of developing tools and techniques to aid the interface designer from the point of view of system, user and design considerations. These were the products of upstream research, and for best value to be made of this work, the project also investigated ways of transferring these results downstream to the design community.

Three main problems bedevil the transfer work. Those described here are those encountered by the team investigating transfer and assay of the research results. Although this example refers to the HCI domain, it is also valid to say that the complex interplay between the form and content of results and the transfer mechanism between the researchers and users repeat themselves in other domains [24].

The first of these problems refers to the nature of the research results. These modelling techniques, coming from a wide variety of disciplines, (computer science, cognitive science, ergonomics, etc.) consequently differed considerably in approach, in scope, and in degree of formality, and although all touched on the problems of usability in the design of computer systems, some covered certain areas more than others, and were in turn less concerned with some areas than others.

Considerable effort was expended to try to integrate the approaches [2] but the diversity of the approaches and the multidisciplinarity of the research did not lend itself to the establishment of an overarching theory. Several strategies were adopted to aid integration and hence transfer. The most important of these being to work on examples. This was to give a common platform to all the modellers and also to allow designers who were invited at intervals to contribute to the research in order to allow easier access to the issues under discussion. A further problematic aspect of transfer attempt was that this was ongoing research and that results were being developed, revised and extended continuously. Thus there was no clear definitive and internally coherent "package" of results to transfer.

A second problem, related to the first, concerned the nature of the design process [21,22,27,28]. In empirical designer studies that were carried out to try to establish how designers design it was repeatedly found that strict notions of design processes were not adhered to in practice. The formal software engineering view of design suggested a linear process expressed as:

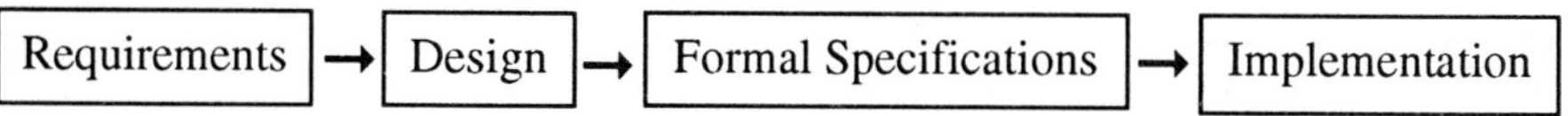

However, empirical research, showed that, with one or two exceptions, the product development process had, in reality, relatively little in common with any product design procedures [23]. In real life, the process was one of "muddling through", and that rather than any clear design decisions being taken, there was a kind of "evolving commitment" [33]; design can only be considered as a heterarchical process, a series of reiterations, switching from high level to low level discussion and back, as the design team seeks and receives answers from various inputs at varying levels of granularity [30,31].

Thus there was not even a conception common to both designers and modellers of what constitutes the design activity, nor for that matter between designers themselves and consequently no well defined place within design activity for usability techniques.

The third problem concerned the interaction between researchers and design practitioners. That is: the practicalities of actually communicating with the end users for whom these techniques were being developed, namely, the design practitioners. One of the transfer mechanisms was to demonstrate the techniques in specially organised workshops [1,5,32]. The designers were introduced to the modelling, in theory by talks and demonstrations, and in practice, by working through examples and by having the modellers work on real life problems which the designers had been invited to contribute. This last activity took place both at workshops and as large scale investigations lasting several months.

However, the pressures of the commercial world being as they are, it was very difficult to get designers to commit to such activities. Even accounting for the fact that the most "enlightened" design teams included Human Factors experts, persons with an especially vested interest in learning about what was going on at the forefront of HCI research, the very richness of the results defied quick and easy transfer.

Since it was difficult to get commitment from commercial designers to participate the techniques were tried out on and by students studying design as part of their curricula. Here the emphasis was on refining training material that would enable the future generation of designers to use the techniques.

Thus within the project, several types of transfer activity took place. These were the workshops, with all the design planning and organisation that they involved; the working on the common exemplars; and the definition and use of "encapsulated" material [6] to pass on the bare essentials of the techniques.

A further aim of the transfer activity was that which forms the main thrust of this paper, that of investigating the concept of a decision aiding system to act as a transfer mechanism. The next section discusses the concept of the Designers' Decision Aiding System (DDAS) and how its design confronted some of the problems that beset transfer activities.

Although the motivation behind the concept of the DDAS was to act as a transfer mechanism, the actual aid the DDAS was designed to give was that of helping designers decide which technique(s) offered the best value for them. This was a problem that was voiced several times by designers. Their situation, typically, was that they did not have the time or the expertise to "wade through" theory, but wanted useful end results in terms of tools and techniques to help them incorporate usability considerations in their designs, and having understood that there was a variety of such techniques needed some way to distinguishing what was useful for what aspect of design, and how it affected usability related problems.

Moreover, it was stated informally in the workshops that, in some cases, the users were not able to articulate satisfactorily what aspect of usability they were interested in. What they knew is that some part of their designs were not easy to use and they wanted to know what was the reason and how they could correct this and avoid future designs having problems.

While not discounting the value of workshops and other means of transfer, it was felt that a decision support system could offer a further valuable means of transferring results.

3. Concept and Design of the Designer's Decision Support System (DDAS)

The first step in undertaking the design and eventual building of the DDAS, was to address the problems engendered by the variety of the modelling techniques as well as the lack of a common perception of the problem space constituted by design activities. Further, the system had to take account of relevant design problems to be able to be useful to designers.

As a starting point for the understanding of the problem situation, a "rich picture" [3,7,9,25] was formed of the design activity space. The views of activities undertaken within design were identified and accommodated in the rich picture in order to form as complete an appreciation of the domain as possible, removing all unsubstantiated referent to sequentiality in design activities. Instead, the elements of the design process are shown as components of the design space. These are the artefact itself, specification of the system (tasks) and the interface elements, the communication between them and a continuum of conceptual views of deliberation activity. The process undertaken for the making of the rich picture was via consultations with the modellers and

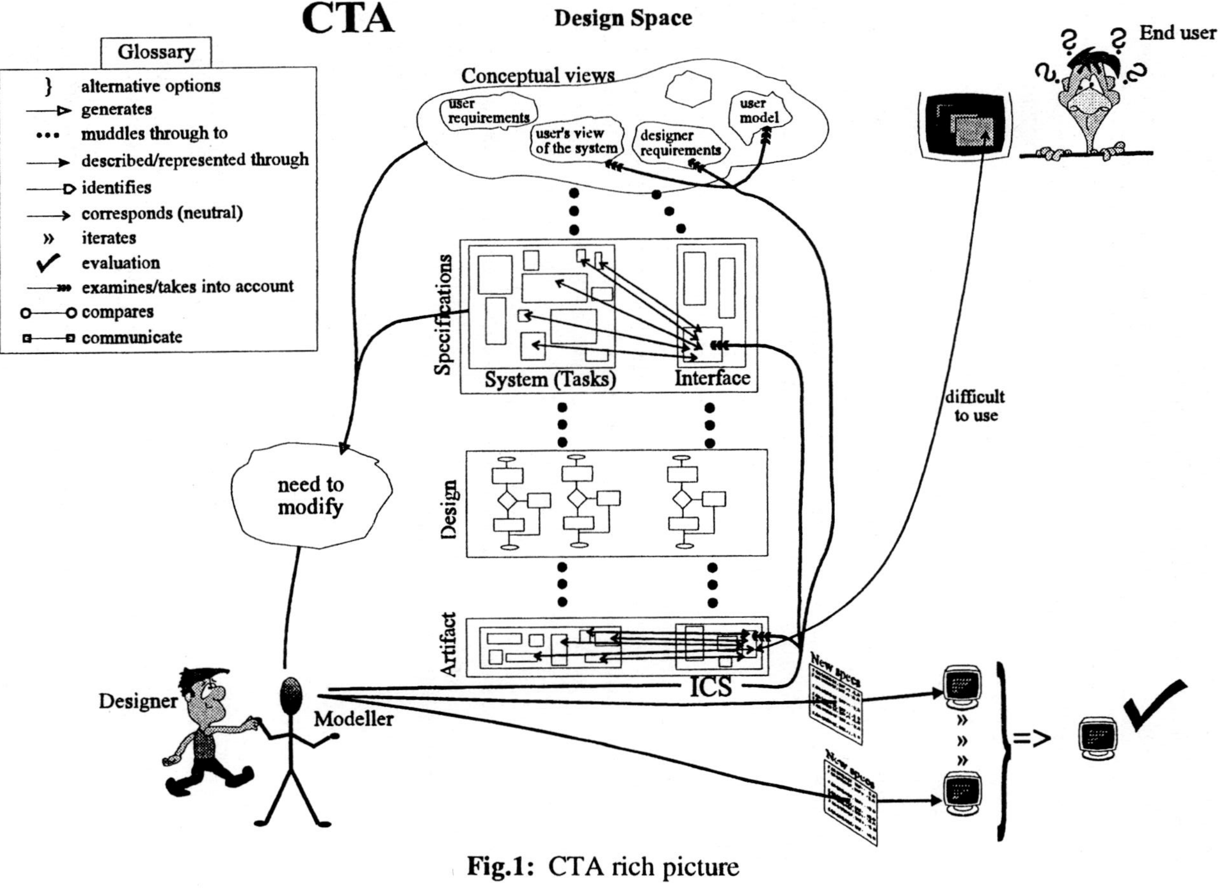

Fig.1: CTA rich picture

reference to the literature until a consensus was reached, as described in more detail in [10,14]. An example of a rich picture is shown in figure 1.

The primary benefit of using such an approach is that of gaining insight from learning and debating about the problem situation. It offered an understanding of the activities which constitute design as well as the relationships between the design activities in the design space and the modelling techniques.

The task of identifying and defining the potential of these modelling techniques to design practice, i.e. identifying the relationship between the modelling techniques and the problem descriptions they can address was next tackled using the same methods of consultations, literature search and verification [12,13]. The outcome is a conceptual systemic view of the design space defined through a set of relevant subsystems which are identified according to the range of problems that the Amodeus modelling approaches can address. The relationships between the relevant activity subsystems and the modelling techniques form the main structural functional component of the DDAS.

With this deeper understanding of the domain and the transfer problem situation that the decision aiding system was attempting to assist with, the task of designing the architecture of the DSS was confronted. In terms of building a DSS, there are three tasks central to development: *i)* representing the expert knowledge, *ii)* user problem formulation, and *iii)* reasoning.

The expert knowledge to be represented is the modelling techniques. As previously stated, these originate from various disciplines and vary in scope of focus: some concentrating on users, some on systems and some on tasks, others on design rationale, etc. Their range of applicability is overlapping and not crisply defined; some techniques are more suited to tackling certain aspects of the design problem space than others. The modelling techniques are research products which are continuously being refined, thus there is no final version of a technique, while the developers of the techniques are variously psychologists, cognitive scientists, computer scientists, etc. whose perspective on design may not necessarily be readily comprehensible to designers. Some techniques require special skills, e.g. knowledge of a programming language; some are aimed at particular members of the design community, e.g. the software engineer, the human factors specialist.

Thus the representation of the expert knowledge needs to be capable of accommodating the multi-disciplinary character of the techniques. It should represent the elements that are common in the sense that they share similar goals, or they explain the same phenomena. It should represent the differences between modelling techniques by capturing their strengths and weaknesses in relation to specific design problems. And finally it should represent the relationships of the various components within a technique and those between different techniques.

In the DDAS this was accomplished by representing the expert knowledge about the modelling techniques and their use in design, through their identified relationships to parts of the possible problems (problem descriptions) they can address. The relevant subsystems and their links form a network of design problem descriptions.

The means of dealing with the question of user problem formulation is closely linked to the representation of the expert knowledge. Two caveats were made here: firstly, decision aid is for use with design problems or classes of problem that the Amodeus modelling techniques can handle; and secondly, the designer user is guided to express his problem by being asked to select descriptions of design problems which relate to his situation of concern. This accords well with recent work in active DSS which show that the user prefers "active" aid from a system, and wants to be prompted [29]. That is to say that a user who has a very well formed idea of what his problem is may not mind expressing it, (though he may wonder if the machine can interpret it as he wants), but a user who just "has a feeling" would have difficulties making that intuitive response to a situation comprehensible to the system. In the case of designers and computer system usability problems this had been shown to be the case. Thus, bearing it mind the above, the question of user problem formulation was tackled by representing the knowledge in the system in such a way that the designer can express his problem within it: i.e. the designer is shown a variety of problem descriptions and selects those which are most closely resemble his concern. The resulting attributes and relationships associated with subsystems selected by the designer, can be separated into groups according to the modelling techniques they are associated to. Each of these groups can now be evaluated in order to provide recommendation as to which modelling technique(s) are more appropriate to be used for the particular problem. The evaluation of these groups of attributes is carried out with the aid of test score semantics, this constitutes the third major task area of the development.

The interaction between user and system actually results in a description of the user problem in terms of the activity subsystems which link back into the modelling techniques. Not surprisingly the output shows that several of the techniques would have something to say about this problem. Such output is not succinct enough to be of use to the designer. He requires more intelligent aid. He would like to know when and where a technique is useful. To refine output, the use of fuzzy reasoning, in the form of test score semantics is used, and a recommendation is made to the designer.

Due to the nature of the problem and the method of representation of the expert knowledge, the evaluation is made on the basis of linguistically expressed qualitative as opposed to quantifiable statements. For instance, "technique x is used to resolve problems of ambiguity". The meaning of each of these "discourses" about what each modelling technique can do for a problem or part of a problem is evaluated using test score semantics [34] where the proposals contained in the discourse about a modelling technique are treated as fuzzy constraints.

Following the test score semantics procedure each relationship (fuzzy constraint) is evaluated in the explanatory database on the basis of specific templates for the relations. The user provides a score for each relationship, which will describe the degree to which, according to him (and not the expert who compiled the database), the relationship is satisfied. These two scores per constraint may be combined to one via an operator, such as the compensation operator [35]. According to this approach the test scores assigned to every relationship will give overall aggregated test scores for the groups of attributes and relationships which correspond to each modelling technique. The highest of these overall test scores may be taken as a very good indication that the corresponding modelling technique is the most appropriate currently. To summarise, the challenges facing the creation of DDAS were threefold:

- to find a common language and use it to describe what each modelling-technique can do,
- to describe design problems in such a way that they can be correlated to the relevant abilities of the modelling techniques, using that language, and
- to find a way for the system to evaluate the appropriateness of each modelling approach to a design problem.

In order to meet these challenges, an approach was developed for a) the elicitation of expert knowledge about the potential of models; b) representing the meaning of that potential to the client and c) from there recommending to the client the most suitable technique(s). The system's architecture and how the user interacts with the system is described in the next section and an example session is given.

4. DDAS Architecture

Figure 2 shows a high level functional architecture of the system. The designer selects the set of subsystems (problem descriptions) relevant to his problem to provide the design problem space knowledge module. The design space module is based on representations in a frame and rule based environment and it is basically retrieved from the general design space contained in the knowledge module. It is the one used by the decision models module. Sets of rules and meta-rules manage the relevant subsystems.

Note that modelling techniques are considered as whole units, in other words the modelling techniques are not broken down into operational parts nor is there any attempt to redefine amalgamated techniques from parts of others. The relationships are identified and defined between subsystems of the design space and whole modelling techniques.

The decision models module contains the function which performs the decision aiding process based on fuzzy sets and in particular on test score semantics. This module, having the set of relevant subsystems selected by the designer describing his problem, requests that all the links (constraints) between the subsystems and the modelling techniques etc. are evaluated either by the designer or retrieved from a data base with expert evaluations for some of the links or both. Then following the test score semantics approach this module proceeds with the aggregation of these evaluations followed by the defuzzification of that aggregation towards the final recommendation.

The interface module controls the interfacing between the user (designer) and the system. It contains six functions which are responsible for displaying the current problem representation, browsing and inputting user selections/ rejections, evaluations of subsystems and constraints (relationships); and communicating the final recommendations.

Implementation was carried out using CLIPS, an expert system environment developed by NASA and HARDY, a hypertext based diagramme editor for

XWindows and Windows 3.1 developed by the University of Edinburgh [20,26]. Using CLIPS enabled the use of a logic based programming environment needed for the task of manipulating qualitative knowledge, combined with required expert systems features. The use of HARDY enabled the utilisation of visual techniques to interact with the user, making use of graphics and labelled nodes within networks.

5. Interacting with the System

The presentation of the problem descriptions to the user; how the user is guided to express/identify his problem and what facilities are available for this; and finally how the system outputs recommendations explained below. The interaction with the user is based upon two types of presentation elements: the graphic display of the problem descriptions, and the commands that manipulate the interaction. The problem descriptions are displayed in the form of labelled shapes and are laid out in a series of screens browsable by the user.

Two types of shapes are used, one to represent the fact that there exist more specific problem descriptions in the knowledge base, while the other shape represents the most specific expression of a subproblem contained in the knowledge base. In the current version, the former are shown as rhombii, the latter as circles. Shapes may be linked by arcs which denote different types of relationships existing between problem descriptions, for example, green arcs represent "high possible concurrency" and blue arcs, "low possible concurrency".

Commands are displayed as buttons on a toolbar which is permanently on screen. These commands aid the user to choose amongst the available facilities of the system, for example the facility of moving to diagrammes/screens that correspond to different levels of analysis is performed by double arrow buttons. During the interaction the problem descriptions are displayed to the user, so that he can search for and identify those that he considers as most relevant to his problem. The objective is for him to make a selection of these relevant descriptions as a way of expressing his situation of concern. Whilst selecting (by clicking on the problem descriptions), the user can also specify the degree of relevance of the descriptions to his problem, and should he change his mind, he can unselect anything he has already chosen. Each time he clicks on a problem description, its colour changes. Each colour shows the degree of importance of the specific problem descriptions to the user. The set of used colours are white, turquoise, yellow, magenta and red, signifying least to maximum importance respectively. This is also the sequence of the colours which appear when clicking. After red, (most relevant) comes white again and the user can go through this cycle as many times as he wants. In order to guide the user through the network of problem descriptions, these are presented to him at various levels of detail. It is possible for the user to go backwards and forwards between screens (by using the buttons << >>).

The user can ask for comments from the system about the set of the problem descriptions he has chosen (*Comments on Choices*). This facility is available any time during the interaction when selections are made. The

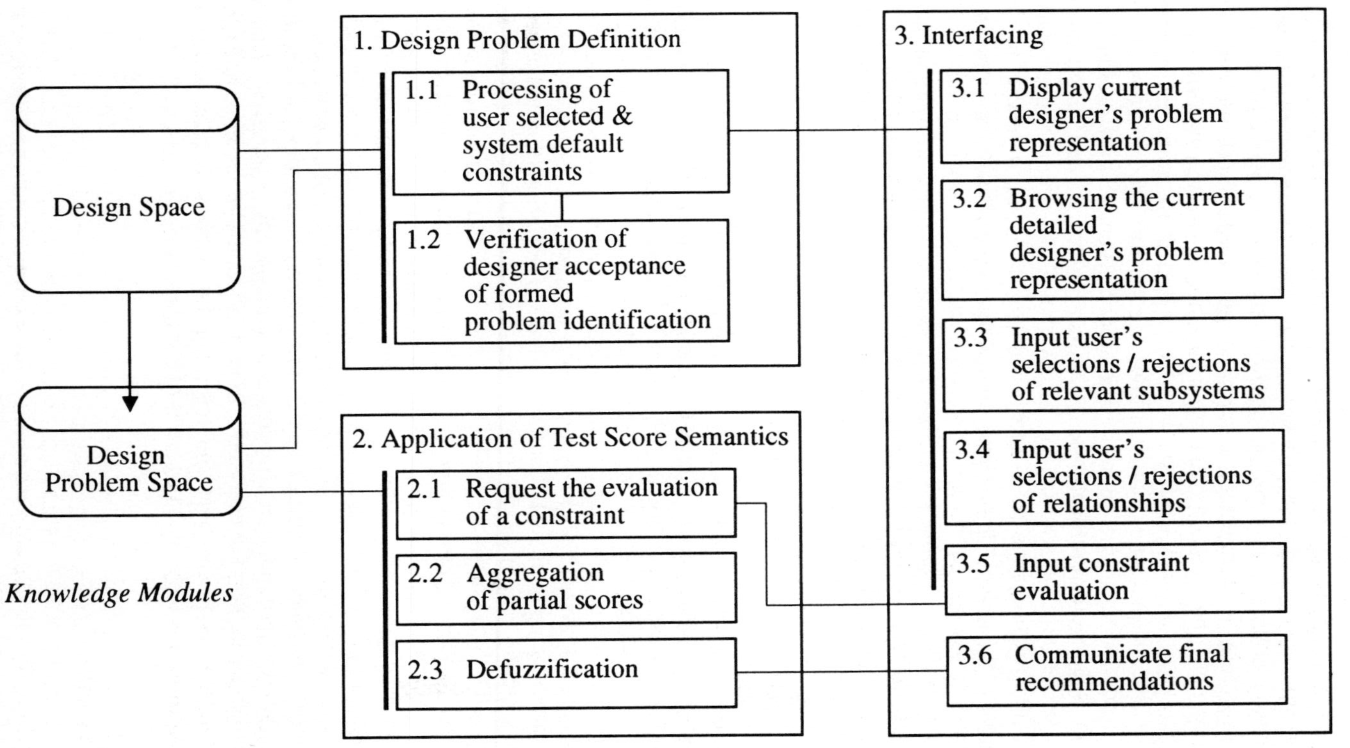

Fig.2: Functional architecture of DDAS

comments that the system is able to give are based on the relationships of the problem descriptions that exist in the knowledge base. For instance, the user who has chosen both of the problem descriptions that are parts of a "low-possible-concurrency" relationship, is warned that these problems are not usually concurrent. The problems that are mentioned in the warning messages are highlighted with a black outline in order to find them more easily. The system is flexible in the sense that it allows the user to ignore the warning messages. Should the user want to follow the advice given, he may decide how he wants to solve the implications, by either selecting and unselecting accordingly. Once all the warning messages that the system has to show according to the relationships have been displayed, the system reverts to the normal interaction state where the user can choose/unchoose problem descriptions or choose one of the other available facilities.

A further facility available at any time is that of providing a formatted text description of the set of problem descriptions chosen (*Current State*). The relationships that exist in the knowledge base form the basis for the text description of the chosen problems. Once the text description of the set of chosen problems has been presented, the system reverts to state where the user can choose/unchoose problem descriptions or select one of the other available facilities.

Should the user want an illustration of a particular problem description, he can obtain examples of use by using the example button (or by shift-left-clicking on the problem descriptions in question). This feature can be useful in helping the user decide about how close (if at all) the specific subproblem description is to his own particular problem. Finally, the user is also able to see instructions regarding the use of the system (*Help button*).

When the designer-user feels that the problem descriptions he has chosen describe his situation adequately, he can request a recommendation from the system. The DDAS recommends which of the modelling technique(s) are suitable for his problem. This facility is available whenever no other facility is active. The recommendation is given as formatted text which recommends to the user the most appropriate technique(s). The reasoning behind this recommendation, based upon fuzzy logic, is also given in the formatted text, in order to give the user the justification of the rationale behind the recommendation. The compensation oriented score operator from test score semantics [34] is used to compute the recommendation. For its computation, the quantifier values (linguistic or otherwise) that specify how important each chosen most specific problem description is to the user and the quantifier values of how well the modelling techniques satisfy each chosen problem description are used.

6. An Example

To illustrate some of the system's capabilities, an example detailing a designer's specific problem and how he can handle it using DDAS follows. In this example, the designer's concern is that interface users are often confused by the outcome of clicking a button X. e.g. there can be two different results of clicking the same button X in two different contexts respectively. The designer wants to solve this problem. For the sake of the example, it is assumed that he wants the solution to enable the users of the interface to distinguish clearly what are the corresponding effects on the system when a button is pressed. It is also assumed that the designer wants to check that this problem of the design of the interface does not start from a confusion in the requirements.

The designer is firstly presented with a diagramme which uses rhombii to represent the most general subproblem descriptions (see figure 3). The designer searches through the diagramme for labels which come closest to his intention of expressing his problem. In this case, he chooses the rhombii with the following labels and assigns to them a degree of relevance, as follows:

- identify features in the design of the interface that need modifications or extensions (red),
- identify problematic features in the requirements (yellow), and
- provide a framework for capturing properties that are generally required to exist between the system and the interface (magenta).

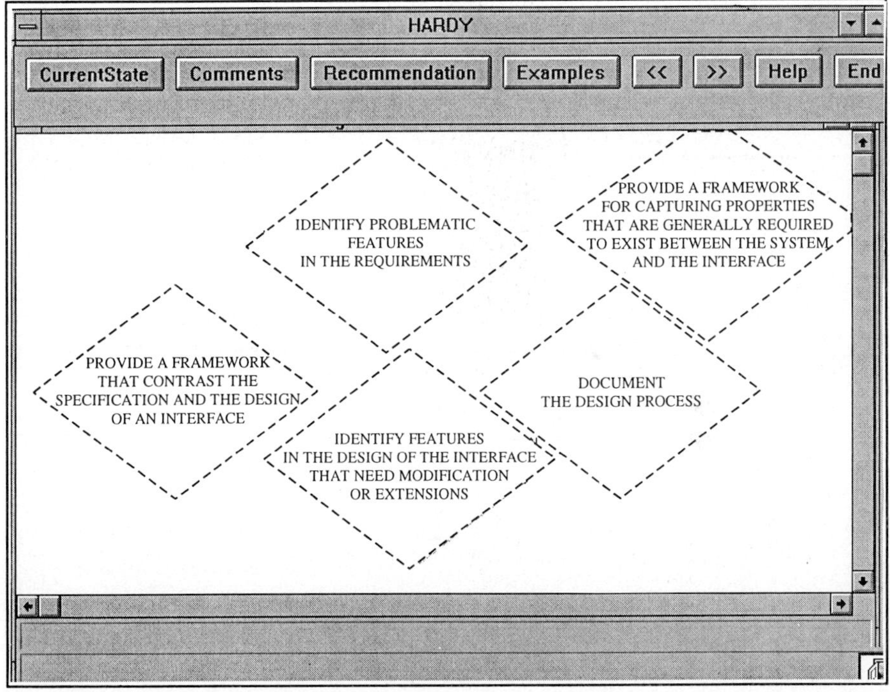

Fig.3: A snapshot of the most general problem descriptions diagramme

The designer presses the button with the label «>>« in order to move to the next diagramme with the more specific subproblem descriptions. He is then presented with a diagramme which uses circles and arcs to represent the possible subproblem descriptions and the relationships between them, such as that given in figure 4. The designer searches through the network diagrammes for labels which come closest to expressing his problem. He chooses the circles with the following labels and assigns to them a degree of relevance (colour):

- identifies features that are sources of ambiguity and confusion (red),
- identifies ambiguities and confusions in the requirements and therefore iterate towards design specifications that are cognitively straightforward (yellow),
- provides a framework for representing and understanding the compatibility between functional (system) state and perceived state (conformance) (magenta),
- provides a framework for representing and understanding the trade-off between what the representation in itself will support and what must be supported by the system (affordance) (turquoise), and
- provides a framework for representing and understanding the property of predictability: supporting the system tasks by providing enough information to indicate to user what effect his new actions will have (magenta).

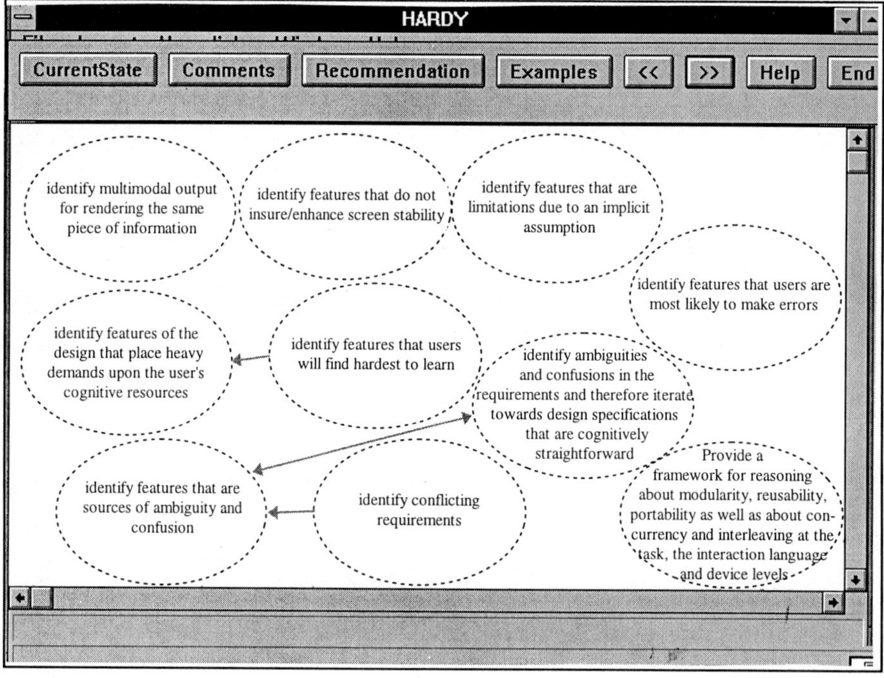

Fig.4: A snapshot of the most specific problem descriptions diagramme

Before going on to choose some more subproblem descriptions from the DDAS diagramme, the designer would like to have comments from the system about his choices. He clicks on the «COMMENTS ON CHOICES» grey button. This advice is given in a message window as shown in figure 5.

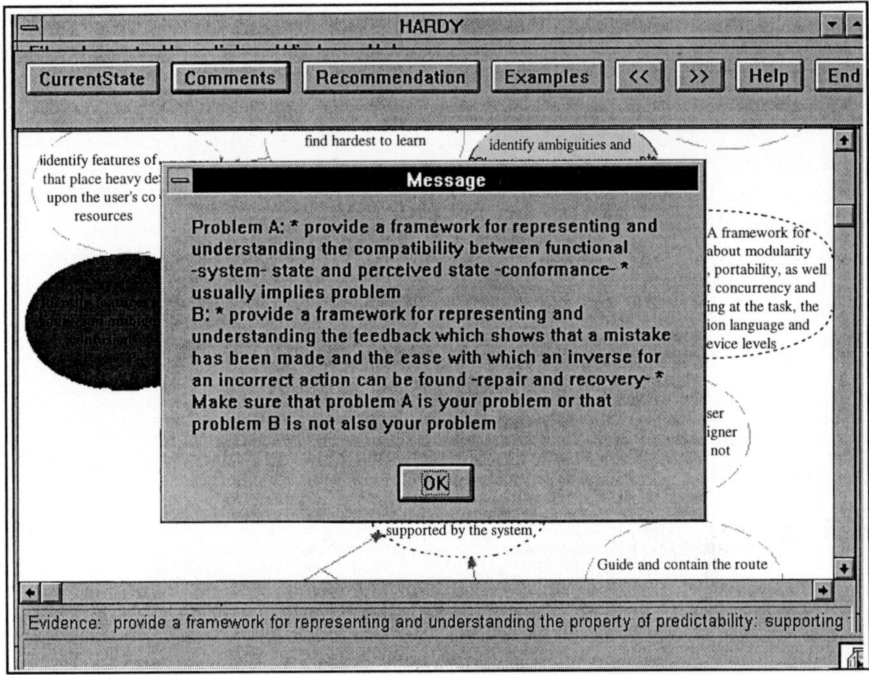

Fig.5: Comments on choices message window

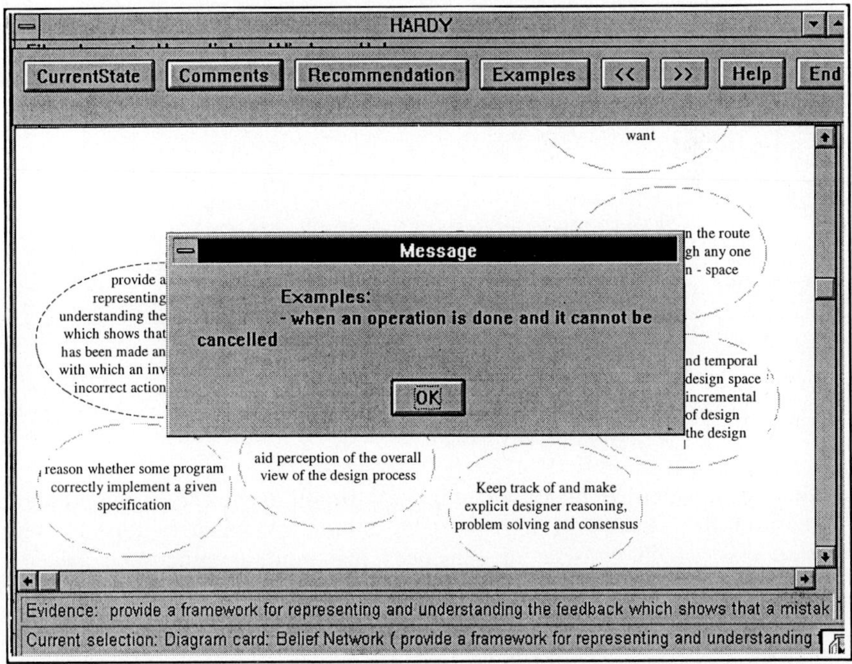

Fig.6: Message window for the chosen specific subproblem

In this particular case the displayed message comments that according to the system, the subproblem description "*provides a framework for representing and understanding the compatibility between functional (system) state and perceived state (conformance)*". Usually it implies that the one with the label "*provides a framework for representing and understanding the feedback which shows that a mistake has been made and the ease with which an inverse for an incorrect action can be found (repair and recovery)*" and therefore the second could also be chosen.

The designer can click on a subproblem in order to see the available examples (if any) of the specific subproblem. The examples are given to help him understand better and see some characteristic situations described by the subproblem. The examples are given in a message window as shown in figure 6.

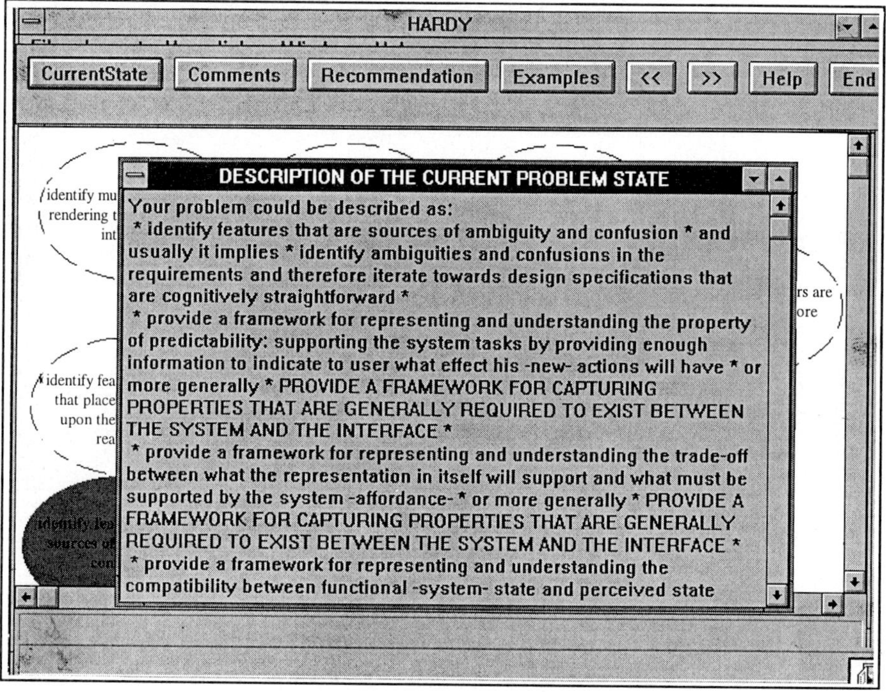

Fig.7: Current state message window

Each time the designer wants to see a text description of the chosen subproblem he clicks on the «CURRENT STATE» grey button. A window appears with formatted text which consists of sentences that contain either one selected problem descriptions description or two selected problem descriptions that are related with a type of relationship expressed in words. In this example, a part of the text description that the designer sees is shown in the window in figure 7. In this way, the system, utilising its knowledge of the design space, and problem descriptions associated with it, prompts the user and aids him to consider subproblem descriptions which may be relevant to his problem of concern and which he has not chosen. The user considers the system's advice and is free to reject it should he not think it relevant. Otherwise, the system highlights the problem descriptions mentioned with a black outline (see figure 8) to help the user find the problem descriptions that the message refers to. The user continues in this way, making selections, reading the comments on current choices and reselecting until he is satisfied with what the current selection represents. During this cycle he can at any time get a text description of the current state.

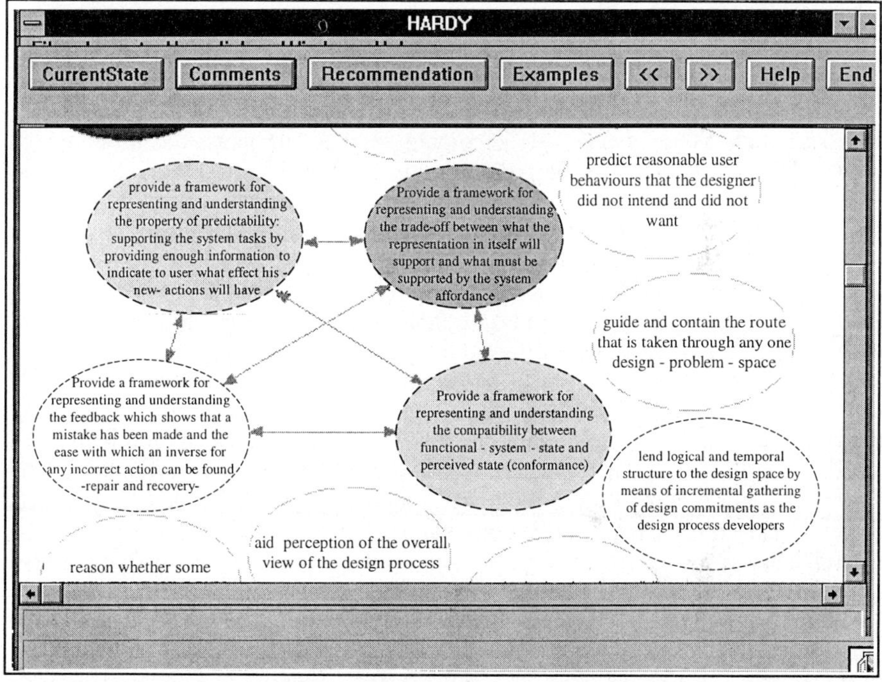

Fig.8: Selected problem descriptions

When the designer is satisfied that he has a final set of chosen subproblem descriptions (i.e. he doesn't want to choose any more subproblem descriptions by clicking on them and that he doesn't want to change his belief about the importance he gave to the selected subproblem descriptions, by changing their colour), he then clicks on the «*Recommendation*» button to get a recommendation about the most appropriate modelling technique(s) for his problem. A window appears with the recommendation. The computation representing the reasoning behind this result is also displayed in the same window for traceability. This can be transformed to formatted text in order to give the user the opportunity to understand and justify the system's reasoning.

7. Discussion and Conclusions

This paper looked at the means of transferring research results in cases where these results are not readily exploitable due mainly to their academic nature. The problems encountered in transfer of such work was discussed, and in this case, the research results concerned the usability of computer systems and what can be done to make systems more comfortable and accessible. A methodology leading to a computer supported aid was given as an example of an effective means of transfer.

The creation of a decision support system to help users chose which results were the most useful for them was a useful tool. Moreover, in addition to the benefits to be gained from other transfer techniques, DDAS offered the following advantageous *features to the user*:

- it was tailored to user needs, cutting straight to the heart of user concerns, without the need to understand theory and rhetoric,
- it acted as a means of accessing the techniques, deciding which technique(s) were most appropriate was the first step, the user then had to find out about how to use the recommended technique(s), and
- it is simple to use and accessible to anyone with appropriate equipment: no need to attend workshops or demonstration sessions, no need for human intervention or travel, it can be used wherever and whenever convenient.

It integrated research results along a common axis, and furthermore that common axis was directly related to user concerns: "what can this tool for me in my situation". In this way it helped to "package" results for *ease of transfer*.

Another important achievement is the fact that the user learned more about his problem, which is an important benefit that was not envisaged but which is a direct result of the type of vehicle used for the transfer i.e. the active DSS. The user learning more about his problem is a significant result since it impacts on the user both in terms of what he learns about the subject (content) and what he was able to see in practice (form): the power of the active DSS to lead the user to question and explore the subject.

The "browsing" skills that in a pre-computer age would belong to the person who leafed through encyclopaedias, and which nowadays are translated to those who use the information highway, are harnessed in DDAS to provide the learning forum of such systems.

The user is able to search the knowledge base looking for descriptions of problems which are most close to his area of concern. This is a skill that is being developed by all who generally seek information, and its advantage is that the user does not have to come with a problem precisely defined but can make "mini-decisions" throughout the process, and learning almost incidentally, what else is on offer.

In terms of transfer and usability the DDAS was conceived specifically to make accessible to the designers techniques for achieving greater degrees of comfort and accessibility. The designers and users of DDAS familiarise themselves with Intelligent Decision Support Systems (Intelligent DSS), and experience for themselves the very real and individually tailored help these systems can provide.

The methodology used to design the DDAS overcame difficulties which have been encountered by other transfer efforts, namely that of how to convey results that are widely differing in terms of discipline, scope and formality and which are not packaged for transfer. This methodology is generalisable to other results where techniques and tools are available to solve problems, but problem owners are unable to efficiently choose which is most appropriate for them.

References

1. Aboulafia A., Nielsen J., Jorgensen A.H. "Evaluation Report on the EnExl Workshop", Amodeus Project Document TA/WP2, 1992.
2. Amodeus ESPRIT Basic Research Action 3066, 1989-1992, Amodeus (Assimilating Models of Designers Users and Systems) and ESPRIT Basic Research Action 7040 Amodeus-2 1992-1995 (Assaying Means of Design Expressions for Users and Systems) Documentation available by (ftp.mrc-apu.cam.ac.uk) or by (http://www.mrcapu.cam.ac.uk/amodeus/qref.html).
3. Avison D.E., Golder P.A.,Shah H.U. Towards an SSM toolkit: rich picture diagramming, European Journal of Information Systems, Vol.1, No.6., pp.397-307, 1992.
4. Bangemann M. et al. "Europe and the Global Information Society" Recommendations to the European Council June 1994, Report available via http://www.echo.lu/eudocs/en/.bangemann.html
5. Buckingham S., S. Hammond, N. Jorgensen, A.H., Aboulafia, A. EnEx3: The ISLE Modelling Transfer Exercise Amodeus Project Document TA/WP22, 1992.
6. Buckingham S., Jürgensen A.H., Hammond N. and Aboulafia A.(Eds), "Amodeus-2 HCI Modelling and Design Approaches: Executive Summaries and Worked Examples, Amodeus Project Document: TA/WP16, 1994.
7. Checkland P.B. "The Development of Systems Thinking by Systems Practice - a Methodology from an Action Research Programme", Progress in Cybernetics and Systems Research, Vol.2, Trappl R., Hanika F., (eds) Hemisphere, pp.278-283, 1975.
8. Checkland P.B. "Systems Thinking", Systems Practice, Wiley, New York, 1981.
9. Checkland P.B., Scholes J. "Soft Systems Methodology in Action", Wiley, New York, 1990.
10. Darzentas J., Darzentas J.S., Spyrou T. Defining the Design "Decision Space: Rich Pictures and Relevant Subsystems", Amodeus Project Document, TA/WP 21, 1994.

11. Darzentas J., Darzentas J.S., Spyrou T. "Fuzzy Reasoning and Systems Thinking in a Decision Aid for Designers", in Proceedings of Second European Conference on Intelligent Techniques and Soft Computing, Aachen, pp.1609-1614, 1994.

12. Darzentas J., Darzentas J.S., Spyrou T. "Designing a Designers' Decision Aiding System (DDAS): a Designers' Decision Aiding System", Journal of Decision Systems, Vol.4, No.1, pp. 9-22, 1995.

13. Darzentas J., Darzentas J.S ., Spyrou T. "An Architecture for Designer Decision Aiding" in Brannback M. and.Leino T. (Eds) Decision Support Systems, Academy Press, Vol.427, pp.115-132, 1995.

14. Darzentas J., Darzentas J.S., Spyrou T. "Towards a Design Decision Aiding System (DDAS)", Amodeus Project Document TA/WP9, 1992

15. Darzentas J., Spyrou T., Tsagaris C. "Evaluating Option-related Text Descriptions for Decision Aiding", in Proceedings of the 6th Meeting of the European Working Group on Decision Support Systems, Samos Greece, May 1995.

16. European Commission "Information and Communication Technologies Partnership", available via http://www.echo.lu, 1995

17. European Commission "Information Society Project Office (ISPO)", Part of Commission's Action Plan in "Europe's Way towards the Information Society", COM 94/347, July 1994.

18. European Commission VALUE 1(1989-1993), VALUE 2 (1992-94) Programmes for dissemination and exploitation of Research Results

19. Gannon P. "Whatever happened to that (Multi-Billion) Thing called RACE?", Network Europe, November 1994.

20. Giarratano J. , Riley G. "Expert Systems: Principles and Programming", PWS Publishing, Boston, MA, 2nd. edition, 1994.

21. Grudin J. "Interactive Users: Bridging the Gaps between Developers and Users", IEEE Computer Vol.24, No.4, pp.59-69, 1991.

22. Grudin J. "Interface: an Evolving Concept", Communications of the ACM pp.83-99, Vol.6, No.4, April 1993.

23. Hannigan S., Herring V. "The Role of Human Factors Inputs to Design Cycles", Deliverable A1.2b, HUFIT CODE HUFIT/8-HUS-11/86, 1986.

24. Laopodis V., Fernandez F.F., Gritzalis D., Darzentas J. "Evaluation of ICT Policy Options by Public, Using the Awareness Scenario Workshops Methodology", 2nd Conf. Evaluation of Inf. Techn., Henley, UK, July 1995.

25. Lewis, P.J. Rich Picture Building in the soft systems methodology. European Journal of Information Systems, Vol.1, No.5, pp. 551-360, 1992.

26. NASA Johnson Space Center, Houston, TX, "Clips Programmer's Guide, Version 6.0", JSC-25012, June 1993.

27. Nielsen J. "A Meta-Model for Interacting with Computers", in Interacting with Computers, pp.147-160, Vol.2, No.2, 1990.

28. Nielsen J. "The Usability Engineering Life Cycle" Vol.25, No.3, IEEE Computer, pp.12-22, March 1992.

29. Raghav R.H., Sridhar R., Narain S. An active Intelligent Decision support system - Architecture and Simulation" Decision Support Systems, 12, pp. 79-91, 1994.

30. Rouse, W.B. and Cody, W.J.: On the Design of Man-Machine Systems: Principles, Practices and Prospects", Automatica, Vol.24, pp. 227-238, 1988.

31. Rouse W.B. and Cody W.J. "A Theory-based Approach to Supporting Design Decision Making and Problem Solving", Information and Decision Technologies, Vol.15, pp.291-306, 1989.

32. Shum S., Hammond N. "The EnEx1 Modeller-Designer Workshop: Implications for Encapsulation", Amodeus Project, Document TA/WP4. 1992.

33. Terrins-Rudge D., Jorgensen A.H. "Supporting the Designers, Reaching the Users" in Byerly P.F., Barnard P.J., May J. (eds) Computers, Communication and Usability: Design Issues, Research and Methods for Integrated Services, pp.87-98, Elsevier, 1993.

34. Zadeh L.A. "Knowledge Representation in Fuzzy Logic", IEEE Trans. on Knowledge and Data Engineering, Vol.1, No.1, pp. 89-100, 1989.

35. Zimmermann H.-J., Zysno P. "Latent Connectives in Human Decision Making", Fuzzy Set and Systems, Vol.4, pp.37-51, 1980.

Coordination of Multiple Input Modes in User Interfaces

G.P. Faconti
CNR - Istituto CNUCE
Via S.Maria 36, I-56126 Pisa, Italy

Abstract

User interfaces of many application systems have begun to include multiple devices which can be used together to input single expressions. Such interfaces are widely labelled multimodal, since they use different types of communication channels to acquire information. In such cases, interface designers have not only to decide on which input modes should be supported, but also how to fuse them into a single representation format that can be processed by the underlying application system. Several informal criteria have been proposed in the literature in order to characterize fusion processes; they allow to analyse and compare existing multimodal interfaces beyond the level of surface aspects. When developing new interfaces, however, full insight into the structure of a fusion process must be guaranteed. In this paper, we show how fusion processes can be characterized by applying methods for formal process modelling. The presented approach can be applied to analyze and compare fusion processes in existing systems, as well as an aid for interface designers, who have to verify the behaviour of their systems.

1. Introduction

User interfaces of many application systems have begun to include multiple devices which can be used together to input single expressions. Such interfaces (and even the whole application systems) are widely labelled multimodal, since they use different types of communication channels to acquire information. For example, early prototype systems such as SCHOLAR [l], or NLG [2], aimed at combining natural language (NL) input from a keyboard with simple pointing gestures on the screen. A more advanced approach has been taken in the XTRA [3] system, where written NL has been combined with several types of pointing gestures of different granularity, e.g., pointing with a pencil or the hand. There are also various systems which allow for speech input accompanied by pointing gestures, e.g., Bolt's *put-that-there* [4], Cubbricon [5], MATIS [6], VoicePaint [7], Talk and Draw [8], and VECIG [9]. Multimodal input does not necessarily include written or spoken NL. The Gesture System [10], for example, allows a user to interact with three-dimensional objects using gestures combined with the use of a force input device, namely a spaceball.

When different parts of an expression are input through different modalities they must be fused into a single expression which can be processed by the underlying application system. Several criteria have been proposed in the literature in order to characterize fusion processes. For example, in [11] two basic definitions of fusion are distinguished. Fusion is defined as:

1. "computation of a process abstracting/concretizing a collection of information types received from distinct processes into a different information type to be transferred to another process "
2. "composition of multiple information types at some level of abstraction into a single information type of the same level of abstraction "

In [12], fusion is characterized with respect to the temporal relationship between input events which have to be fused. If the modalities providing the input expressions are used in parallel, then the multimodal interaction is described as synergistic, if they are used sequentially, it is described as alternate.

Criteria like the above allow to analyse and compare existing multimodal interfaces beyond the level of surface aspects such as supported modalities and application domain. If we, for example, classify the systems mentioned before with respect to the use of modalities, we find that systems which rely only on the keyboard for NL input provide alternate use of modalities, while systems with speech input usually support the synergistic use of voice and pointing devices. Other systems allow both uses of modalities. An example is MATIS which allows users to get information on flight schedules using speech, mouse and keyboard, or a combination of them. For example, a user can input the expression "*show me USair flights from Pittsburgh to Boston*" using speech only, or input the expression "*show me USair flights from Pittsburgh to this city*" using speech and pointing a label for specifying "this" using the mouse. For defining an expression, multiple modalities available for specifying it can be combined in a sequential way. For example, the user can say "flights from", then select Pittsburgh from a menu list, then say "to", and then select Boston from a menu list. Conversely, the multiple modalities can be combined concurrently. For example, one can say "*flights from this city to this city arriving in the afternoon*" while performing mouse clicks on a menu list to denote the two cities referred to in the utterance. Although further criteria may be introduced to get more fine grained descriptions of fusion processes, it may happen that such informal characterizations do not provide a sufficient level of preciseness. When developing new interfaces, however, full insight into the structure of a fusion process must be guaranteed. In this paper, we show how fusion processes can be characterized by applying methods for formal process modelling. In general we want to formally specify [19] aspects of systems in order to:

- formally verify an implementation by successively refining the specification and meeting proof obligations to show that an implementation is a valid interpretation of a specification,

- derive the minimal set of test cases to evaluate a valid implementation in order to show that it indeed has the properties written in the specification,
- gain an insight into the structure of specification and process,
- show the properties which necessarily result from the specification. This stems from the fact that a valid formalism shows that process results are instances in a finite set, that the system is deterministic, and that there can be no unexpected results from an implementation.

2. Specifying Fusion Processes in a Formal Framework

As a starting point for setting up a formal framework to reason about properties of fusion processes, we regard fusion as a transformation process that maps several input units to a single one. The formalism itself is drawn from the *Z* [13], *LOTOS* [14] and *ACTL* [16] notations.

The reason to address more than one formalism finds its justification in that, given the poliedricity of interactive systems, no single formal specification language can today offer a correspondingly flexible expressiveness. Consequently, one is often forced to use different notations to express/investigate different properties of such systems. The claim is that different formal models can have complementary roles in the process of software development and in the broader context of developing a principled approach to the design of interactive systems. Of course the boundary between the types of approach is not exact. Thus, while a Z based specification is primarily analytic, it could also be used as an engineering model to express the requirements on a system at a high level of abstraction. On the contrary, LOTOS supports a constructive approach to specification and thus it is well positioned to fill the role of engineering notations. However, it also plays an analytic role by providing a basis for linking specifications to task models [17].

In the following section, a short introductory remark is given that outlines the foundations to which the notations are grounded. The interested reader may directly address the reference books and papers to gain a deeper insight into the formalism.

2.1 Analytic Model of Fusion

We consider fusion as the composition of multiple information types at some level of abstraction into a single information type of the same level of abstraction [11]. We define the composition of multiple information types as a collection of elements from a set by addressing the *Z* concept of bag:

$$\text{bag}X == X \rightarrow_{p} \mathbf{N}_1$$

where bag$X$ is the set of bags of elements of X and $\rightarrow_p$ denotes a partial function from X to the set of strictly positive integers. Bags are collections of elements of X in which the number of times an element occurs is significant. As an example, given $X := \{x_1, x_2\}$, then bag $X := \{x_1 \mapsto 2, x_2 \mapsto 3\}$ is the bag composed of two occurrences of element x_1 and three occurrences of element x_2.

Multiplicity of elements and bag membership are specified as:

$$
\begin{array}{l}
[X] \\
\hline
count : \text{bag } X \rightarrow_b (X \rightarrow \mathbb{N}) \\
\_in\_ : X \leftrightarrow bag\ X \\
\hline
\forall x : X;\ B : \text{bag } X \bullet \\
\qquad count\ B = (\lambda x : X \bullet 0) \oplus B \wedge \\
\qquad x\ in\ B \Leftrightarrow x \in \text{dom } B
\end{array}
$$

The above specification defines

- *count* as a bijection ($\rightarrow_b$), and _ in _ as a binary relation ($\leftrightarrow$),
- $\_\oplus\_$ is the functional overriding so that $f \oplus g$ is defined on the union of the domains of f and g. On the domain of g it agrees with g, and elsewhere on its domain it agrees with f,
- $\lambda S \bullet E$ denotes a function which takes arguments of a shape determined by S, and returns the result E.

Consequently, we say that the number of times x appears in the bag B *is count* $B\ x$, and the relationship x in B holds exactly, if this number is greater than 0.

We observe that the specification doesn't take into account any ordering relation amongst the elements in the set of bags. In fact, we are not interested in how a bag is composed but only in the expression of the composition. This is justified by considering that bag$X$ identifies a class of equivalence on the set of finite sequences over X. Let's specify

$$\text{seq } X == \{\ f : \mathbb{N} \rightarrow_{fp} X \mid \text{dom } f = 1...\#f\ \}$$

$$
\begin{array}{l}
[X] \\
\hline
items : \text{seq } X \rightarrow \text{bag } X \\
\hline
\forall s\ : \text{seq } X;\ x : X\ \bullet \\
count\ (\ items\ s\ )\ x = \#\{\ i : \text{dom } s \mid s\ (\ i\ ) = x\ \}
\end{array}
$$

where $\rightarrow_{fp}$ denotes a finite partial function. Then, if s is a non-empty sequence, *items* s is the bag in which each element x appears exactly as often as it appears in s. We can define the following relation between sequences:

$$
\begin{array}{l}
[X] \\
\hline
\_=\_ : \text{seq } X \leftrightarrow \text{seq } X \\
\hline
\forall s_1, s_2 : \text{seq } X\ \bullet \\
\qquad s_1 \approx s_2 \Leftrightarrow items\ s_1 = items\ s_2
\end{array}
$$

that defines a partition over seq X whose elements are identified by bag$X$.

From the above specification, we can easily derive the following law

$$\forall s_1, s_2 : \text{seq}\, X \bullet s_1 \approx s_2 \Leftrightarrow (\exists f: \text{dom}\, s_1 \rightarrowtail_b \text{dom}\, s_2 \bullet s_1 = s_2 \circ f)$$

that is, any sequence can be rewritten as any other sequence in its class of equivalence defined by =.

We can now speak of fusion within the framework so far introduced. In our account of fusion, we shall need to deal with both information types and information values, and correspondingly, two given sets are introduced. Each names a set of values that are of interest in the specification, but whose structure is unimportant.

[*infovalues*] - information values
[*infotypes*] - information types

The first aspect of fusion to describe is its state space. Although the abstract of fusion is small, it is useful to break it into three sections, each defined by a Z schema. The first schema introduces observations about the information to be fused:

FusionStateInput

incharacteristic : bag *infotypes*
information : *infotypes* $\rightarrow_{fp}$ $\mathbf{F}_1$ *infovalues*

(P1) $\#incharacteristic > 1 \lor$
$(\#incharacteristic = 1 \land$
$(\exists_1 t : infotypes \bullet (count\ incharacteristic\ t) > 1))$
(P2) $\text{dom}\ information = \text{dom}\ incharacteristic$

This schema consists of a part above the central dividing line, in which the state variables are declared, and a part below the line which gives the relationship between the values of the variables.

- *incharacteristic* is a characteristic identifier of fusion; it is the bag of information types that uniquely identifies the composition of information to be fused. As discussed in section 2.1, the concept of bag is suitable to represent the fact that the fusion of information is independent from the order in which they enter into the system;
- *information* is a function which, when applied to certain types, gives the values associated with them.

The predicates of the schema, the part below the central line, give a number of relationships which are true in every state of the system and are maintained by every operation on it. They are referred as the invariants of the system, and have been numbered to be easily referred.

- From predicate (P1) we say that the cardinality of incharacteristic must be either greater than 1 or equal to 1 in which case there exists a unique information type in the bag, and this type must occur more than once. The invariant has been introduced in order to express that a fusion has to deal with multiple information. Note that this is a free intelpretation of the wording multiple information types given in the second definition of fusion (see section 1). In fact we allowed to fuse either multiple information of different types or multiple information of the same type;

- predicate (P2) says that information can be validly applied only to the set of types exactly defined by *incharacteristic*.

The second schema introduces observations about the result of the fusion:

```
┌─ FusionStateOutput ─────────────────
│ resulttype : infotypes
│ resultinfo : F1 infovalues
└─────────────────────────────────────
```

FusionStateOutput

resulttype : *infotypes*
resultinfo : $\mathbf{F}_1$ *infovalues*

The schema is very simple; it just introduces two variables that can get values respectively from the set of *infotypes* and of the finite subsets of *infovalues.*

- *resulttype* is a second characteristic identifier of the fusion. It defines the type of the information which is the result of the fusion;
- *resultinfo* carries the content of this information.

The next and last schema completes the description of the state space:

FusionStateAll

FusionStateInput
FusionStateOutput
transform : (*infotypes* $\rightarrow_{fp}$ $\mathbf{F}_1$ *infovalues*) $\rightarrow_{fp}$ $\mathbf{F}_1$ *infovalues*

(P1) $\forall T$: dom *transform* • T = *information*

The schema includes the definition of the state space given in *FusionStateInput* and in *FusionStateResult*, and adds one more observation:

- *transform* is a function which, when applied to certain functions that return values associated to types, gives functions of the same kind. The definition is very abstract and represents values from a set of the type **P** ((**P** (*infotypes* $\times$ (**P** *infovalues*))) $\times$ (**P** *infovalues*));
- predicate (P1) defines an invariant so that *transform* can be successfully applied only to *information.* Consequently, only those sets of values can be transformed which are associated with types in *incharacteristic* bag;

Having defined the (abstract) state space, we can now start to define a number of operations on fusion. The first of these is to add a new information, and we describe it with the following schema:

FusionAddInfo

Δ*FusionStateInput*
inputtype? : *infotypes*
inputvalue? : $\mathbf{F}_1$ *infovalues*

(P1) *inputtype?* $\in$ dom *incharacteristic* $\Rightarrow$
information '(*inputtype?*) = *information* (*inputtype?*) $\cup$ {*inputvalue?*}
$\wedge$ {*inputtype?*} $\lhd$ *information* = {*inputtype?*} $\lhd$ *information*'
(P2) *inputtype?* $\notin$ dom *incharacteristic* $\Rightarrow$
information' = *information*

The declaration $\Delta FusionStateInput$ indicates that the schema is describing a state change; it introduces a pair of variables for each variable in the state, e.g., *information'* and *information.* The primed variables are observations of the state after the change, the unprimed ones are observations of the state before the change. Each pair of variables is implicitly constrained to satisfy the invariants, so they must hold both before and after the operation.

The next declarations introduce two inputs to the operation defined as an information type and an information (by convention, the name of inputs ends in a question mark).

Both predicates give a pre-condition and a post-condition respectively on input type and on inputt values to be satisfied for the success of the operation. The predicate (P1) says that if the pre-condition "$inputtype? \in \mathrm{dom}\ incharacteristic$" is satisfied, then after the operation *information'* extends *information* to include $\{inputvalue?\}$ and the set of information types doesn't change. Predicate (P2) says that if the pre-condition "$inputtype? \notin \mathrm{dom} incharacteristic$" is satisfied then the state doesn't change. In other terms, only values that are of a type defined by the characteristic bag of the fusion are considered by the system. This is reasonable, since we are not able to handle types of data that we don't know about.

Another operation is to fuse the information so far entered into the system. Again we describe the operation with a schema.

FusionTransform

$\Delta FusionStateAll$

(P1) $resultinfo' = transform\ (information)$

(P2) $\forall t : \mathrm{dom}\ incharacteristic$

$\exists_1\ default : \mathbf{F}_1\ infovalues \bullet information'\ (t) = default$

This schema describes the core of the fusion in predicate (P1): that is the computation of a *resultinfo'* by transforming the set of information available before the operation is performed. The predicate (P2) says that after the operation the function *information'* returns a default value for all the types defined by the bag *incharacteristic.* Since the operation has no pre-conditions, it can be applied in any state of the system. This fact introduces a non-determinism in the system with respect to the ordering of the execution of operations. We already recognize here the problem and will resolve it within the engineering model. The non-determinism could also be solved in a refinement of this specification by using the same formalism. However, Z is as powerful in developing state based specifications as it is weak in dealing with the system behaviour. The exact contrary applies to process algebras where the strengths in describing system behaviour are coupled with the weaknesses in describing system state.

The last operation, specified with the next schema, describes the output of the fusion system. The operation has two outputs (by convention, the name of outputs end in a exclamation mark): *outvalue!*, which takes values from the finite subsets of *infovalues*, and *outtype!*, which takes values from *infotypes*.

There are no pre-conditions, as in the previous case, so that the operation can be applied in any state of the system.

FusionGiveResult

Δ*FusionStateAll*
outvalue!: $\mathbf{F}_1$ *infovalues*
outtype!: *infotypes*

(P1) *outvalue!* = *resultinfo*
(P2) *outtype!* = *resulttype*
(P3) $\exists_1$ *default* : $\mathbf{F}_1$ *infovalues* • *resultinfo'* = *default*

However, we don't want to output information that have not been fused. To solve this problem we will later define.

FusionTransform ; *FusionGiveResult*

in order to specify that the two operations can only be executed in sequence. That guarantees that only fused information can be provided as output. The schema (S; T) is defined as follows:

$\exists$*State*"
($\exists$*State*' • [S | θ*State*' = θ*State*"])
($\exists$*State* • [T | θ*State* = θ*State*"])

where the value of the expression θS in any situation is a binding. If *p* and *q* are distinct identifiers, and *x* and *y* are objects of type *t* and *u* respectively, then there is a binding *z* with components *z.p* equal to *x* and *z.q* equal to *y*. In other terms, the primed components of the first operation in the sequence correspond exactly to the unprimed components of the second operation, and this state is called the *hidden state*. The informal semantics of the sequential composition of operations is an operation where the state before the operation is the state before the first operation, and the state after the operation is the state after the second operation in the sequence. For this reason we have included Δ*FusionStateAll* in the schema declaration, even if the inclusion of Δ*FusionStateOutput* was sufficient for the specification of the operation by itself. Here *outinfo!* carries the value of *resultinfo* and it is assigned a type of *resulttype*, carried by *outtype!*. After the operation the value of *resultinfo'* is assigned to a default value. It should be noted that since *resulttype'* never changes, it uniquely determines the type of the information given as output once it has been initialized. Finally, we can affirm that the more abstract fusion is defined as

FUSION $\widehat{=}$ *FusionAddInfo* $\vee$ (*FusionTransform ; FusionGiveOutput*)

that is its behaviour is an interleaving of the *FusionAddInfo* operation and of the sequence of the *FusionTransform* and of the *FusionGiveOutput* operations. So far we have described in the same mathematical framework both the state space and the operations that can be performed on a fusion system. The data objects where described in terms of mathematical data types such as sets and functions.

The descriptions included invariant relationships between the parts of the state that are vital to understanding the fusion. The effects of the operations are described in terms of the relationship which must hold between input and output through transformation, rather than giving a recipe to be followed.

We complete the specification by specifying the initial state of the system (i.e. when it is first started). In defining the initial state, we implicitly define what kind of fusion we are describing by giving (more) concrete values to *incharacteristic* and to *resulttype*. The initialization is clearly dependent from the context in which the fusion is performed. Since we are not addressing any specific application domain, we will not define exactly what the given sets are and how they are structured. Consequently, the initialization of the state is given semi-formally in the following schema.

FusionInit

$\Delta FusionStateAll$

(P1) $\exists_1\, defaultbag : \text{bag}\ infotypes \bullet incharactristic' = defaultbag$
(P2) $\forall t : \text{dom}\ incharacteristic' \bullet$
$\quad \exists_1\, default : \mathbf{F}_1\ infovalues \bullet information'(t) = default$
(P3) $\exists_1\, defaulttype : infotypes \bullet resulttype' = defaulttype$
(P4) $\exists_1\, defaultinfo : \mathbf{F}_1\ infovalues \bullet resultinfo' = defaultinfo$

The predicates in the above schema just specify that there must exist default values for the variables in the state of the fusion. These values are also used to reset *information'* and *resultinfo'* after they have been actually used by operations. On the contrary, the initial values assigned to *incharacteristic'* and to *resulttype'* are never updated by operations.

A semi-formal definition of *transform* can be given to describe the class of functions addressed by the fusion.

Let *information* be so that for $\forall t \in$ domain, *incharacteristic* it contains a set of *infovalues* of the form $y_{ti} = f_t(x_j)$, y_{t1} = default. Let $f_t(x_j)$ be computed for $x_j \in \aleph_t \subset \aleph$. Let be a set of all possible *m*-tuples $(x_1, .. x_m) \in \Pi \aleph_{ti}$ so that *items* $< t_1, .. t_m >$ = *incharacteristic* and

$$(x_{t1}, .. x_{tm} \underset{g}{\mapsto} \left| \max(x_{ti}) - \min(x_{ti}) \right| \text{ for } i, j = 1, ..., m$$

then the value returned by *transform* is

$$someinfo \Leftrightarrow \forall\ (x_{t1}, .. x_{tm}) \bullet \exists\, y_{ti} = default$$

$$T(\bar{y}_{t1}, .. \bar{y}_{tm}) \Leftrightarrow$$

$$\forall\ (x_{t1}, .. x_{tm}) \bullet \exists\, (\bar{x}_{t1}, .. \bar{x}_{tm}) \bullet g(\bar{x}_{t1}, .. \bar{x}_{tm}) \leq g(x_{t1}, .. x_{tm})$$

In other words, the result of the fusion is some "application defined information" in the case of incomplete input, or a transformed m-tuple, so that the distance between the points at which the information is computed is minimized. The minimum itself can refer to different spaces, i.e. minimal distance in a sequence, or minimal distance in time.

2.2 Engineering Model of Fusion

Starting from the analytic model of fusion developed in the previous section, we will give a refinement of its behaviour by developing an engineering model, by using specifications in the LOTOS process algebra [14]. Following the methodology introduced by Milner's Calculus of Communicating Systems (CCS) [18], LOTOS provides a notation for defining the temporal relation among the interactions representing the externally observable behaviour of a system.

In LOTOS a concurrent system is seen as a process able to perform internal, unobservable actions, and to interact with other processes by means of external, observable actions (interactions). Actions are atomic entities that occur at interaction points or gates, without consuming time (i.e. they occur instantaneously). Processes may interact with each other by performing the common actions defined at their gates. A process definition specifies the behaviour of a process by defining the sequences of observable actions that may occur at the process gates. Complex behaviour is expressed by composing simpler behaviour expressions via operators such as interleaving (P ||| Q), parallelism with synchronization (P |[G]| Q), where P and Q are process instances and G is a set of synchronization gates. Behaviour of processes, described in a process definition, are specified by means of the composition constructs, already described, and additional constructs such as *a: B* meaning that the process must perform action *a* and then behave like B, B1 [] B2, meaning that the process can act either as Bl or as B2 and hide G in B where each action in G is transformed into an internal non-observable action. Communication is specified by giving a structure to actions like in CSP [20], such as *g ? x : Nat* defining action *g* as the assignment to variable *x* of a natural number, and *g ! v* defines action *g* as the output of value *v*. Extensions to the notation are under consideration that allow to introduce quantitative measurements of the time at which an action occurs in a system [15]. In Timed-LOTOS, a process can make action transitions as in the standard notation as well as time transitions. *a{tl,t2}; B* means that can perform action *a* within the time interval *{tl,t2}* and then behave like B. When the action occurs, the time information is captured by a variable (as in *a* ^{t} @ *x*, where *x* is assigned the value of time).
In rewriting the Z specification in LOTOS, we apply the following rules:

- for every non-sequential composition of Z operations, we define a corresponding LOTOS process,
- for each sequence of Z operations, we define a unique process where the behaviour of an operation is prefixed to the behaviour of the next operation in the sequence, and
- we recover the global state space of Z by the LOTOS synchronization with value passing constructs.

Moreover, we introduce the following notational conventions:

- T is the characteristic fusion bag, each type in the bag is denoted by T_i
- GS is the set of gates at which the fusion process receives inputs from its environment. There is a gate, denoted by g_i, for each the structure of the actions occurring at the gate is $g_i\ ?\ x\colon T_i$,
- o is the gate at which the fusion process makes available to its environment the information resulting from fusion, and T_o is the type assigned to that information. The structure of the actions occurring at the gate is, consequently, $o!\ v \in T$
- S is a list of information (any information received at gate g_i in the set GS of gates is added to the list),
- $[]_i$ is defined in the context $[]_{i=1,\dots n} Bex_i \Leftrightarrow Bex_1\ []\ \dots\ []\ Bex_n$
- $|||_i$ is defined to be $|||_{i=1,\dots n} Bex_i \Leftrightarrow Bex_1\ |||\ \dots\ |||\ Bex_n$

Finally we define the operations *add*, and *transform*, as follows:

- add : S T → S   that returns a list from a list and an information so that #S' = #add (S, T_i),
- transform : S → T_o transforms a list to an output information of type T_o .

The definition of the fusion process is consequently:

```
FUSION [GS, o] (s : S, to : To) :: =
hide synch in
    FusionAddInfo [GS, synch] (S)
    |[synch]| FusionTransformAndGiveResult [synch, o] (To)
    where
        FusionAddInfo [GS, synch] (s:S) :: =
         []i gi ? add (s, x: Ti ); FusionAddInfo [GS, synch] (s)
         [] t; synch ! s; FusionAddInfo [GS, synch] (S)
        FusionTransformAndGiveResult [synch, o] (to : To) :: =
         synch ? transform ( s : S, to); o ! to ;
           FusionTransformAndGiveResult [synch, o] (To)
```

The specification says that the FUSION process is defined over the set *GS* of gates and the *o* gate; its state is defined by the variable *s* of sort *S* and by the variable t_o of sort T_o; its behaviour is the parallel composition with synchronization on the hidden gate synch of the FusionAddInfo and the FusionTransformAnd GiveResult processes. The FusionAddInfo process is defined over the set *GS* of gates and the *synch* gate; its state is defined by the variable *s* of sort *S* and it is initialized by the *FUSION* process to be the distinguished value *S*; it behaves as to receive inputs $x : T_i$ that are added to the actual list *s*, or to perform an internal action.After that it offers to its environment the actual value of *s* at the gate *synch*. After the synchronization, the state of the process becomes the initial state.*FusionTransformAndGiveResult* is defined over the *synch* and *o* gates; its state is defined by the variable t_o of sort T_o which is initialized at T_o by the FUSION process; it behaves as to synchronize on the gate *synch*, receiving the list *s* and transforming it to a value t_o from the set defined by T_o, and to subsequently offer to its environment this value at the gate *o*. Then, the process restarts its behaviour with the initial state.

With respect to the analytic model, the engineering model hard-wires the types defined in the characteristic bag of the fusion by means of the set GS of gates and ensures that the fusion is correctly applied to the actual set of input information by synchronization. Moreover it relaxes the effect of the $\vee$ operator in following specification:

FUSION $\triangleq$ *FusionAddInfo* $\vee$ (*FusionTransform* ; *FusionGiveOutput*)

by allowing that input and output operations are freely interleaved without danger for the safety of the system. However, this engineering model is, as well as the analytic one, non-deterministic in that the *FusionAddInfo* process decides autonomously whether to receive a new input or to synchronize with the *FusionTransformAndGiveResult* process in order to produce a fused piece of information. We want to keep the non-determinism for its effect on the ordering in which input is received, but we want also to be able to control when output information is given.

Consequently, we refine the specification by substituting the internal action with the observable action *trigger* that we offer to the environment for synchronization, so that an external process can constrain its occurrence following a pre-defined behaviour. The refined definition of the FUSION process is expressed as follows:

```
FUSION [GS, trigger, o] (s : S, t_O : T_O) :: =
hide synch in
      FusionAddInfo [GS, trigger, synch] (S)
      |[synch]| FusionTransformAndGiveResult [synch, o] (T_O)
      where
         FusionAddInfo [GS, trigger, synch] (s:S) :: =
          []_i g_i ? add (s, x: T_i ); FusionAddInfo [GS, trigger, synch] (s)
          [] trigger; synch ! s; FusionAddInfo [GS, trigger, synch] (S)
         FusionTransformAndGiveResult [synch, o] (t_O : T_O) :: =
          synch ? transform ( s : S, t_O); o ! t_O ;
            FusionTransformAndGiveResult [synch, o] (T_O)
```

The process is still non-deterministic, but we are able to resolve the non-determinism by defining constraints on the process behaviour by imposing a synchronization on the trigger gate, as it will be shown in the following sections.

2.3 Necessary Properties of Fusion

In the following section we will examine a number of properties of the LOTOS specification, which uses the ACTL [16] notation, a branching time temporal logic [21] based on actions that allows for qualitative reasoning about systems.

1. Delivery of fused Information: The first property we express is that after a trigger event has occurred, a corre sponding action occurring at gate *o* and delivering fused information will always be generated, and we write

[*trigger*] **AF** {*o*} true

This property guarantees that the FUSION process will always deliver a result.

2. *Incompleteness of Information:* A further property is particularly relevant since it addresses an issue of interest in this context; it is written

$$\mathbf{AG} < trigger > \text{true}$$

The formula says that it is always possible for a trigger event to occur, even if no input has occurred. This property is necessary to insure that any process behaviour, constraining the *FUSION* process to deliver fused information at a certain moment, can be safely applied (i.e. deadlock avoidance). The consequences of this property are that the *FUSION* process must be able to deal with incomplete data in order to deliver always valid results. The minimal heuristics we can develop for this purpose, is to address the classical solution to this problem by defining a lifting operation

$$\forall T_i : T \bullet \text{ lifting } (T_i) = (T_i \cup \bot, \leq_f)$$

$$\forall x_i, x_j \in d \cup \bot_d \bullet x_i \leq x_j \Rrightarrow x_i = \bot \vee x_i = x_j$$

that allows us to distinguish the specific symbol $\bot$ in the set of values bound to a data type. Since an actual instance of the FUSION process is dependent on the problem domain space; nothing more can be said other than that we have recognized the existence of this problem.

3. *Redundancy of Information:* The last property we are considering is written

$$\forall i : \#T \bullet [\, g_i \,] < g_i > \text{true}$$

The formula says that after any information has been input, other information of the same type can be again accepted as input. The consequences induced by this property are that in a fusion process one has to deal with redundancy of data, since many tokens of the same type can in general be introduced into the system before an actual fusion takes place, and consequently data may be redundant. Redundancy is itself not a problematic property of the fusion process, since when duplicated symbols are detected a simple deletion rule can be applied resulting in a single symbol (e.g. $A \wedge A \Rrightarrow A$).

Equally this phenomenon is clearly observed in users of multimodal systems. For example, the user of a travel reservation system will persist to use the verbal modality in addition to the selection, by selecting the town name and saying it at the same time, when selecting a journey destination from a menu having issued the commands verbally.

However, users are imperfect and make errors. The introduction of redundancy with an error by a user in one of two instances, results in a contradiction in input between two channels. This possibility of contradiction would not exist without the redundancy. Without redundancy, an error by the user in a symbol which results in an otherwise valid message would not be detected, since the message would be interpreted as valid. That is to say, without redundancy at the level of the message from the user to the system, contradictions between a user intention and a user action would not be detected since the action in itself would be valid. Redundancy in the message allows the refinement of the contradiction between a user intention and the resulting user action, and also between two linked user actions in different modes. Therefore the introduction of redundancy at the message level permits the introduction into the system of a mechanism to repair temporarily inconsistent knowledge. That is a mechanism to choose between two inconsistent messages.

2.4 Temporal Coordination of Fusion

The truth of the formulae, given in the previous section, raises a non-trivial issue expressible as an answer to the question: "When does the trigger firing occurs within the FUSlON process?"

A possible way to proceed is to categorize a number of basic modes of fusion and to define a composition operator that builds more complex modes starting from the basic set. This actually exceeds the scope of the present paper and, consequently, we only give a flavour on how it might work.

Starting from the generic FUSION process, we add constraints to the specification by defining further processes that are composed in parallel with synchronization gates. In this way the behaviour of the *FUSION* process must agree with the behaviour of the processes in the parallel composition.

Let's give a couple of examples for two basic modes of fusion in order to explain this fact . The first basic mode, called *pivot mode*, is defined by the following property:

$$\exists_1 i : \#T \bullet [\, g_i \,]\ \mathbf{AX} < \mathit{trigger} > \text{true}$$

saying that after an information of a specific type has been accepted as input in the next state of the system, a trigger event will occur that will direct the delivery of a fused information. A corresponding process definition is

$$\text{PIVOT}\,[\, g_i , \mathit{trigger} \,] \ ::= \ g_i \,;\, \mathit{trigger}\,;\ \text{PIVOT}\,[\, g_i , \mathit{trigger} \,]$$

that when instantiated in the expression

$$\text{FUSION}\,[\mathit{GS, trigger, o}] \mid [\, g_i , \mathit{trigger} \,] \mid \text{PIVOT}\,[\, g_i , \mathit{trigger} \,]$$

directs the FUSION process to deliver information on action "$o \,!\, t_o$ " after the action " g_i ? add (s, x: T_i) " has occurred and internal synchronization on gate *synch* has taken place.

The second basic mode, called *complete mode*, is defined by the following property:

$$\exists_1 i : \#T \bullet \mathbf{A}\ [\text{ true } \{\sim \mathit{trigger}\ \}\ \mathsf{U}$$
$$\{\, g_i \,\} \text{ true }] \ \wedge\ \{\, g_i \,\}\, \mathbf{A}\ [\text{ true } \{\sim g_i \,\}\ \mathsf{U}\ \{\ \mathit{trigger}\ \}\ \text{true }]$$

Here no trigger events can occur until the set of information to be fused is complete and information of a type cannot be input twice in between the occurrence of two trigger events.

Clearly, this operating mode avoids both incompleteness and redundancy but it might be much to restrictive for most applications, and we suggest following process definition:

COMPLETE [*GS, trigger*] ::=

($|||_i$, GS_i ; *exit*) >> *trigger* ; COMPLETE [*GS, trigger*]

an instance of which is used to constrain the behaviour of the fusion as in

FUSION [*GS, trigger, o*] | [*GS, trigger*] | COMPLETE [*GS, trigger*]

Up to this point, we performed of qualitative reasoning about some facts of fusion. The fusion itself was expressed by abstracting from modalities. On the contrary, a number of systems considered in the informal sections of this paper deal with the synergistic use of different modalities. These systems heavily rely on models of time that cannot be expressed by only capturing the temporal ordering of events in which a process is executed. We must address concrete models of time as the one proposed in the time enhancement of LOTOS [15] in order to express effective time constraints.

3. Applying the Framework to characterize MATIS

Let's now give an example of application of the framework so far developed to a system, namely MATIS [6]. MATIS was developed at University of Grenoble to experiment on multimodal interfaces. It allows an end user to obtain information about flight schedules from a data base that respond to queries built by using speech, mouse and keyboard, or a combination of them.

The system has been the object of deep investigation within the ESPRIT Basic Research Action AMODEUS [22], [23], [24]. A full analysis of MATIS is beyond the scope of the present paper due to the inherent complexity of the system.

Here we will address only the issue related to fusion when using in a synergistic way a speech recognition system and a pointing device to generate input information. Moreover we feel free to abstract from the current implementation of MATIS and to confine our analysis to the building of a query out of two slots respectively containing information on the departure and on the arrival city of flights. This simplification doesn't influence the results of the analysis that can be easily extended to the case of more complex queries.

3.1 Fusion Requirements in MATIS

The user may ask the system both by speaking (i.e., "give me all the flights from London to Lamezia Terme") and by pointing to a menu and selecting a city name from a list of city names (i.e., Lamezia Terme). The system uses the user input and fills both a from and a to slot that will be processed later to compose a query to the data base. It should be noted that the transformation of the information entered in the slots into a query is also a fusion; however we will not discuss this operation. Both speech and pointing input modalities could in principle be used separately in filling the slots. Their synergistic use is justified by the fact that a user who chooses to start an input operation by speaking may not know how to pronounce a city name. In this case, he/she can simply refer to the city name with the word this and supply the true name by pointing to it. Both modalities are addressed in the informal requirements of the system can be modelled by two corresponding processes, respectively named *POINT* and *SPEECH*, that receive a token and deliver a new token. The *POINT* process is defined over the gates

- *p_in* where actions of the structure *p_in ? x: Point* occurs or, in other terms, a value from the sort *Point* is read from the environment and it is assigned to the variable *x*,
- *s_value* where actions of the structure *s_value ! Point_to_CityName (x)* occur; that is, the function *Point_to_CityName* is applied to the actual value of *x* and the result is offered to the environment.

The two action types are performed in an endless sequence by recursion of the process. The process definition is accordingly, as follows:

POINT [*p_in, s_value*] : := *p_in ? x: Point ; s_value ! Point_to_CityName (x) ;*
POINT [*p_in, s_value*]

The SPEECH process is defined over the gates

- *s_in* where the input values of sort *String*, read from the environment, are assigned to the variable *x*,
- *slot* where a complete slot of information is made available to the environment by transforming the actual value of *x* into an information slot with the application of the function *String_to_Slot.*

The process requires the definition of a state variable to store the input strings until a complete phrase is available for parsing. Since this fact doesn't add any information to the understanding of the fusion, we will hide the parsing operation in the process definition.

SPEECH [*s_in, slot] : := s_in ? x: String ; slot ! String_to_Slot (x) ;*
SPEECH [*s_in, slot*]

Using these assumptions we can give the following definitions

[*Point, String, Departure, Destination, CityName*]
Slot ::= *Departure* $\times$ *CityNnme* | *Destination* $\times$ *CityName*
incharacteristic = { *Slot* $\mapsto$ 1, *CityName* $\mapsto$ 1}
resulttype = *Slot*

Given the POINT and SPEECH process definitions, and the generic FUSION process defined in section 2.3 we can describe the behaviour of MATIS with the following specification

MATIS [*s_in, p_in, s_value, slot, fused_slot, trigger*] ::=
(SPEECH [*s_in, slot*] ||| POINT [*p_in, s_value*])
|[*s_value, slot*]|
FUSION [*s_value, slot, trigger, fused-slot*] ($\perp_{CityName}$, $\perp_{Slot}$)
where
FUSION[*s_value, slot, trigger,fused_slot*]
(*sl*: seq *CityName*, s2: seq *Slot*, t_O: *Slot*) ::=
hide *synch* in
FusionAddInfo[*s_value, slot, trigger, synch*] ($\perp_{CityName}$, $\perp_{Slot}$) |[*synch*]|
FusionTransformAndGiveResult [*synch, fused_slot*] ($\perp_{Slot}$)

where

FusionAddInfo [*s_value, slot, trigger, synch*]
(sl : seq CityName, s2 : seq Slot) ::=
s_value ? addCN (sl, x : CityName) ;
FusionAddInfo [*s_value, slot, trigger, synch*] *(sl, s2)*
[]*slot ? addS (x2, x : Slot) ;*
FusionAddInfo [*s_value, slot, trigger, synch*] *(sl, s2)*
[] *trigger ; synch ! s1* $\cup$ *s2 ;*
FusionAddInfo [*s_value, slot, trigger, synch*] ($\bot_{\mathrm{CityName}}$, $\bot_{\mathrm{Slot}}$)
FusionTransformAndGiveResult [*synch, fused_slot*] (*t* $_0$, *Slot) ::=*
synch ? transform (*s: seq CityName* $\cup$ seq *Slot,* t_0); *fused_slot!* t_0 *;*
FusionTransformAndGiveResult [*synch, fused_slot*] ($\bot_{Slot}$)

where the state of the FUSION process is properly initialized with the $\bot_{\mathrm{CityName}}$ and $\bot_{\mathrm{Slot}}$ values that, according to the discussion in section 2.4, are the distinguished values respectively for the *CityName* and *Slot* sorts. It receives information of these types at the gates *s_values* and slot and returns a value from the sort *Slot* at the gate *fused_slot.*

Following graphical representation of the specification clarifies the composition of the processes.

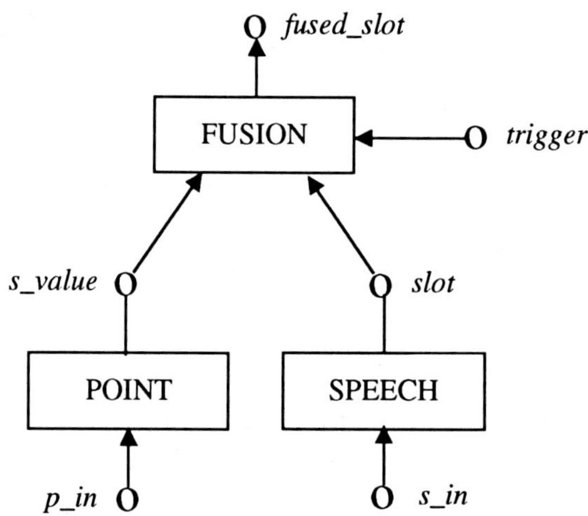

Fig. 1: Composition of the processes *POINT and SPEECH*

It is easy to verify that the above specification has the properties discussed in section 2.2 and, consequently, we must be prepared to deal with incompleteness and redundancy of information.

Moreover, following the discussion on the temporal coordination of fusion, we are asked to provide a further process to constrain the actions at the trigger gate to occur in a deterministic way.

3.2 Handling Redundancy and Incompleteness

The obvious motivation for having redundancy in the system, is that the user is free to enter a city name by pointing while speaking. The effect of this freedom is that a city name entered by pointing may not match the spoken name of that city leading to an inconsistent state of the system. Several solutions to the problem can be explored, as follows:

- The implementors of MATIS have adopted a solution that leads to results that might be not desired by the user. In fact, MATIS resolves the inconsistency outside of the fusion process by considering the actual state of the query. We will explain this with two examples.
  Let the two slots composing a query be empty, and let the user point to *London* while saying *from Lamezia Terme*, then the system fills the *Departure* slot with the value of *Lamezia Terme* and the *Destination* slot with the value of *London*.
  Let the *Destination* slot be filled with the value *London,* and the user repeats the previous input, then the system fills the *Departure* slot with the value of *Lamezia Terme* and presents a new query where both slots are filled with the value of *London*.
  Obviously, the results given by the system in such cases will appear to the user as non-deterministic answers. Furthermore, this approach has the disadvantage of depending from the semantic of the application.
- The simplest approach is to provide the distinguished value from the sort *Slot* as the result of the fusion and to notify the user of the inconsistency of input data. In this case, we will define

  $$\begin{aligned}&\mathit{transform\,(information)} = \bot \Leftrightarrow \\ &\qquad \mathit{last\,(Slot)} \neq \mathit{CityName} \wedge \mathrm{Slot} \neq \bot \wedge \mathit{CityName} \neq \bot\end{aligned}$$

- A further solution is to give higher priority to one of the processes providing the fusion process with information. We will define

  $$\begin{aligned}&\mathit{transform\,(information)} = \mathrm{Slot} \Leftrightarrow \mathrm{Slot} \neq \bot \\ &\mathit{transform\,(information)} = \mathit{first(Slot)} \times \mathit{CityName} \Leftrightarrow \\ &\qquad \mathit{last(Slot)} = \bot \wedge \mathit{CityName} \neq \bot \\ &\mathit{transform\,(information)} = \bot \Leftrightarrow \mathrm{Slot} = \bot \wedge \mathit{C\,yityName} = \bot\end{aligned}$$

  in the case of speech priority, and

  $$\begin{aligned}&\mathit{transform\,(information)} = \mathrm{Slot} \Leftrightarrow \mathrm{Slot} \neq \bot \wedge \mathit{CityName} = \bot \\ &\mathit{transform\,(information)} = \mathit{first(Slot)} \times \mathit{CityName} \Leftrightarrow \mathit{CityName} \neq \bot \\ &\mathit{transform\,(information)} = \bot \Leftrightarrow \mathrm{Slot} = \bot \wedge \mathit{CityName} = \bot\end{aligned}$$

  in the case of pointing priority.

- More complex solutions can be explored, which will not be addressed here. As an example, one can think of having a knowledge base system embedded within the *transform* function that could find solutions by applying inference rules.

The specification previously developed is already able to deal with incomplete data. The minimal heuristic provided by the lifting operation discussed in section 2.3 is powerful enough to provide a solution to this problem.

3.3 Temporal Coordination of Fusion in MATIS

The specification of the fusion applied to MATIS is actually non-deterministic, since the trigger action can occur at any time in the system. We observe that the basic modes of fusion previously discussed don't apply to MATIS. In fact, here the fusion cannot be directed by a pivot, and the complete mode would break the requirement of freedom for the user in using the preferred modality for the building of queries. Since the user effectively coordinates her speech with the pointing gestures, the most appropriate solution for the coordination of fusion in MATIS is to explicitly introduce a model of time. This is achieved by defining the following process

```
TIMED_FUSION [s_value, slot, trigger] (waittime: Time) ::=
    slot; (s_value { 0, waittime }; trigger;
        TIMED_FUSION [s_value, slot, trigger] (waittime)
    [] ι{waittime}; TIMED_FUSION [s_value, slot, trigger] (waittime))
    [] s_value; (slot {0, waittime}; trigger;
        TIMED_FUSION [s_value, slot, trigger] (waittime)
    [] ι{waittime }; TIMED_FUSION [s_value, slot, trigger] (waittime))
```

that, when composed in parallel with the MATIS process, constrains the FUSION process to give up after a time span equal to waittime has elapsed. The new behaviour of the system is consequently

```
MATIS [s_in, p_in, s_value, slot, fused_slot, trigger]
|[s_value, slot, trigger]|
TIMED_FUSION [s_value, slot, trigger] (waittime)
```

The above solution only solves a part of the problem. What is really needed is to relate the user input from both the considered devices and not just a "timeout mechanism".

We observe that the user might be requested to synchronize his/her actions so that a pointing event occurs at the same time the related word is spoken. Issues from the domains of ergonomics and cognitive psychology are raised at this point. In fact we cannot express by means of our formalism any user perception of time nor any property related to the usability of specific devices.

Nevertheless, we can introduce a constraint in the specification by allowing input from both devices to occur only in precisely defined temporal windows. This constraint is consequently added to the specification, as follows:

```
TIMED_INPUT [s_in, p_in] (inputtime: Time, waittime: Time) ::=
    time p_in, s_in in
    (p_in @ p; stop ||| s_in @ s; stop) [> ι { inputtime};
        exit (age_to_waittime (p, s, waittime))
```

The above process declares *s_in* and *p_in* as timed events (i.e. each event has an age). They can occur once at any time and in any order as soon as the process is activated. After a time interval equal to inputtime, the events are disabled until the new activation of the process. The process then exits by exporting a value for waittime computed from the age of the registered events.

When TIMED_INPUT is composed in sequence with TIMED_FUSION it describes the requested behaviour of the system. The TIME_FUSION process must also be an exiting process so that recursion in the process definition is replaced by the exit action.

TIMED_CONTROL [*s_in, p_in, s_value, slot, trigger*] ::=
TIMED_INPUT [*s_in, p_in*] (inputtime, waittime)
>>
(TIMED_FUSION [*s_value, slot, trigger*] (waittime)
||| TIMED_CONTROL [*s_in, p_in, s_value, slot, trigger*])

The final behaviour describes the entire system and is specified as follows:

MATIS [*s_in, p_in, s_value, slot, fused_slot, trigger*]
|[*s_in, p_in, s_value, slot, trigger*]|
TIMED_CONTROL [*s_in, p_in, s_value, slot, trigger*]

The above specification is, in some sense, the best we can do to reason about systems when unknown quantities and unpredictability are an intrinsic part of the problem to be described. A number of issues are in fact unsolved that do not depend from the specific style of specification adopted. In particular, we cannot make any claim on the perception that the user has of the existence of temporal windows. Consequently, we cannot predict how usable such a system will be. A further non-trivial issue is the exact definition of

$$age\_to\_waittime : a \ @ \ x \times b \ @ \ y \rightarrow \text{Time}$$

computing the value of system timeouts for the fusion process from the age of input events. It is clear that only an approximate solution can be found here since we are dealing with a large number of different metrics of time when considering the user mental model of time, the physical performance of the user either as an absolute values or in specific conditions, the timing of input devices, the timing of the physical computer, etc.

4. Conclusions

This formal approach allows specification of multimodal interactive systems and gives us the possibility of gaining insights into the fusion problem, and also of finding solutions by exploiting different viable scenarios whose potential capabilities are well understood. Following this perspective, we have formally specified fusion in its most general form as a many-to-one transformation process. The specification was then used to derive necessary properties of fusion. In particular, we showed that redundancy and incompleteness are unavoidable properties of any fusion process. However, there is an inherent difficulty in applying classical formal description techniques of software systems in order to describe the interaction between users and systems. The reason is obvious: whereas computer systems are finite and deterministic, users are notoriously unpredictable, and discussing interactive behaviour is dealing with an unknown quantity. Consequently, while formal system modelling is able to provide a description of the structures and properties that relate to design, it cannot produce an explanation of why a particular option would be most appropriate. Nevertheless, a formal modelling approach helps to clarify design issues and provides insights to potential problems.

Acknowledgements

The work reported in this paper has been partially funded by the European Commission under the programmes Human Capital and Mobility Program (Contract CHRX CT93-0085) and ESPRIT Basic Research Action (Contract AMODEUS 7040).

References

1. Carbonell J.R. "Mixed-Initiative Man-Computer Dialogues", BBN Report No. 1971, Bolt, Beranek, and Newman, Cambridge, MA 1970.
2. Brown D.C., Kwasny S.C., Chandrasekaran B., and Sondheimer N.K. "An Experimental Graphics System with Natural-Language Input", Computer and Graphics", Vol. 4, pp. 13-22, 1979.
3. Wahlster W. "User and Discourse Models for Multimodal Communication", Sullivan J.W. and Tyler S.W. (eds), Intelligent User Interfaces, ACM Press, pp. 45-67, 1991.
4. Bolt R.A. "Put-That-There, Voice and Gesture at the Graphics Interface", Computer Graphics, Vol. 14, pp. 262-270, 1980.
5. Neal J.G. and Shapiro S.C. "Intelligent Multi-Media Interface Technology", Sullivan J.W. and Tyler S.W. (eds), Intelligent User Interfaces, ACM Press, pp. 11-43, 1991.
6. Nigay L., Coutaz J., Salber D. "MATIS: A Multi-modal Airline Travel Information System", AMODEUS Project - ESPRIT BRA 7040, Report SM/ WP 10, 1993.
7. Salber D., Coutaz J., Nigay L. "VoicePaint: a Voice and Mouse controlled Drawing Program", AMODEUS Project - ESPRIT BRA 7040, Report SM/WP 9, 1993.
8. Salisbury M.W., Hendrickson J.H., Lammers T.L., Fu C., Moody S.A. "Talk and Draw: Bundling Speech and Graphics", IEEE Computer, Vol. 23/4, pp. 59-65, August 1990.
9. Sparrel C.J. "Coverbal Iconic Gesture in Human-Computer Interaction", Ms Thesis, MIT, 1993.
10. Bordegoni M., Hemmje M. "A Dynamic Gesture Language and Graphical Feedback for Interaction in a 3D User Interface", Computer Graphics Forum, Vol. 12, pp. 1- 11, NCC Blackwell, 1993.

11. Salber D., Coutaz J., Nigay L., Faconti G.P., Paterno F., Duke D.J., Harri son M.D., Duce D. "The System Modelling Glossary", AMODEUS Project - ESPRIT BRA 7040, Report SM/WP 26, 1994.
12. Coutaz J., Nigay L., Salber D. "The MSM Framework: A Design Space for Multi-Sensory-Motor Systems, in Bass L., Gornostaev J., Unger C. (eds), Lecture Notes in Computer Science 753, pp. 231-241, Springer-Verlag, 1993.
13. Spivey J.M. "Understanding Z: a specification language and its formal semantics", Cambridge University Press, 1988.
14. Bolognesi T., Brinksma E. "Introduction to the ISO Specification Language LOTOS", Computer Networks and ISDN Systems, Vol.14/1, 1987.
15. Bolognesi T., Lucidi F., Triglia S. "Converging towards a Timed-LOTOS Standard", Technical Report CNUCE-1993, submitted for publication to Computer Standards and Interfaces, North-Holland, 1993.
16. De Nicola R., Fantechi A., Gnesi S., Ristori G. "An Action-based Framework for Verifying Logical and Behavioural Properties of Concurrent Systems", Proc. of 3rd Workshop on Computer-Aided Verification, Aalborg, 1991.
17. Duke D. J., Faconti G.P., Harrison M. D., Paterno F. "Unifying Views of Interactors", Proceedings of Advanced Visualization Interfaces (AVI'94), 1994.
18 Milner A.J.R.G. "A Calculus of Communicating Systems", Prentice-Hall, 1990.
19. Ehrig H. , Mahr B. "Fundamentals of Algebraic Specification - I, Springer-Verlag, 1985.
20. Hoare C.A.R. "Communicating Sequential Processes", Prentice Hall International, 1985.
21. de Bakker, de Roever, Rozemberg (eds), "Linear Time, Branching Time and Partial Order in Logics and Models for Concurrency", Lecture Notes in Computer Science 354, Springer-Verlag, 1989.
22. Coutaz J., Faconti G. P., Paterno F., Nigay L., Salber D. "A Comparison of Approaches for Specifying Multimodal Interactive Systems", Proc. of the ERCIM Workshop on Multimodal HCI, Nancy, 1993.
23. Duke D. J., Harrison M., D. MATIS. "A Case Study in Formal Specification", The AMODEUS Project - ESPRIT BRA 7040, Report SM/WP 17, 1993.
24. Paterno F., Mezzanotte M. "Analyzing MATIS by Interactors and ACTL", AMODEUS Project - ESPRIT BRA 7040, Report SM/WP 36, 1994.

Developing User Interfaces for Hypermedia Data Bases

Umberto Cavallaro
EDS - Systems & ManagementVia Alfieri 19, I- 10121 Torino, Italy

Paolo Paolini and Franca Garzotto
Politecnico di Milano, Electronics and Information Sciences
Hypermedia Laboratory
Piazza L. da Vinci 32, I-20133 Milano, Italy

Abstract

Implementing hypermedia applications is becoming an organized, engineered and efficient process, supported by methodologies, models and tools. One of the main results of HIFI (EP 6532) is the structured approach to hypermedia design. HIFI considers design as the task of specifying representation structures, dynamic behaviour, navigation patterns and layout features. The goal is to provide a guideline to make hypermedia design more systematic and to improve consistency and usability of the resulting complex applications. The technical relevance of HIFI stems from the possibility of using a hypermedia navigational interface in order to access external data Bases, possibly managed by traditional Data Base tools, and supporting traditional, operational Information Systems. The HIFI approach allows end-users to access, much more easily and effectively both already existing Data Bases, and new applications alike.

1. Introduction

An enormous amount of information stored in computers today is managed by data bases. The information access interfaces of most data base systems are essentially query based: users specify what they search for, in some form of declarative or graphical language, and the interface displays the data "matching" the user's query.

However, this question-answering style is not always the most appropriate to access the data base content. Oftentimes, the end user cannot characterise precisely the data he or she is interested to; he or she finds more intuitive to "explore" the base of information, progressively and in an interactive way. In these cases, the most natural style of information access is "navigation", or "browsing", in which the user can move from one piece of information to another simply by following an interactive representation of links that connect pieces.

Furthermore, in many situations query and navigation should be interplayed. We can imagine, for example, that the user wants to access to the items returned as a result of a query, and to continue navigation from here to related elements. In this case, therefore, the query results are used as "entry points" for further navigation. Or, during navigation, the user might desire to restrict the set of connected elements, specifying selection conditions on the link destinations.

The interactive navigation style of accessing information, typical paradigm of hypertext and hypermedia, is becoming more and more popular, perhaps because it is so intuitive. We may expect that, in a short term, it will be fully integrated with query mechanisms and will be part of future data base management systems. Some object oriented data base management systems already provide some form of navigation, but in a limited and crude way consisting of traversing one-way pointers among objects. In the mean time, the question is, *how can we achieve similar results with today's systems,* to allow accessing the information of existing data bases in a *navigational form ?*

1.1 Requirements

The above problem can be addressed by developing navigational interfaces that present the data of external data bases as hypermedia networks of nodes and links. Nodes display simple or structured values stored in the data base. Links represent relationships among these data, explicitly or implicitly represented in the data base. To access data base information through the interface, users can browse across the network according to various patterns, eventually interplaying query and navigation. Several requirements should be taken into account when developing a database navigational interface, as follows.

Dynamic Network Construction

Reasonably, the external data base is updated along the time; thus the number of nodes and links of the interface, as well as their content, is not known a priori, but must change as the data base evolves. This implies that the interface must guarantee the consistency between the network structure and the actual data of the external data base. This can be achieved by a dynamic network construction. Whenever a user's command requiring a new piece of information is activated, the interface must be able, at execution time, to translate user's command into the proper sequence of data base retrieval commands, and to dynamically create node and link structures presenting the data returned from the data base

Data Structuring

A major problem is interface information structuring, both in-the-small (i.e., in the way of organizing information inside nodes) and in-the-large (i.e., in the way of mutually organizing nodes and links) [2,3,4,5,9,13,15].

In fact, the in-the-small structure of nodes does not necessarily reflect a single data structure of the underlying data base. For example, each node does not necessarily store a single tuple of a relational data base table, or a set of tuples from the same table, since the design criteria in the data base and in the interface are radically different. In the former, the organization is system oriented, focusing on efficiency and consistency (which lead to strongly normalized structures, that are hard to read and to use by humans). In the latter, the organization must be centred to the needs of end users. Therefore, data presented in nodes must be re-structured (i.e., dis-aggregated and re-aggregated) with respect to the way they are stored in the data base, to provide a presentation that is as much as possible close to the user's intuition and needs. For a similar reason, links, which define the in-the-large structure of the interface, do not necessarily correspond to a single "relationship" in the database, but might involve a complex chain of connections among data.

Query support
Query based access can and must be integrated with navigation, as discussed in the introduction.

1.2 Technical Approach

To meet the above requirements, we have identified some critical logical elements in a database navigational interface: the interface schema, the data base mapping, the layout schema, and the layout mapping. In principle, a navigational interface also is composed by many other constituents, including a navigation engine managing the behaviour of links and nodes when activated. These constituents will not be discussed here. The reader is referred to [1] for a detailed description on the architecture of a navigational interface.

The interface schema specifies the information structure of the navigational interface, both in-the-large and in-the-small. The data base mapping relates the interface schema structures with the representation structures of the external data base. The layout schema defines a set of visual templates that describe how interface schema objects are presented on the screen. The layout mapping defines how interface schema elements correspond to the various constituents of the layout templates.

It is important to notice that the way information are structured in the interface, and the way of presenting them and navigating across them, must be independent from the logical and physical models of the underlying data base. Of course, the interface schema, the layout schema, and the lay out mapping, can be defined only if the designer knows the content of the data base, but any change in the logical and physical schema of the data base must have no effect on these interface elements.

Only the data base mapping is dependent from the logical organization of data in the external data base (but of course, it is not dependent from the physical schema). The mapping, that can be defined only if the designer understands the logical schema of the data base, must necessarily change if the data base schema is modified.

Finally, we must observe that the interface schema is totally independent from the development system of the hypermedia interface; all other design choices (but the mapping to the data base) are instead constrained, at different degrees, by the presentation and programming facilities of the chosen implementation and delivery platforms(s).

In the rest of this section, we will briefly illustrate some technical issues related to each of the above mentioned constituents of a navigational interface.

2. Interface Schema

To support the design of interface schemas [7], we have created a model - HDM+ which extends the primitives of the Hypertext Design Model [4, 5] specifically for navigational interfaces to data bases. The major features of HDM+ are:

- the distinction among different *levels of abstractions* in the schema structures (i.e. in-the-large and in-the-small) which helps designers in rationalizing the design process and in making it more systematic
- the distinction among different *uses of the information* retrieved from the data base: to be presented in a single node, to be collected with others in entry points for further navigation, to be used for query definition by the end user
- *navigational interpretation* of the schema structures, and the identification of different categories of links and consequently, of different navigation patterns [6, 8].

2.1 Main Primitives of HDM+

Technical details on HDM+ can be found elsewhere [12,15]. In this paper, we will summarize the major primitives of the model.

According to HDM+, the interface schema is defined by a set of entity types and a set of web types. An *entity type* denotes a collection, or class, of information structures called entities, representing abstract or conceptual objects of the application domain. A *web type* denotes a class of connection structures called webs. An *entity* is viewed as organised as a tree shaped structure, each node of the tree denoting a "subtopic" or a "constituent" of the object represented by the entity. A node has one or more contents, called *data segments* (or simply segments). A segment is an aggregate of slot values, defined by a frame structure. A slot can be a simple value, or it can have a hierarchical structure, because each slot value can be structured in turn as frame. Values can range from simple data (like numbers and text) to images or video clips, whatever types are needed. Value typing is not concern of HDM+, but of the external database.
There are several categories of segments, depending on their intended use:

- *Visual segments,* which contain enough data to describe a given object constituent in a single "node" of the interface. Different visual segments define different perspectives, i.e., different ways to look at the same piece of information.

- *Query segments,* which define sets of possible items that can be used in the query conditions. They are presented in interface nodes representing query masks.
- *List segments,* which contain little data about a given object constituent. List segments are intended to be presented in tabular format, typically when several logical pieces of information are to be shown simultaneously (e.g. as a result of a query).

The entity structure defined by HDM+ induces a variety of links among the nodes corresponding to visual segments and different navigation patterns:

- two visual segments *of the same component* are connected by perspective links, allowing the user navigate among different perspectives of the same piece of information, or
- two visual segments that belong to components *of the same entity* are connected by structural links. Structural links denote topological relationships (e.g. parent-of, sibling-of, etc.), and allow the user navigate among different constituents of the same entity.

A *web* connects visual segments of entities, or other webs. Optionally, it might have a centre, storing information about the web itself. If a web represents a semantic relationship among pieces of information, it induces several links, joining each pair of the connected items, eventually traversing the center, if any. These links are called applicative; differently from perspective and structural navigation, applicative navigation allows the user move across different entities (and can be therefore more disorienting than structural and perspective navigation). If a web simply glues a collection of elements, according to some application-oriented criteria, it must have a center and it is used as an entry point that can be navigated as an *index* or a as *guided tour*. Index navigation consists into moving from the web center to any of the connected items, and the other way around. With guided navigation, users move linearly, along the sequence of elements connected by the web.

2.2 Example of HDM+ Design

We have developed a navigational interface for an Italian Bank (BIPOP - Banca Popolare di Brescia) which has the purpose to support sales persons and managers of the marketing department in accessing and analysing data about customers and their relationships with the bank, about the bank sales force, about the financial products and the marketing and sales strategies [14]. The entity types of this system are Customer, Salesperson, Product, Visit, and Relation.

For lack of space, we will shortly discuss only the entity type Customer, which describes the main information concerning a bank customer. The Customer tree structure is defined by a root and two or more children tree nodes, describing the synthetic data about all accounts of, visits to, and products of, a customer. The visual segments of the root node are "Short Banking Data", "Personal Data", "Extended Banking Data". Its list segment includes the slots Customer Banking Code, Fiscal Code, and Customer Name. One of its query segments includes the slots Customer Banking Code, Fiscal Code, Customer Name, Customer Geographic Area, Job Type, Account Type, Investment

Amount, Credit Amount, and Debt Amount. Among others, some webs of the BIPOP interface connect entities of type Customer to entities of type Products, to denote the relationship among customers and the bank products owned by those customers.

3. Data Base Mapping

The mapping that relates HDM+ schema structures into database structures can be split into two elements: segment mapping and link mapping.

The segment mapping is defined for each "type" of segment, i.e., for each segment in a given entity type structure. Its purpose is to identify the data base items corresponding to the various segments of entity instances. The link mapping has the purpose to identify the destination of links, given the identification of the link source.

For each type of segment, the segment mapping identifies:

- the actual domains the values of a segment belong to
- the relationships among these data that defines their dependencies and therefore how they must be re-aggregated.

3.1 Segment Mapping

In the context of this paper, we will refer to relational data bases only. In relational data base terminology, a segment mapping can be defined by a relational expression, combining *a set of projections* on the data base relations (one for each simple slot occurring in the frame of the segment) and a set of *equi-joins*. The projections identify the value domains, partitioning each frame into a number of sub-aggregates, and the joins define the dependencies among such values, and ensure that a consistent aggregation (frame) can be later reconstructed. In SQL language, the same mapping can be expressed by a query statement:

select A1,..., An **from** R1, ..., Rk **where** JC

Here *A1,..., An* denote all the table attributes from where the values must be retrieved (i.e., the attributes involved in the projections) and all the attributes involved in the joins. *R1, ..., Rk* denote all tables involved in the projections and in the joins, and *JC* is the SQL statement corresponding to the joins.

The execution of a segment mapping retrieves all data for all segments of a given type. Given the identification of a specific segment of an entity, its data are retrieved by "qualifying" the corresponding segment mapping, i.e.,by selecting the specific data item corresponding to the segment identifier or joined with it.

The following examples define the mapping for two visual segment templates ("Personal Data" and "Short Data") of the root component of entity type Customer in the BIPOP bank interface. Data must be retrieved from various tables, here renamed A, B, C, and D for simplicity. Sex, phone, ISTAT code, etc. correspond to the slots of the frame visual segment "Personal dataî; CUST-CODE in the where-condition denotes the customer code and it is the primary key in tables A and B; it corresponds to the identification slot of the segment frame, as illustratted below.

```
%Customer Personal Data - Segment Mapping %

SELECT        A.SEX ,
              A.PHONE ,
              A.ISTAT-CODE ,
              B.DOC-TYPE ,
              B.DOC_NUMBER
              A.FISCAL-CODE ,
              D.JOB-TYPE-DESCRIPTION ,
              C.JOB-CATEGORY-CODE ,
              A.VAT

FROM          A, B, C, D

WHERE
              A.CUST-CODE= B.CUST-CODE
        AND
              B.JOB-TYPE-CODE = C.JOB-TYPE-CODE
        AND
              B.COD-TYPE-CODE = D.CODE-TYPE-CODE
```

```
%Customer Short Data - Segment Mapping %

SELECT        A.BIRT-DATE,
              A.FIRST-NAME,
              B.JOB-TYPE-DESCRIPTION,
              C.EMPLOYEMENT-COMPANY-CODE

FROM          A, B, C

WHERE
              A.CUST-CODE= C.CUST-CODE
        AND
              C.JOB-TYPE-CODE = B.JOB-TYPE-CODE
```

Let us now consider a segment of customer "Mario Rossi", identified by the Customer Code, say 100. At execution time, the following query must be evaluated, in order to retrieve the actual values of the segment "Personal Data" which can be displayed in a node of the interface :

```
SELECT      A.PHONE ,
            A.ISTAT-CODE ,
            B.DOC-TYPE ,
            B.DOC_NUMBER
            A.FISCAL-CODE ,
            D.JOB-TYPE-DESCRIPTION ,
            C.JOB-CATEGORY-CODE ,
            A.VAT
FROM        A, B, C, D
WHERE       A.CUST-CODE= B.CUST-CODE
        AND
            B.JOB-TYPE-CODE = C.JOB-TYPE-CODE
        AND
            B.COD-TYPE-CODE = D.CODE-TYPE-CODE
        AND
            A.CUST-CODE = 100
```

3.2 Link Mapping

All links of a given link type are identified by the identifiers of their source and target nodes. Thus, given a link type and the segment values identifying a source node, the purpose of the mapping is to retrieve the data base values identifying the target node. Given those values, the target node can be created by "specializing" the segment mapping as described in the previous section.

Let us assume that the term "source domains" of a link type refers to the set of domains for the values identifying, eventually through some joins, the source nodes for the links of that type. Similarly, the term "target domains" refers to the set of domains for the values identifying, eventually through some joins, the target nodes for the links of that type.For each link type, the problem of link mapping definition consists into defining a set of equi-joins operating on source domains and target domains, and then applying the projections on the target domains only. Given the identification of an actual source node (i.e. segment), the target node is then identified by applying to the result a selection condition, which expresses that the values of the source domains are equal to the identifications of the source node.

4. Layout Schema

Nodes of a navigational interface are graphical objects on the screen filled in with data retrieved from the data base. The layout schema has the purpose to describe a set of *visual templates*, that define the visual pattern of classes of nodes in the navigational interface. Nodes are defined as instances of *layout templates.* A template is described by a (typically, full screen) window, composed of several constituents in different positions. In this paper, we will not discuss the layout attributes (e.g. size, colour, texture, etc.) of templates and their constituents, or aesthetic criteria to define them. In general, we will abstract from any layout design issue, and will focus on the logical constituents of layout templates.

In our approach, template constituents are of two categories: fields (denoting containers of information which display data values when a node, instance of a template are created), and buttons (denoting active areas on the template, that are sensitive to user's actions).

We have identified three basic categories of buttons, that differ in their meaning and intended use: navigational in-the-large (structural and context-dependent), control in-the-small, and functional buttons.

Navigational in-the-large buttons

A button of this category is a placeholder of links among different nodes. It shows the existence of a link or a set of links and can be activated to traverse the corresponding link(s). There are two "subcategories" of navigation in-the-large buttons. In the first category are the buttons denoting structural, perspective, and applicative links, defined according the HDM+ model. These links depends only on the state of the underlying data base, i.e. on the actual values of the data stored in the data base. In the second category are buttons representing context dependent links, that are generated according to the current navigation context, on the basis of the actual visited nodes and on the actions performed by the user up to a given time. Example of context dependent links are backtracking links, that connect, in inverse temporal order, all visited nodes.

Control in-the-small buttons

They denote commands to control the behaviour of node constituents. Examples are the buttons to scroll, or to zoom in/out, the content of a field, to control a video element. They are "in-the-small" in the sense that they leave the user in the current node, changing the state of the current node, but not the current point of navigation.

Functional buttons

They represent functionalities other than navigation (e.g. printing facilities, query functions, help, etc.).

5. Layout Mapping

The layout mapping relates the segments and their constituents to visual templates and their components. Mapping a set of visual segment templates into a set of visual templates is done at three levels:

- assignment is injective; in fact, different segment types can be associated to the same visual template.
- for each frame defined in a segment type, assigning one, some, or all its slots to a field of the corresponding visual template. We will assume that neither two different frames of the same segment, nor two different sets of slots (of the same or different frames) can be assigned to the same field.

- assigning each type of link, outgoing from a nodes of a given type, to a navigation in-the-large button. Non necessarily this assignment is injective; in fact, different link types can be associated to the same button (as we will see in many examples in the next sections).

5.1 Layout Mapping Examples

An example of node, corresponding to the visual template "Customer-T" is shown in the figure 1. It displays the visual segment "Personal Data" of an entity of type "Customer".

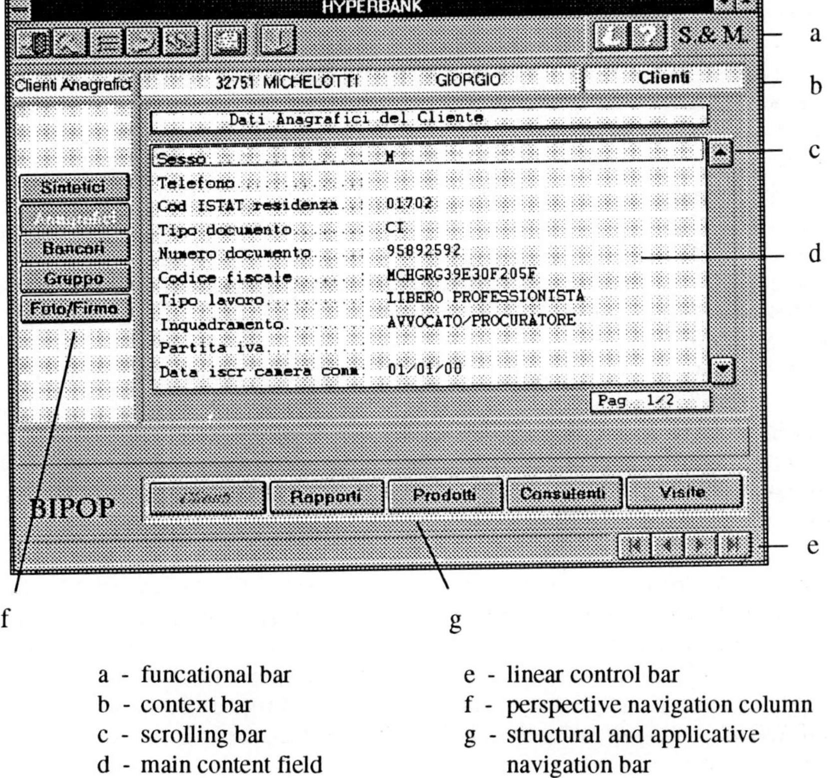

a - funcational bar
b - context bar
c - scrolling bar
d - main content field
e - linear control bar
f - perspective navigation column
g - structural and applicative navigation bar

Fig. 1: Node corresponding to visual segment "Personal Data" of the entity type "Customer"

Its template is structured in various fields and groups of buttons, as follows.

- *Main Content Field:* On the central area of the window, there is a field that will store the actual slots of the corresponding visual segment. It can be structured in subfields, one for each slot.

- *Perspective Navigation Column:* One the left side area there is a "column" of navigation-in-the-large buttons for perspective links, allowing to move across different perspective of the same piece of information (i.e. across nodes corresponding to different visual segments of the same component).
- Structural and applicative navigation bar. On the bottom, there is a sequence of navigation-in-the-large buttons, for structural and applicative links.
- Linear control bar. On the bottom right end side, there are some buttons to control in-the-small the execution of video elements, similar in their look to buttons in analogic video players and recorders, or to move back and forth in guided tours.
- Scrolling bar. On the right end side, close to the main content field, there are buttons to control in the small the presentation of the content of the main field, allowing to scroll up and down.

6. Conclusions

The work presented in this paper has been developed within the ESPRIT project HIFI [10]. HIFI stands for "Hypertext Interface For Information: Relational and Multimedia Data Bases" and denotes the ESPRIT project P 6532 which started in June 1992 and ended in September 1994.

The consortium consisted of EDS-Systems & Management in Torino (I) as Coordinating Partner, and following partners: EPSILON in Athens (G), SIEMENS AG in Munich (D), SYNTAX Sistemi Software in Bari (I), BENAKI Museum in Athens (G), GMD-IPSI in Darmastadt (D), MUSIC-FORTH in Chania (G) and POLITECNICO DI MILANO (I).

Aim of HIFI was to provide a set of tools supporting the development of hypermedia interfaces to information systems. This set of tools also allows to cheaply and quickly create a navigational interface on top of an external data base information systems.

So far, there are three major contributions of this project: *(1) the identification of various steps* in the design of a navigational interface to data bases, *(2) definitions of the interface* schema, of the mapping from interface structures to data base structures, of the lay our schema, and of the layout mapping; the specification of an interface schema design model (HDM+) that supports a systematic approach to interface schema design, and finally, *(3) the identification of a set of rules* to map HDM+ interface structures into relational database structure.

The HIFI approach has been tested by the HIFI partners in the development of a number of interfaces to pre-existing, real life data bases (i.e. the information system of an Italian bank, a medical data base of a German Hospital, and a cultural data base of a Greek Museum [11]), and has been proved extremely effective. In all these systems, the interface implementation environment has been Asymmetrix ToolBook, integrated with Q+E library functions in order to manage the access to the external SQL data bases. A prototype version of the overall architecture of HIFI has been implemented in C++ under Windows, and is described in detail in [1].

References

1. Cavallaro U., Garzotto F., Paolini P., Totaro D. "HIFI: Hypertext Interface for Information Systems", In IEEE Software (November 1993), pp. 48-51.
2. Garzotto F., Paolini P. and Schwabe, D. "Authoring-in-the-large: Software Engineering Techniques for Hypertext Application Design", In Proceedings 6th IEEE Int. Workshop on Sw Specification and Design, pp. 87-98, Como, Italy, Sept. 1991.
3. Garzotto F., Paolini P., Schwabe D., and Berstein M. "Tools for Designer". In Hypertext/Hypermedia Handbook, Berk, E. and Devlin, J. Eds., pp. 179-207, McGraw Hill, 1991.
4. Garzotto F., Paolini P., and Schwabe D. "HDM - A Model for the Design of Hypertext Applications". In Proceedings ACM Hypertext '91, S. Antonio, TX, pp. 313-328, Dec. 1991.
5. Garzotto F., Paolini P., Schwabe D. "HDM - A Model Based Approach to Hypermedia Application Design," in ACM Transactions on Office Information Systems, Vol. 11/1, J pp. 1-26, 1993.
6. Garzotto F., Mainetti L., Paolini P. "Navigation Patterns in Hypermedia Data Bases, in Proceedings 26th IEEE Int. Conf. on System Sciences, pp. 370-379, Maui, USA, Jan.1993.
7. Garzotto F., Mainetti L., Paolini P., "HDM2: Extending the E-R Approach to Hypermedia Application Design". In Proceedings 12th International Conference on the Entity-Relationship Approach Arlington, USA, Dec. 1993.
8. Garzotto F., Mainetti L., Paolini P., "Navigation in Hypermedia Applications: Modelling and Semantics", In Journal of Organizational Computing - to appear.
9. Garzotto F., Mainetti L., Paolini P. "Hypermedia Application Design: A Structured Approach". In Designing Hypermedia User Interfaces, W. Schuler, J. Hanneman, N. Streitz (eds.) Springer-Verlag, 1995.
10. HIFI Project ESPRIT P6532. "Technical Annex", 1991.
11. HIFI Project ESPRIT P6532. "Deliverable D5: HIFI Applications: Specification and Design", June 1993.
12. HIFI Project ESPRIT P6532. "Deliverable D12: The HDM+ User Manual", Jan. 1994.
13. Schwabe, D., Caloini, A., Garzotto, F., and Paolini, P. "Hypertext Development Using a Model-based Approach", In Software Practice and Experience, Vol. 22/11, pp. 937-962, Nov. 1992.
14 Cavallaro U. Tentori M. "HIFINBIPOP: Hypertext Interface to Financial Data in BIPOP (Italy)", In Designing Hypermedia User Interfaces, W. Schuler, J. Hanneman, N. Streitz (eds.) Springer-Verlag, 1995.
15. "HYPED" U. Cavallaro, P. Paolini (eds.), EDS-Systems & Management, ISBN IT 88-900063-9-0, (hypertext version of HIFI official document deliverables, video clips, HIFI literature on CD-Rom),Torino-Milano 1995.

Achieving Comfort and Security in the Use of Software Systems

Simon Lambert, Gordon Ringland
Knowledge Engineering Group
Rutherford Appleton Laboratory
Chilton, Didcot
Oxon OX11 0QX, U.K.

Abstract

The terms "comfort" and "security" when applied to a software system refer respectively to the sensations of the user and to attributes of the user's performance. Comfort describes the user's feeling of ease when interacting with the system, which can be partly achieved by familiarity, e.g. a consistent look-and-feel with other systems, but at a deeper level requires that the user be happy (at some sufficient level of understanding) with the workings of the system, the significance of its outputs, etc. Security means that the user is less likely to make mistakes due, for example, to a flawed understanding of the system's limitations. These qualities can be achieved by the provision of co-operative explanatory behaviour, which is the goal of the I-SEE project (ESPRIT P6013). The detection of and response to implicit information needs, the tailoring of the response to the user's knowledge and interests, and the justification of system reasoning in domain terms are all important ways of achieving this behaviour.

1. Comfort and Security for Software: an Application from I-SEE

The ESPRIT project I-SEE (P6013) is developing a toolkit for adding co-operative, explanatory capabilities to software systems. One of the I-SEE applications is a knowledge-based system called GEANT, developed by the I-SEE partner Lyonnaise des Eaux, for monitoring and diagnosis of problems in the operation of sewage plants. It uses quantitative and qualitative models of the sewage plant to perform its task, and provides assistance to sewage plant engineers. As well as diagnosis, it allows them to assess the consequences of modifications of the settings of the plant, and thereby helps the users to solve the problems that GEANT has detected. GEANT thus improves the performance of sewage plants.

However, in its original state, GEANT could not be said to be an environment with "comfort and security" for the user. A GEANT session normally proceeds in a prescribed sequence of steps whose results form the input to the next step, yet there was no explanation of the significance of the results of each step, either in terms of the overall purpose of the step or in domain terms justifying individual results. For example, in the second step of GEANT's reasoning, contradictory hypotheses are eliminated. For example, a user observation may clash with a simulation result, in which case the user observation is considered more reliable and is kept. GEANT in its original form could offer no explanation for the reasons for preferring one hypothesis to another. This is a perfect example of knowledge that is hard-coded into the application but not explicitly represented, and yet is crucial for convincing the user of the validity of the GEANT's reasoning. This is an aspect of the user's comfort when using the system: systems which ask the user for input and use it to reach conclusions which are then presented to the user without the ability to question or critique them may lead to discomfort, particularly in users who have experience of the domain.

Another example occurs in the third step of GEANT, which establishes a causal network to identify which of the various problems are the original, underlying causes (the others being consequences of these). It displays its results graphically. The user may wish to see a justification of reasoning which leads to a particular causal connection being made. This may be presented either as an explanation of the general causal relation between problems on the plant, or as an explanation of a particular inference carried out by GEANT in this case, rather than a statement of general truths about the domain. (Incidentally, this illustrates that a single "information need" may be satisfied by more than one "explanation technique".) In either case, the security of the user/system is increased, in the sense that the user becomes better informed, and may be able to assess the system's conclusions and detect limitations in its reasoning.

2. The I-SEE Architecture

The I-SEE architecture is shown in figure 1. This architecture represents a system (the application) with the I-SEE co-operative explanatory facilities added above it. The I-SEE project is developing a generic toolkit which will permit the addition of such facilities to applications: the toolkit will consist of software components, libraries, methods and where appropriate tools.

The architecture of an I-SEE explaining system is based on two generic modules, the explanation engine and the co-operative interaction engine. These lie between the user and the application. In general, an application may include some explicit representations of domain knowledge used in its processing. It will also operate with internal representations which may be either a "projection" of domain knowledge, i.e. based on domain knowledge but represented implicitly in the data structures and procedures of the system, or a purely internal representation, containing all the details of the implementation that are not relevant to explanations. For generating an explanation no access to this latter part of the application is needed. This analysis is based on Newell's ideas of the knowledge level [3].

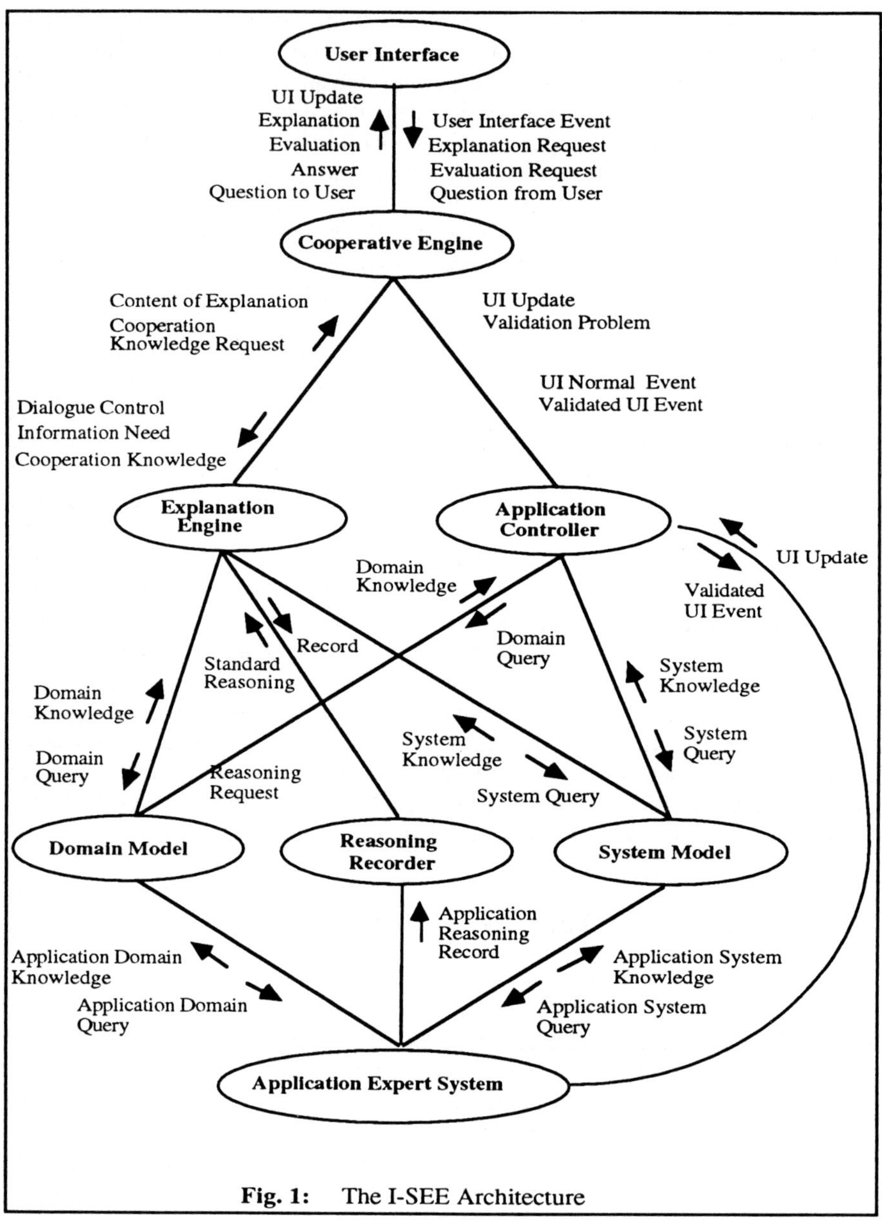

Fig. 1: The I-SEE Architecture

There are three types of knowledge that might be necessary to generate an explanation:

- knowledge about the domain of the application;
- knowledge about how the application performs a task in general—for example, how GEANT performs its diagnosis of the malfunctions on a sewage plant;
- knowledge of how it has solved a particular problem.

Knowledge about the application domain is represented in the domain model and knowledge about how the application reasons is represented in the system model. These models each consist of two parts: knowledge that is already present in the application and knowledge that has to be added for explanation. The former part is knowledge that is already represented explicitly, the knowledge level part of the system. It is not necessary to duplicate this knowledge in the system by building another model of it.

The second parts of these two models consist of knowledge not represented in the actual application. It is not in the application because it is not required for the application to perform its task. In a sense, it represents knowledge about the knowledge in the application. In other words, the knowledge which is present in the application is being augmented with knowledge that is not present but is necessary for generating explanations. The last source of information is the reasoning recorder, which is responsible for recording the dynamic processing of the application as it works on a particular case.

The Explanation Engine is the heart of the system. The task of the explanation engine is to generate the content of an explanation using the domain and system model and the reasoning record. To do this it needs a different kind of knowledge, knowledge of how to explain, how to generate the content of answers to satisfy different information needs, which explanations are the most appropriate in different contexts, etc. The domain model, the system model and the reasoning record are utilised by the explanation engine and should provide sufficient knowledge for the potential content of an explanation.

Given a user's information need it selects the content of an explanation. It does so by first generating a general explanation plan to satisfy the user's need. It then selects information from the models according to this plan. Finally the explanation is assessed and if necessary, replanning is initiated until the content of the explanation is considered satisfactory.

The co-operative interaction engine takes care that all user needs are satisfied in an appropriate way. It is firstly responsible for detecting information needs and for passing them on to the explanation engine. Secondly, the co-operative interaction engine takes the content of an explanation from the explanation engine and decides how to present what it wants to say. One of its major responsibilities is the generation of a textual form of the response from the internal representation which is used to communicate between all the components of I-SEE. Rhetorical predicates (after Pilkington [5]) are employed to help structure the text.

The use of rhetorical predicates in I-SEE is innovative and overcomes some of the problems associated with their use in earlier work. The work of McKeown [2] and Paris [4] employs rhetorical predicates to analyse text structures by classifying individual utterances. However, their approach suffers from confusing a number of different functions of rhetorical predicates. To take an example from the domain of GEANT: the explanatory sentence:

"*The brown foam means the presence of anaerobic bacteria*
which means that the amount of oxygen in the tank is too low"

could be analysed in terms of instances of McKeown's *Cause-effect* rhetorical predicate, of *Inference* and of *Evidence*. Yet these fulfil different functions: the first is a factual statement about the domain; the second defines the role in the wider context of the explanation, while the third describes the overall way in which the explanation is presented. From the point of view of generating explanations, the resulting problem is one of lack of clarity in generating explanations: the task of the explanation planner (in I-SEE's terms) would be complicated by confusing elements of the explanation which convey facts about the domain with those which express these facts in a particular way, and with those which structure the overall explanation. In fact, it would be very hard to create a generic toolkit for the explanation planner.

The I-SEE architecture has overcome this problem by representing the three different elements in different ways. The factual content is obtained from the domain and/or system models. The role is defined by the primitive explanation techniques which form a set of basic methods for presenting content information and which may be built up into larger structures.

Examples of primitive explanation techniques are *GiveSuperConcept* (in terms of a hierarchy of domain objects) and *GiveJustification* (in terms of rules that have implied the fact in question). The overall structure of the explanation is then handled by the explanation planner, which assembles sequences of primitive explanation techniques into coherent structures. In the I-SEE architecture, the rhetorical predicates are structures returned from the primitive explanation techniques and passed to the co-operative interaction engine where they are used in text generation.

The advantage of this clear distinction is the separation of and reusability of explanatory knowledge and techniques across different domains and systems. The domain models will need to be redeveloped for new domains, but the range of explanation techniques and explanation plans will be independent of the domain and therefore available for reuse, at least potentially—of course not all explanation techniques used in one application will be suitable for another, and likewise some new ones may be required, but the point is that a library of techniques is available.

3. Explanations in I-SEE: an Example

We now present an example of user interaction with the GEANT system enhanced with I-SEE. Figure 2 shows a stage in a consultation with GEANT when the system has just completed the third step of its reasoning, the "results section", which identifies the underlying or original problems on the plant and indicates the other problems which are a consequence of them. The results are presented diagramatically.

The I-SEE explaining system is totally integrated with the GEANT application, in that the user requests explanations by interacting with the GEANT interface. In the case shown, the user has used the mouse to click on the node labelled "BOD5 outlet", which stands for the problem that the biological oxygen demand at the outlet is too high. I-SEE displays a pop-up menu corresponding to various information needs that the user may have concerning the node. Each of these is associated with one or more explanation techniques permitting a variety of explanations.In this example, the user chooses to ask "WHY is this NOT an original problem?" (i.e. it is not at the beginning of the causal chain of problems). The explanation is shown in Figure 3.

A statement of the significance of the queried node in context (i.e. that it is a potential problem on the plant).

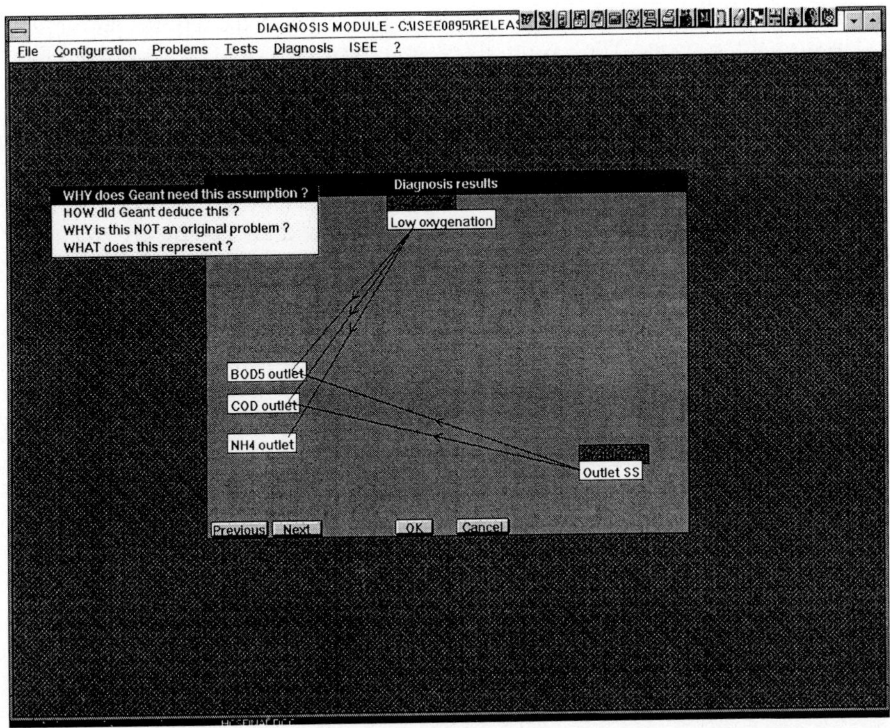

Fig. 2: A stage in the consultation with GEANT

The explanation illustrates the use of rhetorical predicates to structure an explanation, and the trace from the reasoning recorder to explain a particular inference. The explanation is structured as follows.

- A statement of the purpose, inputs and outputs of the results section of GEANT, setting the scene for the particular explanation that follows.
- A statement of which other problems on the plant cause the BOD5 problem.
- A conclusion which refers back directly to the user's question.

It should be emphasised that the coverage of I-SEE applied to GEANT is very high, i.e. for each of the screens through which the user interacts with the application, it is possible to use the mouse to click on most of the entities of interest and to obtain I-SEE explanations. All these explanations are generated from the I-SEE system in a consistent way.

4. User Assessment

A thorough user assessment of the I-SEE-enhanced application has been undertaken within the scope of the project [1]. Here the findings are summarised and related to the comfort and security of the users as defined above.

The user assessment took the form of a number of structured exercises performed by each of three users. They were asked to carry out a number of tasks using GEANT, the tasks having been designed by Lyonnaise des Eaux experts to be fairly typical of the kind of tasks that would face a user in practice. These tasks included understanding and justifying the system's reasoning and conclusions, for which the I-SEE explanatory capabilities were required. The users were asked to give their opinions of the combined I-SEE/GEANT system on a number of seven-point scales, which were analysed and summarised to produce evaluative conclusions.

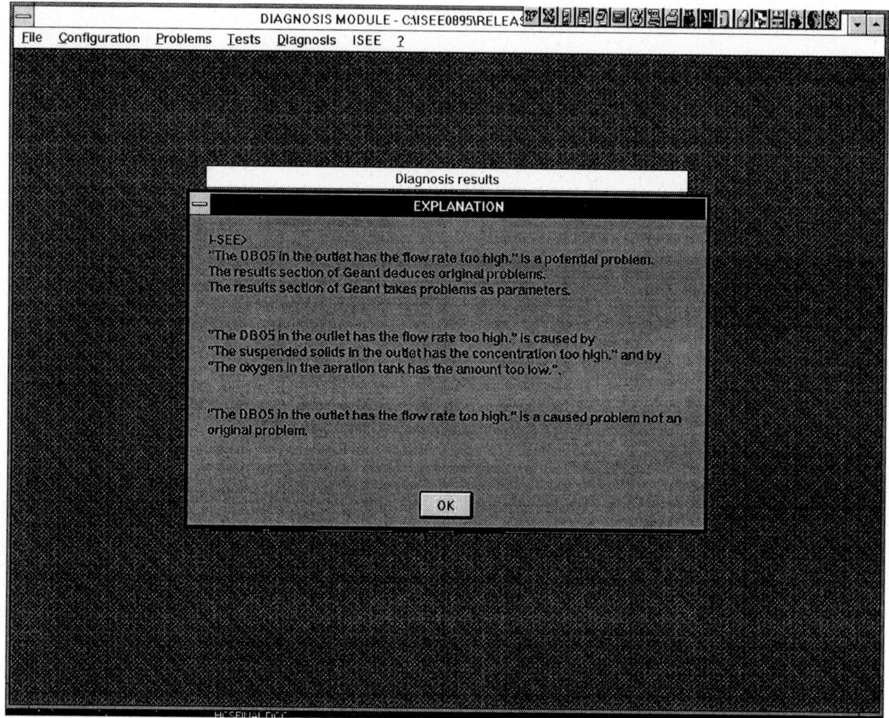

Fig. 3: An explanation produced by I-SEE

The main result was that the users' confidence in GEANT was much increased, and hence the likelihood that in practice the GEANT system will be used to assist in the diagnosis and control of real-life problems.

- The system was assessed on criteria of *Readability*, *Navigation*, *Explanation Content*, *Depth of the Knowledge Base*, *Functioning*, *Usability*, *Integration* and *User Acceptance*.
- According to the assessment of *Functioning*: "All of the question types deemed necessary existed in the system. A context-dependent selection menu ensured that only „logical“ questions could be asked about a given object. This in turn ensured that only relevant explanations were provided."
- According to the *User Acceptance* assessment: "The system provided explanations that were accurate, easy to accept and increased the confidence in the

GEANT results. The explanations will provide a significant aid in increasing the confidence that a user will place in the GEANT results."

- The overall summary concludes that: "The vast ambiguity that naturally exists in the domain is reduced by the explanations provided. The explanations can reduce the number of possible solutions, thereby guiding the user to select the most appropriate response to a dysfunction."

We can conclude from these results that users' comfort with using a software system, and the security of the interaction, can be enhanced by the addition of carefully designed co-operative explanatory capabilities, and that such capabilities may be developed using the I-SEE generic toolkit and added to existing applications.

References

1. Cinq-Mars S. "I-SEE System Assessment, Deliverable D470.1", 1995.
2. McKeown K.R. "Text Generation: Using Discourse Strategies and Focus Constraints to Generate Natural Language Text", Cambridge University Press, 1985.
3. Newell A. "The knowledge level", Artificial Intelligence, 1982: 82-17.
4. Paris C. "Tailoring object descriptions to a user's level of expertise", Computational Linguistics 14(3): 64-78, 1988.
5. Pilkington R. "Intelligent Help: Communicating with Knowledge-Based Systems", Paul Chapman Publishing Ltd. 1992.

OPX2 Intelligent Help: an Example of Intelligent Interfaces

Jean-Yves Quéméneur, Florent Brossier
SYSECA
66-68, avenue Pierre Brossolette
F-92247 Malakoff Cedex, France

Abstract

Intelligent interfaces are the result of continuous evolution of man-machine interfaces. The aim of an intelligent interface is to communicate actively and co-operatively with the user, and to give him the information he needs in order to achieve his tasks efficiently. The company SYSECA participated to the ESPRIT project 6013 I-SEE (Interactive Self-Explanation Engine) and developed intelligent interfaces within a customized framework. The developed Intelligent Help System for the OPX2 environment uses the I-SEE toolkit, which allows users to access quickly and selectively the required information. An individual access is also supported, since the user is allowed to describe his requirements by a focussed question. The access is fast, since the Intelligent Help for OPX2 is able to extract information from its knowledge base quicker than an usual consultation of the manual.

1. Introduction

The intelligent interfaces are based on the logical evolution of the man-machine interfaces. Their existence is the result of the observation that we need programmes which are capable of a better communicatiuon with their users, rather than programmes with additional functions. In general, existing programmes are used to a fraction of their capabilities, since they become too complex to use.

The main objective of an intelligent interface is to support co-operatively communication with the user, and to supply the information required for completion of an user task. Here the intelligence is focussed primarily on the improvement of the man-machine communication, but it also provides in a comfortable way the information content, which is in this context only a secondary achievement.

An intelligent interface should also be co-operative. The co-operation is usually supplied by a dialogue manager, as well as by special features of the knowledge representation with the aim of solving both the "*no answer*" and the "*too many answers*" problems. The intelligence is here supplied by an expert system [8], and knowledge representation. The main objectives of an intelligent interface are as follows:

- improvement of the communication with the user,
- co-operation with the user,
- improvement of the user productivity, and
- increasement of the number of potential users, due to the "*easy to understand*" facilities.

The improvement of the communication with the user is here the central objective. It can be achieved in two ways: by a *question answering* facility [5], and by the *use of explanation knowledge*. These two mechanisms provide both the presentation of the conclusions provided by a complex software or expert system, and intelligent help to the user.

The co-operation with the user is implemented by the detection of the information needs, and by special features in the knowledge representation [1].

The need for information can be explicit or implicit. An explicit information need is expressed by a direct question. An implicit information need is, for instance, an user asking the same question twice. In this case clearly the first answer wasn't satisfactory. A intelligent interface could supply different information the second time. Some special features in the knowledge representation allow the control of the generalization versus specialization ratio, when answering. This help is used in problem solving of the "*no answer*" and "*too many answers*" problems [4].

The user's productivity improvement is ensured by the improvement in understanding software. A better understanding could come, depending on the application, from an intelligent help or from the explanation of complex results. In many domains the explanation [2], [3] of how a solution has been obtained is as important as the solution itself

A shorter learning time is also a factor that improves user productivity. This reduction of learning time must not be here neglected. For instance, the usual text processing tools are already too complex: the average user masters less than 10% of their functionality. The learning time is then very long if you consider that the effective use of a new functionality begins by a learning phase. Finally, an increase in the number of users is a logical consequence of the three previous points. When you take into account the market and the long term evolution, this last point is important. In fact, more and more people must learn to use computers, either as working tool, or as an instrument of daily life. The transition to the information highway society imposes "easy to use" computer systems, i.e. the design of user-friendly interfaces.

2. Explanation Toolkit

The I-SEE project (Interactive Self-Explanation Engine, EP6013) was partly financed by the European Commission under the ESPRIT programme, and was focussed on providing efficient explanations to the user. The consortium has developed an explanation toolkit allowing the construction of explanation modules, as well as intelligent interfaces. SYSECA has developed, in co-operation with other partners, the "OPX2 Intelligent Help" system. The I-SEE explanation toolkit consists of *an adaptable and customizable architecture* which contains a domain model of the application, a dialogue manager, an individual explanation knowledge base, and the explanation adaptation system to the user needs. The architecture developed by the I-SEE project is adaptable to different domains [7]. The adaptation is carried out by different models:

- the model of the application domain,
- the application control model, and
- the reasoning model.

2.1 Application Domain

The application domain model allows the description of domain knowledge which is necessary for the explanation. The studies carried out have clearly demonstrated that "the necessary knowledge for solving a problem", and that necessary for explaining "how it has been solved", are different. The application control model allows the description of the control in the application itself. This information is necessary in order to be able to explain how a conclusion has been reached. The reasoning model allows the memorizing of the rules which are carried out by the application (if the application is an expert system). Unlike the two previous ones, this model is dynamic and processes information specific to each case.

2.2 Dialogue Manager

The dialogue manager contains a user model and the generalization level adjustment mechanism. Clearly, an expert prefers short explanations. But on the other hand, a beginner needs more detailed explanations. This knowledge allows an explanation to be built, which is adapted to the user's needs. Additionally, the dialogue manager controls the generalization versus specialization ratio. This mechanism provides partial answers when the "no answer" problem or the "*too many answers*" problem occurred. These partial answers help the user to figure out the problem, to express the question, and to adjust the level of generality of his question.

2.3 Explanation Knowledge

The explanation engine includes specific knowledge to the explanation. This knowledge takes the form of explanation plans, which are able to satisfy a particular information requirement. These plans call themselves explanation primitives. The explanation primitives are gathered in an extendible library. The library contains explanations which are general enough to be applicable in the majority of the cases. However, each new domain will probably request the introduction of specific explanation primitives and specific explanation plans.

3. OPX2 Intelligent Help

The I-SEE project develops three demonstrators:

- GEANT,
- OSIS, and
- OPX2 Intelligent Help

The first two demonstrators are here briefly presented. The third one is presented in more detail in the rest of this paper. *GEANT*, the diagnostic expert system developed by the Lyonnaise des Eaux/Dumez company, concerns the domain of waste water processing. It provides advice on waste water plant monitoring. The *OSIS* software is dedicated to the oil dispersal modelling of sea pollution. The problems which occur and which justify the use of I-SEE are the following. The configuration of the dispersal model is complex, and interpreting the raw data supplied by the numerical simulator is difficult.

The objective of the third demonstrator, called the *OPX2 Intelligent Help*, is to facilitate the use of complex software systems [6]. The chosen software for the demonstration of I-SEE results is OPX2, a scheduling tool developed and marketed by SYSECA. It is a high level tool, and consequently it is rich in functionality. A consequence of this richness is unsatisfactory usability. The main objective of the OPX2 Intelligent Help is to increase the usability of the OPX2 software system, and to improve in this way the market position of OPX2, since the usability is a key "buying and acceptance" criteria for customers. The availability of intelligent help is of great importance to many customers.

A Help System [6] can have several levels of functionality. The first and the most simple level supplies on-line access to the user manual. The second level also supplies hypertext links. This capacity accelerates the access to the information and produces more dynamic help. The third level is the one proposed by I-SEE: the intelligent help. In this case, the help is even more specific and dynamic. It is more specific, because the user can construct a question, describing his information request. The intelligent help is able to build an specific answer to his question. In conclusion, the user rapidly obtains the requested information.

The aim of the Intelligent Help System, which was designed for OPX2, is to fill the gap between a "general planning knowledge" facility and the OPX2 specific knowledge.

The intelligent help supplies the guiding functionality and the error explanation functionality. The user's guide is implemented by using the method recommended by OPX2. The explanation of the error causes allows minimizing their consequences. The expected results are the improvement of the user productivity, and a reduction in the error number. In addition, the time needed for error recovery is also reduced. All these factors cause a reduction in the learning time.

The general operation of the Intelligent Help System is the following: the user builds a question by selecting a question type and adding complementary information. This question is then transformed into a particular logical formalism, the common meaning representation (CMR), a knowledge representation formalism based on first order logic with typed variables. This formalism is used as a general mean of complex information exchange in the I-SEE architecture. The domain model is then interrogated with questions of CMR format.

The domain model is mainly based on the QUEST model presented by Graesser in [5]. The QUEST model contains interconnected hierarchies which are equivalent to a semantic network. This mode of representation is simple enough and adapted to the knowledge type necessary for intelligent help. In addition, the QUEST model contains information search algorithms able to answer specific questions. The QUEST model has been adapted to I-SEE needs. For instance, the information attached to a semantic network node is coded in CMR. The answers are obviously supplied in CMR form. This logical representation is then translated to text by using a specific algorithm.

3.1 User Interface

The Intelligent Help user interface allows the user to build semi-open questions. This interface type gives some freedom to the user but alleviates the difficulty of a natural language interface. The user interface should be very user-friendly and support fast interaction. The intelligent help for OPX2 user interfaces should support both hypertext links and graphics, due to OPX2 graphics capability. We selected the hypertext engine Mosaic, in agreement with the OPX2 team. Mosaic is based on the HTML language and is used as a browser in the Internet. This choice opens interesting possibilities concerning the supported platforms, and also the evolution to a World Wide Web information server with intelligent access to distributed information. The current version of the OPX2 intelligent help is a full HTTP server, and can be connected to the Internet in order to provide remote information to international customers. The user interface allows each user to build his individual questions based on HTML language constructs, and this information is sent to the Intelligent Help System. The user selects a group of questions among the options: "know-how", "know-what" or "know-why". These options group the questions according to the type of provided information. The user may select a question from one list, and also add complementary information. The complementary information indicates, for instance, the object or the action to which the question refers (see figure 1). The HTML page is returned to the user, and contains now the answer elaborated by the intelligent help engine, additional to the initial user's question. The system expression of the question allows the user to verify if the question processed by the system is the question that he wants to ask. The answer may also contain hyperlinks to the on-line documentation.

In order to provide a quick overview of the architecture at work, let's suppose that the user selects the type of question "*how do you do <action>?*". Then he selects the complementary information "define" and "project". The question is expressed again: "*how do you define a project?* ".

3.2 Knowledge Representation

The CMR is a knowledge representation formalism based on first order logic with typed variables. This formalism is used between the high level modules in the I-SEE architecture in order to support the exchange of complex information.

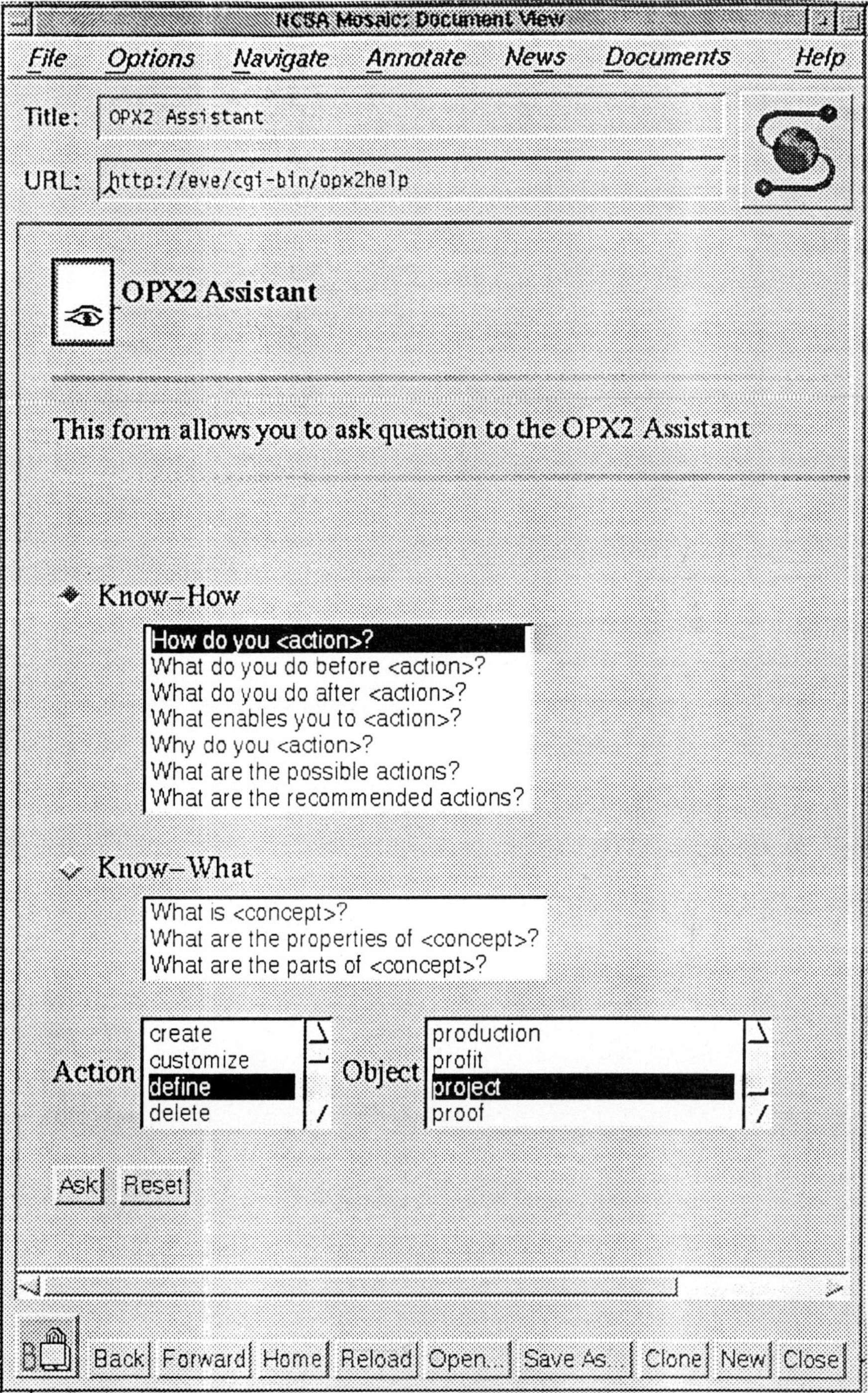

Fig. 1: User Interface of the Intelligent Help System of OPX2

The most significant feature of the CMR is *variable typing*, which refers to the conceptual hiererchy. The conceptual hierarchy is divided in two parts, the root and the domain-dependent part. This hierarchy also defines the vocabulary known by the Help System. It structures the vocabulary and allows for some semantic control. The root hierarchy is common to all applications.

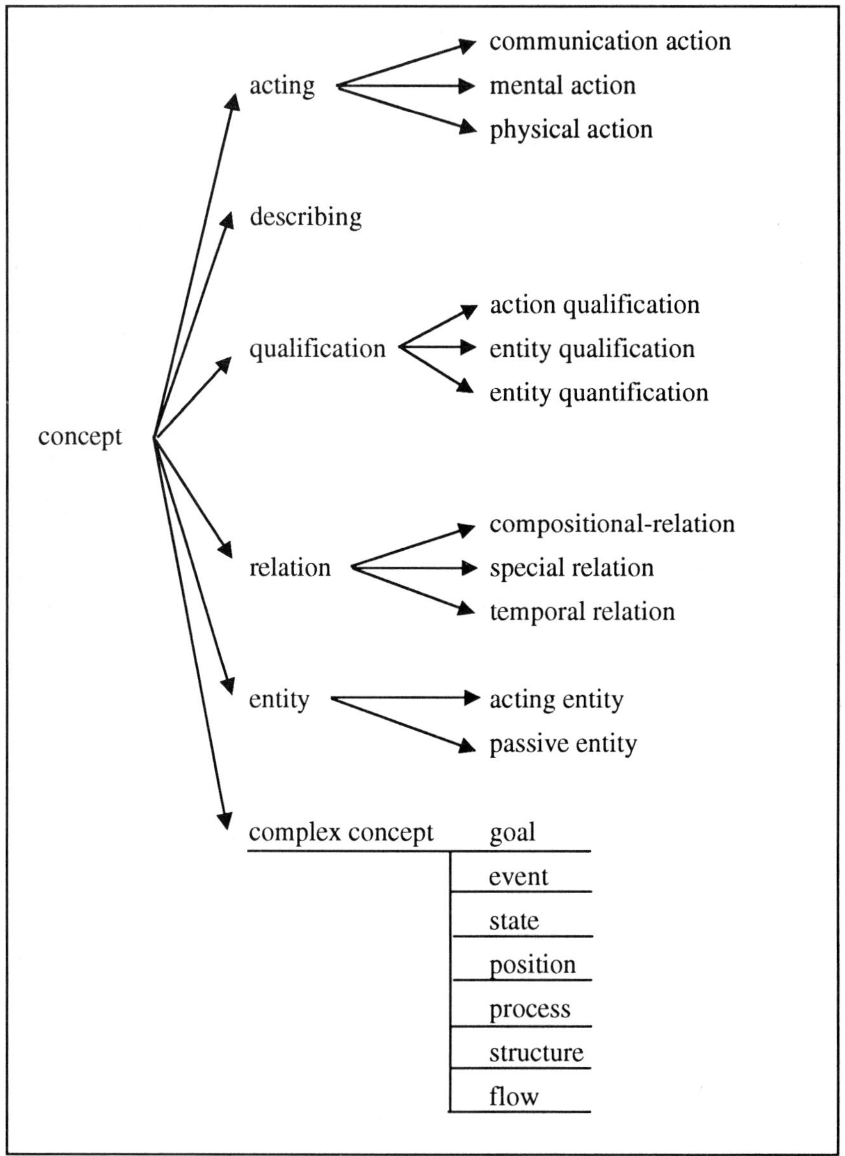

Fig. 2: Root of the Conceptual Hierarchy

The hierarchy is composed mainly of concepts and links. In addition each concept has some characteristic (due to link property) which distinguishes this concept from its sibling concepts. This building constraint is significant because it constitutes a distinctive part of the concept definition. Another type of link which occurs frequently in the conceptual hierarchy is the "*HasAsPart*" link. This type of link describes the concept components.

CMR is a formalism which is well adapted to the representation of complex knowledge and relatively easy to transform into text. However it is less adapted to the reasoning. This choice is consistent with the project objective concerning the support of a good level of communication with the user. Despite that, the reasoning capacity of CMR is satisfactory when compared to the user needs. In particular, the unification mechanism was extended to take into account the variable typing. The capacity of subtyping is here very useful for obtaining specific information by asking general questions. The subtyping implements, at the unification level, the semantics of the IsA link. If two concepts are linked by a *IsA* link, then the subconcept is included in the super-concept. So it is logical to accept the subconcept when a super-concept is requested.

The QUEST model contains interconnected hierarchies that are equivalent to a semantic network. In the OPX2 Intelligent Help System the domain model is mainly based on the QUEST model [5]. This representation mode is simple enough, and also well adapted to the knowledge type which is necessary for intelligent help. The search algorithms of the QUEST model are able to answer specific questions.

The important characteristics of the QUEST model are expressed by the knowledge structuring and search algorithms, and both are well adapted to our needs. In fact, QUEST is a model that originates from cognitive psychology studies, and reproduce the capability of an adult to answer general questions. QUEST simulates the answers of adults when they answer questions of the type: *why, how, or when,* etc. One of the most interesting properties of this model is that it was designed to be psychologically plausible. This point is crucial, because it means that if the internal information is present, the user will generally be satisfied by the answer produced by QUEST.

The QUEST model contains following hierarchies: conceptual, goal, event (including a causal network), state, position, process, structure and flow. If necessary, even more specific hierarchies can be integrated. All these hierarchies capture specific information. For instance, the goal hierarchy is able to represent the domain goals and to break down these goals into subgoals. This hierarchy is used for answering questions of the type "*how to do*" and "*why*".

3.3 Co-operation

The normal interrogation of a goal hierarchy with a CMR appropriate to the user's question: "how do you define a project?" can be performed by simple matching. It finds the goal "*define_project*". Then, the use of the "r*eason*" links in the reversed direction allows to find the subgoals associated to the initial goal. The co-operation of the I-SEE toolkit is specially effective when the normal interrogation process fails.

The co-operation process in the question answering task is based on following three mechanisms:

- general goals supplemented by follow-up questions,
- generalization of too specific questions, and
- specialization of too general questions.

The general goals and follow-up questions solve a problem introduced by a design choice. The user interface is kept simple in order to allow rapid interaction; in fact, too simple to allow complex goals to be expressed. In this case we cannot reach these non-expressible goals. For this purpose we introduced the general goals, that are connected to inexpressible goals, and allow general goals to be built by the user interface. In addition the "follow-up question mechanism" helps speed up execution process. We add a button to each goal when an answer is provided to the user, and by clicking on a button the user is able to build a question based on these answers.

The last two mechanisms rely on the capability of subtyping matching, and help the user when the simple matching fails by providing "*no answer*" or "*too many answers*". The two cases are interpreted as a wrong position on the generality scale.

The simplest way to present these mechanisms is to give two examples. The first example regarding the subtyping mechanism illustrates the generalization of a question that is too specific. The exact matching raises a problem of the class "*no answer*". The *too specific* action is then replaced by a very general action, allowing the retrieval of all the possible actions on the object, according to the direct match in the knowledge base.

In the first example the CMR expression query is equivalent to the task "*how do you construct a link?*". In this case there is no direct match in the knowledge base. The dialogue manager here enlarges the scope of the question in order to obtain some answers. These answers are presented to the user in a summarized form. With these elements he could reformulate his question using an existing piece of knowledge, which fits his requirements. In this case the co-operative answers are as follows:

> *"There is no answer with the construct verb but possible actions on links are: create, edit, remove."*

> *"There is no answer with this link object but possible objects with the construct verb are: project, work break down structure, network chart, resource break down structure."*

The second example deals with the subtyping mechanism, and illustrates the specialization of "*too general*" questions. Exact matching raises a problem with the type "*too many answers*". The different answers are here presented to the user in a summarized form, which allows him to focus his question on an existing piece of knowledge that fits to his requirements.

In the second example the CMR expression query is equivalent to:

> *"How do you modify a work break down structure?"*

In this case the answer is:

> *"There are answers with verb more specific than modify:*
> *construct, configure, edit."*

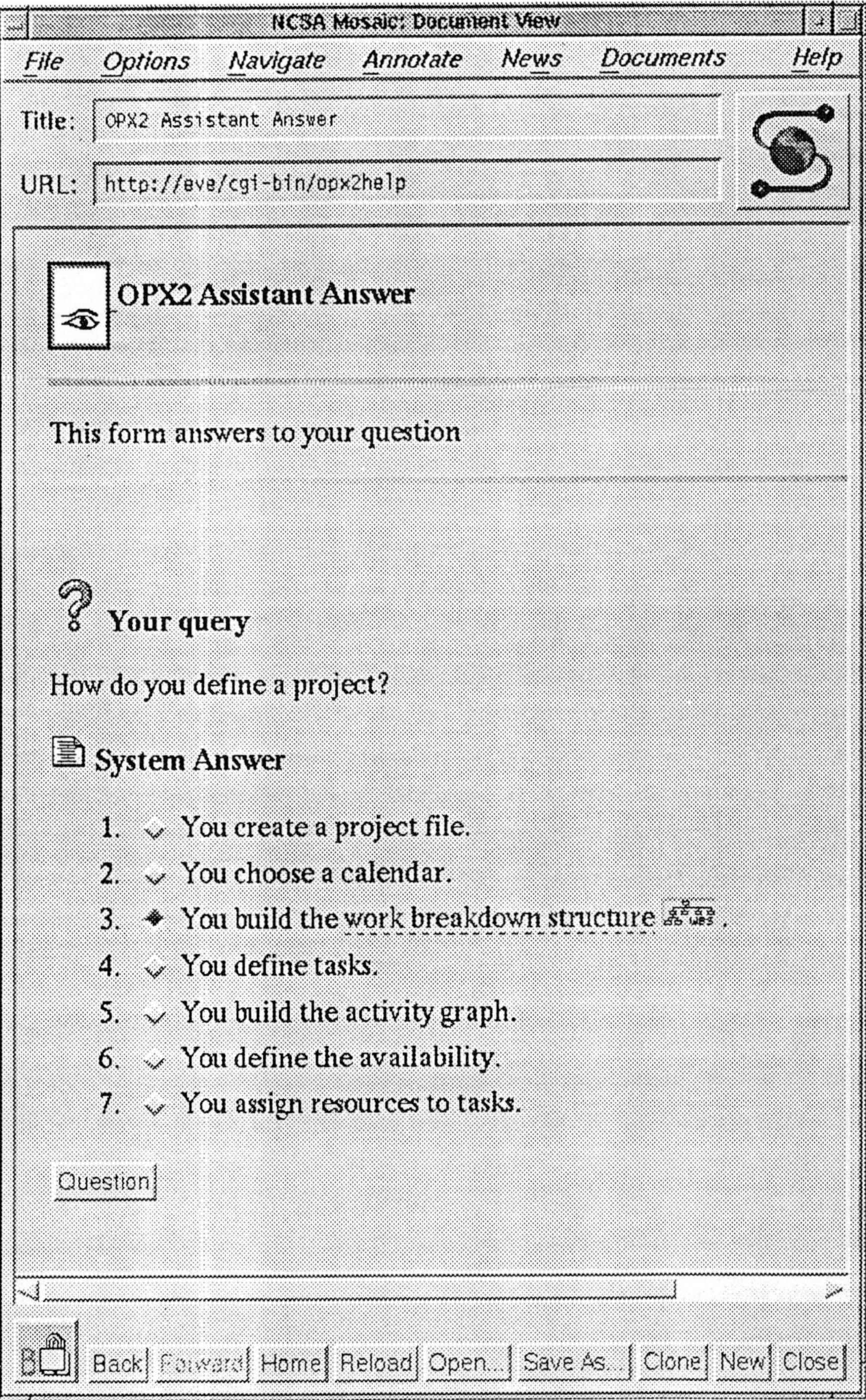

Fig. 3: Answer presented by MOSAIC

3.4 Text Generation

The logical answer produced by the explanation engine is transformed into text by the text generation algorithm, which is a relatively complex part of the architecture. In fact, the problem complexity requests the application of several techniques and knowledge representations. The first step is, of course, the adaptation of the CMR to the text generation. The second step is the use of rhetorical predicates, which provide the argumentative part of the discourse. The third step is the use of syntactical trees, as the intermediate stages. The combination of all these elements makes the text generation algorithm feasible.
The transformation of a syntactical tree into text is a relatively simple step. This transformation takes into account the English syntactical rules. The syntactical tree transformer implements a sub-set of the English grammar. A French version of the OPX2 Intelligent Help System is already available.

Two approaches were considered during the development process. The first approach, and the most simple, consists of a translation of the internal knowledge from English to French. The French syntactical tree transformer programme is requested in both approaches.

The second approach dynamically translates the syntactical tree. This solution suppresses the translation of all the internal knowledge. From the maintenance point of view, this issue is important, especially if the extension to more than two languages is envisaged. In order to evaluate the difficulty of the dynamic translation, we keep in mind following factors that simplify the problem: *(1)* only a subset of the French grammar is supported, *(2)* the information is supplied in the form of a syntactical tree, and *(3)* the domain is limited and well defined. The problem of the translation quality is minimized by these three factors. Moreover an efficient management of the dictionary or, in the most difficult cases, rewriting of the internal knowledge will solve most of the quality problems. For the other problems, we must weigh up the pro and the contra points, as follows: the advantage of an unique knowledge version, versus text quality. Our main decision was to evaluate the quality of the dynamic translation; if the quality was evaluated as insufficient, the backup solution was simply the translation of the knowledge into French.

4. Conclusions

The I-SEE project led to the development of an explanation toolbox which allowed the construction of intelligent interfaces. SYSECA used it to develop the OPX2 Intelligent Help System. This scheduling software is presented on the market as a high level software tool, and consequently it is very rich in functionality. A consequence of this richness is unsatisfactory usability. The main objective of the OPX2 Intelligent Help System is to increase the usability.

The usability is a key "buying and acceptance" criteria for customers. This improvement will increase the marketability of OPX2. The user interface of the Intelligent Help System allows the user to build semi-open questions. This type of interface gives some freedom to the user, but alleviates the difficulty of a natural language interface. The presented user interface is user-friendly and also supports quick interaction. As OPX2 is a graphic system, the Intelligent Help System supports both hypertext links as well as graphics. In agreement with the OPX2 team, the chosen hypertext engine is Mosaic. The QUEST model and the common meaning representation formalism are used to represent the knowledge.

The search algorithms of the QUEST model are able to answer specific questions like *how, why, what is, where, when.* The text generation algorithm transforms the internal representation into text. Finally, the same internal knowledge can be transformed into English or French text. The co-operation of the I-SEE toolkit is especially efficient when the normal interrogation process fails. The co-operation in question answering is built on three mechanisms: general goals supplemented by follow-up questions, generalization of too specific questions, and specialization of too general questions.

The success of the OPX2 Intelligent Help System is ensured by its advanced characteristics, and the rapid information access. The access is specific too (since the user describes his requirement by a specific question), and also fast (since the Intelligent Help is able to extract only the required information from its knowledge base). The co-operation in question answering allows the system to deal with normal interrogation process failure. This first application of the intelligent interfaces of the OPX2 Intelligent Help, led us to envisage this approach for other applications. In the long term we hope to improve the capabilities of "*easy to use*" and the "*friendliness*" of various classes of software systems using the advanced OPX2 technology.

References

[1] Anand T. and Kahn G. "Focusing Knowledge-based Techniques on Market Analysis", IEEE Expert, August 1993.

[2] Charlie Ellis "Expert Knowledge and Explanation", Ellis Horwood Books, 1989.

[3] T. R. Fennel, J. D. Johannes "An Architecture for Rule-based System Explanation", Fifth Conference on Artificial Intelligence for Space Application, NASA Marshall Space Flight Center, 1990.

[4] Frainier R., Groleau N., Hazelt L., Colombano S., Compton M., Statler I., Szolovits P., Young L. "Pi-in-anBox, a Knowledge-based System for Space Science Experimentation", AI Magazine, March 1994.

[5] Lauer T. W., Peacock E., Graesser A. C. "Questions and information systems", Lawrence Erlbaum Associates, 1992.

[6] Pilkington R. "Intelligent Help: Communicating with Knowledge-based Systems", Oxford University Press, New York, 1992.

[7] Tanner M., Keuneke A. "The Roles of the Task Structure and Domain Functional Models", IEEE Expert, June 1991.

[8] Turban E. "Decision Support and Expert Systems", Maxwell Macmillan, 1993.

Interaction Objects for Explanation

D.W. Thomas, E.A. Edmonds, R.M. Junes
LUTCHI Research Centre Loughborough University of Technology
Loughborough, Leicestershire, LE11 3TU, UK

J. L. Cunningham
British Maritime Technology
Orlando House, 1 Waldgrave Road, Teddington, Middlesex, TW11 8LZ, UK

Abstract

The ability of a computer system to provide intelligent explanation about its output and reasoning methods is important for user confidence. In this context user interface tools that enable the definition of interaction objects dynamically are essential. This is due to the unpredictable nature of the dynamically produced explanations. It is therefore impossible to fully pre-define the dialogue and determine which interaction objects will be required for any given explanation. User modelling within the explanation system compounds the indeterminate nature of the dialogue. This paper describes how the FOCUS (ESPRIT 2620) User Interface System, which offers dynamic dialogue definition, has been used to front end explanation tools in the I-SEE project (ESPRIT 6013). Using this approach, the explanation system can create output for the user in a form determined "on the fly". The results are illustrated by examples from an explanation system connected to the OSIS application.

1. Introduction

An explanation engine is the component of a computer system that provides the user with explanations about the results produced by an application. It relays information as to why certain conclusions have been reached by the system and may also be able to give explanation about its own reasoning behaviour. The aim of a system that has the ability to do this is to provide the user with confidence in the results it produces. For an explanation engine that produces explanations by simply delivering strings of "canned" text and graphics in response to a particular input, the output can be determined before runtime for all possible inputs. Where an explanation engine produces meaningful explanations from inbuilt reasoning techniques and knowledge held in user and domain models, its output for any given input will depend on the current context of the query and therefore cannot be determined before runtime. In this case it is essential that the interaction objects can be adapted or created by the explanation engine to display the results in a suitable form.

There are many user interface tools that have been produced both for research and commercial purposes that help an application developer when they are creating a user interface for a particular application. These tools aid the developer by offering high level definitions of objects. This makes the construction of user interface objects (interaction objects) easier than if they were created by merely programming the user interface in some low level language. Many tools such as the NeXT's Interface Builder and Apple's HyperCard offer graphical definitions whereas others, the ALGAE [1] system for example, offer a high level textual definition of interaction objects. However despite their many advantages most of these tools are severely limited by only allowing the programmer to statically define interaction objects before runtime. That is, to get the full benefit out of these tools the interface needs to be able to be fully definable before the application is run.

Most tools do not have the ability to specify the user interface whilst the program is running (dynamic definition) as a high level description. For applications like the explanation engine described above where the output cannot be determined before runtime the user interface developer usually has to revert to a lower level programming language to alter the interaction objects dynamically. This paper describes one solution to the problem offered by the FOCUS user interface system [2], which allows both static and dynamic definition of interaction objects in a high level abstract description language.

2. User Interfaces for Explanation Systems

In order to specify the user interface for an explanation engine the developer first needs to look at the requirements of that system. In common with most IT systems, explanation engines have both input and output interface requirements. These are considered below:

Input

There are several ways in which a user is likely to be able to interrogate an explanation engine. The most instinctive method would be for the user to pose questions in natural language [3]. This allows the user to ask the exact question they want in the form they want to ask it. However current natural language processing limitations mean that a user is likely to ask a question in a syntax that the system does not recognise. A worse case is when the system gives an incorrect reply because the user has not phrased the question in a form that the system could understand. There are other problems concerning ambiguity that also arise in natural language input [4],[5].

A more constrained way of interrogating the explanation engine knowledge-base is to let the user construct a question from various parts of grammar. For example, the user could select "Why" from a list of "type of questions", "water" from a list of "objects" and "cold" from a list of "attributes" to form the question to be asked, "Why water cold?". For this method the system must know which questions are sensible in a given context, for instance the user should not be able to pose the meaningless question 'Why water empty?' from lists containing the items "Why", "water" and "empty".

A yet more constrained method of interrogating the knowledge base is when the explanation engine actually produces the questions that a user can ask within the current context. In this case their is no fear of the user asking the system a question that it cannot give a sensible response to but it may limit the amount of questions that a user can ask or present a question in a form unrecognisable to the user. For this method the application that the explanation engine is connected to may formulate the comment 'A'. The explanation engine would then construct a question 'Why A?' and so on. The questions that could be asked for this form of input could be listed as items on a menu or a series of radio button selections. It would be impossible to pre determine either the order or form of questions presented to the user in a particular context before the application is run.

Output

An explanation system that constructs explanations dynamically from inbuilt reasoning techniques and domain and application models is unable to determine exactly what form its output will take or indeed what that output will be. For any given question posed by the user an explanation may produce a response of several words, sentences or paragraphs. Furthermore, if an explanation can be presented with the aid of graphical representations the output may be a mixture of both text and graphics [4],[6]. There may also be a different answer to the same question depending on the context in which that question is asked.

User Models

The presence of user models within an explanation engine compounds the indeterminate nature of the interaction object requirements with regards to both input and output of the user interface. For user interrogation of the engine, models within the engine may restrict the questions that can legally be asked in a given context by a particular user. The questions may also be displayed differently, for example as items on a menu for one user and selections within a group of radio buttons for another user, depending on their personal preferences.

A user model within the engine could affect the detail of the explanation given. For example if a member of a management team poses a question the engine may only produce a small amount of text describing a top level response that will be satisfactory for them to make a decision. For a technician posing the same question a longer explanation may be presented, giving more technical detail. The size of the window displaying the text object in the first instance need only be small whereas for the technician the system may produce a larger text window which may possibly require scroll bars.

As can be seen, explanation engine input and output requirements cannot be determined before runtime if the system is to produce explanations in a versatile manner. User models within the explanation engine can alter the content of the explanations whilst models within the user interface specify the way in which the output is presented. Thus user interface tools enable the definition of initial interaction objects but do not easily accommodate dynamic alteration of those objects.

3. Programming the User Interface: Solutions and their Limitations

Despite ongoing advances in user interface development [7], such as end user programming [8], object oriented user interfaces [9],[10] and automatic generation of interaction objects [11], there still remain only two normal ways to construct a user interface for an application. These are, firstly, low level programming in a specific user interface language or using libraries with a general purpose language and secondly, constructing interaction objects in a user interface tool with high level textual or graphical descriptions.

Very often a mixture of the two methods has to be used to produce a complete user interface. The advantages and disadvantages of both low and high level specification are outlined below with a brief description of how both "*html*" browsers and the FOCUS system have overcome some of the disadvantages.

Low Level Programming

The traditional way to create graphical user interfaces for an application has been to construct different objects within the low level program code and then display them on screen in specified positions relative to other objects.

This involves using tool kits such as Xt [12] and Tk [13] for X which provide a library of procedures that the programmer can make calls to. Interaction objects can be constructed on the fly comprised of smaller objects with their attributes being altered as required using the control mechanisms within the programming language.

Using this approach all explanation engine user interface requirements can be satisfied. For example, the number of radio buttons that an application may need to display can be determined by creating the buttons within a loop and then placing then relative to one another. This method allows for maximum flexibility as the user interface developer can create his own look and feel for interaction objects and also specify his own standards as to where menus, buttons and windows should appear within windows.

However, constructing a user interface in this manner has several disadvantages. The user interface developer has to write specialised low level code for each interaction object to be created from low level graphical primitives. This must be done for every application that is to be front ended which makes programming the interface difficult and time consuming and often requires specialised knowledge to write hundreds of lines of code.

The interaction object attributes can be specified in great detail providing flexibility but the programmer gets very little feel for what the user interface will finally look like and fast prototyping cannot be done easily. Difficulties persist when the user interface has to be modified for maintenance purposes as the developer must alter many lines of low level code. Because of these disadvantages user interface tools that offer a higher level of interaction object definition have become increasingly popular.

User Interface Tools

Due to the high costs in developing user interfaces from low level graphical primitives user interface tools have appeared over recent years for both research and commercial purposes which offer several advantages over traditional programming methods [14]. Many of these allow the user interface developer to define the interaction objects that will be required by the application in a high level textual or graphical description providing relatively quick and easy construction of the user interface. Where the interaction objects are constructed graphically within a user interface builder, such as Borland's Resource Workshop, or NeXTs Interface Builder, the graphical description is often translated into a high level textual description of the object. This is then interpreted into lower level graphical primitives which are compiled.

These tools enable early prototyping of the user interface so that the programmer can get an idea of the look and feel of the objects before the functionality of the application is written.

A trade is often made between ease of development using the tool and the functionality offered by the interaction objects created with the tool. Within a graphical interface builder once an object is placed on the screen, the developer commonly has the option of specifying several attributes for the object via a dialogue box. The attributes are often limited although developers have more and more choices offered all the time. Programs such as Microsoft's Visual Basic provide whole lists of attributes that can be applied to interaction objects.

Although there are obvious benefits to this kind of tool, problems arise when the user interface cannot be defined statically before application runtime. For example, most tools would not allow the construction of an arbitrary number of radio buttons on the fly as in the example given above.

To get around this particular problem developers may be forced to use a LISTBOX interaction object (a rectangle, with scroll bars, containing a list of strings (such as filenames) from which the user can select). The LISTBOX is always the same size no matter how many items are contained so the layout of the rest of the window need not be affected by new entries.

However, entries made to the LISTBOX dynamically have to be carried out in a low level programming language.

A common situation that arises with user interface tools is that the developer has to define a default interaction object and then provide routines in a low level programming language to make alterations to the object when the details become known during runtime. Situations when this problem could arise are when a developer does not know before runtime what text will appear on control buttons, how many control buttons will be required within a window, what will be the necessary structure of menus or what the size of a text field is to be. These are typical situations that a developer of a user interface for an explanation engine is presented with and hence often needs to resort to programming at a lower level to make alterations to the interaction objects.

Maintenance of the user interface may or may not be trivial depending on whether the interaction objects can be amended using the tool.

Browsers

With the arrival of the Internet as a major information resource great effort has been paid on how to present the data received to the user. Users often access this resource via the World Wide Web (WWW) - a global network of servers holding information on almost anything one cares to think of. Currently there are browsers that can be used to present the information downloaded from across the network to the user, such as Mosaic and Netscape. Although these browsers are intended for use with the WWW they can also be used to display information that is held within files on the local machine.

To construct the interaction objects that will appear in the browser the user interface developer uses the Hypertext Mark-up Language (*html*). Until recently this has meant learning another language to create the desired user interface but with the advent of tools such as Microsoft Word's Internet Assistant the user can construct the majority of the interface using Word's style sheets, templates and wizards, making this task easier. The interfaces produced using *html* are restricted in that they must be contained within the browser that is presenting them and because these browsers have been designed and developed for the purpose of accessing the Internet they are more suitable for some types of application area than others. The interaction objects that *html* allows the developer to display are text, hypertext, images, forms and control buttons. Video and audio objects can be incorporated into *html* and displayed using external viewers to the browser. Once the *html* is written it is translated by the browser into the lower level graphical primitives that produce the interaction objects the user sees on screen.

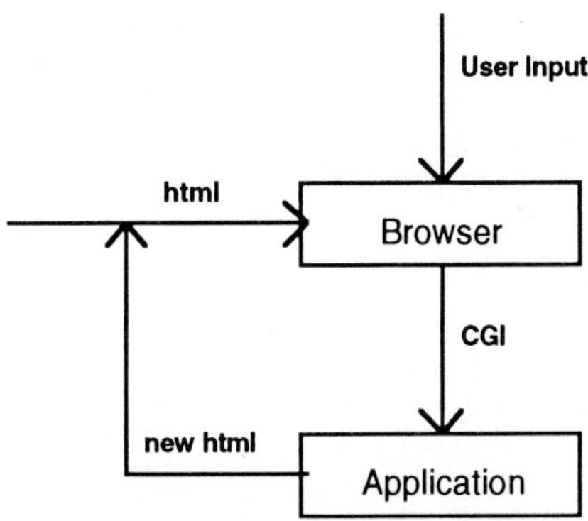

Fig. 1: Browser interfaces

For a system using a browser and *html* to produce the user interface to be able to construct interaction objects "on the fly" the browser must be connected, via a Common Gateway Interface (CGI), to an application that can produce files containing html. The Common Gateway Interface, or CGI, is an interface for running external programs, or gateways, under an information server [15]. As shown in figure 1 the browser takes information entered by the user and converts it into a form recognisable by the CGI which can then be used as input into applications written in general purpose programming languages. These applications could dynamically generate new files of *html* which could then be used as input for the browser. In this way browsers such as Netscape can be used to display interaction objects that could not be specified before runtime and front end applications with user interface similar to explanation systems. However browsers are currently limited to an event driven interaction mode. This means that the state of the user interface can only be updated after a user has carried out some action such as pressing a control button. This way of making use of browsers is not yet widely practised.

FOCUS

The FOCUS user interface management system offers advantages over both of the methods outlined above. Interaction objects can be defined both statically (i.e. before runtime) and also dynamically (i.e. during runtime), by the FOCUS presentation component, as a high level description. The ability of a system to create its user interface "on the fly" is a great benefit, in cases such as ours, where the program cannot fully specify before runtime what user interface requirements will be needed as is the case with explanation systems. Within the FOCUS system an interaction object is described as an abstract definition in which the details of the presentation are not specified. Each definition details the contents and attributes that an object may have but says nothing about the appearance of the object on screen. High level abstract definitions are interpreted into low level graphical primitives by the system at runtime as with virtual tool kits [16] allowing the same definition to realise objects on different platforms. Maintenance of the user interface involves amending high level definitions of objects. Figure 2 shows how the FOCUS user interface system can dynamically define interaction objects.

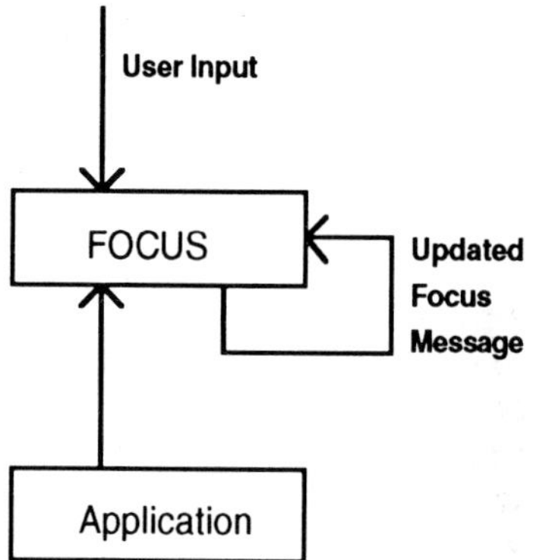

Fig. 2: The FOCUS User Interface system

As mentioned earlier, there is a often a trade off between ease, speed and flexibility of the creation of the user interface and the details with which the objects can be realised. For example, within FOCUS, an application developer can specify which control buttons are needed within a window but does not have any say over where they will be placed. This however provides the benefit that a standard look and feel can be created over several applications without the application developer worrying about these details. The FOCUS user interface system also accommodates several interaction modes. As well as the event driven interaction mode offered by browsers, the state of the user interface can be obtained and amended either on request from another application or by sampling the interaction objects periodically.

Below is a table of the some of the features offered by the various user interface development paths, focusing on the characteristics that have an influence on the ease with which interaction objects can be dynamic updated.

	Low Level Programming	High Level Description	Browsers (*html*)	FOCUS
Functionality offered by objects produced.	Good	Fair	Fair (limited interaction modes)	Fair
Ease of development	Difficult	Easy	Fair	Easy
Prototying ability	None	Good	Fair	Good
Multi-user interfaces	Yes- much more work involved	Tool dependent	Yes	Yes
Platform Independent	None	Tool dependent	Yes	Yes
Maintenance of User Interface	Difficult (low Level)	Static objects (Easy) Dynamic objects (Difficult)	Fair	Easy
Learning curve	Steep	Shallow	Medium	Medium
Dynamic Definition	Yes (complex)	None	Yes (non trivial)	Yes (easy)

Table 1: Features of the interface development parts

4. Using FOCUS to front end an Explanation System

As we have seen, for an explanation engine that produces explanations dynamically a user interface system that can define interaction objects "on the fly" is necessary if the explanations are to be presented to the user in a flexible manner. As has been shown, user interface tools, whilst easing the creation of interaction objects, have limitations in that the objects constructed need to be fully defined before the application is run. When using a tool to produce the user interface, traditional programming methods can be used to alter the interaction objects dynamically but this has to be done by reverting to a lower level and involves lengthy descriptions of all objects that have to be altered. Browsers offer a slightly better method of dynamic definition of interaction objects. The FOCUS system allows the user interface developer to define interaction objects at a high level before the application is run but the application can then alter these objects "on the fly" using the same high level object description language.

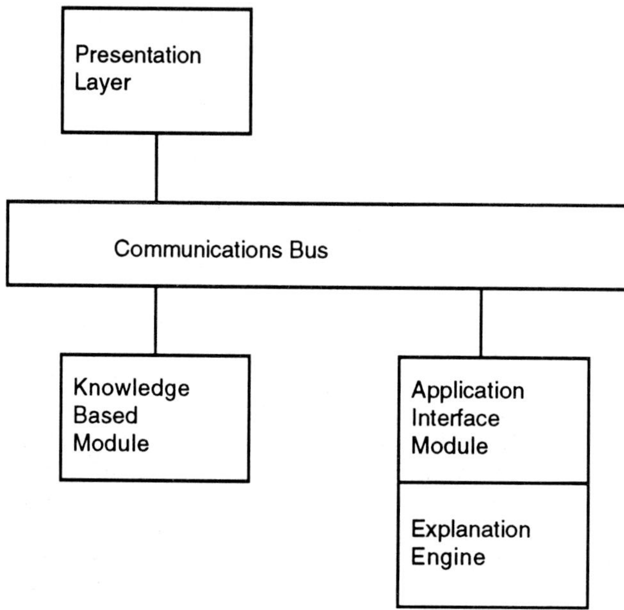

Fig. 3: FOCUS Architecture

The diagram in Figure 3 shows the architecture of the FOCUS user interface system connected to an explanation engine.

The system is distributed and can be run over several machines with different processes on different platforms (UNIX, PC, Mac). Messages are passed from one FOCUS module to another via the communications bus which controls all communication flow. The explanation engine is connected to the FOCUS architecture by an application interface module which packages the output supplied by the engine into FOCUS messages and converts user actions at the user interface into interrogations of the engine. The output messages are sent to a dialogue knowledge based module which uses the information to define abstract interaction objects which will be used to display the explanation given by the engine. The abstract interaction objects chosen to display the results depend on the type and amount of data to be shown as well as models of the user preferences stored within the knowledge based module. Once the abstract interaction object has been defined it is passed in a message to the Presentation Layer module which interprets the high level definition into low level graphical primitives for realisation on the screen as interaction objects such as windows, menus, text, bitmaps and radio and control buttons.

Interaction Object Definition within FOCUS

The abstract interaction objects that can be defined under the FOCUS system fall into two categories, standard interaction objects which are designed to be components of interaction and container interaction objects which allow developers to group standard interaction objects logically and apply attributes (controls, menus etc.) to the whole group [17]. The top level object in a definition must be a container interaction object with the form :

ContainerAIO(ContainerId, ContainerContents, ContainerAttributes)

The ContainerContents parameter may be a list of standard interaction objects of the form :

StandardAIO(StandardId, StandardContents, StandardAttributes)

An example definition of an interaction object in the FOCUS language is described below in figure 4. The container interaction object used is a group which is a general purpose container for holding one or more standard objects. The group has an identifier "group_id", contents and attributes. The attributes are the list of control buttons that will appear at the bottom of the container, here there is just one. The button has the identifier "gothere" and itself has a list of attributes, external specifies the text that will appear on the button (this becomes the identifier if external is not explicitly specified) and disposal specifies what happens to the container when the button is pressed - either being destroyed immediately or postponed (default).

The contents of the group container is a selection interaction object. Again, each standard interaction object has its own identifier, here "selection_id". The contents of the selection object contains a list of the items that will appear within the selection - either as radio buttons or check box. Each selection item has optional attributes specifying the external text that will appear next to the button and the state (on/off/disabled) of that button. If the external text is not specified then the selection items identifier it used (as in the example). Each standard interaction object has a list of optional attributes. Here the only attribute included is the limits attribute. This specifies what is the minimum and maximum number of items that can be selected at once. When the case is (0,1), as below, the selection is realised as a list of radio buttons whereas when more than one selection can be chosen the items are realised as a list of check boxes.

```
group( group_id,
        selection ( selection_id,
                [ 'Up', 'Down', 'Left', 'Right'(state:on) ],
        [ limits:(0,1)] ),
controls :['gothere'(external:'Go There', disposal: immediate ) ]
] ).
```

Fig. 4: Definition of an interaction object in FOCUS language

This definition creates the interaction object below in figure 5. The interaction object is realised under Windows 3.1 but the specific look and feel depend on the platform and environment that the user interface is realised on. Once the FOCUS user interface system has realised the interaction object on the screen, the end user is free to interact with it.

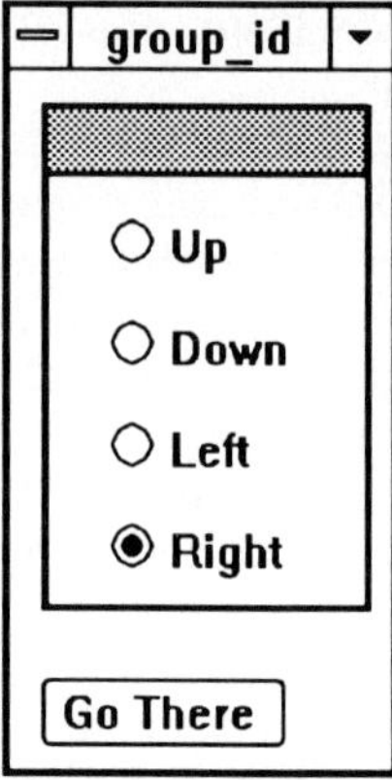

Fig.5: Created interaction object

Example Interaction with the OSIS Application Explanation Engine

The OSIS application is a numerical modelling program that predicts what happens when oil is spilt at sea, providing valuable information for reducing the damaged caused when a spillage occurs. The application contains tidal and geographic information about the area of concern well as data about the properties of different oils. The user must supply information about the oil spill and OSIS will attempt to predict the flow of the spill. OSIS is designed to be used by non experts and is, in essence, a numerical model that provides results either in tabular or graphical from about a spill without giving an explanation about how or why it has come to the conclusion presented.

One of the goals of the I-SEE project (Esprit 6013) was to provide the OSIS application with explanation capabilities to explain the graphical output it produced. The user simply clicks on a results graph within the OSIS application and the explanation engine is invoked allowing the user to interrogate it about the graph by presenting the user with relative questions such as 'Why is the slick volume rising?'. Information presented quantitatively by the application is converted into qualitative explanations by the engine. For example if the application shows that "wind speed = 6 knots" the explanation may state that "the wind speed is fairly low".

User Interaction with the OSIS Explanation Engine

In the most basic query type, the OSIS explanation interaction will begin when the user is examining one of the graphs summarising the results of the numerical simulation. In this example, we will assume that the user is looking at the "Slick Volume" graph (Figure 6). The user wants to know why the graph volume is falling more steeply after an initial slow fall, and so clicks on the graph for an explanation.

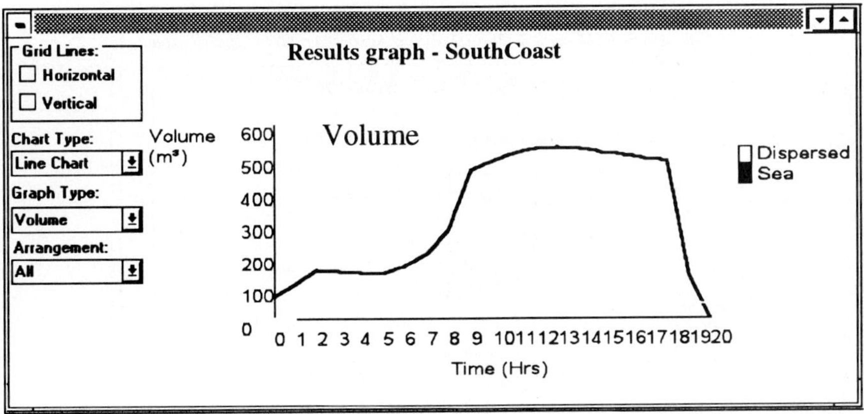

Fig. 6: "Slick Volume" graph

Clicking at this point on the graph, the user could be intending one of two questions: why the graph is falling, or why it is (still) high. The explanation engine constructs a simple dialogue (see figure 7) to allow the user to indicate which question the system should answer.

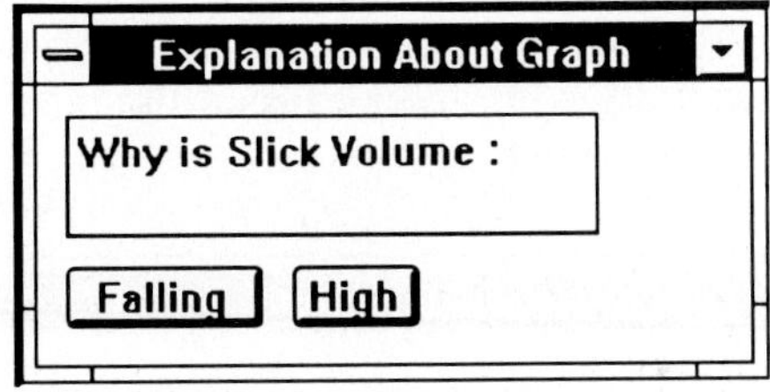

Fig. 7: Dialogue contructed by the explanation engine

This dialogue is standard, and could be constructed statically using conventional UI tools, except that the text in the dialogue, and the labels on the buttons may be different. Thus, as described earlier, even with this simple dialogue, some low level programming to set the contents of the dialogue can be avoided using FOCUS.

Next the user selects the "Falling" question by clicking on the "Falling" button. The explanation engine calls FOCUS to create an explanation window (see figure 8). As can be seen there are several contributing causes in the explanation: the slick volume is falling because some oil is evaporating from the slick, some is dispersing into the sea, and some (unfortunately) is "beaching" i.e. coming ashore. (This last cause is why the graph is falling more quickly.) The number of causes for any question will vary depending on the context in which the question is asked. Therefore, using FOCUS to display the explanation engines output saves the developer using low level programming to dynamically create and place the selections and alter the size of the window containing them.

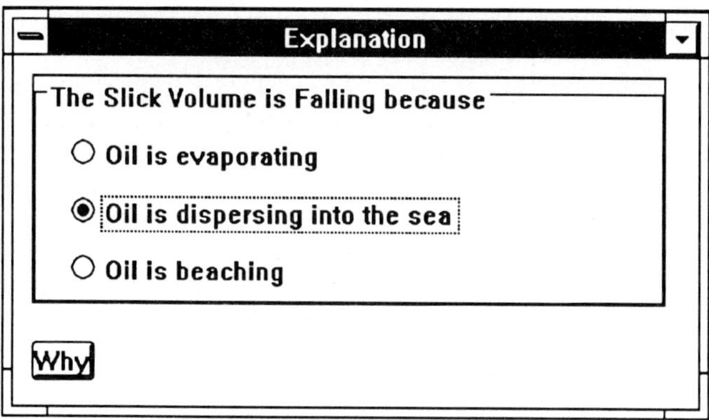

Fig. 8: Explanation window

There is also a "Why" button in the explanation window, which allows the user to seek a deeper level of explanation. Since the answer to the first question requires more than a single phrase, the user must indicate to the explanation system which part of the answer the system should expand upon. For this reason, the explanation was split into separate phrases, and the set of phrases was sent to FOCUS as a "selection" abstract interaction object, so that the user can select which phrase is the topic of the "Why" button. Figure 8 shows that FOCUS has realised this choice as a set of radio buttons. The user has chosen the "Oil is dispersing" button, so that the "Why" button would allow the user to send the question "Why is the oil dispersing?" back to the explanation engine.

History List

Previous question topics

- Oil is evaporating
- Oil is dispersing into the sea
- Oil is beaching
- the wind speed is high
- the wave height is large

Close Why

Fig.9: History window

After following a line of questioning, the user may wish to go back to an earlier part of the explanation, and expand upon a different choice. To allow this, when the user first selects the "Why" button the original choice set from the explanation window is added to another window: a history window. Each time the user selects another question, the history window is updated with the current choices from the explanation window.

Figure 9 shows the history window after it has been initialised with the original contents (items one to three) of the explanation window (as in figure 8) and then updated with the possible causes to the "Why is the oil dispersing?" question (item four and five). The high level description needed to add these last two entries to the history window is shown below in figure 10.

```
group( hist_window ,
        selection ( select_hist ,
                update([‘the wind speed is high‘,‘the wave height is large‘ ] ),
        [ ] ) ,
controls :[ ]
] ).
```

Fig.10: High level description

Note that the attributes for the selection and the containing group abstract interaction object do not need to be specified in an update message unless these are to changed from what they were originally. Hence the windows control buttons ("Close" and "Why") were specified when the object was initially created. FOCUS automatically places the new selections as new radio button items within the window and re-sizes the window.

5. Conclusion

Despite the overwhelming number of user interface programming tool kits and builders that have appeared over recent years, very few tackle the problem of providing the interface developer with the ability to construct systems that define interaction objects in a high level language dynamically. Therefore developers of computer systems incorporating such components as explanation engines, where the form of output cannot be determined before runtime, often need to revert back to a lower level language to be able alter these objects. The FOCUS user interface system offers one way in which tools can be provided that enable both static and dynamic definition of the user interface for such purposes.

References

1. Flecchia M.A. and Bergeron D.R. "Specifying Complex Dialogues in ALGAE", in Human Factors in Computer Systems, CHI+GI'87, Toronto, Ontario, Canada, pp.229-234, April 1987.

2. Edmonds E.A. and McDaid E. "An architecture for knowledge-based front ends", in Knowledge Based Systems, vol.3 /4, pp.187- 190, 1990.
3. Sparck Jones K. "Natural language interfaces for expert systems: An introductory note.", in Research and development in expert systems: Proceedings of the 4th technical conference of the British Computer Society Special Group on Expert Systems, University of Warwick, edited by M.A. Bramer, pp 85 -94. Cambridge: Cambridge University Press, Dec 1984.
4. Berry, D.C. and Broadbent, D.E "Expert Systems and the man-machine interface part two: The user interface." In Expert Systems, vol.4/1, pp.18-28, 1987.
5. Shneiderman B. "Human Factors experiments in designing interactive systems.", in Computer, pp.9 -19, New York: IEEE Computer Society Press, 1979.
6. Montazemi A. R. "The impact of experience on the design of the user interface." In International Journal of Man-Machine Studies 34, pp.731-749, 1991.
7. Myers B.A. "User Interface Software Tools.", in ACM Transactions on Computer-Human Interaction 2 (1), pp.94-103, 1995.
8. Myers, B.A. "Demonstrational interfaces: a step beyond direct manipulation", in People and computers VI. Proceedings of the sixth conference of the British Computer Society HCI Specialist Group, HCI'91 Usability Now, pp 20 - 23, Heriot-Watt University, Edinburgh, Aug. 1991.
9. Six H. W. and Voss J. "DIWA: a hierarchical object-oriented model for dialogue design", in Engineering for human-computer interaction: Proceedings of the IFIP TC2/WG 2.7 working conference. Napa Valley, California, USA. August, pp.21-25, 1989.
10. Nakatsuyama H., Murata M., Kusmoto K. "A new framework for separating user interfaces from application programs.", In SIGCHI Bulletin, vol.23/1, pp.88 - 91, 1991.
11. Vander Zanden B. and Myers B. A. "Automatic, look-and-feel independent dialog creation for graphical user interfaces", in Empowering people: human factors in computing systems: CHI '90 conference proceedings. Seattle, Washington, April 1-5, 1990.
12. McCormack J. and Asente P. "An Overview of the X Toolkit", ACM SIGGRAPH Symposium on User Interface Software and Technology, Proceedings UIST'88, Banff, Alberta, Canada, pp.46-55, 1988.
13. 0usterhout J.K. "An X11 Toolkit Based on the Tcl Language", Winter, USENIX, pp.105-115, 1991.
14. Myers B.A. and Rosson M.B. "Survey on User Interface Programming", in CHI'92 Proceedings, Addison Wesley, May 3-7, pp.195-202, 1992.
15. McCool R. "The Common Gateway Interface", http://bcn.boulder.co.us/docs/cgi/overview .html
16. Chimera R. "Evaluation of Platform Independent User Interface Builders", Tech report working paper 93-09, Human-Computer Interaction Laboratory, University of Maryland, March 1993.
17. Heggie S. et al. "FOCUS Messages User Guide", Esprit 2 Project 2620, Ref: FOCUS/LUTCHI/ 16/4.1 -C, LUTCHI Research Centre, Loughborough University of Technology, 1992.

Haptic Interfaces for Improving Interaction in Virtual Environments

Massimo Bergamasco
PERCRO
Scuola Superiore S.Anna
Via Carducci, 40, Pisa, Italy

Abstract

Present developments of Virtual Environments outline the importance of the Interaction Component of the VE system: by means of the interface system, the user can directly interact with the simulated entities, belonging to the virtual scenario. In order to achieve a high degree of realism during the interaction, it is important that the interface system can accurately record the movements of the human operator as well as provide him adequate sensory stimuli as occurs in real activities. In the control of the physical interaction with virtual objects, the interface system should provide to the user both tactile and force information related to the contact conditions. An interesting research trend in the field of Virtual Environments deals with the design of haptic interfaces: these are interface systems devoted to replicate cutaneous stimuli to the human hand. In this paper we indicate the functionalities that a haptic device should possess and, by taking into account specific applications, introduce some considerations for its design. In particular force and tactile feedback systems will be analyzed and the systems developed by PERCRO in the framework of the Information Technology of the European programmes are presented.

1. Introduction

Tasks related to the interaction with Virtual Environments (VE) require the capability for the human operator to acquire knowledge about the features of objects belonging to the simulate scenario. Common object's features refer to shape, hardness, surface temperature, surface texture, presence of holes on sight-occluded sides, etc. In a real environment, the acquisition of such information is performed by haptic exploration procedures exploiting cutaneous and kinesthetic inputs [1]. The rendering to the human operator of the sensation of a physical interaction with a virtual environment can be achieved by utilizing appropriate interface systems capable of generating adequate sensory stimuli to the operator. However, since a strict correlation exists between the typical hand movement pattern related to a specific exploratory procedure and the particular object knowledge associated, the interface system should allow the human operator to execute such a procedure by exploiting correct, natural movements.

The possibility for the human operator to execute realistic movements and to achieve adequate sensory stimuli is a fundamental requisite for achieving a satisfactory operation control. Realism of interaction, especially for haptic perception tasks, is strictly related to the capabilities of the interface system to allow natural movements to the human operator's hand as well as to the fidelity in reproducing adequate cutaneous stimuli on them. Such a transparency of the interface system can be achieved through appropriate design.

The basis for haptic perception is represented by cutaneous and kinesthetic inputs. During the execution of an exploratory procedure of a virtual object, the kinesthetic inputs that are presented to the operator's perceptual systems are real kinesthetic information he/she achieves from the movements of his/her hand. Adequate kinesthetic inputs should then derive from the correct exploratory movements executed by the human operator.

The other essential issue to be considered for haptic perception is represented by cutaneous inputs. Under this type of sensory information we include force and tactile inputs. Usual interface systems are devoted to the rendering of force and tactile information during the interaction with the VE, have been separately developed as force and tactile feedback systems. However, we believe that a correct approach should address the design of force and tactile feedback systems as an integrated Haptic Interface System, embedding the replication of both functionalities. Recently an important trend in the design of interface systems is the development of "Haptic Interfaces" [2][3]. Hier the human operator usually interacts with an actuated external device by means of an handle or a stylus. In this way the force stimuli perceived are generated by the devices, while the tactile input is completely real (and not realistic) since the user grasps the end-point of the real device. Hand controllers allow only a limited control of manipulative or exploratory procedures that do not require the presence of a tool in the hand; natural movements of the human hand working in free conditions cannot be easily performed. We are interested in the ultimate concept of haptic interfaces that allow a large spectrum of natural pattern of mevements of the human upper limb, and capable of replicating adequate cutaneous inputs. The design of the FDD (force display devices) and TDD (tactile display devices) developed in out laboratory followed this last approach.

2. Force Feedback Systems

The importance of force replication, or force feedback, on the human operator is well recognized since the first telemanipulation experiments carried out in US in late 1950s [4]. At present, a boosting action for the design of new man-mchine interfaces has been induced by the innovative research in the field of the interaction with VE. The problem of the design of the interface system, especially in terms of afferent sensory information replicated to the human operator's hand, can be considered in VE as very close to those to be tackled for the control of teleoperators for telemanipulation tasks [5]. We assume that a Force Feedback System is composed of one or more *Force Display Devices* (FDD), their *control* system, and a *modelling module* which generate the force to be replicated. The set of general features that force feedback systems must possess for allowing a good control of the task by the human operator, comprehends issues such as:

a) *manoeuvrability:* the interface system must allow a natural mobility to the human hand and arm. This requirement can be seen in terms of the natural workspace of the human-hand arm complex which must not be restricted by the presence of the FDD mechanical structure. This condition is difficult to be achieved from the design point of view because the FDD possesses its own workspace whose intersection with the human hand workspace must be optimized;
b) *fidelity:* the interface system must be able to reproduce in a faithful way to the human hand-arm the forces modelled in the VE. In previous papers we have analyzed how the forces (wrenches) which can be replicated depend on the kinematics of the FDD [6];
c) *impedance:* the impedance offered to the human hand-arm complex by the force feedback system must match the same condition of impedance seen by the human hand-arm complex during the performance of a real manipulative operation. This condition of passivity of the force feedback system subtends also the need of rendering, for whatever kinematic configuration of the structure, a complete inertial and weight compensation;
d) *wearability:* wearability and also portability of the FDD represent also two important features for the synthesis of the final mechanism.

From the topological point of view we distinguish two main categories of FDDs with several DOF, depending on their structure

External SAtructure with respect to the Human Limb

Only the FDD end-point is connected to the human limb and through thi point the forces are transmitted. Since the human limb is constrained to be connected with the FDD end-point (which base frame is fixed to the ground), the resulting manoeuvrability is limited to the intersection of the FDD's and limb workspaces. In terms of force replication, however, the force exerted by the FDD is perceived by the human operator as an external force, without side effects; in the case that multiple contact points with the human limb has to be considered, an equivalent number of FDDs must be utilized;

Structure Wraping up the Human Limb

In this case the FDD kinematic reflects the one of the limb since the joint axes are the same (Exoskeletons). Exoskeletons can be designed with one or more point of attachment to the human limb as well as with their base frame fixed to the ground (external to the body) or to the human limb (e.g. shoulders). In the last condition side effects phenomena due to the presence of reaction forces at the level of the base frame attachment point are present. When the interaction between the human operator and the VE comprehends grasping, manipulative as well as exploratory procedures, the set of virtual forces that can be modelled in the virtual environment can belong to a large spectrum, in terms of magnitude, direction and also point of application [7]. At PERCRO of Scuola Superiore S.Anna, a complete Force Feedback System consisting of a) two serially connected FDD components, b) their control systems. c) a modelling module for generating the forces and d) a graphical module for the representation of the VE scenario, has been designed and realized. The FDD components consist of two exoskeleton systems devoted to replicate forces at the level of the arm and of the operator's fingers. The main components are as follows:

1 a FDD component, called Arm Exoskeleton System, with 7 DOF which are coincident with the principal joint axes of the human arm. The Arm Exoskeleton has been designed to be completely supported by the operator's body by means of a purposely designed trunk structure or by a fixed frame structure which allows easier wearing conditions in case of repeated experimental tests;

2 a FDD component, called Hand Force Feedback System, consisting of 4 parallel FDDs wrapping up four fingers of the human hand (little finger excluded) and each one possessing 3 DOF in correspondence of the finger joint axes (the total number of DOF is then 12). The 4 FDD are connected to a base plate located at the metacarpus and corresponding to the end-point of the Arm Exoskeleton.

Both FDD components have been designed in order to maximize the resulting workspaces of the human arm and hand during operation. In case the Arm Exoskeleton is supported by the trunk structure, the complete FDD system becomes portable and allows a large physical mobility to the human operator inside the control space. This fact extends its use also for augmented reality applications.

3. Arm Exoskeleton

As outlined in the previous Section, the forces at the level of the arm and the external forces acting against the hand are replicated by means of a FDD component called Arm Exoskeleton. The Arm Exoskeleton consists of a mechanical structure wrapping up the whole human arm and composed of links connected through 7 DOF located in correspondence of the human arm joints.

The DOF of the Arm Exoskeleton follow the configuration of the arm joints: there are two DOF at the shoulder (flexion-extension and abduction-adduction movements); one DOF in correspondence of the arm (arm rotation); one DOF at the elbow (flexion-extension); one DOF in correspondence of the forearm (prono-supination movement); two DOF at the wrist level (flexion-extension and abduction-adduction). The structure follows the movements of the human arm atlhough limited constraints due to the mechanical limits in some joints do not allow to span the complete workspace of the arm. However very good mobility is allowed around an initial refernce position assumed as significant for manipulative operations. The appearance of the Arm Exoskeleton is depicted in figure 1.

Each joint is actuated by means of DC servomotors located on the structure; gear boxes have been integrated and a cable transmission system transmits the output of the gear box to the joint. Position sensors are located at each joint. The arrangement of the actuators and sensors allows the system to be completely portable, i.e. the user, wearing the arm exoskeleton, can freely move in the real control space. The total weight of the structure is around 9.7 kilograms, and gravity compensation is performed during the control of manipulative operations. A purposely conceived control architecture, based on transputer technology , has been designed and implemented. Integration with a VGX440 graphical workstation has been obtained.

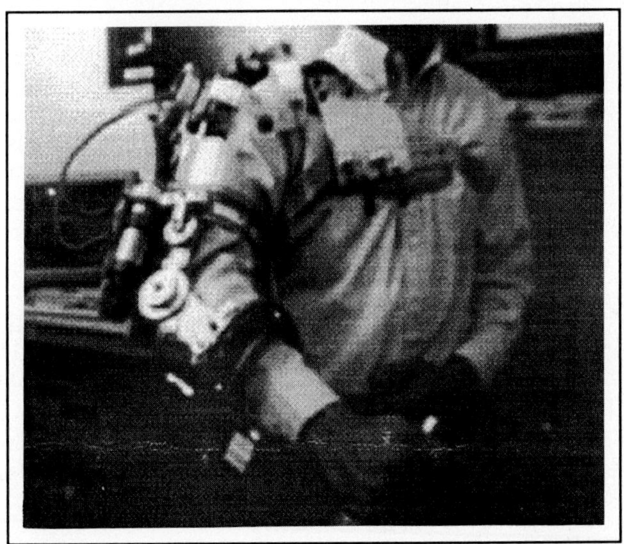

Fig. 1: The arm exoskeleton in the five DOF configuration

Experimental tests have been performed with the aim of reproducing two basic interactions with a rigid surface: the collision with a virtual surface and the following of the virtual surface. Experiments have been carried out by varying the parameters of the VE such as the system sampling time, the virtual surface elastic and viscosity coefficients. Results have been extensively reported in [8][9].

4. Hand Exoskeleton

The second component of the complete FDD system is called Hand Exoskeleton and consists of four FDD capable of exerting forces to the phalanges of the hand's fingers (little finger excluded). Each finger exoskeleton consists of four links connected by revolute joints. For each joint of the finger exoskeleton, the joint axis has been designed in order to approximate the instantaneous position of the flexion-extension axis during operation. At the metacarpo-phalangeal joint a passive abduction -adduction movement has been also integrated. The actuation system for one finger exoskeleton is based on three DC servomotors and associated tendon tension transmission systems. Each tendon is pulling on the middle point of each phalanx of the finger in order to execute the extension movement; at each joint, the flexion movement is obtained by a passive torsion spring integrated on the joint axis. The three motors are located on a cantilever structure fixed with the base frame of each finger exoskeleton. Rotation sensors, based on conductive plastics technologies, are integrated at each joint while force sensors, capable of recording the interaction force between the exoskeleton structure and each phalanx, are located directly on the dorsal surface of each phalanx link.

The kinematic structure of the thumb exoskeleton is slightly different to those of the other fingers. In particular, from the construction point of view, the cantilever supporting the three motors of the thumb assumes a completely different aspect with respect to the one of the other fingers. Also the Hand Exoskeleton system is controlled by a transputer-based control architecture.

One of the critical factors encountered during the design of the system has been that of obtaining a system possessing limited weight and volume, in such a way as to allow good manoeuvrability of the hand. During wearing conditions, the ranges of motion of the fingers can be considered very close to those of the free human hand. In terms of the mechanical performances of the Hand Exoskeleton system, we obtained a maximum extension force of 0.3N, being the force sensor range of -0.5 N to 3.0 N. Force resolution is 0.0025N, while the force feedback bandwidth is 0.5 Hz, with an angular displacement of 90deg. for all the three DOF. In order to test the performances of each finger exoskeleton, a purposely designed test-bed actuated structure has been realized. Isometric and isotonic tests of each finger exoskeleton are in progress [10].

5. Tactile Feedback Systems

The problem of tactile feedback in VE can be seen as decomposed in two main domains, geometric and thermal feedback. The *geometric feedback* generates the sensation related to the geometry of the touched virtual object surface, at both macroscopic and microscopic level. In general terms this domain includes the problem of the indentation of the user's skin during static and dynamic contact with the virtual object; in particular the aim is the replication of macroscopic geometrical features, such as planar surfaces, edges or vertices, as well as microcopic features, such as surface texture patterns. The*thermal feedback* generates the appropriate sensation of the thermal conditions of the virtual object.

The basic assumption in tackling the above problems refers to the way in which tactile stimuli are generated. Although different ways are theoretically possible (electrical stimulation, direct stimulation of afferent nerves, etc.) we refer to the reproduction of external mechanical stimuli to the user's skin. The goal is in fact that of reproducing the exact physical phenomena that elicit the same sensation in the same real condition. Although the approach we have followed is based on the defintion and on the separate theoretical study and development of geometrical and thermal feedback domains, it is obvious that it allows to implement realistic conditions of contact with the virtual object by means of the superposition effect of both stimuli, as it happens in a real operation.

A basic assumption we have introduced for the design of a tactile display device (or tactile effector system) refers to the fact that the tactile effectors will be located on the palmar surface of a glove-like advanced interface which possesses kinesthetic sensors for the detection of the movements of each joint of the hand. Although the utilization of a glove-like advanced interface, worn by the human operator, is extremely successful in terms of naturalness of movements, some drawbacks, such as wearability conditions and consequent non-exact correspondence between the surface of the glove (where the effectors are assumed to be integrated) and the external surface of the human hand, can be devised. At first we have analyzed in detail the problem of the collision detection in VE between the virtual hand and the virtual object. An appropriate collision detection procedure allows to obtain a real-time behaviour for the calculation of the contact areas of the virtual hand correspondent to the areas of the real hand where tactile stimuli should be replicated. In order to detect such contact areas independently of wearability conditions, a reference surface has been introduced: in this way the palmar surface of the virtual hand is seen as a very dense set of control points to be utilized for the collision detection procedure.

The model for the indentation and texture feedback is based on the hypothesis that the tactile effector consists of an array of indentors satisfying the following characteristics: the *indentors* perform a controllable stroke with respect to a reference point; the *size area* of the indentors is assumed to be known, and *the spatial density* of the indentors is enough to reproduce, through indentation patterns, a perception of a continuous surface on the subject.

Different technological solutions have been tested in order to realize a prototypical version of the tactile effector system. In particular, after having tested arrays of pins actuated through a pneumatic system, a definitive solution has been obtained by exploiting a 4x4 array of microsolenoids integrated on a mechanical case located in correspondence of each fingertip. Experimental tests are now in progress for the determination of this TDD performances.

The thermal feedback problem has been approached by developing accurate models of the heat transfer between the human hand and real external objects made by different materials. This theoretical modelling effort has been then utilized in order to implement the analytical functions describing the temperature and heat flow courses when the virtual hand enters in contact with a virtual object. A first solution has been obtained by integrating Peltier cells into the same effector case of indentors array located on the fingertip. Also in this case experimental tests are in progress.

6. Future Applications

The interfaces developed at PERCRO have been recently exploited in two main fields of application: rehabilitation technology and educational-entertainment. The first, rehabilitation technology seems a more promising area since, at present, medicine-related applications are requiring more and more inputs from VE and multimedia technologies. The field of rehabilitation represent one of the few areas in which, due to the particular context and methodologies the user (patient) is forced to operate with, present VE technologies can be preliminary applied in to allow an iterative process of further refinement and development. The idea of utilizing VE techniques as one of the new tools for Rehabilitation is acquiring growing interest, in limited research environments, as a result of the preliminary applications of such a technology in other areas of medicine (e.g. simulated surgery intervention, navigation inside the virtual body, etc.).

Justification of the introduction of VE technologies in rehabilitation can also be derived by considering the technical improvements and commercial expectations that can be estimated from such a transfer. Clearly, the utilization of the VE technologies cannot be considered a crude porting operation of one technology into a well defined application domain. Although this operation could be the preliminary step to be followed, a further methodological approach consisting of an iterative technical specification definition process based on results of practical rehabilitation testing experiments on the patient should follow for the implementation of an effective rehabilitation VE system. From such an approach, different aspects can be outlined as benefits for the VE technologies; in particular:

a) due to intrinsic features and particular working conditions, rehabilitation procedures can help to focus and define all the categories of human factors tests for validation and assessment of VE systems;

b) the strong requirements for a high degree of interaction between the patient and the VE system could lead to boost the design and realization phases of VE systems (ranging from advanced interfaces to behavioural modeling components);

c) just to mention an example, features of the interaction component (e.g. actuation systems devoted to implement force feedback capabilities as those described in the previous Sections) could be re-utilized as direct sources of mobility aid for the user's limbs (active otheses); the same consideration is valid also for other components of the interface system such as joint rotation sensors, position trackers, etc.;

d) high costs of VE systems could be considered as a secondary aspect (for large institutions, hospitals or rehabilitation centres) with respect to possible improvements (both in terms of ultimate results on the patient and also in terms of resultant time) the whole rehabilitation procedure could achieve; moreover it is expected that in the near future communication systems could be accessible to a large number of patients who, at their home, could be linked to a central high performance information system.

At present, PERCRO is addressing the utilization of VE technologies in a specific area of Rehabilitation, i.e. motor dexterity disabilities. In this framework, motor dexterity issues are in fact related to primarily assess, restore and enhance manipulation capabilities of the user by the utilization of advanced interface directly worn by the patient such as, joint rotation sensors, gloves, hand exoskeleton.

The interfaces systems described above have been re-designed for direct use of disable people and will be construed and validated in the course of the present year.

The same VE methodologies can be fully utilized also for research on ergonomical factors and employment risks; these studies can be performed through the simulation of usual working operation in order to evaluate appropriate ergonomical modifications (postural, dynamical, related to different tools to be utilized, etc.).

By considering the application of the VE technologies to the other fields, it is possible to take into account problems related to teleoperation and telepresence. VE technologies offer in fact intrinsic capabilities for extending the user‘s functions remotely, thus improving his/her access and interaction with places and persons which are not physically reachable due to his/her reduction in mobility or hostility of the environment.
To this purpose, two different levels of implementation can be considered for the utilization of VE technologies in this area: *Televirtuality* and Supervisory-Control of Robotics Aid.

The concept of *Televirtuality* implies that two or more users can interact with the same Virtual Environment. In this case each user possesses an individual interface system while the same VE is shared by all the control architecture. Televirtuality is a new concept of man-to-man interface which can be exploited for interpersonal and group communication.

In the framework of the *direct control of robotics aid* performed by the user, VE technologies (in particular both interface systems and mainly software simulation and modeling techniques) can be utilized in order to relieve, at least in part, the burden of attention required to the same user. The whole operation performed by the robot in a real, also remote, environment could be in fact previously simulated by the user in the virtual environment through the use of basic interface systems and, when complete safe and reliable conditions have been verified, commands can be issued to the robotics system for autonomous completion of the task. The utilization of supervisory-control of robotics aid can be thought for tele-working thus allowing people to remotely interact and operate in his/her working place.

7. Conclusions

In this paper the work performed at Scuola Superiore S.Anna on the development of Haptic Interfaces has been presented. The design and development of Haptic Devices has been approached by considering both Force and Tactile Display Devices. The goal of the research activity in progress at PERCRO of Scuola Superiore S.Anna is that of obtaining Haptic Interfaces capable of allowing the human operator to faithfully control exploration procedure of virtual objects. This goal has been devised as essential in order to increase the performances of the interaction component of VE systems. Only by augmenting the complete sense of presence of the user during the interaction with VE it will be possible, in the future, to boost the utilization of VE systems in wide areas of applications.

Acknowledgements

The work described in this paper has been funded by the European Union in the framework of the ESPRIT project n.5363 GLAD-IN-ART and in the ESPRIT Basic Research project n.6358 SCATIS.

References

1. Lederman S.J., Klatsky R.L "Haptic Exploration and Object Representation", in M.A.Goodale (Ed.), Vision and Action: the Control of Grasping, Ablex Publishing Corporation, Norwood, NJ, 1990.
2. Hayward V. "Toward a Seven Axis Haptic Device", Proc. of 1995 IROS, Pittsburgh, PA, Aug. 1995.
3. Massey T. H., Salisbury J.K. "The PHANToM Haptic Interface: a Device for Probing Virtual Objects", Proc. of ASME Winter Annual Meeting, Chicago, IL, Nov. 1994.
4. Goertz R.C. "Manipulator Systems Development at ANL", Proc. of 12th RSTD Conference, 1964.
5. Bergamasco M. "Design of Hand Force Feedback Systems for Glove-like Advanced Interfaces", Proc. of the 1st IEEE Intern. Workshop on Robot and Human Communication ROMAN'92, Hosei University, Tokyo, Japan, 1992.
6. Bergamasco M. "Theoretical Study and Experiments on Internal and External Force Replication", Lecture Notes Workshop on Force Display in Virtual Environments and its Application to Robotic teleoperation (A.Bejczy, G. Hirzinger, K. Tanie, Eds.) 1993 IEE Conf. on Robotics and Automation, May, Atlanta, GA, 1993.
7. Bergamasco M. "Haptic Interfaces: the Study of Force and Tactile Feedback Systems", Proc. of IEEE Workshop on Robot na d Human Communication ROMAN'95, Waseda University, Tokyo, Japan, 1995.
8. Bergamasco M., Prisco G.M. "Virtual Surface Contour Following: an Experimental Approach Exploiting an Arm Exoskeleton as Haptic Interface", Proc. of 1995 ASME Winter Annual Meeting, San Francisco, CA, Nov. 1995.
9. Bergamasco M., Prisco G.M. "An experimental Approach to Virtual Surface Exploration Exploiting an Arm Exoskeleton as Haptic Interface", Proc. of SPIE 1995, Philadelphia, Oct. 1995.
10. Bergamasco M. "Force Replication to the Human Operator: the Development of Arm and Hand Exoskeletons as Haptic Interfaces", Proc. of 7th Intern. Symposium of Robotics Research ISRR 1995, Munich, Germany, 1995.

Facial Interaction for Human Machine Interface

P. Kalra, I.S. Pandzic, N. Magnenat Thalmann
MIRALab, CUI, University of Geneva
24, rue du General Dufour
1211 Geneva, Switzerland

Abstract

Interaction in graphical systems is becoming more and more multimodal. Use of the conventional mode of 2D widget-mouse or keyboard interaction is not very natural for many applications. For the comfort of disabled persons who may not be able to use the hand input devices, it is necessary to explore means for interactive controls for them. In this paper, we discuss real time interaction through facial input and face-to-face communication in a virtual dialogue. The paper presents our method of extracting dynamic facial movements which can be hooked as controls for a desired application. For example, in performance driven facial animation, the method enables recognition of facial expressions of a real person which are appropriately mapped as controlling parameters to simulate facial expressions of a synthetic actor in real time. In other applications, the extracted parameters can provide real time estimates of positions and orientations in a virtual scene. The method requires a video camera input and extracts motion parameters through a small set of visually tracked feature points. In the face-to-face virtual dialogue, recognition acts like a module for acquiring emotional states of a real actor. This can be integrated with other modules for the interpretation of the response with voice and emotions of the virtual actor. This gives potential for an interface system with human like agent interacting with user in spoken language with facial expressions.

1. Introduction

Human interface for computer graphics systems is taking an evolutionary turn where it would involve multimodal approach [1] using human like agent. It is now moving from typical keyboard operation to more natural modes of interaction using visual, audio and gestural means. This paper discusses real time interaction using visual input from a human face. It describes the underlying approach for recognizing and analyzing the facial movements of a real performance. The output in the form of parameters describing the facial expressions can then be used to drive one or more applications running on the same or on a remote computer. This enables the user to control the graphics system by means of facial expressions. This is being used primarily as a part of a real-time facial animation system, where the synthetic actor reproduces the animator's expression. This offers interesting possibilities for teleconferencing as the requirements on the network bandwidth are low. Experiments are also done using facial movements as means of controlling a walkthrough or performing simple object manipulation. Recognition of facial expressions is a very complex and interesting subject. However, there have been numerous research efforts in this area [2]. Mase and Pentland [3] apply optical flow and principal direction analysis for lip reading. Terzopoulos and Waters [4] reported on techniques using deformable curves for estimating face muscle contraction parameters from video sequences. Waters and Terzopoulos [5] modeled and animated faces using scanned data obtained from a radial laser scanner and used muscle contraction parameters estimated from video sequences. Saji et al. [6] introduced a new method called "Lighting Switch Photometry" to extract 3D shapes from the moving face. Kato et al. [7] use isodensity maps for the description and the synthesis of facial expressions. Most of these techniques do not perform the information extraction in real time. There have been some implementations of the facial expression recognition using colored markers painted on the face and/or lipstick [8], [9], [10]. However, the use of markers is not practical and the methods are needed to perform recognition without them. In another approach Azarbayejani et al. [11] and Saulnier et al. [12] use extended Kalman filter formulation to recover motion parameters of an object. However, the motion parameters include only head position and orientation. Li et al. [13] use the Candid model for 3D motion estimation for model based image coding. The size of the geometric model is limited to only 100 triangles which is rather low for characterizing the shape of a particular model. Magnenat-Thalmann et al. [14] propose a real time recognition method based on "snakes" as introduced by Terzopoulos and Waters [4]. The main drawback of this approach, is that the method relies on the information from the previous frame in order to extract the next one. This can lead to the accumulation of error and the "snake" may completely loose the contour it is supposed to follow. We adopt a different approach [15] where each frame can be processed independently from the previous one.

First we describe our recognition method for facial movements. Then facial animation system using real performance as input is briefly discussed. Some other applications of controlling movements and manipulation are also outlined. The prototype system for face-to-face communication in a virtual dialogue is briefly presented. A short note on implementation provides the communication protocol between the different modules. Finally, we give the concluding remarks.

2. Expression Recognition Method

Accurate recognition and analysis of facial expressions from video sequence requires detailed measurements of facial features. Currently, it is computationally expensive to precisely acquire these measurements. Our primary concern was the extraction of the features in real time, for which we have focussed our attention on recognition and analysis of only a few facial features.

The recognition method relies on the "soft mask", which is a set of points adjusted interactively by the user on the image of the face as shown in figure 1. Using the mask, various characteristic measures of the face are calculated at the time of initialization. Color samples of the skin, background, hair etc., are also registered.

Recognition of the facial features is primarily based on color sample identification and edge detection. Based on the characteristics of human face, variations of these methods are used in order to find the optimal adaptation for the particular case of each facial feature. Special care is taken to make the recognition of one frame independent from the recognition of the previous one in order to avoid the accumulation of error. The data extracted from the previous frame is used only for the features that are relatively easy to track (e.g. the neck edges), making the risk of error accumulation low. A reliability test is performed and the data is reinitialized if necessary. This makes the recognition very robust.

The following sections describe the initialization of the system and the details of the recognition method for different facial feature, as well as the verification of the extracted data. The recognition of the features and the data verification are presented in the order of execution.

2.1 Initialization

Initialization is done on a still frame of the face grabbed with a neutral expression. The soft mask is placed over the image as shown in figure 1. The points of the mask are interactively adjusted to the characteristic features of the face, such as mouth, eyes, eyebrows etc.

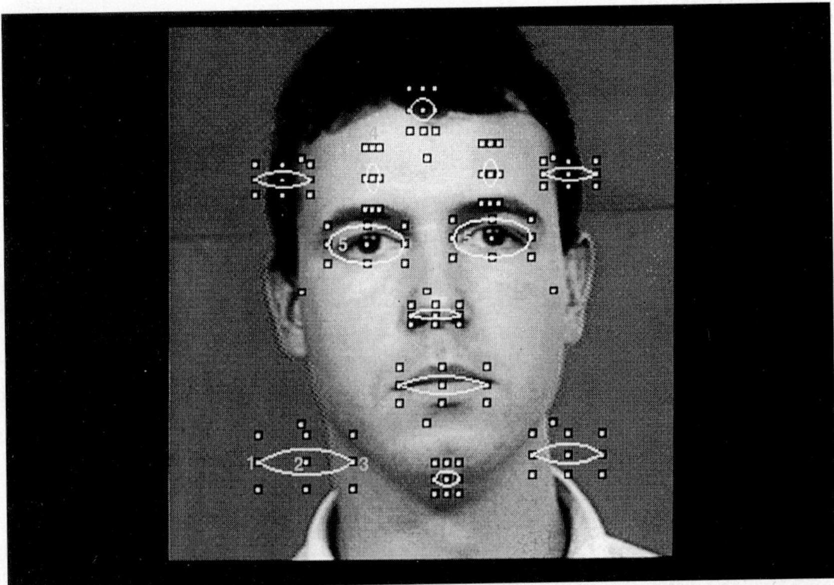

Fig. 1: Soft mask for initialization

These points determine the measures of the face with neutral expression and provide color samples of the background and the facial features. The process of setting the mask is rather simple and usually takes less than half a minute.

2.2 Head Tracking

First step is to find the edges of the neck (shown as circles in the neck region in figure 2). During the initialization, color samples are taken at the points 1, 2 and 3 of the mask (see figure 1). Points 1 and 3 are aligned over background and skin respectively, and point 2 over the hair falling on the side of the face, if any. During recognition, a sample taken from the analyzed point of the image is compared with those three samples and identified as one of them. As each color sample consists of three values (red, green and blue), it can be regarded as a point in a three dimensional RGB space. The distance in this space between the sample being analyzed and each stored sample is calculated. The closest one is chosen to categorize the point. This method of sample identification works fine in the areas where the number of possible different colors is small and where there is sufficient difference between the colors.

Next step is to find the hairline (marked with circles in sides of forehead in figure 2). The samples of the hair and skin color are taken and edge between the two is detected. The horizontal position of the starting point is halfway between the neck edges, and the vertical position is taken from the previous frame. At a fixed distance below the hairline the edges of the hair seen on the sides of the forehead are detected using the sample identification method.

2.3 Jaw Rotation

To extract the rotation of the jaw the position of the chin has to be found. We exploit the fact that the chin casts a shadow on the neck, which gives a sharp color change on the point of the chin. Once again the sample identification is used to track this edge.

2.4 Data Verification

At this point the data extracted so far is checked against the measurements of the face made during initialization. If serious discrepancies are observed the recognition of the frame is interrupted, the warning signal is issued and the data is reinitialized in order to recognize the next frame correctly. This may happen if the user partially or totally leaves the camera field of view or if he takes such a position that the recognition cannot proceed.

2.5 Eyebrows

The starting points for the eyebrow detection are positioned above each eyebrow, sufficiently high that the eyebrows cannot be raised above them. They are adjusted interactively during initialization (points marked 4 in figure 1) and kept at fixed position with respect to the center of the hairline. Also during initialization, the color samples of the skin and the eyebrows are taken. The search proceeds downwards from the starting point until the color is identified as eyebrow. To avoid wrinkles on the forehead being confused with the eyebrows, the search is continued downward after a potential eyebrow is found. If that is the real eyebrow (i.e. not just a wrinkle), the next sample resembling the eyebrow will be in the eye region, i.e. too low. The points on eyebrows are marked with circles in figure 2. The relative position of each eyebrow with respect to the hairline is compared with the eyebrow position in the neutral face to determine the eyebrow-raise. The eyebrow squeeze is calculated from the distance between the left and right eyebrow.

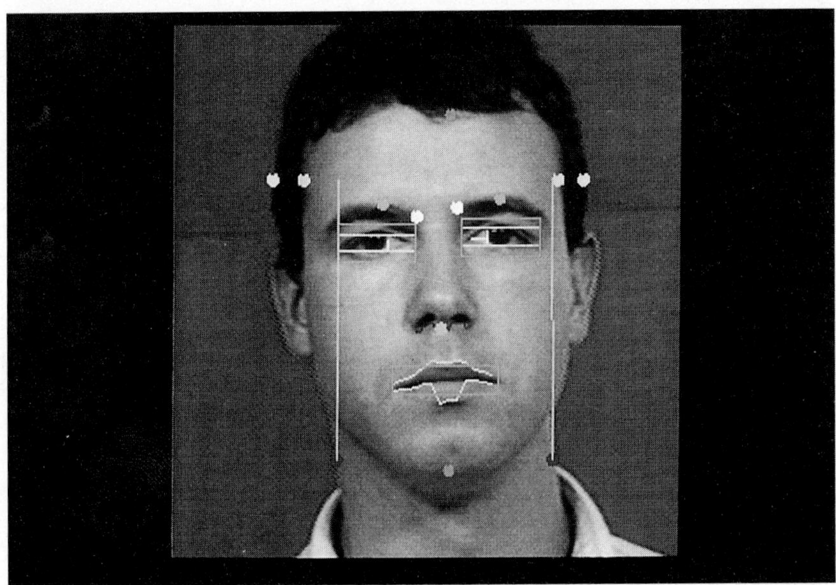

Fig. 2: Face with circle marks from the recognition

2.6 Eyes

During initialization, a rectangle (marked as 5 in figure 1) is placed over each eye and its position relative to the center of the hairline is measured. During recognition the rectangles (outlined in figure 2) are fixed with respect to the center of the hairline and stay around the eyes when the user moves.

We exploit the fact that the sides of the iris make strong vertical edges in the eye region in order to determine the aperture of the eye. The points lying on vertical edges are found as the local minima of a simplified color intensity gradient function. The edges are found by searching for the groups of such points connected vertically. The largest vertical edge is a side of the iris. To find the aperture of the eye we search for the eyelid edges upwards and downwards from the extremes of the vertical edge found earlier. To determine the horizontal position of the iris we find the distance between the iris and the edge of the eye using simple edge detection.

2.7 Nose and Mouth

The distance between the nose and the hairline is measured during initialization. Using this value the approximate position of the nose is determined. Edge detection is used for locating the nose. A point where the vertical color intensity gradient is above a certain threshold, is considered to lie on a horizontal edge. A 3x3 pixels gradient operator is used. The threshold value is determined during initialization by exploring the gradient values in the area.

For acquisition in the mouth region we search for a horizontal edge downward the nose point to find a point on the upper lip. At the same horizontal position the search is performed from the chin in upward direction to find a point on the lower lip. This process is repeated on the next horizontal position n pixels to the right, *n* being 1/10 of the mouth width. The search starts in the proximity of the found vertical positions. We continue to move to the right, each time storing in memory the points on the lips edges found, until the corner of the lips is passed. This is detected when no edge is found in the area. The corner of the lips is then tracked more precisely by decreasing the step to *n/2, n/4, n/8,...,1*. The same process is repeated for the left side. All the points found together thus form the mouth curve. It is shown in figure 2. However, due to shadows, wrinkles, beard or insufficient lip-skin color contrast, the curve is not very precise. Therefore the average height of the points in the middle third of the curve is taken for the vertical position of the lip. The bounding rectangle of the mouth is also outlined in figure 2. This rectangle provides measures for the nose and chin heights, relative vertical positions of both the lips, and squeeze/stretch of the mouth etc.

3. Real Time Facial Animation

Facial animation, as any other animation, typically involves execution of a sequence of a set of basic facial actions. We use what we call a Minimum Perceptible Action (MPA) [16] as a basic facial motion parameter. Each MPA has a corresponding set of visible movements of different parts of the face resulting from muscle contraction. Muscular activity is simulated using rational free form deformations [17]. MPAs also include actions like head turning and nodding. An MPA can be considered as an atomic action unit similar to AU (Action Unit) of FACS (Facial Action Coding System) [18], execution of which results in a visible and perceptible change of a face. We can aggregate a set of MPAs and define expressions and phonemes. Further these can be used for defining emotion and sentences for speech. Animation at the lowest level, however, is specified as a sequence of MPAs with their respective intensities and time of occurrence. The discrete action units defined in terms of MPAs can be used as fundamental building blocks or reference units for the development of a parametric facial process.

Development of the basic motion actions is non specific to a facial topology and provides a general approach for the modeling and animation of the primary facial expressions. In our facial model the skin surface of the face is considered as a polygonal mesh. It contains 2500-3000 polygons to represent the shape of the model. Hence, the model considered has sufficient complexity and irregularity to represent a virtual face, and is not merely represented as crude mask as considered in many other systems.

For the real time performance driven facial animation the input parameters to the facial animation are the MPAs. These MPAs have normalized intensities between 0 and 1 or -1 and 1. The analysis of the recognition module is mapped appropriately to these MPAs. In most cases the mapping is straightforward. Due to the speed constraint we have concentrated on only few parameters for the motion. This reduces the degrees of freedom for the animation. However, we believe that complete range of facial motion is practically not present in any particular sequence of animation. To mimic the motion of a real performance only a set of parameters is used. Figure 3 shows some frames of the real time facial animation.

With the input from real performance we are able to reproduce individual particular feature on the synthetic actor's face (e.g. raising the eyebrows, opening the mouth etc.) in real time. However, reproducing these features together may not faithfully reproduce the overall facial emotion (e.g. smile, surprise etc.). In order to achieve this a better interpreting/analyzing layer between recognition and simulation may be included. Use of a real performance to animate a synthetic face is one kind of input accessory used for our multimodal animation system. The system can basically capture the initial template of animation from real performance with accurate temporal characteristics. This motion template then can be modified, enhanced and complemented as per the need by other accessories for the production of final animation.

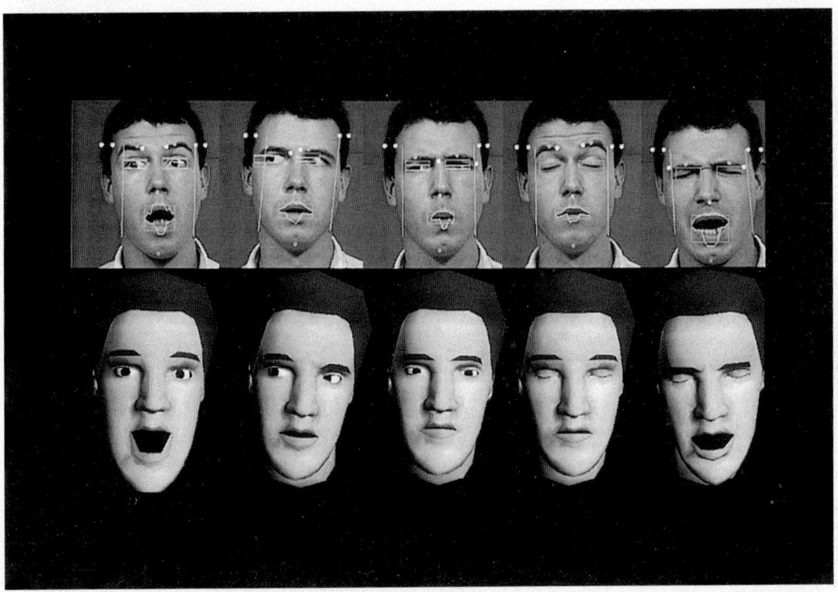

Fig. 3: Real time facial animation

4. Other Applications

We are currently experimenting with some other applications, like walkthrough and simple object manipulation. We also discuss some potential applications that may be included in the future.

4.1 Walkthrough or Navigation

Input from facial movement may be used for controlling the movement in the virtual environment. We have experimented controlling the virtual camera by the appropriate rotations of the head. At the same time user can perform a move forward in the direction of his/her view by opening the mouth. While it is very natural to turn the head in the direction we want to look at, it is relatively difficult to co-ordinate the head rotation around all the three axis at the same time. Consequently, we have reduced the complexity of the controls which is more natural and easy to learn. Figure 4 shows the user "walking through" a virtual environment using the face to control the movement.

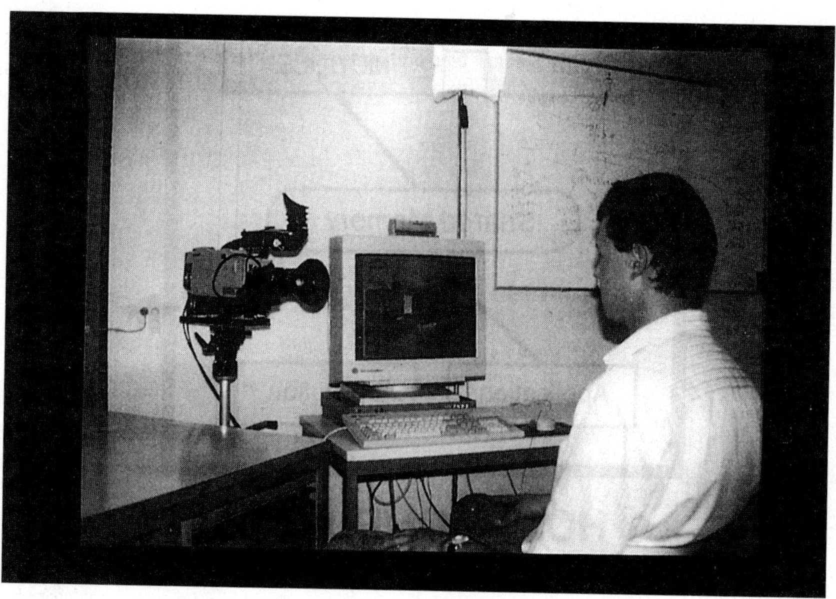

Fig.4: Walkthrough control with facial input

4.2 Simple Object Manipulation

In a 3D object environment the user can control the rotation of the object around all the three axes by appropriate movements of the head. At the same time user can stretch or squash the object horizontally by stretching or squeezing the mouth, and vertically by raising or lowering the eyebrows. These controls are quite natural for the user.

Another input is in the form of the voice of what user says. The system at present does not have the working module of the voice recognition. The input for the voice is therefore created through the text. In order to make the virtual actor respond to the real person, a data base or dictionary is used which contains words with emotional states. These are defined in terms of constituent phonemes and facial expressions, and are referred to as phono-emotional entries. These entries also contain temporal information, for example, precaliberated duration of words, relative position of emotional states with respect to the words.

In the analyzer, for the search of the response of the virtual actor, from the user input theory of automata is used. This conducts syntactic and semantic analysis of the input sentence.

The final state in the automata refers to the response, which is an index to the response data base. The propagation from one state to another is done by making comparison of word in a sentence. A meta state is defined where, the virtual actor would wait for a particular or specific response. The output of the analyzer in the form of phono-emotional entries of the response and the words to be spoken by the virtual actor go to the actuator. In the actuator first the entries are timed, i.e. the time-scale is changed from the relative to absolute time of the clock. This series of timed phonemes and expressions are then compiled and decomposed into the basic action units (MPAs) in order to produce the visual changes to be done on the virtual actor's face. The words to be spoken are transmitted to the vocal synthesizer module. A module of synchronizer is used to allow the visual and audio synchronization of the speech.

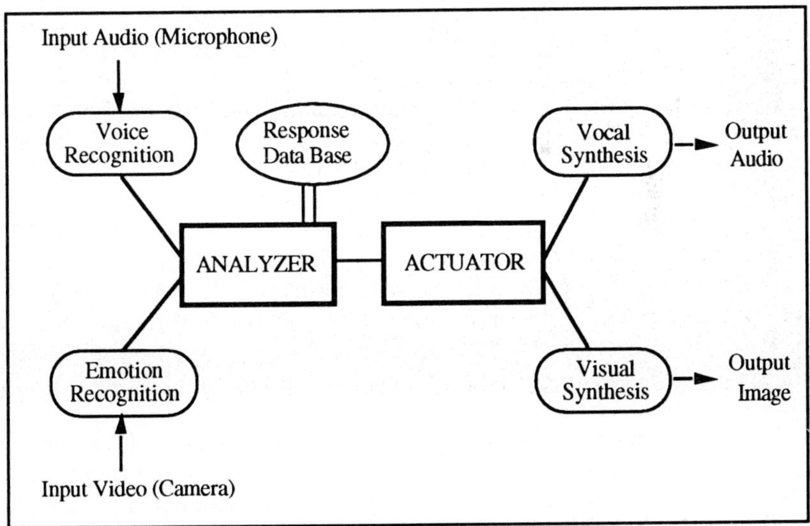

Fig.5: Schematic diagramme for virtual dialogue

Figure 6 shows display of facial communication in a virtual dialogue, where virtual actor is saying "hello everybody".

4.3 Visual Communication

With some extensions, our real time facial animation system can be used as a communication system [19]. Since the recognition of the facial expression is done on the host machine, and the rendering of the synthetic actor on the remote machine, this already provides one way communication. For a two ways dialogue it would be necessary for the person on the other side to have a camera and the recognition module.

4.4 Aid for Disabled Persons

Our experiments with the simple applications like walkthrough and object manipulation show that it is possible to control the computer by means of facial movements. Potentially, this could aid the disabled persons, enabling them to control an application by whatever limited movements they can do. Warner [20] uses the bio-electric signals from eye, muscle and brain activity as input and thus enables the severely disabled persons to control their environment by means of limited movements. He reports several successful applications. We would like to explore a similar path, using the facial expression recognition as input.

5. Facial Communication in Virtual Dialogue

The system is well suited for developing an autonomous virtual actor who may communicate and exchange the dialogue with a real person or even another virtual actor. This requires an intelligent and knowledge based interpreter for the communication process. This interpreter would perform much more task than just merely copying other's facial expression.

We are developing a prototype for a virtual dialogue system where a virtual actor communicates with a real person (user). This involves face-to-face communication integrating visual and acoustic signals. This seems a natural way of human machine communication as the analysis and comprehension rely on bimodal perceptive mechanism.

Over the past decade, research on man-machine dialogue has become an increasingly important subject. Here, it is not our intention to offer an exhaustive list of different attempts in the field. Instead, we want to propose a simple architecture of such a system which can give a framework for a complex speech-emotion-voice dialogue between human and machine. Figure 5 shows the global structure of the proposed system.

There are two main modules to the system: analyzer and actuator. The analyzer is like the brain of the system which takes inputs from different sources and analyses the interpretation for the response. The actuator does the job of processing the response so that the modules for visual and audio output can produce the results synchronously.

The two inputs to the analyzer are the emotion-recognition module, which has been elaborated earlier. Here the analysis is more toward the emotional expressions and the head movements. The result of the analysis can provide the emotions of the user (real actor), and head gestures for "yes" or "no".

6. Implementation

In our implementation, the communication protocol is designed in such a way that one or more applications can easily connect to the recognition module. The applications can run on the same machine and/or on a remote machine connected through a standard network supporting TCP/IP.

The applications running on the local machine connect through shared memory. On the remote machine there is a communication process whose only task is to read the data coming from the recognition module over the network. Applications get the data from the communication process through shared memory. This type of asynchronous communication enables the application to use the data at it's own speed. This is important when the application is slower than the recognition module -- otherwise there would be accumulating delays. The communication process allows more applications to use the same data from the shared memory.

We can use any Silicon Graphics workstation for the motion capture of the facial features with Live Video Digitizer facility. The recognition speed is 10 frames per second on a SGI Indy workstation which we consider enough for all the current applications. For the animation of a virtual actor we use a faster SGI workstation (e.g. Reality Engine) to obtain real time display and match with the speed of the recognition module. The system is developed in C and uses Fifth Dimension Toolkit [21] for the interface. For facial communication in virtual dialogue, the voice recognition and synthesis are done on IBM R6000, and communication is done through socket.

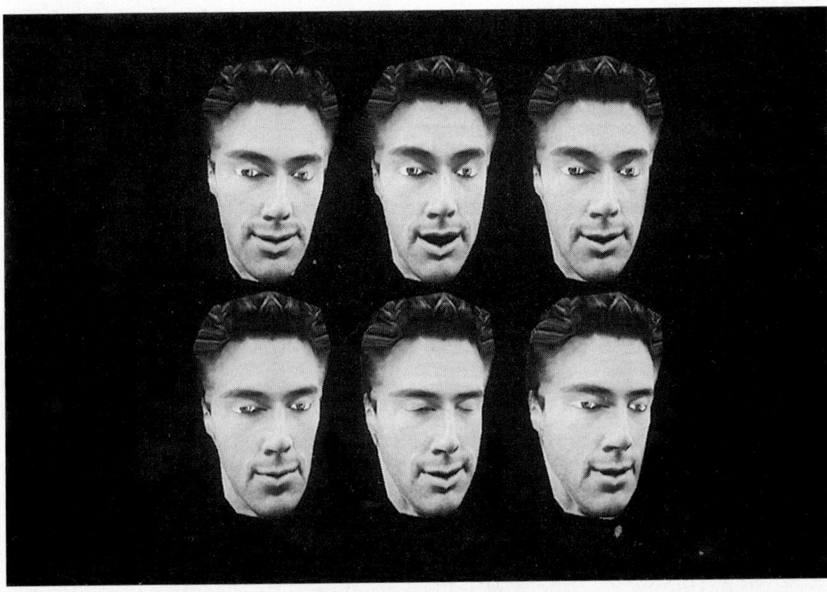

Fig.6: Display of facial communication in a virtual dialogue

7. Conclusions

This paper presents a prototype system for human-machine interface which uses facial input. The recognition module in our system does not require use of any special markers or make-up on the users. It also does not need "training" the system by executing the entire set of expressions. The system is reasonably robust, adequately fast, and adaptable to a new user. Several applications using such interaction are given. The face-to-face communication in virtual dialogue is also presented, this demonstrates the importance of facial interaction for a natural human-machine interaction.

Acknowledgment

The research is supported by Fonds National Suisse pour la Recherche Scientifique, part of it was supported by the ESPRIT Project 6709 HUMANOID. Authors would like to extend thanks to Hugues Cazeaux, Marc Escher, Nicolas Ruscon, Jean-Marc Tribet for their help in the development of the system.

References

1. Kalra P (1993) "An Interactive Multimodal Facial Animation System," PhD Thesis, Swiss Federal Institute of Technology, Lausanne, 1993.
2. Blake A. "Applying visual curve tracking to graphics" Proc Computer Animation '95, Geneva, Switzerland, pp.67-71, 1995.
3. Mase K, Pentland A (1990) "Automatic Lipreading by Computer" Trans. Inst. Elec. Info. and Comm. Eng., vol. J73-D-II, No.6, pp.796-803, 1990.
4. Terzopoulos D, Waters K (1991) "Techniques for Realistic Facial Modeling and Animation" Proc. Computer Animation, Geneva, Switzerland, Springer-Verlag, Tokyo, pp.59 - 74, 1991.
5. Waters K, Terzopoulos D (1991) "Modeling and Animating Faces using Scanned Data" Journal of Visualization and Computer Animation, vol.2 /4, pp 123-128, 1991.
6. Saji H, Hioki H, Shinagawa Y, Yoshida K, Kunii T. "Extraction of 3D Shapes from the Moving Human Face using Lighting Switch Photometry" in Magnenat Thalmann N, Thalmann D (Eds) Creating and Animating the Virtual World, Springer Verlag Tokyo, pp.69-86, 1992.
7. Kato M, So I, Hishinuma Y, Nakamura O, Minami T. "Description and Synthesis of Facial Expressions based on Isodensity Maps" in Tosiyasu L Kunii(Ed) Visual Computing, Springer-Verlag, Tokyo, pp.39-56, 1992
8. Magno Caldognetto E, Vagges K, Borghese N A, Ferrigno G. "Automatic Analysis of Lips and Jaw Kinematics in VCV Sequences" Proceedings of Eurospeech 89 Conference, vol.2, pp.453 - 456, 1989.
9. Patterson E C, Litwinowich P C, Greene N (1991) "Facial Animation by Spatial Mapping", Proc. Computer Animation 91, Magnenat Thalmann N, Thalmann D (Eds.), Springer-Verlag, pp.31 - 44, 1991.

10. Kishino F, (1994) "Virtual Space Teleconferencing System - Real Time Detection and Reproduction of Human Images" Proc. Imagina 94, pp.109-118, 1994.
11. Azarbayejani A, Starner T, Horowitz B, Pentland A. "Visually Controlled Graphics" IEEE Transaction on Pattern Analysis and Machine Intelligence, June 1993, vol.15/6, pp.602-605, 1993.
12. Saulnier A, Viaud M L, Geldreich D. "Analyse et Synthèse en temps réel du Vsage pour la Télévirtualité" Proc Imagina '94, pp.175-182, 1994.
13. Li Haibo, Roivainen P, Forchheimer R. "3-D Motion Estimation in Model Based Facial Image Coding" IEEE Transaction on Pattern Analysis and Machine Intelligence, June 1993, vol.15/6, pp.545-555, 1993.
14. Magnenat Thalmann N, Cazedevals A, Thalmann D. "Modeling Facial Communication Between an Animator and a Synthetic Actor in Real Time" Proc Modeling in Computer Graphics, Genova, Italy, June 1993 (Eds Falcidieno B and Kunii L), pp 387-396, 1993.
15. Pandzic I S, Kalra P, Magnenat Thalmann N. "Real Time Facial Interaction", Displays, vol.15/3, pp.157-163, 1994.
16. Kalra P, Mangili A, Magnenat-Thalmann N, Thalmann D. "SMILE: A Multilayered Facial Animation System", Proc IFIPS WG 5.10, Japan (Ed Kunii Tosiyasu L), pp.189-198, 1991.
17. Kalra P, Mangili A, Magnenat-Thalmann N, Thalmann D. "Simulation of Muscle Actions using Rational Free Form Deformations" Proc Eurographics '92, Computer Graphics Forum, vol.2/3, pp.59-69, 1992.
18. Ekman P, Friesen W.V. "Facial Action Coding System", Investigator's Guide Part 2, Consulting Psychologists Press Inc., 1978.
19. Pandzic I, Capin T, Magnenat-Thalmann N, Thalmann D. "VLNET: A Networked Multimedia 3D Environment with Virtual Human, Proc. Multi-Media Modeling '95, Singapore 1995 .
20. Warner D."Biologically Responsive Interactive Interface" Proc. Imagina 94, pp.52 - 59, 1994.
21. Turner R, Gobbetti E, Balaguer F, Mangili A, Thalmann D, Magnenat-Thalmann N. "An Object Oriented Methodology using Dynamic Variables for Animation and Scientific Visualization' Proc. CGI '90, Springer-Verlag, pp.317-328, 1990.

A Comparison of Design Strategies for 3D Human Motions

Ronan Boulic, Zhiyong Huang, Daniel Thalmann
LIG - Computer Graphics Lab, Swiss Federal Institute of Technology
CH-1015 Lausanne, Switzerland

Abstract

Three-dimensional character animation and especially human animation becomes everyday more popular for simulation, multimedia applications, and games. However the specification of human motion in a computer animation system is still a tedious task for the user in most commercial systems. Based on the experience on the ESPRIT projects HUMANOID and HUMANOID-2, we compare in this paper the various strategies for describing and interacting with complex motions of the human body. We especially analyze the advantages and disadvantages of the associated interfaces. A case study of object grasping and handling is detailed within the framework of the TRACK system.

1. Introduction

In this paper we compare the design strategies for 3D human motion. We choose to concentrate on the constraints, the objectives and the methodologies adopted for the body skeleton animation thus excluding the facial animation field from our investigations. The comparison is organized according to the major trade-off between the interaction refresh rate and the desired realism of the resulting motion. Although, it is a major factor of computing cost and final realism of the human motion, we don't address in detail here the problem of the human envelope deformation, either skin or cloth. It is clear that the same trade-off also applies to that feature and we keep it in mind when comparing the different strategies. We can order the various methodologies along a scale beginning at high realism for the motion design process in a production context, then middle realism for the interactive process provided by a wide range of motion modeling systems and finally low realism for real-time applications as simulators, virtual reality and games. We review the characteristics of these various approaches by describing the strategies used to animate and interact with 3D human characters.

We first examine the design process of realistic motions for productions as films, commercials and more recently games. Then, in the second part we focus on the wide range of systems providing interactive response time basically for design purpose or for some of them dedicated to human factors evaluation. The objectives of the ESPRIT project HUMANOID 2 are recalled in that context. In this class of systems the integration of the end user interaction flow is depending on the system load. Conversely, in the simulators and the games a high input-output rate tightly constraints the system architecture as developed in the third part. We especially stress the problems which have found recent improvements and those intrinsically difficult to solve in a near future. The fifth part recalls the methodology of the TRACK system developed in the framework of the ESPRIT project HUMANOID. We focus on a case-study of complex goal-oriented grasping and handling motions. Finally, we conclude by summarizing the general trends of the field.

2. Motion Design in Film Production Context

What is required in movie productions is much more than the mere physically-based realism ; it is rather a high believability conveying the intention of the motion and the emotional state of the character. Animating a 3D human with that objective in mind makes the whole process extremely difficult as the models are still desperately simple compared to any real actor.

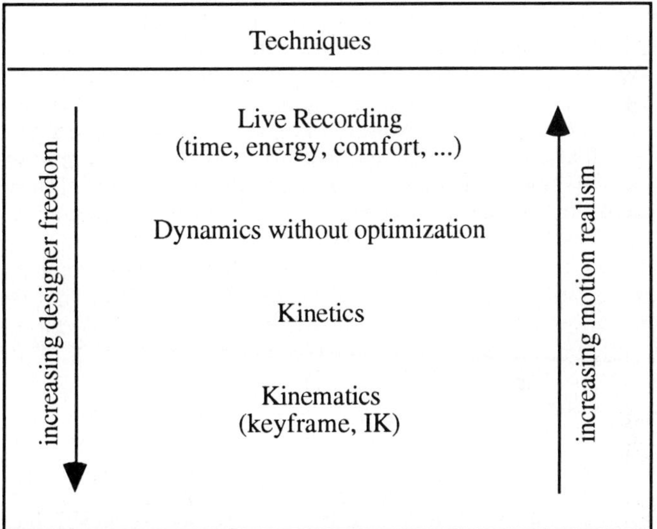

Fig. 1: Designer freedom Vs motion realism

The animators and directors know very well that the body postures and movements express nearly as much as the face and the speech themselves [1]. This has been partly exploited in traditional 2D animation together with other observations regarding subjective interpretation of object proportions and relative motion. Such practical knowledge can now guide the 3D animators [2][3] in bringing to "life" cartoon-like or toy-like characters as recently demonstrated with the movie "Toy Story" [4].

Apart from that masterpiece which involved an important team (110 persons at Pixar [4]), this type of work is limited to short pieces for cost reasons. At this moment, most of them are special effects, commercials and, more and more, some sophisticated games [5].

In the production context, the animators have very detailed specifications of each individual motions to design from the storyboard and artistic directives about the characters. The logical requirement on the software tools is to ask both for the highest realism and the greatest freedom of design in order to edit and improve any detail of the motion. However, as appears on Figure 1 (inspired by [6]), the techniques providing highly realistic motions, at least from the physical aspect of the problem, are the ones providing the least design freedom. We now review them and analyze why the live recording, also known as Performance Animation, is now the most popular technique is that field. In a second part we recall what still prevent performance animation systems to be more widely accepted in 3D human animation.

2.1 Physics alone does not bring "Life"

The major commercial systems for 3D human animation, as Alias-Wavefront-TDI and Softimage, propose various degrees of motion realism from the standard Keyframe techniques, Inverse Kinematics, Direct and Inverse Dynamics to the option of live recording. They ignore Optimization techniques and Inverse Kinetics (see details in section 3). In the film production context, the motion design is an incremental process that require the possibility for the animator to fine tune any *degree of freedom* (further noted *DOF*) of the animated structure at any point in time. This is achieved with the large set of tools manipulating keyframes [4]. Such fine control is also mandatory in cartesian space for fine positioning and orienting of end effectors (hands, feet, head, others...). This is now very common practice with Inverse Kinematics (further noted IK) [7][5]. Furthermore, the animator needs interactive specification and a fast response system to work within an efficient "look, feel and adjust" design loop. Such requirements discard language-based interfaces in this context [8][9]. Commercial systems now integrate these techniques and design requirements on standard graphic workstations, allowing to handle 3D human figures with usually around 30 DOFs.

Although impressive results have been obtained with optimization techniques [10], [11] they still face severe computation costs for such high dimension of animation space. As appears on Figure 1, the second limitation of that technique comes from the insufficient amount of animator control over the resulting motion. A recent advance in that field [6] improves these two aspects by combining the optimization with the keyframe technique:

- the animator has a greater control by specifying keyframed postures, eventually with their associated key time, as constraints. It is also possible to specify higher level constraints as velocity of the center of mass or any end effector.
- the type of in-between interpolation is fixed, so it remains only the first derivative at each DOF and the time of most keyframes to be optimized thus greatly reducing the computing cost.

Perhaps the most difficult problem faced by this approach, in term of designer control, is how to express the objective function in order to reflect the character's intentions and mood, i.e. what makes the character looking *alive* while performing a desired motion.

This is a general problem also faced by more standard techniques (IK, Dynamics, functional models as walking, grasping, etc...). At the moment it is solved by sampling the resulting motions into keyframe motions and use the various techniques available at that bottom level of representation [12],[13]. Figure 1 has put the Live Recording technique at the top of the scale as providing the most realistic motions while, at first sight, freeing the animator from any intervention. Indeed, recording the motion from a performing actor allows to capture its natural dynamics along with the subtle attitudes and motions that are so important to convey the underlying message of the shot [5].

On the other hand, it seems that this technique transfers the responsibility of the character design from the animator to the actor. In fact, the actor usually does not match the skeleton features of the virtual creature. Even in case of ideal measurements, this technique still induces significant work of the animator after converting the motion into the standard keyframe representation. So, in short, it provides both the realism and the design freedom. This explain why the Performance Animation approach has been widely adopted in the film production context [14][5]. We now explore more technically the limitations preventing a larger acceptance.

2.2 Live Recording Techniques are still too "superficial"

Most of the Performance Animation systems dedicated to the recording of human body motion belong to two groups depending on the sensing technologies they rely on, either optical or magnetic. Both allow the real-time registration of the human motion, practically speaking from around 20Hz to 100Hz for magnetic, and from 50Hz to 200Hz for optical.

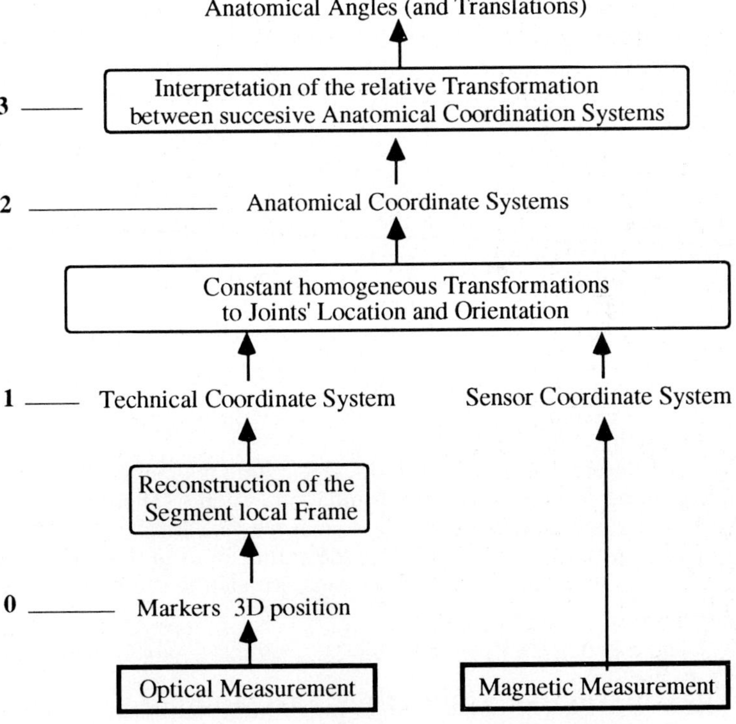

Fig. 2: The live motion recording process with performance animation systems

Although the optical technology is also suited to record the hand motion, dedicated devices are proposed which are discussed in section 4. An extensive discussion about their relative merits can be found in [14] ; we just recall here the major facts :

- Both approaches place the sensors on the external surface of a human performer.
- The magnetic technology provides the position and orientation of sensors while the optical technology provides the 3D position of reflective markers.
- From the first point we can state that the measurement is "superficial" and this has essential consequences for its use.

Figure 2 recalls the general process of translating the raw 3D trajectories into anatomical joint angles trajectories (based on the methodology of clinical motion analysis [15],[16]). We can distinguish three fundamental transformations through the different levels of information :

- constructing the so-called *technical frames* associated with the body segments from the raw 3D position of at least three *markers*.
- locating the *anatomical frame* at each joint of interest by applying a rigid transformation from the *technical frame* (or magnetic *sensor frame*)
- deriving the *anatomical angles* from the relative orientation between *anatomical frames* belonging to successive segments at a given joint.

At this time, the animated character calibration seriously hamper the effective reflection of the performer's motion, generating uncertainties at the three processing levels :

A) The rigid segments assumption is weak due to the deformation of muscles and the dynamics of human tissues (see [17],[18] for comparative measurements).

B) The performer's skeleton parameters are difficult to identify, inducing inaccurate positioning of the technical or sensor frame relative to the anatomical frame. Using bony landmarks is convenient but subject to errors (see [19] for the hip joint or [15] for the knee).

C) The Biomechanics of the human joints should be reflected in the virtual character as well. It is rarely the case as real joints often exhibit complex behaviors as integrating translation DOFs, varying axis of rotation, non mutually perpendicular axis, etc. (see [16] for the knee joint).

All these factors alter the realization of the cartesian constraints effectively performed by the real actor, e.g. the animated character body may exhibit various self-collisions and external collisions (foot into floor, etc...) or, conversely, no more realize some important contacts (hand in hand, hand on face etc.). Moreover, in some cases, the imaginary character may have no real performer counterpart thus amplifying these artifacts.

As a conclusion, the animator is still left a large responsibility in the editing of motion coming from Performance Animation systems. There is also a need to improve motion editing methods in order to enforce the cartesian constraints lost in the acquisition process while retaining the initial motion dynamics [20],[12]. Recent advances in motion signal processing are also worth mentioning in that respect [21],[13].

3. The interactive simulation environment

Apart from the wide range of commercial systems providing interactive response time for the purpose of animation design, we can consider here the systems dedicated to human factors evaluation, ergonomics, human behaviors studies and autonomous agent simulations. In this paper we focus only on this second class of systems. It is more rooted in robotics as the desired result is more quantitative than in the production class of application. In that context the realism is more a matter of conformance with the situations potentially faced by populations of future users of public environment [22], working place or device [23]. Recent advances focus on extending the human model to allow a larger autonomy of the virtual human agent. In the ESPRIT project HUMANOID II, the perception faculties of vision, audition and general collision detection are basic features of the human model [24]. Modeling the perception of balance is also very useful for motion design as developed later [9],[25].

In the interactive simulation context, a large use of functional models is made to access to a higher level of specification and control of the human motion [9],[26]. Such motion modeling is usually kinematic due to its low computation cost. As such it may lack the realism requested for full believability. However, it is the price to pay for the flexibility, the higher levels of control and the longer duration of simulation. Compared to the production context where one has to pay a high price for a high quality live recording of says, a single walking motion, we have here models providing flexible and infinite duration of a walking motion at low cost. Although the resulting motion is less artistic, it remains nearly as realistic as a recorded one in term of space, time and phase characteristics [27],[28],[29]. The same remark is globally valid for other classical functional models as grasping [30] or general goal-oriented motion with IK [31] and general balance control with Inverse Kinetics [25],[7]. Regarding the evaluation of behaviors in complex environments, the language-based interface now becomes a suitable approach to structure the functional models activation resulting in a higher level plan similar to robots task planning [9].

The balance control is a fundamental problem in realistic human motion design as human subjects perform a large class of motion while standing in equilibrium on one or two feet. Inverse Kinematics is not suited to handle that problem as the mass distribution information is not integrated in the kinematic jacobian [9]. Conversely, Inverse Kinetics evaluates the exact influence of each joint on the displacement of the total center of mass [25]. An equally important property of this technique is the ability to combine it with goal-oriented motions (defined with Inverse Kinematics) in a hierarchical fashion [7]. Such tool can of course be used to design realistic postures later used as keyframes in a production context. An important issue in that context is the management of the transition between successive actions. This is generally made with the ease-in and ease-out technique realized with simple cubic steps. Such approach is used in games where realistic prerecorded animation sequences, possibly with performance animation systems, can be combined on the fly to provide fluid behaviors [5]. Some interesting generalization of the transition management between multiple postures have be proposed to define simple behaviors that can also be used in real-time applications [32]. Basically, a set of postures is structured in a so-called Posture Transition Graph defining which posture can success to which posture with associated transition conditions. The technique has been applied to model a simple soldier behavior with postures as stand, squat, kneel on one knee, kneel on both knee, supine, crawl and prone.

Another branch of these systems focuses on the study of group and population behaviors for security assessment of public environments. This branch has begun with simple flock of birds and animal herds behaviors and now turns to simulate believable human behaviors in complex environments [22]. The theoretical background behind complex behaviors involving multiple agents are grounded in AI studies with recent applications to group behaviors of mobile robots [33]. In the human simulation context we clearly need either language-based or finite state automata structures to represent complex behaviors emerging from the interaction of elementary behaviour. Intended applications are scenario testing in multimedia applications and games with multiple human models.

4. The Real-Time Simulation Environment

The real-time simulation environment fully integrate the end-user within the animation loop in order to drive strategic simulation parameters. In that context, only very small system lag is acceptable in response to user input. So human motion control shrinks to: *the playback* and combination of prerecorded realistic motions (see section 2) according to a scenario integrating user generated events (games [5]), and *the use of Inverse Kinematics* [34], functional models [35] and posture-based behavioral automata [32] (see section 3).

In some highly sophisticated real-time environment the system can integrate a real-time performance animation system to either simulate a virtual character interacting with the end user (interactive TV or real-time production environment [14]), or to simulate the virtual body of the operator in the virtual environment [34], or to have bi-directional interaction between operator and virtual character in the virtual world [36]. The techniques used there are the magnetic sensor technology (see section 2), the real-time image analysis [36] and various dedicated approaches to measure the hand posture with digital gloves. The use of digital glove for real-time production of character animation is called digital puppetry for two reasons :

- the interaction metaphor is close to puppetry as the movement is measured on a articulated structure (the hand) rather different from the controlled one (the character) thus requiring some adjustment on the part of the performer [14].
- only simple characters can be animated in such a way due to the limited number of measured DOFs (even if more than one puppeteer are coordinating their performance, one usually animates the body, the other the face).

At the moment very few real-time simulation environments integrate the full human body representation for an operator immersed and interacting with a virtual world [34],[35]. Most VR applications limit the representation of the operator to the display of the hand posture when wearing a digital glove. Even in that limited context it can be desirable to automatically alter the displayed hand posture in order to reflect the virtual hand interaction with the virtual objects [37]. In such a way, the operator gets a feedback about the relative position of the hand-object system and is able to perform grasping with a higher efficiency.

5. The HUMANOID Environment

The HUMANOID environment is dedicated to the development of multimedia, VR and CAD applications involving virtual humans [26]. This environment integrates highly heterogeneous components such as the environment model, the humanoid model and various motion generators. Among others, it supports the TRACK application providing :

- interactive manipulation of multiple humanoids on standard SGI workstations
- skin deformation of a human body, including the hands and the face•
- collision detection and correction between multiple humanoid entities
- keyframing, inverse kinematics, dynamics, walking and grasping

In TRACK the motion designer can generate sequences with high level functional models as walking [27] and grasping [30],[38] and later refine or blend them at the lower keyframe level (figure 3) [12]. Inverse Kinematics is also one key component of the system especially regarding the ability to perform goal-oriented motion with grasped objects.

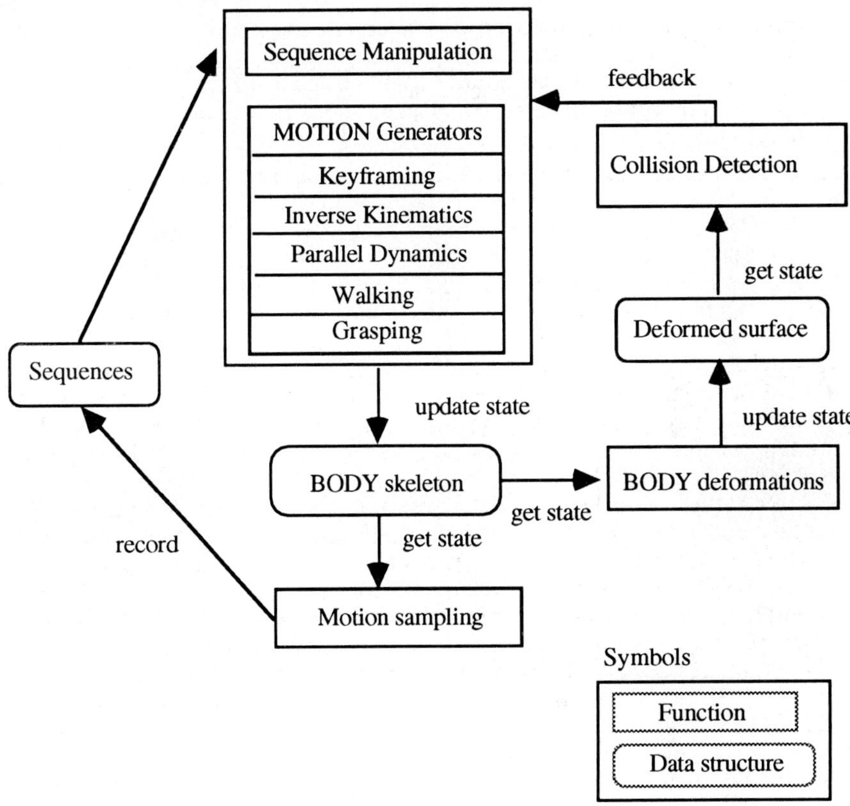

Fig. 3: The System Control Flow of TRACK

Owned to the hierarchical nature of its solution [7], we can integrate secondary behaviors which significantly improve the realism of the resulting motion. In this paper we especially focus on two major design issues:

- integrating self-collision avoidance and gravity optimization with IK.
- combining IK and keyframe for goal-oriented motions with grasped objects.

Self-collision is difficult to avoid when the goal-oriented motion is close to the body as can be seen on figure 4a,b. With standard Inverse Kinematics the end effector usually performs a collision-free trajectory as it is directly specified by the animator (in figure 4a, the hand first grasps the sphere and then moves to the target on the left of the body). The self-collision occurs frequently with unused end effectors [39] or intermediate segments of the articulated figure (figure 4b).

For that problem, we propose to generalize an approach introduced in Robotics for articulated robot arm [40] thus freeing the animator from tedious adjustments in such context. In our approach, spherical sensors are placed at strategic location of the body and they generate a correction displacement when entering into other body parts (as the elbow sensor in figure 4c). The displacement is realized as an automatic secondary behavior of the Inverse Kinematics solution [7]. It is achieved, for each step of the end effector behavior, in a two stages process :

1) construction of each sensor's kinematic jacobian which is inverted and multiplied to the correction displacement to get the correction posture variation of the character.
2) the sum of the correction posture variations due to all the sensors is projected on the null space of the end effector behavior thus not disturbing its realization [7].

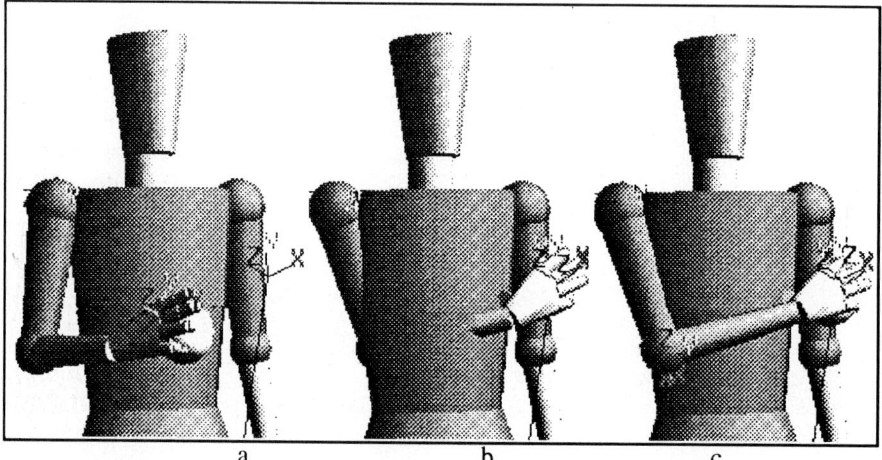

a b c

Fig. 4: Moving the hand without (b) and with (c) self-collision avoidance

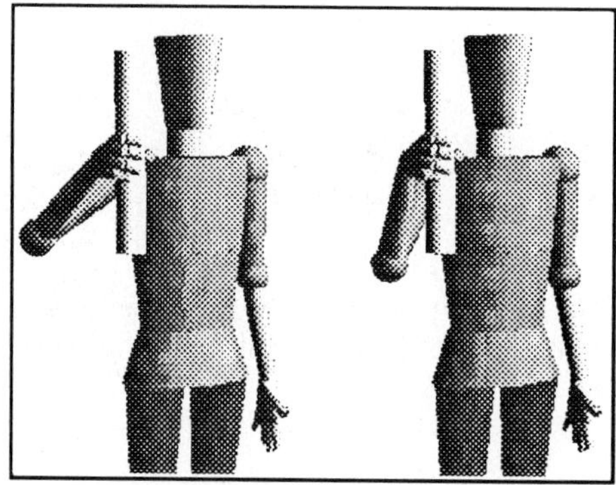

Fig. 5: Applying the gravity secondary behaviour

That correction process may have to be repeated a few iterations before converging as its priority is lower than the one of the end effector. Moreover, if there are multiple sensors the final solution is a compromise providing the smallest collision among the sensor set.

In fact, our approach is very general as it can be applied to avoid any collision, including with the environment, or to simulate the gravity as presented now. The gravity effect on a human being is to generate torques that the human being has to counter balance in order to maintain a given posture. For this reason a real human being naturally adopts the postures inducing the best comfort for a desired behavior [41]. Designing such natural postures requires a great experience from the animator.

We propose to use the same principle as for the secondary behavior of collision avoidance. In the present case, we automatically define a desired constant downward displacement for the sensors. The displacements are only partially realized as they belong to the secondary task. So the control converges to the posture realizing the main behavior with the least gravity torques (figure 5). The gravity and collision avoidance can be added thus automatically producing realistic postures as a background behaviour.

The second issue we want to highlight here is the interest of specifying the body motion from keyframed motion assigned to grasped objects. A large class of human behavior is related to the manipulation of manual tools and mechanical devices. It is often easier to specify the desired motion on these objects as they are designed to perform a specific function associated with a limited set of positions and/or orientations in space. So, we propose to set keyframes on these objects rather than on the human end effector. Combined with the Grasping function and Inverse Kinematics, we are able to obtain a coherent resulting behavior by applying the following algorithm: *First,* apply the full grasping process for the object in the initial keyframe [30], this includes the selection of the grasp, the first guidance of the hand with IK and closing of the fingers on the object [38].*Then,* for each time step of the keyframe sequence associated with the object: (i) move the object independently of the articulated figure, (ii) attract the hand frame to the new object location with IK, (iv) adjust the hand closure to the new relative position

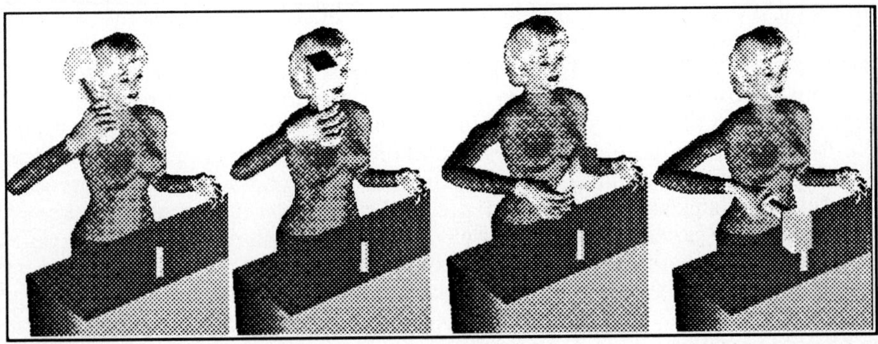

Fig. 6: Goal-oriented motion with a grasped object (hammer) with one hand

Two examples illustrate that approach. In figure 6 two keyframes have been defined for the hammer which is used to guide the right arm motion. In figure 7 we show a two hands grasp of a turning wheel. Again the keyframes are easier to specify on the object itself.

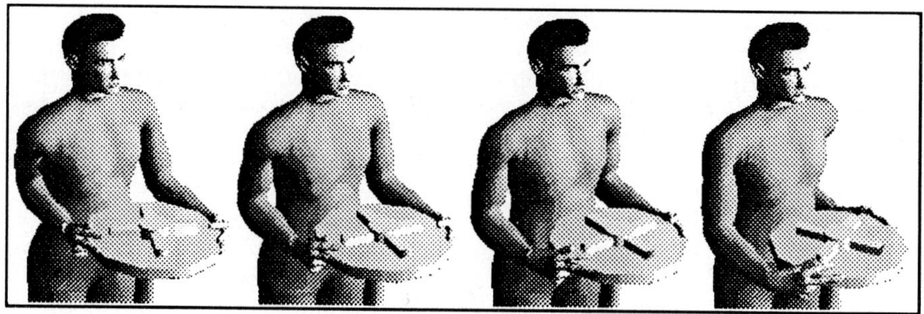

Fig. 7: Turning a grasped object (wheel) with two hands

6. Conclusions

We have reviewed the various strategies used to animate 3D human characters by grossly classifying them in three classes of compromise between the requirements of motion realism and real-time interaction. When scanning these different classes of applications, the end-user profile gradually changes from the film production animator to the human behaviors analyst and finally to the Virtual Environment operator interacting with virtual humans (they all are referred as viewers in the following lines). Real-time animation of 3D human motion with convincing realism and high interaction with the viewer is far from now. The viewer has the natural skill of detecting a synthetic motion, or the synthetic mixing of recorded motions, or a synthetic display of a motion performed in real time by partners in virtual worlds. On the other hand, some class of viewers can accept the imperfection of the displayed motion, whatever the production tool, if it allows a greater interaction.

The design strategies for 3D human motions have been the object of important researches since the beginning of the 80s. Now and for the years to come, the considerable interest which has supported them is still raising as the computing power only begins to allow convenient handling of these classes of problems. However, according to productions standards, we predict a slow improvement in the direction of designing more *lively* animations out of scratch. On the other hand, more motion manipulation methods are emerging thus soon allowing a greater reusability and generalization of recorded material. Moreover, significant advances are soon to emerge in the direction of autonomous agents reacting to each other and to their environment. As a consequence these results should directly benefit to real-time simulation environments. So, if one can accept to still distinguish the real from the virtual motions and behaviors, we think that the great challenge of cooperative work between operators and virtual humans is a reasonable objective for the five years to come.

Acknowledgments
We wish to thank our colleagues Hansruedi Noser, Tom Molet, Pascal Becheiraz, Serge Rezzonico, Tolga Capin and Ramon Mas for many fruitful discussions on related topics. We are also very grateful to Roberto Maiocchi for sharing his experience in the production context. The research was supported by the Swiss National Science Research Foundation and the Federal Office for Education and Science.

References

1. Mindpower, Communicate with Confidence, TIME-LIFE BOOKS, Amsterdam, ISBN 0 7054 1623 2.

2. Van Baerle S. (1986) Character Animation : Combining Computer Graphics and Traditional Animation, SIGGRAPH 86 Course Notes.

3. Lasseter J. (1987) Principle of traditional Animation Applied to 3D Computer Animation. Computer Graphics 21(4), 1987, pp.35-44.

4. Robertson B. (1995) Toy Story : A Triumph of Animation, Computer Graphics World 18(8), August 1995, pp.28-38.

5. Coco D. (1995) Breathing Life Into 3D Humans, Computer Graphics World 18(8), August 1995, pp.41-49.

6. Liu Z., Cohen M.F., Keyframe Motion Optimization by Relaxing Speed and Timing, Proc. of 6th EUROGRAPHICS Workshop on Animation and Simulation, September 95, Maastricht, Springer Verlag Wien.

7. Boulic R., Mas R. (1995) Hierarchical Kinematic Behaviors for Complex Articulated Figures, in "Advanced Interactive Animation", Magnenat-Thalmann & Thalmann (eds.), Prentice Hall, To Appear in October 1995.

8. Magnenat-Thalmann N., Thalmann D (1985) Computer Animation, Theory and Practice, Springer-Verlag Tokyo.

9. Badler N., Phillips C. and Webber B. (1993) "Simulating Humans, Computer Graphics Animation and Control", Chapter 4 "Behavioral Control", Oxford University Press 1993.

10. Witkin A., Kass M. (1988) "Spacetime constraints", Computer Graphics 22 (4),1988, pp.159-168.

11. Zajac F.E., Winters J.M. (1990) Modeling Musculoskeletal Movement Systems: Joint and Body Segmental Dynamics, Musculoskeletal Actuation, and Neuromuscular Control, In “Multiple Muscle Systems: Biomechanics and Movement Organization”, J.M. Winters and S.L.Woo (eds.), Chapter 8, pp.121-148, Springer-Verlag.

12. Boulic R., Huang Z., Magnenat-Thalmann N., Thalmann D. (1994) Goal-Oriented Design and Correction of Articulated Figure Motion with the TRACK System , Computer. & Graphics, Vol. 18, No. 4, pp.443-452.

13. Witkin A., Popovic Z. (1995) "Motion Warping", Computer Graphics Proceedings, Annual Conference Series, 1995, pp.105-108

14. Maiocchi R. (1995) 3D character Animation Using Motion Capture, In "Advanced Interactive Animation", Thalmann&Magnenat-Thalmann (eds.), Prentice-Hall, to appear in october 1995, 23 pages.

15. Cappozzo A. (1991) Three-Dimensional Analysis of Human Walking : Experimental Methods and Associated Artifacts, Human Movement Science 10 (1991) pp589-602, North-Holland.

16. Pennock G.R., Clark K.J. (1990) An Anatomy-Based Coordinate System for the Description of the Kinematic Displacements in the Human Knee, Journal of Biomechanics 23(12), pp.1209-1218.

17. Rab G.T. (1991) Flexible Marker Set for Human Gait Analysis, Technical Note, Journal of Electromyography and Kinesiology 1(2), pp.139-145, Raven Press Ltd, New-York.

18. Ramakrishnan H.K., Kadaba M.P. (1991) On the Estimation of Joint Kinematics During Gait, Technical Note, Journal of Biomechanics 24(10), pp.969-977.

19. Davis R.B.III, Ounpuu S., Tyburski D., Gage J.R. (1991) A Gait Analysis Data Collection and Reduction Technique, Human Movement Science 10 (1991), pp 575-587, North-Holland.

20. Boulic R. , Thalmann D. "Combined Direct and Inverse Kinematic Control for Articulated Figure Motion Editing", Computer Graphics Forum ,2(4), pp , October 1992, partly integrated in Course notes n°80, SIGGRAPH 93, Anaheim, California, August 93.

21. Bruderlin A., Williams L. (1995) Motion Signal Processing, Computer Graphics Proceedings, Annual Conference Series, 1995, pp.97-104.

22. Potel M.J. (1995) See How they Run: Modeling Evacuations in VR, IEEE CGA march 1995, pp.11-13.

23. Philips C. B., Zhao J., Badler N. I. (1990) Interactive Real-Time Articulated Figure Manipulation Using Multiple Kinematic Constraints, Computer Graphics 24 (2), pp.245-250.

24. Noser H., Thalmann D. (1995) Synthetic vision and audition for digital actors, Computer Graphics Forum special issue of EUROGRAPHICS'95 Proc., pp 325-336, Maastricht.

25. Boulic R. and Mas R. "Inverse Kinetics for Center of Mass Position Control and Posture Optimization", Technical Report 94/68, 40 pages, Computer Sciences Department, EPFL, DI-LIG, Switzerland, September 1994.

26. Boulic R., Capin T., Huang Z., Kalra P., Lintermann B., Magnenat-Thalmann N., Moccozet L., Molet T., Pandzic I., Saar K., Schmitt A., Shen j., Thalmann D. (1995) "A system for the Parallel Integrated Motion of Multiple Deformable Human Characters with Collision Detection" , Computer Graphics Forum special issue of EUROGRAPHICS'95 Proceedings, pp.337-348, Maastricht.

27. Boulic R., Thalmann D., Magnenat-Thalmann N., A global human walking model with real time kinematic personification, The Visual Computer, 6(6), Dec. 1990.

28. Bezault L, Boulic R, Thalmann D, Magnenat-Thalmann N (1992) A Interactive Tool for the Design of Human Free-Walking Trajectories,*Proc. of Computer Animation 92*, Geneva

29. Ko H, Badler NI (1993) Curved Path Locomotion that Handles Anthropometrical Variety, Technical report MS-CIS-93-13,University of Pennsylvania, Graphics Lab .

30. Mas R., Thalmann D. (1994) A Hand Control and Automatic Grasping System for Synthetic Actors, Proceedings of Eurographic'94, pp.167-178.

31. Badler N., Manoocherhi K. and Walters G. (1987) "Articulated Figure Positioning by Multiple Constraints", IEEE CGA, 7(6), pp.28-38.

32. Badler N., Bindiganavale R., Granieri J.P., Wei S., Zhao X. (1994) Posture Interpolation with Collision Avoidance, Proc. of Computer Animation'94, Geneva, IEEE Press, pp.13-20.

33. Mataric M. (1994) Group behaviors and group learning, Conf. “from Perception to Action” Proc., Sept. 1994, pp.326-329, IEEE Press.

34. Badler N., Hollick M.J., Granieri J.P. (1993) Real-Time Control of a Virtual Human Using Minimal Sensors, a Forum short paper in Presence 2(1), pp.82-86, MIT.

35. Capin T., Pandzic I.S., Magnenat-Thalmann N., Thalmann D. (1995) Virtual Humans for Representing Participants in Immersive Virtual Environments, in Proc. of FIVE Conference, December 1995, London

36. Pentland A., Darrell T., Irfan Essa, Azarbayejani A., Sclaroff S. (1994) Visually Guided Animation, Proc. of Computer Animation'94, IEEE Press.

37. Rezzonico S., Boulic R., Huang Z., Magnenat-Thalmann N., Thalmann D. (1995) Consistent Grasping in Virtual Environments Based on the Interactive Grasping Automata, in "Virtual Environment", M. Gobel Edt, Springer Verlag,

38. Huang Z., Boulic R., Magnenat-Thalmann N., Thalmann D (1995) A Multi-sensor Approach for Grasping and 3D Interaction, Proc. of CGI 95, Leeds.

39. Zhao X., Badler N.I. (1994) Interactive Body Awareness, Computer Aided Design 26(12), pp.861-867, December 94, Butterworth Heinemann Ltd

40. Espiau B., Boulic R. (1985) Collision avoidance for redundant robots with proximity sensors, Proc. of Third International Symposium of Robotics Research, October 1985, Gouvieux, O.D. Faugeras and G. Giralt (eds.), The MIT Press Series in Artificial Intelligence.

41. Lee P.L.Y. (1993) Modeling Articulated Figure Motion with Physically- and Physiologically-based Constraints, Ph.D. Dissertation in Mechanical Engineering and Applied Mechanics, University of Pennsylvania.

Authors' Index

Research Reports Esprit

Area *Peripheral Systems, Business Systems and House Automation*

Learning in Man-Computer Interaction. A Review of the Literature.
T. Bösser. XI, 218 pages. 1987 (Project 385 HUFIT, Human Factor Laboratories in Information Technologies, Vol. 1)

Automatic Tools for Designing Office Information Systems. The TODOS Approach. Edited by B. Pernici, C. Rolland. IX, 321 pages. 1990 (Project 813 TODOS, Vol.1)

Integrated Management of Technical Documentation. The System SPRITE. Edited by J. Hoppe. VIII, 244 pages. 1992 (Project 2001 SPRITE, Storage, Processing and Retrieval of Information in a Technical Environment, Vol. 1)

Integration of Graphics and OSI Standards. Edited by R.A. Day, D.A. Duce, J.R. Gallop, D.C. Sutcliffe. X, 157 pages. 1993 (Project 2463 ARGOSI, Applications-Related Graphics and OSI Standards Integration, Vol. 1)

The COMANDOS Distributed Application Platform. Edited by V. Cahill, R. Balter, N.R. Harris, X. Rousset de Pina. XVII, 312 pages. 1993 (Project 2071 COMANDOS, Construction and Management of Distributed Open Systems, Vol. 1)

Ultra-wideband Coherent Optical LANs. Edited by S. Forcesi. X, 97 pages. 1993 (Project 2054 UCOL, Vol. 1)

Cooperation Among Organizations. The Potential of Computer Supported Cooperative Work. Edited by R.J.D. Power. VII, 140 pages, 1993 (Project 5660 PECOS, Perspectives on Cooperative Systems, Vol. 1)

The OSI95 Transport Service with Multimedia Support. Edited by A. Danthine. VIII, 515 pages. 1994 (Project 5341 OSI95, High Performance OSI Protocols with Multimedia Support on HSLANs and B-ISDN, Vol. 1)

The Translator's Workbench. Tools and Terminology for Translation and Text Processing. Edited by M. Kugler, K. Ahmad, G. Thurmair. IX, 183 pages. 1995 (Project 2315 TWB, Vol. 1)

Advances in Human-Computer Interaction. Human Comfort and Security. Edited by S. Pfleger, J. Gonçalves, K. Varghese. XI, 323 pages. 1995 (Project Group HCI, Vol. 1)

Human Comfort and Security of Information Systems. Advanced Interfaces for the Information Society. Human Comfort and Security. Edited by K. Varghese, S. Pfleger. XIII, 320 pages. 1997 (Project Group HCI, Vol. 2)

Printing: Weihert-Druck GmbH, Darmstadt
Binding: Theo Gansert Buchbinderei GmbH, Weinheim